Second Edition

Family Therapy
Theory and Practice

Second Edition
Family Therapy
Theory and Practice

Joseph H. Brown
Dana N. Christensen
University of Louisville

Brooks/Cole Publishing Company

I(T)P®*An International Thomson Publishing Company*

Pacific Grove • Albany • Belmont • Bonn • Boston • Cincinnati • Detroit • Johannesburg
London • Madrid • Melbourne • Mexico City • New York • Paris • Singapore • Tokyo
Toronto • Washington

Sponsoring Editor: *Eileen Murphy*
Marketing Team: *Steve Catalano, Aaron Eden, and Jean Vevers Thompson*
Editorial Assistant: *Julie Martinez*
Production Editor: *Laurel Jackson*
Manuscript Editor: *Jean Thurman*
Permissions Editor: *Mary Kay Hancharik*
Indexer: *Jane Farnol, Astor Indexers*

Interior and Cover Design: *Christine Garrigan*
Art Editor: *Lisa Torri*
Typesetting: *CompuKing Typesetting*
Cover Printing: *Phoenix Color Corporation*
Printing and Binding: *Quebecor/ Fairfield*

For more information, contact:

BROOKS/COLE PUBLISHING COMPANY
511 Forest Lodge Road
Pacific Grove, CA 93950
USA

International Thomson Publishing Europe
Berkshire House 168-173
High Holborn
London WC1V 7AA
England

Thomas Nelson Australia
102 Dodds Street
South Melbourne, 3205
Victoria, Australia

Nelson Canada
1120 Birchmount Road
Scarborough, Ontario
Canada M1K 5G4

International Thomson Editores
Seneca 53
Col. Polanco
11560 México, D. F., México

International Thomson Publishing GmbH
Königswinterer Strasse 418
53227 Bonn
Germany

International Thomson Publishing Asia
60 Albert Street
#15-01 Albert Complex
Singapore 189969

International Thomson Publishing Japan
Hirakawacho Kyowa Building, 3F
2-2-1 Hirakawacho
Chiyoda-ku, Tokyo 102
Japan

Printed in the United States of America

10 9 8 7 6 5 4 3 2

Library of Congress Cataloging-in-Publication Data
Brown, Joseph H.
    Family therapy : theory and practice / Joseph H. Brown, Dana N. Christensen. — 2nd ed.
        p.   cm.
    Includes bibliographical references and index.
    ISBN 0-534-34651-0
    1. Family psychotherapy.   I. Christensen, Dana N., [date]
II. Title.
    [DNLM: 1. Family Therapy. WM 430.5.F2 B878f 198]
RC488.5.B76   1998
616.89'156—dc21
DNLM/DLC
For Library of Congress   98-22364
                                                              CIP

To our parents,
Joseph W. Brown
Margaret J. Brown
Edwin H. Christensen
Marilyn F. Christensen

Contents

Preface

In writing this text, we were guided by our view of what is most important for the beginning student of family therapy to learn. Because this required a process of selection, we present a brief discussion of the decisions we made regarding the organization and content of the book and the philosophy behind them.

A systemic perspective   We have chosen to look at each theory we discuss from the overall systems perspective so that the reader can see problems not as intrapsychic occurrences but as relationship-oriented events. Some of the theories presented in the text are not typically classified as "systems." However, we have included them because, in recent years, these theories have undergone many adaptations that make them more consistent with a systemic perspective and because their techniques have found their way into regular use by mainstream systems therapists. Rather than use the term *systems* in its narrowest sense and be constrained by the fine points of what is a systemic theory and what is not, we have chosen to emphasize the systemic characteristics of each major group of theories.

A developmental perspective   All the major schools we discuss share not only a certain degree of systemic thinking, but also a developmental approach. The developmental perspective has become increasingly important to the field in recent years, and we consider education in issues of the family life cycle a necessary foundation for understanding and using any applied theory.

Major schools   Because the practitioners of early family therapy used to develop their own training programs and schools—each with its own labels and terms—this text could have contained twice as many chapters if we had treated each approach as a separate school. Aside from the fact that diversification in the field is now giving way to integration, we believe that it is very important for the beginning student of family therapy to recognize the breadth of the field before arriving at any one "true" form of therapy. We also think it useful for the student to attempt to integrate the various theoretical orientations that have much in common. To assist the reader, we have therefore elected to present the theoretical approaches to family therapy under five major "umbrella" groups: structural, strategic, transgenerational, experiential, and behavioral. We have also chosen not to include all theorists and clinicians so that, by narrowing our range slightly, we could examine in greater depth each major theoretical group. By doing so, to give interested students a solid groundwork for study.

Example of theory integration   Rather than present our own model, another model, or a cross-section of models for integrating family theory, we offer an example of how the various theories might work together on a specific case. We based our decision on he experience of watching students settle too quickly on an integrative approach as a way of dealing with information over-load. Beginning students must experiment with ideas and techniques on their own so that they can discover for themselves what works and makes sense, given their own particular personality and caseload. We offer the example of theory integration in the hope that it will lend structure to the reader's creativity. As students begin to develop theoretical integration, they should also consult primary sources and read the individual theorists' writings to broaden the scope of their conceptual base.

Format

The organization of this book is a result of the decisions we have just discussed. Chapter One introduces systems thinking and its historical evolution, presenting the concepts of family therapy and the contexts in which they apply throughout the book. Chapter Two lays the foundation for thinking developmentally about the family and using the developmental approach to understand symptoms and conflict from a relationship point of view.

Each of the next five chapters (Chapters Three through Seven) presents one of the five major theoretical approaches that form the core of this book, and Chapter Eight (which is new to this edition) contains a discussion of postmodern theoretical models. These chapters follow similar outlines to aid in comparison: A summary of theoretical concepts precedes a description of techniques used in practice. Although beginning students of family therapy may not be clinically ready to apply the technique, awareness of it helps to deepen their understanding of the theory.

Chapter Nine ushers the reader through a detailed case illustration that was first introduced at the end of Chapter Two. The treatment described in Chapter Nine makes use of aspects of each of the major theoretical approaches. Although this case study is not meant to represent a paradigm of integration, it illustrates how practitioners can blend concepts and techniques from the various approaches.

In Chapters Ten and Eleven, we examine the current professional field of marital and family therapy. The practice of marital and family therapy in diverse settings is discussed in Chapter Ten. Chapter Eleven offers an overview of contemporary issues in the profession, covering important concerns for the therapist in this field and projecting some future trends.

Students will find the glossary at the end of the book useful when they need a quick definition of a term. Glossary terms are printed in boldface when they appear in the text for the first time.

Finally, a word about the case illustrations throughout the book. Unless otherwise noted, all of them are actual cases of families seen in clinical practice either by one of the authors or by their students. In every case, only identifying information has been changed to preserve the family's privacy.

Acknowledgments

We are grateful to the following reviewers for their helpful comments and suggestions: Martin Fiebert, California State University, Long Beach; Alisabeth Buck Marsh, Tacoma Community College; and Donna Wheeler, California State University, Long Beach/Humboldt State Distance Program.

Joseph H. Brown
Dana N. Christensen

PART ONE

FOUNDATIONS OF FAMILY THERAPY

Chapter One

The Family Organism

Imagine for just a moment that you had been asked to write a report about what makes human beings tick. Think about how you would go about writing such a report. Most people say they would go to the literature of psychology or philosophy and read about values and attitudes and also about how early life experiences might combine to create a particular personality. Some people add that they would think about what motivates them personally and what angers and frustrates them in life. Their soul-searching would give them clues about what makes human beings tick. A smaller group of people say that they would interview people about what they thought was important and significant in life. A still smaller group comes up with the idea that observing people doing things in their everyday work life might provide some important information about why people do the things they do and feel the things they feel.

If you thought of any of these ideas, then you are certainly in good company. Human life has been studied in just these ways throughout history. It wasn't until halfway through the 20th century that another idea began to interest and excite people who were trying to figure out what makes human beings tick.

This new idea was that maybe we were all trying to answer questions about human life by thinking about, interviewing, or observing the wrong organism—the individual human being. Maybe we needed to expand our focus on the subject and try to think about studying a larger organism, an organism in which the human individual is but a part, a member. This larger organism is, of course, the family.

If you think of the family as an organism, you too will quickly see that it is a particularly interesting one. Its parts are not nuclei as in an amoeba, or organs as in an individual; rather, it is made up of individuals. These individuals (parts) are not connected by tissue or vessels, nor are they encased in a tangible outer membrane. And yet, as we shall see later in the text, they are connected for life, and each part is aware of the family's outer edge or boundary. The family also changes appearance over time by evolving; it transforms itself, and it may divide and form another associated branch. The **family organism** can continue to exist and function even when its parts (members) are distributed over vast geographical distances. It can withstand enormous pressure, and, because it keeps generating new parts and evolving new inner structures, it is very difficult to detect when the life of the organism begins and ends.

This new idea—that, by studying the family organism or system, we could learn more about what makes human beings tick—has come to be known as the family systems perspective.

The movement toward a family systems perspective developed not from a single source but rather in response to far-ranging social needs. Technological advances, a mobile society, and the baby boom following World War II produced tremendous pressures in the family. Families began to receive special attention on account of rising rates of juvenile delinquency and divorce (Broderick & Schrader, 1981). Family members increasingly sought help from mental-health professionals for emotional problems. Although most of those professionals were still studying the individual, many joined a growing trend to treat the individual in the context of the family. The shift toward viewing the family as a social system evolved primarily out of three independent movements: (1) marriage counseling, (2) psychiatry, and (3) research on schizophrenia. Beginning with a historical discussion of these movements, this chapter will first trace the shift from treatment of the individual to treatment of the family system and then describe some of the fundamental concepts employed in the new family systems perspective.

Historical Evolution
Marriage Counseling

Throughout history, people have discussed their marital problems. They discussed their problems, however, with clergy, lawyers, and doctors, rather than with mental-health professionals. Some change occurred with important developments in gynecology and obstetrics. The new knowledge resulted in an increase of professionals who consulted on sex-related marital issues (Broderick & Schrader, 1981). Increasing popularity of marriage courses on college campuses also generated interest in this field.

The first marriage centers were actually established in 1930. Paul Popenoe, a biologist, developed the American Institute of Family Relations in Los Angeles. He did much to popularize marriage counseling through articles published in the *Ladies' Home Journal*. At the same time, two physicians, Abraham and Hannah Stone, started a similar clinic in New York City. Two years later, another such center was added when Emily Hartshorne Mudd opened the Marriage Council of Philadelphia. She did extensive research in marriage counseling and was one of the original founders of the American Association of Marriage Counselors in 1945.

The American Association of Marriage Counselors helped to establish professional standards for marriage counselors. Later, standards were established for training centers and advanced-degree programs in marriage counseling. In

1956, the Marriage Council of Philadelphia, the Merrill-Palmer School in Detroit, and the Menninger Clinic in Topeka, Kansas received professional accreditation in marriage counselor training (Broderick & Schrader, 1981).

In the middle 1950s and early 1960s, therapists moved from individual analysis to **conjoint marital therapy** (with both spouses present). Bela Mittlemann, of the New York Psychoanalytic Institute, had been the first to publish papers on concurrent analysis in marital therapy. He argued that individual marital problems were "anchored" in the marital relationship (Mittlemann, 1944, 1948). In 1956, Victor Eisenstein, Director of the New Jersey Neuropsychiatric Institute, edited and published a volume entitled *Neurotic Interaction in Marriage*, which included several articles on marital interaction. At the same time, Don Jackson (1959) was describing "conjoint therapy" through a communications perspective.

Psychiatry

The second major movement involved in the shift toward family treatment was spurred by individual pioneers within psychiatry. Among the most influential were Nathan Ackerman, Carl Whitaker, and Ivan Boszormenyi-Nagy.

Nathan W. Ackerman   Nathan W. Ackerman has often been referred to as "the grandfather of family therapy" (Framo, 1972). Ackerman was a child psychiatrist trained in psychoanalysis. In 1938, he became the chief psychiatrist for the Child Guidance Clinic at the Menninger Clinic in Topeka, Kansas. Ackerman initially followed the traditional model of the psychiatrist's seeing the child and the social worker's seeing the mother. In the mid-1940s, however, he experimented with interviewing the entire family and eventually came to see the family as the central unit for diagnosis and treatment.

Ackerman helped to move family therapy toward further prominence in the l950s. In 1955, Ackerman organized and directed the first meetings on family therapy at the American Orthopsychiatric Convention. In 1957, he opened the Family Mental Health Clinic at Jewish Family Services in New York City. Three years later, in 1960, he founded the Family Institute, renamed the Ackerman Institute after his death in 1971.

Ackerman emphasized family roles in psychoanalysis and saw family therapy as a way of focusing on the broader context of human relations and interactions (Hansen & L'Abate, 1982). He believed that the therapist must relate to individual personalities as well as to interactions among family members. Ackerman noted that each family member is, at one time, an individual, a member of various subgroups, and a member of the family system as a whole (Nichols, 1984). Ackerman continued to give equal weight to the **intrapsychic** process and the systems process. This combination of emphases separated him from other systems practitioners whose ideas of "pure" family systems therapy were continuing to gain popularity (Okun & Rappaport, 1980).

Carl Whitaker Carl Whitaker has often been considered the most radical and flamboyant founder of family therapy. Whitaker did much of his early work with schizophrenics and their spouses at Emory University in Atlanta, Georgia. In 1953, Whitaker helped to organize the family therapy movement by convening Gregory Bateson, Don Jackson, John Rosen, and Albert Scheflen at Sea Island, Georgia. At that gathering, each met separately with the same family while the others observed and analyzed the case. This open interaction led to further discussion and exchange of ideas.

Whitaker left Emory University in 1955 and entered private practice. He continued to develop an atheoretical style of therapy that focuses on provocation and stress. Whitaker is totally spontaneous and at times purposely absurd. His interventions are designed to help family members become more open and flexible. Since 1965, he has served in the Department of Psychiatry at the University of Wisconsin Medical School, where he has continued to practice, teach, and serve as mentor to the field.

Ivan Boszormenyi-Nagy In 1957, Ivan Boszormenyi-Nagy founded the Eastern Pennsylvania Psychiatric Institute (EPPI). Boszormenyi-Nagy was a psychoanalyst who attracted an impressive staff to the institute. Among those colleagues were James Framo, psychologist, who coauthored *Intensive Family Therapy* with Boszormenyi-Nagy in 1965; David Rubenstein, psychiatrist; and Geraldine Spark, who coauthored *Invisible Loyalties* with Boszormenyi-Nagy in 1973. In 1960, Ray Birdwhistell joined Albert Scheflen (EPPI) to study body language in therapy. At about that time, Ross Speck did his internship at EPPI and, along with Carolyn Attneave, developed **network therapy**, which includes others (for example, friends and neighbors) outside the family system in the treatment process.

Boszormenyi-Nagy has continued to make major contributions to the integration of the intrapsychic and systems approaches to family therapy. He has studied the unconscious needs of parents and their importance to an understanding of child-parent relationships. More recently, Boszormenyi-Nagy has studied the concepts of loyalty and justice within relational systems over several generations (Boszormenyi-Nagy & Spark, 1973).

Research on Schizophrenia

The third major movement leading to the family perspective in treatment emerged from the groups that formed to study schizophrenia. In the 1950s, there were at least four major research groups, along with a number of individual researchers and practitioners, who studied the etiology and communications patterns of schizophrenia in families (Goldenberg & Goldenberg, 1983).

The Palo Alto group The Palo Alto group started with Gregory Bateson, an anthropologist on the faculty at Stanford University. In 1952, Bateson was awarded a grant to study paradoxical communication in animals and humans at the Palo Alto V.A. Hospital. In 1953, Bateson was joined by Jay Haley, a graduate student studying communication, and John Weakland, a chemical engineer who had become interested in cultural anthropology. In 1954, Bateson received a two-year grant from the Macy Foundation to study schizophrenic communication. Soon afterward, Don Jackson, a psychiatrist who worked with people with schizophrenia and their families, became affiliated with the group.

The presence of Don Jackson and his clinical expertise helped greatly to influence the Palo Alto group. Jackson emphasized the importance of mechanisms that control family stability. For example, a mechanism that occurs in all families to varying degrees when the parents begin to argue is the feigning of illness or incompetence by their child to attract their focus and to stabilize the conflict. The child's symptom serves as a mechanism to maintain peace or equilibrium in the family.

In 1956, Bateson, Jackson, Haley, and Weakland published an important article, "Towards a Theory of Schizophrenia," in which they introduced the communications concept of the "double bind." Briefly, a **double bind** could be defined as the situation of a person who receives two related but contradictory messages at the same time, response to either of which is inappropriate (that is, there is no escape). Bateson offers the example of a young man who was visited by his mother in the hospital while recovering from a schizophrenic episode. When the man put his arms around her, she stiffened. However, when he withdrew his arms, she asked, "Don't you love me any more?" When he blushed, she commented, "Dear, you must not be so easily embarrassed and afraid of your feelings." Shortly after his mother left, the man became upset and assaulted an aide. Unable to respond directly in such a dilemma, the person with schizophrenia often withdraws from the external world. Jackson reported on the group's research in 1957 at the American Psychiatric Association's meeting in Chicago, where he met Lyman Wynne, Theodore Lidz, Murray Bowen, and Nathan Ackerman (Goldenberg & Goldenberg, 1983).

In 1959, Jackson founded the Mental Research Institute (MRI). Shortly thereafter, he asked Virginia Satir from Chicago to work with him. Haley and Weakland joined the MRI group in 1962. While Bateson continued to focus on the theory of the double bind, Jackson, Haley, and Weakland were more interested in various other patterns of communication in families. All, however, agreed that a theory about families was necessary to understand the rules and communication processes they were observing (Nichols, 1984). Individually oriented psychodynamics theory was insufficient. Many of these ideas were presented in *Pragmatics of Human Communication* (Watzlawick, Beavin, & Jackson, 1967). In the mid-1960s, Satir moved away from MRI, eventually to become the first director of the Esalen Institute at Big Sur, California. In 1967, Haley also left MRI to join Salvador Minuchin at the Philadelphia Child Guidance Clinic. The emerging field lost one of its greatest pioneers in 1968 when Don Jackson died.

The Theodore Lidz group   In the early 1950s, Lidz, a psychoanalyst, was studying hospitalized people with schizophrenia and their families at Yale.

Lidz viewed schizophrenia as resulting from inappropriate personality integration and role differentiation in families. Lidz emphasized the critical role fathers play in the development of the child. In some schizophrenic families, he found fathers who were in conflict with their wives and who tried to win their daughters' affection. Such inappropriate demands often meant that the schizophrenic daughter failed to develop a sense of autonomy or role differentiation. In other cases, fathers were extremely "hostile" or "passive," and their behavior made forming an identity difficult for their children (Lidz, Cornelison, Fleck, & Terry, 1957).

Lidz also focused on two patterns of marital discord in schizophrenic families. In the first pattern, there was severe conflict. He found parents competing for the child's affection. Lidz referred to this pattern as **marital schism**. In the second pattern, **marital skew,** the mother often dominated the father, and the children attempted to balance the marriage. Lidz's research suggested that marital schism led to schizophrenia in daughters, while marital skew led to schizophrenia in sons.

The Lyman Wynne group   Wynne was a pioneer researcher and therapist who studied patterns of communication and role relationships in schizophrenic families. Wynne's study of schizophrenics began in 1954 at the National Institute of Mental Health (NIMH). Wynne was primarily interested in how individuals formed identities in the family. Wynne observed that there was often conflict between the needs of the child to develop an identity and, at the same time, to develop intimate relationships with others in the family. The former need propels the individual out of the family, while the second need pulls the individual back into the family. The issue of separation becomes critical if these conflicting needs are not resolved. Wynne referred to this separation conflict as *pseudomutuality* in families (Wynne, Ryckoff, Day, & Hirsch, 1958).

The concept of **pseudomutuality** means that family members develop masks to relate to each other. In pseudomutual families, the person with schizophrenia fails to develop a separate identity. Family members are assigned roles that have the appearance of mutuality, and any deviation is met with disapproval. Hence, the person with schizophrenia becomes dependent on his or her assigned role. Involvement outside the family is also restricted. In this context, the person with schizophrenia fears outside relationships, preferring to stay within the rigid boundaries of the family. Schizophrenia was thus viewed as an attempt to separate, which often failed and excluded the member from the family. Wynne and his group succeeded in offering still another view of how schizophrenia might not reside just within the individual but might somehow be part of the entire family (Singer & Wynne, 1965).

In 1954, when Wynne was developing his theories about schizophrenia, Murray Bowen joined the staff at NIMH (Broderick & Schrader, 1981). Wynne was influenced by Bowen, and together in 1956–1957 they began collaborating with Don Jackson, Theodore Lidz, and Nathan Ackerman at the American Psychiatric Association conventions in Chicago. Ultimately, Jackson and Wynne began to exchange videotapes of counseling sessions in 1959. Bowen left NIMH in 1956, and Wynne moved to the University of Rochester Medical School in 1971, where he continued to study family role communications patterns and their contribution to schizophrenia. Although the pioneers worked for the most part separately, they slowly began to establish a professional network.

The Murray Bowen group   Bowen was a psychiatrist who began conducting research on schizophrenia in the early 1950s. In 1954, when he joined Lyman Wynne at NIMH, he designed a project in which he hospitalized entire families to examine their role designations and patterns of communication. Initially, Bowen saw family members individually, but soon he began treating the family as a unit. Bowen learned that progress was more rapid when the family was treated as a unit (Bowen, 1976a) . Although that project is considered to be a general forerunner of family therapy (Guerin, 1976), it failed to win continued NIMH approval, and in 1956 Bowen moved to Georgetown University. Bowen continued to do research and train family therapists at Georgetown Family Therapy Center.

As a part of his study in 1954, Bowen observed that parents of children with schizophrenia would often vacillate between "over closeness" and "over distance." This emotional distance often leads to what Bowen termed *triangulation* of the child. When **triangulation** occurs, spouses attempt to dissipate conflictual tension through the child (or third person). Bowen believed that if a couple were forced to solve its own problems, it would prevent **scapegoating** or triangulating of the child—an antecedent condition to schizophrenia.

The early research on communication was thought to pertain only to schizophrenic families. However, later investigations demonstrated that the same patterns of communication found in schizophrenic families also existed to some extent in normal families (Okun & Rappaport, 1980). Bowen (1976b) notes that "the results of the early studies on normal families might be summarized by saying that the patterns originally thought to be typical of schizophrenia are present in all families some of the time and in some of the families most of the time" (p. 61). This realization obviously accelerated the profession's shift toward thinking "family" rather than thinking individual.

The early 1960s saw exciting innovations and collaborations among the pioneers and new professionals entering the field. Their converging views were provided a forum in which to take shape when, in 1962, Nathan Ackerman and Don Jackson founded the *Journal of Family Process.* Jay Haley was appointed the first editor of the journal, which sought to bring major family clinicians and researchers together. The clinicians came from diverse backgrounds, such as group therapy, psychoanalysis, communications theory, and child guidance. The result was a preponderance of techniques for clinical intervention, exciting exchanges of methodology, and very little research on theory. One exception to that pattern was the work of Salvador Minuchin and his associates. Minuchin came originally from Argentina, where he was trained as a psychiatrist. Minuchin developed a family treatment approach for delinquent boys at the Wiltwych School for Boys in New York. He studied the communications patterns of twelve families, nine of which had no father. The families were poorly organized and were characterized by parental overinvolvement or under-involvement. Treatment sessions were designed to change transactional patterns and thereby change the structure of the family. Minuchin's findings were published in *Families of the Slums* in 1967 (Minuchin, Montalvo, Guerney, Rosman, & Schumer, 1967) and led to his appointment as director of the Philadelphia Child Guidance Clinic in 1967. Minuchin brought Brauho Montalvo and Bernice Rosman to the clinic, and later that year, they were joined by Jay Haley. Together, they developed a model of therapy called structural family therapy. In the 1970s, the Philadelphia Child Guidance Clinic became a major center for family therapy and training.

The Systems Perspective

The contributions of Minuchin, Bowen, Ackerman, Whitaker, Boszormenyi-Nagy, Lidz, the Palo Alto group, and others combined to produce a paradigmatic shift in thinking. Rather than viewing symptomatic behavior as residing within the individual, therapists increasingly saw problems within family relationships and increasingly referred to themselves as family therapists.

General Systems Theory

The new paradigm was greatly influenced by **general systems theory** (Bertalanffy, 1969), a theoretical perspective that had its origins in biology and medicine. This theory placed its emphasis not on the parts that go to make up a whole but on the interrelationships of the parts to one another. Applied to families, general systems theory replaced the notion of focusing on each individual in the family, and then somehow adding all the individuals together to get a picture of the family, with the idea that one could not understand any family member (part) without understanding how all the family members (whole) operate together. The process by which all the family members operate together is what is referred to as the *family system*. Taken a step further, general systems theory sees each system itself as just a part of a larger system (for example, the family system is part of the community, which in turn is a part of the larger societal system) and likewise as comprising smaller systems, or subsystems (for example, the family system is composed of individuals, who are in turn made up of organ systems that consist of tissues).

There are four other concepts in general systems theory that have influenced mainstream thinking about the family: wholeness, feedback, homeostasis, and equifinality.

Wholeness   The concept of **wholeness** takes interrelatedness further. It states that a system cannot be understood by dissection and study of its individual parts. Nor can one study an individual action within the system without a complex understanding of how that action relates to the total transactions of the system. The commonly used expression "the whole is greater than the sum of its parts" refers to this concept of wholeness. If one member in the system changes, then all members of that system will change because of that one member's behavior and the reverberating change created as each member responds to other members' changes. Like ripples from pebbles thrown into a pond, the ripples created interactionally are greater than the sum of ripples created if each pebble had been thrown in individually.

Feedback   Feedback refers to how individual units in the system communicate with each other. Feedback in a system is **circular** rather than linear. **Linear causality** is based on a Newtonian model in which communication occurs in one direction (change in *A* produces a change in *B*, which produces a change in *C*, and so forth) . However, if one examines communication through a circular model, one finds that a change in *A* may produce a change in *B*, which produces a change in *C*, which in turn produces a change in *B* and *A* and so on.

The thermostat is an example of a circular feedback loop. When the temperature in the room decreases (*A*), it triggers the sensor in the thermostat (*B*), which sends a message to the furnace (C), which in turn sends warm air through the heat vent (*D*), which increases the temperature in the room (*A*) and again triggers the thermostat (*B*) (Okun & Rappaport, 1980). Likewise, in family therapy, we can observe how the therapist and family members can influence one another in a circular fashion. A husband may feel that his drinking is caused by his wife's nagging. She in turn may feel that his drinking causes her to nag him. Each person's behavior becomes reinforcing feedback for the behavior of the other. From the perspective of general systems theory, the interaction is circular, and it makes little difference whether his drinking results in her nagging or her nagging results in his drinking.

Homeostasis   Feedback either reflects change (**positive feedback**) or reinstates stability (**negative feedback**). The tendency of a system to seek stability and equilibrium is referred to as **homeostasis.** The thermostat is an example of a negative feedback loop. It is homeostatic because feedback is designed to decrease any deviation in the system. For instance, when a family tries to maintain the status quo by attempting to keep a child from leaving home, it is using negative feedback to keep the system in balance, or homeostatic. How a family actually attempts to maintain the status quo and avoid the shifts inherent in individual and family development is not always clearly apparent, nor was it apparent to the early pioneers in family thinking. Because clinicians had been traditionally trained in viewing pathology as intrapsychic, it was a slow process to discover the system dynamics that could account for what they were observing in developmentally delayed individuals. In the case of the family who presents its young adult son for treatment because he is depressed, listless, and uninterested in the world of work, the rest of the family typically appear to be *wanting* the boy to "grow up." They can recite a long litany of examples of how the boy simply is not capable of doing anything adult-like. Such families appeared to the early researchers, and still do to many uninformed contemporary clinicians, as eager to change their situation. It was not until the researchers observed the patterns of communication *between* family members (feedback) that they learned something of how each member of the family contributes to the whole process of keeping the young adult more "young" than "adult."

The homeostatic tendency of a family system to seek stability by reducing deviations in process (negative feedback) has been an enormously helpful concept for family therapists in understanding a family's reluctance to change. However, family process and structure do, under the proper conditions, transcend homeostasis by encouraging deviation and diversification (Maruyama, 1968). Within the field of family therapy, increased attention is being focused on the intertwining of change and stability processes that cooperate within the family system.

Paul Dell (1982) has argued that homeostasis as a concept does not fully explain the evolutionary tendencies of a family system. On the basis of the work of Humberto Maturana (1980), many family theorists are challenging the concept of homeostasis and the psychotherapy that is based on the view that the family organism is self-regulated. We hope that students of families and family therapy, as they become more familiar with the field, will participate in this theoretical debate through continued study.

Equifinality   The concept of **equifinality** simply implies that there are many paths to the same destination. Applied to the family system, it means that the particular path a family takes as it evolves its form is less significant than the final form itself. This is so because the equifinality characteristic of systems determines that there is always more than one set of events leading up to a certain end state and therefore that studying the events will not produce as much useful information as studying the end state. (The end state, of course, is only the current state, for families are continuously evolving.) This idea brings us to a discussion of how systems thinking has viewed the origins and causes of human problems and Bateson's question: Which is more important, current interactional patterns or antecedent conditions?

Etiology

The influence of systems thinking altered the way family therapists viewed symptomatic behavior. Bateson's studies of schizophrenia concluded that symptomatic behavior was not negative, but instead was quite functional in schizophrenic families. Similarly, Jackson's concept of homeostasis helped to explain why someone else in the family became symptomatic when the patient showed improvement. The concept of circularity helped family therapists to view unwanted behaviors not as something caused by prior **intrapersonal** events (such as mental or physical illness) but as something that was part of the family's current interactional pattern (Nichols, 1984).

From a systems perspective, the etiology of a problem has evolved into one in which the symptom and "cause" are now seen to operate on one another. Weakland (1960), expanding on Jackson's (1967) concept of "family homeostasis," found that the schizophrenic child contributes to the dysfunctional pattern of communication by sending incongruent messages. Thus, what one considers to be symptom and cause depends on one's perspective (Pentony, 1981). Pentony notes:

> If we consider a person who becomes ill from a stomach ulcer, we might regard the illness as the symptom and the ulcer as the cause. At this point, we have a choice as to whether we seek an explanation in terms of social determinants or seek it in terms of physical and chemical determinants. In either case, we can move further away from our initial point of departure, with, at each successive step, what was previously seen as being the cause becoming the symptom and the related process at the more remote level becoming the cause. So, if the physician in the case of the stomach ulcer seeks biochemical explanations, he may account for the ulcer in terms of excessive acid in the stomach. In that case, the ulcer is the symptom. He may then proceed to account for the acid, in which case it becomes the symptom and that which accounts for it, the cause.
>
> However, if the person responsible for treatment is behaviorally oriented, he may see the ulcer as the result of interpersonal stress arising from an unhappy home life with a nagging, bad-tempered wife, in combination with a relatively demanding work situation. In such a case, the behavior of the wife might be seen as the major causal factor. Then the ulcer would be the symptom and the interpersonal stress the causal factor. But the behavior of the wife may be seen to be the outcome of a family structure which denies her an opportunity for the fulfillment of her needs and hence leaves her frustrated and embittered. Now the family organization is the cause and the interpersonal stress the symptom. But, the family organization does not exist in a vacuum. It is a consequence of the wider community system or pattern of which it is a part. So the family structure becomes a symptom and the pattern of a wider order the cause. And so we might proceed to the point where we are, through a series of steps, attributing Mr. X's ulcer to the sociopolitical-economic system in which he lives. (p. 103)

In short, knowledge of cause and symptom is not very productive. Rather, knowledge of the system, its parts, their interrelatedness, the communication feedback between the parts, and the system's homeostatic functioning is far more useful to an understanding of the problem and a search for its resolution.

Amalgamation and Integration of Systems Thinking

In the late 1960s, an ideological conflict erupted between the psychoanalytic approach and the approach influenced by general systems theory. That conflict focused on certain psychoanalytic concepts that were incongruent with systems concepts such as circular causality and homeostasis. The psychoanalytic approach posits that clients' intrapsychic disturbances disrupt family interactions, whereas the systems approach views those same disturbances as occurring to maintain a functional balance in the family. Although this conflict still exists today, there seems to be an effort to balance a systems approach with an integration of clinical knowledge of individual dynamics (Okun & Rappaport, 1980).

The confluence of these two paradigms centers on several key issues: past versus present, content versus process, and intrapsychic versus interpersonal context.

Past versus present   Traditionally, psychoanalysts have focused on early life experiences as the cause of problems. Psychoanalytic therapists use their knowledge of the past to help the client better understand what is going on in the present. Systemic therapists, in contrast, view behavior within the current interactions in the family.

The historical approach, however, has been expanded to include the integration of systemic thinking. For example, Framo's transactional approach suggests that past relationships with loved ones are used as models for the development of current relationships. Boszormenyi-Nagy has attempted to integrate the psychoanalytic systems concepts into family therapy. In seeking an understanding of the relationships between the child and his or her parents, Boszormenyi-Nagy has focused his attention on the unconscious needs of parents. Minuchin, while concerned primarily with the current family structure, considers early experience in the development of pathology in the family. All family therapists focus on current relationships, but some give more attention to the past than others (Nichols, 1984).

Content versus process   When family members come to therapy, they usually focus on the content of their concerns. Parents may say that their child will not come home on time or is "hyperactive." A couple may describe their relationship as being "empty." Although the therapist listens to what family members say about each other (content), he or she is chiefly interested in how family members interact with each other (process). Do family members speak for each other? When the child begins to speak, does Mom or Dad interrupt him or her? Do parents agree about how to solve the problem? The therapist who focuses only on content is not able to help the family function better as a system.

Various approaches to family therapy emphasize in-session process differently. For instance, strategic therapists focus on dysfunctional sequences of interaction that contribute to the problem, whereas structuralists center their attention on how family members interact to carry out specific functions within each subsystem. Attending to family process occurs whether the conversation is about dinnertime rules or a visit by the relatives. Family therapists work in the area of content the family provides (such as dinnertime or a visit by relatives); however, their assessment and intervention will be based on their observations of family process.

Intrapsychic versus interpersonal context Whereas the psychoanalyst focuses on the individual's past to encourage insight (intrapsychic), systemic approaches focus on the current interactions (interpersonal) to alleviate symptomatic behavior. Systemic therapists tend to look at the interpersonal context in order to understand behavior. Family therapy sessions serve as the most significant context for altering interactions, but most systemic approaches treat family members in other contexts as well. Transgenerational therapists, such as Murray Bowen, include extended family members (grandparents) to change interactions in the nuclear family. Structural family therapists involve teachers, social workers, and friends in the treatment process.

In short, family therapists share the assumption that symptomatic behavior can be understood as a manifestation of the interactional processes in the family system (Bross & Benjamin, 1982). Each family systems approach finds it useful and sometimes necessary to include **extrafamilial members** in treatment. They appear to differ, however, in how each conceptualizes family systems to alter dysfunctional interactions.

Classifying Approaches to Family Therapy

Because the field of family therapy evolved from the work of diverse individuals, there have been a number of attempts to classify its approaches beginning with Jay Haley's sketches (1962) of major family therapists. Three years later, the Committee on the Family, of the Group for the Advancement of Psychiatry (GAP) (Group for the Advancement of Psychiatry, 1970), conducted a survey of the field of family therapy and identified three types of family therapists: Position A therapists (psychodynamic), Position Z therapists (family systems), and Position M therapists (psychodynamic and family systems). Beels and Ferber (1969) attempted to group family therapists according to the personal style of the therapist. They classified therapists as **conductors** and **reactors**. Conductors were dominant and forceful leaders, such as Ackerman, Satir, Bowen, Minuchin, Paul, and Bell. Reactors were more nondirective and tended to follow the family's pattern of interaction. However, this schema appears to be more appropriate for classifying family therapists than for subdividing the field of family therapy (Nichols, 1984).

Foley (1974) categorized family therapists by integrating the Group for the Advancement of Psychiatry's classification system (1970) with Beels and Ferber's classification of family therapists (1969). His two-dimensional model permitted classification of therapists according to the theoretical dimension, from psychoanalytic to systemic, and the therapeutic dimension, from activator to observer.

Guerin (1976) developed a comprehensive theoretical classification system in reaction to the atheoretical systems developed earlier. On the basis of the GAP report, he divided therapists into two groups: psychodynamic and systems. Each group then was divided into subgroups. Guerin's classification system is more advanced than previous systems; however, it has several limitations. First, classifying schools according to theoretical orientation along one dimension (systems versus psychodynamic) does not consider the other major theoretical approaches. Levant (1984) notes that categorizing Bowen's multi-generational approach with the systems approaches fails to consider the commonalities between Bowen's theory and the psychodynamic approach.

Levant (1984) classified schools of thought into three clusters: historical, structural/process, and experiential. The historical model consists of the psychodynamic (Wynne, Lidz, Ackerman, Framo), the multigenerational (Bowen), and the intergenerational-contextual (Boszormenyi-Nagy) schools of family therapy. According to Levant, those approaches are concerned with "the individual within the system, with particular attention to those elements of their interpersonal functioning that represent attachments to figures in the past that will be transmitted to future generations" (pp. 80–81). Levant notes that this model goes beyond traditional psychodynamic theory to include the systemic interactions transmitted over generations.

The structural/process model is derived from communications systems. The model includes brief problem-focused therapy (Watzlawick, Weakland, Bodin, Risch), problem-solving therapy (Haley), structural family therapy (Minuchin), paradoxical therapy (Mara Palazzoli-Selvini and colleagues), triadic therapy (Zuk), problem-centered systems therapy (Epstein and associates), integrative therapy (Duhls), behavioral family therapy (Patterson and Stuart), structural strategic therapy (Stanton and Andolfi), and structural-strategic-behavioral approaches (Rabkin and Alexander). These approaches are concerned with current family interactions and their relationship to the presenting problem or symptom bearer.

The experiential model in Levant's classification system consists of the Gestalt (Kempler), experiential (Whitaker), and client-centered (Rogers) approaches to family therapy. The work of Virginia Satir is also included in this model. These approaches are concerned with facilitating personal growth in individual family members rather than with altering the family system. The process of therapy focuses on affective experiences to achieve self-actualization.

The comprehensive classification system designed by Levant is useful for conceptualizing and evaluating different approaches. However, Nichols (1984) notes that the conceptual distinction between historical and ahistorical models is not valid. Bowen focuses both on history and on change in the current family system. Moreover, by classifying behavioral therapists in the structural/process category, Levant fails to consider that behavioral family therapists do not alter family systems. Likewise, other therapists, such as Bandler and Grinder, have failed to base their therapeutic approach on theoretical principles.

As this review of the field's attempt to classify shows, it is very difficult to categorize various models of family therapy. Gurman and Kniskern (1981) comment on this dilemma: "Just as, in our view, the boundaries between the intrapersonal and interpersonal domains of experience are subtle, so, too, are the boundaries between the various family therapies unclear" (p. xiv). Because a proliferation of both family therapy approaches and taxonomies exists, we have chosen to divide the approaches into the following theoretical groups:

Structural (for example, Minuchin, Stanton, Montalvo)
Strategic (for example, Jackson, Haley, Watzlawick, Erickson, Hoffman, Palazzoli-Selvini)
Transgenerational (for example, Ackerman, Bowen, Framo, Boszormenyi-Nagy)
Experiential (for example, Satir, Whitaker)
Behavioral (for example, Stuart, Patterson, Jacobson)

In selecting this method of classification, we have attempted to combine those approaches that have both a common theoretical heritage and a common method of practice. Each theoretical group certainly includes diversity; however, far more similarities exist within a theoretical category than between categories. Selection criteria also include a theoretical group's comprehensiveness, so that we could focus on the principal stages of therapy in each (that is, problem identification, goals, techniques, and evaluation). By examining how the various groups handle each stage of therapy, you can develop a comparative frame of reference for understanding family therapy. In addition, you can compare your own views of therapy with those of each theoretical group.

References

Bateson, G., Jackson, D., Haley, J., & Weakland, J. (1956). Towards a theory of schizophrenia. *Behavioral Science, 1,* 251–264.
Beels, C., & Ferber, A. (1969). Family therapy: A view. *Family Process, 8,* 280–332.
Bertalanffy, L. V. von. (1968). *General system theory.* New York: Braziller.
Boszormenyi-Nagy, L., & Spark, G. M. (1973). *Invisible loyalties.* New York: Harper & Row.
Bowen, M. (1976a). Family therapy and family group therapy. In D. H. L. Olson (Ed.), *Treating relationships.* Lake Mills, IA: Graphic.
Bowen, M. (1976b). Theory in the practice of psychiatry. In P. Guerin (Ed.), *Family therapy* (pp. 42–90). New York: Gardner Press.
Broderick, C. B., & Schrader, S. S. (1981). The history of professional marriage and family therapy. In A. S. Gurman & D. P. Kniskern (Eds.), *Handbook of family therapy* (pp. 5–38). New York: Brunner/Mazel.
Bross, A., & Benjamin, M. (1982). Family therapy: A recursive model of strategic practice. In A. Bross (Ed.), *Family therapy: Principles of strategic practice* (pp. 2–33). New York: Guilford Press.
Dell, P. (1982). Beyond homeostasis: Toward a concept of coherence. *Family Process, 21,* 21–42.
Foley, V. D. (1974). *An introduction to family therapy.* New York: Grune & Stratton.
Framo, J. L. (1972). *Family interaction: A dialogue between family researchers and family therapists.* New York: Springer.

Goldenberg, I., & Goldenberg, H. (1983). Historical roots of contemporary family therapy. In B. B. Wolman & G. Stricker (Eds.), *Handbook of family and marital therapy*. New York: Plenum.

Group for the Advancement of Psychiatry. (1970). *Treatment of families in conflict: The clinical study of family practice*. New York: Aronson.

Guerin, P. J. (1976). Family therapy: The first twenty-five years. In P. J. Guerin (Ed.), *Family therapy: Theory and practice* (pp. 2–22). New York: Gardner Press.

Gurman, A. S., & Kniskern, D. P. (Eds.). (1981). *Handbook of family therapy*. New York: Brunner/Mazel.

Haley, J. (1962). Whither family therapy? *Family Process, 1,* 69–100.

Hansen, J. C., & L'Abate, L. (Eds.). (1982). *Values, ethics, legalities, and the family therapist*. Rockville, MD: Aspen Systems Corporation.

Jackson, D. D. (1959). Family interaction, family homeostasis, and some implications for conjoint family therapy. In J. Maserman (Ed.), *Individual and family dynamics*. New York: Grune & Stratton.

Levant, R. F. (1984). *Family therapy: A comprehensive overview*. Englewood Cliffs, NJ: Prentice Hall.

Lidz, T., Cornelison, A., Fleck, S., & Terry, D. (1957). The intrafamilial environment of schizophrenic patients: Marital schism and marital skew. *American Journal of Psychiatry, 114,* 241–248.

Maruyama, M. (1968). The second cybernetics: Deviation-amplifying mutual causal processes. In W. Buckley (Ed.), *Modern systems research for the behavioral scientist*. Chicago: Aldine.

Maturana, H. R. (1980). *Autopoiesis and cognition: The realization of the living*. Boston: D. Reidel.

Minuchin, S., Montalvo, B., Guerney, B. G., Rosman, B. L., & Schumer, F. (1967). *Families of the slums*. New York: Basic Books.

Mittlemann, B. (1944). Complementary neurotic reactions in intimate relationships. *Psychoanalytic Quarterly, 7,* 479–491.

Mittlemann, B. (1948). The concurrent analysis of married couples. *Psychoanalytic Quarterly, 17,* 182–197.

Nichols, M. P. (1984). *Family therapy: Concepts and methods*. New York: Gardner Press.

Okun, B. F., & Rappaport, L. J. (1980). *Working with families. An introduction to family therapy*. Belmont, CA: Wadsworth.

Pentony, P. (1981). *Models of influence in psychiatry*. New York: Free Press.

Singer, M. T., & Wynne, L. C. (1965). Thought disorder and family relations of schizophrenics: III. Methodology of using projective techniques. *Archives of General Psychiatry, 12,* 201–212.

Watzlawick, P., Beavin, J. H., & Jackson, D. D. (1967). *Pragmatics of human communication*. New York: Norton.

Weakland, J. (1960). The "double bind" hypothesis of schizophrenia and three-party interaction. In D. Jackson (Ed.), *The etiology of schizophrenia*. New York: Basic Books.

Wynne, L., Ryckoff, I., Day, J., & Hirsch, S. (1958). Pseudomutuality in the family relations of schizophrenics. *Psychiatry, 21,* 205–220.

Chapter Two

Family Life Cycle

The principal task of any family is to provide for the development of its members. All families must perform certain basic tasks; for example, providing food and shelter, carrying out developmental tasks (including fostering individual and family growth), and accomplishing tasks related to crises such as illness, death, or the birth of a handicapped child. (Carter & McGoldrick, 1980)

The first detailed description of the family life cycle from a systemic point of view occurred in Jay Haley's (1973) book *Uncommon Therapy*. Haley outlined the therapeutic techniques of Milton Erickson across six stages of the family life cycle. Haley highlighted the fact that symptoms are likely to occur at points of transition between stages. More recently, Betty Carter and Monica McGoldrick (1980) have edited a popular book entitled *The Family Life Cycle: A Framework for Family Therapy*. Carter and McGoldrick propose that problems are the result of an interruption in the family life cycle and that the goal of therapy is to get the family back on track. The book provides a clinical overview of the family life cycle and offers clinical suggestions for working with families at each developmental stage.

Perhaps the greatest contribution of Carter and McGoldrick is their conceptualization of the **nuclear family** as a three-generational system that reacts to pressures from generational tensions as well as developmental transitions. Carter and McGoldrick (1980) use a vertical and horizontal axis in their model to describe this interactive process (see Figure 2.1). Anxiety is transmitted vertically across the generations through emotional triangulation, family expectations, and myths. Anxiety is also transmitted horizontally through changes in the developmental life cycle. Developmental stresses can be both predictable (for example, leaving home or getting married) and unpredictable (for example, illness, loss of job, or death). When a certain amount of stress occurs on both axes, then a crisis in the system often follows. The following case illustrates the relationship between horizontal and vertical levels of stress.

A 40-year-old single man sought family therapy for severe depression. The man had recently lost his mother; his father had died ten years previously. The man had always felt the need to please his mother. He was a full

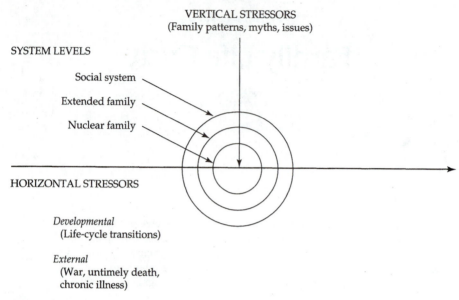

FIGURE 2.1
Horizontal and vertical stressors

professor at a major university and had an international reputation in his field. He had been triangulated into the conflict between his mother and father and continued to have a close relationship with his mother through his adult life. He had remained single and often reported that he couldn't find "a good woman like [his] mother." At the time of his mother's death, he was dating a woman who had recently gone through a divorce. The mother had expressed to her son her tacit approval (**vertical stressor**) of the girlfriend as her own replacement. Shortly following the mother's death, the **generational legacy** became too stressful for the relationship to withstand, and the man and woman broke it off (**horizontal stressor**). At that point, stress at the vertical level (the man's obligation to please his mother by marrying the woman) intersected with stress at the horizontal level (unexpected loss of both his mother and the woman he wished to marry), together producing depression and disruption in the system.

The level of stress on both axes is much greater for families today than for those of past generations. The increasing divorce rate, the women's movement, and sexual and technological revolutions have had a profound impact on families moving through the life cycle. The vast amount of change produced by these events puts a great deal of stress on families today. The loss of a job or a divorce often precipitates a crisis that sends the family to therapy. However, if therapy focuses only on the symptom or the interactional patterns at the time of the crisis then the therapist may be missing information about relationship patterns transmitted from previous generations' struggle with developmental hurdles—patterns that may be contributing to the current crisis.

This chapter deals primarily with the predictable developmental stages of the American family. Special attention is given to variations in the family life cycle based on ethnic and socioeconomic class membership. Family rules and interactional patterns vary greatly for different cultural groups and socioeconomic classes.

The first stage of the family life cycle begins with marriage and lasts until the first child is born. Some attention is given at the beginning of this section to the unattached adult who must separate from his or her **family of origin** and establish intimate peer relationships before forming a new family. If the marital bond is to be formed, both spouses must differentiate themselves from their families of origin. The role of son or daughter must become secondary to the role of husband or wife. The newly married couple must negotiate boundaries with extended families, relatives, and friends. Moreover, more mundane issues must be resolved, such as the division of household chores.

In the second stage, the family must renegotiate rules and relationships to allow for the entry of children. Parenting roles and relationships with extended family must be redefined to include parenting and grandparenting. As the child grows, parents must establish interpersonal boundaries and maintain safety and parental authority while encouraging growth.

The third stage begins approximately when the first child enters school and continues in some form until the last child enters puberty. At this stage, parents must decide how to deal with the school establishment. Who helps the child get ready for school? Who makes contact with the school when there is a problem? Children must learn about peer relationships and new authorities. The system may need to shift at this time to allow mothers to go back to work or pursue other vocational interests.

The adolescent family begins when the first child enters puberty. Depending on the distribution of children, this stage will often overlap earlier and later stages. Some form of the stage will continue, however, until the last child leaves home. In this stage, family boundaries must allow for the adolescent's autonomy. Parents must continually alter their relationships and rules to allow the adolescent to move in and out of the family system. At the same time, the parents are facing midlife decisions and emotions. The way in which critical tasks of communication and boundary negotiation have been resolved in previous stages will affect resolution of challenges in this stage.

To the degree that previous developmental tasks have been mastered, the family can move into the launching stage. It is at this stage that the parents and the adolescent are, one hopes, in a position to attain greater independence from one another. This is now the longest stage because present-day families have fewer children to launch than their grandparents did and people are living longer (Carter & McGoldrick, 1980). Parents must develop adult relationships with their children and renegotiate their marital relationship without children. Stress occurs when parents are alone for the first time in 20 to 25 years and must renegotiate their time, new careers, and so forth.

The postparental family must deal with its own declining health. Spouses must reappraise their own life structures and explore new ways of living. All members of the family at this stage must deal with the loss of a spouse, loss of vitality, and the threat of senility and death in oneself or a loved one.

This chapter will address each of these stages in detail, and the final section will deal with the developmental stages of remarried families. Specific attention is given to the tasks that a family must resolve in order to move through the developmental process of life.

Stages of the Family Life Cycle
Beginning Family

The beginning family commences with the marriage and continues until the first child is born. It is a task to become a couple in our rapidly changing society. Sociological shifts, including the changing role of women and the invention of contraceptives, have produced later marriages. Between 1960 and 1978, the median age for first marriages increased from 22.8 to 24.2 years for men and from 20.3 to 21.8 years for women (Wolman, 1983). In addition, couples are delaying the arrival of children longer than they used to. In 1960, the average couple waited 14 months to have a child, whereas in 1979 the average delay before childbirth was 24 months (Glick, 1979).

Even though many people are deciding to marry later, there appears to be an optimal range for coupling. Glick and Norton (1977) note that women who marry before the age of 20 are twice as likely to divorce as those who marry in their twenties. Likewise, those who marry in their thirties are 50% more likely to divorce than those who marry in their twenties. Monica McGoldrick (1980) suggests that "while it may be better to marry later than sooner those who fall too far out of the normative range on either end are more likely to have trouble making the transition" (p. 95).

The first major task of the family is for both spouses to function as a branch of the family **system** (see Table 2.1). Spouses must establish different relationships with **extended families**; their roles as sons or daughters must become secondary to those of husband and wife. The degree to which a couple is able to develop intimacy and independence often depends on how each spouse has developed a separate personal identity in his or her own family. Spouses who have failed to develop a solid autonomous relationship in the family of origin will often either withhold themselves emotionally or develop an intense couple relationship that takes precedence over their own personal interests (Meyer, 1980). One must become a separate "self" before joining with another to form a couple.

Spouses who have failed to develop a separate "self" in their own family remain dependent on their extended family. Often a spouse will develop **pseudoindependence** from his or her family (Bowen, 1978). Bowen (1978) notes that a spouse will often distance himself or herself from the family of origin to avoid emotional intensity, yet the negative need for closeness leads the individual into marital relationships that are likewise reactive. When the tension in the marital relationship reaches a certain level of intensity, the spouse may again

❀

TABLE 2.1
Some Developmental Stages and Tasks in the Family Life Cycle

Stages of the family life cycle	Developmental tasks
1. Beginning family	a. Differentiating from family of origin
	b. Negotiating boundaries between friends and relatives
	c. Resolving conflict between individual and couple's needs
2. Infant/preschool family	a. Reorganizing family to deal with new tasks
	b. Encouraging the child's growth while maintaining safety and parental authority
	c. Deciding how to implement personal and family goals
3. School-age family	a. Renegotiating work load
	b. Sharing feelings when child can't handle school
	c. Deciding who helps child with school work
4. Adolescent family	a. Renegotiating autonomy and control between adolescents and parents
	b. Changing parental rules and roles
	c. Preparing to leave home
5. Launching family	a. Separating from family
	b. Leaving home appropriately
	c. Entering college, military, or career with assistance
6. Postparental family	a. Renegotiating marital relationships
	b. Renegotiating time and work
	c. Adjusting to retirement

remove himself or herself emotionally. Thus, emotional cutoff can result from the family's need for togetherness and the spouse's unresolved closeness with his or her family of origin.

According to McGoldrick (1980, pp. 108–109), several other factors appear to make marital adjustment during this beginning phase more difficult:

1. The couple meets or marries shortly after a significant loss.
2. The wish to distance from one's family of origin is a factor in the marriage.
3. The family backgrounds of each spouse (for example, religion, education, social class, ethnicity, the age of partners and the like) are significantly different.
4. The couple has incompatible sibling constellations.
5. The couple resides either extremely close to or at a great distance from either family of origin.
6. The couple is dependent on extended family members either financially, physically, or emotionally.

7. The couple marries before age 20 or after age 30.
8. The couple marries after an acquaintanceship of less than six months or more than three years of engagement.
9. The wedding occurs without family or friends present.
10. The wife becomes pregnant before or within the first year of marriage (Bacon, 1974; Christensen, 1963).
11. Either spouse has a poor relationship with his or her siblings or parents.
12. Either spouse considers his or her childhood or adolescence as an unhappy time.
13. Marital patterns in either extended family were unstable.

Another difficulty is reflected in the common cultural/religious expression "and then they were one." Often repeated in marriage ceremonies, the phrase is based on the assumption that an individual can become complete by "fusion" with another person. Bowen (1978) suggests the contrary. He writes that couples who are fused together have failed to differentiate from their family of origin and do not feel free to develop a separate intimate relationship with another. They are afraid to accept differences in the other because these differences would be too great a threat to their own poorly developed "self."

When two people are fused with each other, they often fail to take responsibility for themselves in the relationship. In a **fused relationship,** each spouse feels that his or her happiness is the other person's responsibility and often blames the other for problems in the relationship. It is common for a spouse to feel that if the other spouse would change his or her behavior, then the problem would go away and they would be happy. When spouses blame each other, they are failing to take responsibility for themselves in the relationship.

Couples who are fused also have trouble negotiating in the relationship. Negotiation means that each spouse must give in to some degree. A spouse who is fused in the relationship often fears that "giving in" means "caving in" and risking the fearful emotions of losing one's identity. Thus, fusion inhibits couples from sorting and resorting priorities and from developing spoken and unspoken rules about all the little ways they wish to live together. Moreover, such couples even have difficulty resolving mundane issues, such as "Should we leave the toilet seat up or down?" or "Who puts the dishes away?" or "Who takes out the trash?" Such minor issues become identity struggles.

The resolution of major and minor issues in this initial stage of family life can establish major patterns that will endure over the life cycle ("How do we deal with conflict?" "How will control and feelings be handled in this family?" "Who is responsible for whom and under what conditions?"). Couples must develop rules for closeness, cooperation, and specialization. Each spouse must know what is important to the other and appreciate the other's thoughts and feelings even when they are different. The ability to appreciate differences in the other person, however, can come only when a person has developed an autonomous identity, and an autonomous identity can come only when a person is emotionally independent of one's parents. The following case illustrates this important task of the family during the first stage of the family life cycle.

A young couple sought counseling after three years of marriage because the wife was convinced that her husband was having an affair. The wife had met her husband when she was 15 and had married him the following year. She was attracted to his "free-wheeling" independence and charm. Two months before her marriage, she lost her older brother, who had been living at home. Her father had died when she was 10 years old. The husband was the youngest of seven children and was attracted to her "affection and warmth," something he did not receive in his own family. Married when both were still adolescents, neither had time to develop a separate sense of self. After the first year of marriage, the characteristics that attracted them to each other had become the problem. The husband showed his independence by spending more time with his friends. He spent little time at home and rarely consulted his wife about financial and household decisions. The husband complained that his wife was "smothering" him; she asked too many questions and "nagged" constantly. When a problem arose, the husband would withdraw and, frustrated, the wife would pursue him. Each blamed the other for their unhappiness. In the second year of their marriage, their problems were compounded when they had a child. Therapy initially focused on each spouse and his or her family of origin. The wife reported that she had had bad feelings about herself during adolescence and had often depended on her older brother for help. When her older brother died, she expected her husband to take care of her. The husband reported that his family showed little affection. When conflict occurred, each seemed to go his or her own way. The therapist attempted to show how patterns in the extended family were carried over into the marriage and that each spouse was responsible for his or her own happiness.

In this case, each partner was attempting to complete himself or herself through the other. Each spouse's role and the patterns of communication in their extended families contributed to their inability to develop a relationship as a couple. It is also common for people to marry shortly after the loss of a parent or other family member. When the wife lost her father and brother, she expected her husband to take their place. However, such desires are unrealistic and often lead to disappointment and failure to appreciate the spouse for what he or she is. When a couple cannot successfully negotiate their own needs, they will often move from a **dyad** to a triad by having a baby. However, if a couple cannot resolve their differences before the baby arrives, they will have more difficulty in doing so afterwards.

Infant/Preschool Family

The developmental tasks for the family of young children begin with the decision to start a family and continue until the children enter school. The successful transition to this stage of the family life cycle requires that spouses have mastered the primary tasks of the couple stage of the life cycle. Couples who have achieved a sense of intimacy without extreme costs to autonomy and have been able to resolve conflicts will be more likely than others to accept their roles as mother and father.

The transition to the parenting role often begins with the decision to have children. It appears that women are much more ambivalent than men about having children (Campbell, 1975). Today an increasing number of couples are agreeing to remain childless (Wolman, 1983). The decision to have children is compounded by the changing role of women in our society. Furthermore, pregnancy forces the couple to deal with expected changes in lifestyle. Women also fear that their spouse will not share child-rearing responsibilities (McGoldrick, 1980). Parenting roles are easier when couples have at least a year of courtship before marriage and ample time after marriage to prepare for having a child.

When a couple has a child, the three automatically form a triangle. The mother becomes close to the child. If the mother gets too involved with the child, the father will often distance himself by getting more involved with his work: "The traditional shift of the husband away from the home and fatherhood has been determined not only by society but also by the process of pregnancy, which literally puts distance between mother and father by the omnipresence of the baby between them, even in the privacy of the marriage bed" (Bradt, 1980, p. 129). The husband often feels that the wife spends a disproportionate amount of time with the new member of the system. In some instances in which distance exists, however, the baby may serve to bring the couple closer together. The baby, then, can play a key role in monitoring the distance in the parental triangle.

Whatever their level of preparation, the couple is quickly faced with the strong attachment needs of the newborn baby. In the first two years of life, the child's primary developmental need (beyond survival needs) is to form an attachment to one or more family members. Attachment evolves over a repeated set of steps during the first six months of life. Infants can often discriminate among their mothers, fathers, and strangers by 2 months (Yogman, Dixson, Tronick, Als, & Brazelton, 1977). At 6 or 7 months, infants seek contact primarily with the mother. Infants are more likely to become attached when adults respond immediately to their emotional needs and interact with them (Schaffer & Emerson, 1964). Moreover, infants will become more attached to an attentive father than to an unattentive mother, even when there is greater contact with the mother. When infants have a secure attachment to the care-giver, they are more likely to develop problem-solving and social skills at from 2 to 5 years of age (Sroufe, 1978). Thus, the emotional sensitivity of parents during infancy provides a foundation for good psychological functioning in later years.

Infants develop attachments not only to their mothers but also to their fathers. There is some evidence to suggest that fathers' play behavior is particularly influential (Parke & O'Leary, 1976). Fathers spend four to five times as much time playing with their infants as they do in taking care of them (Lamb, 1977). The attachment of the infant to the father is particularly important in the development of the infant's sexual identity and self-image. The father's attachment to the child also helps to separate the mother-infant dyad and provide the infant with an alternative love object (Berman, Leif, & Williams, 1981).

In summary, when parents are sensitive and nurturant, the infant develops trust in others. The infant learns that his or her behavior has consequences and that his or her world is orderly. When parents do not provide care, the infant often becomes lethargic and unresponsive. Infants who receive care and stimulation from their parents are more likely than others to develop optimally during the early years of life (Belsky, 1981).

As the child grows, parents must establish rules that maintain safety and parental authority and still encourage growth. During toddlerhood, children begin to develop their sense of autonomy or separateness. Toddlers develop autonomy by climbing and pulling to get things without asking. To achieve autonomy, the toddler needs the parents' support. Children need to be encouraged to make choices and take responsibility for feeding and dressing themselves. Nevertheless, reasonable and consistent limits must be set while the child is learning to explore his or her environment. The parents' developmental tasks include learning the balance between limits and freedom, a balance that will change continually through each developmental stage.

As children become more autonomous during toddlerhood, gradual separation from parents is healthy. Children need to spend more time away from their parents exploring their environment. Accordingly, parents must provide adequate room for the child to be himself or herself, to experiment, to make mistakes. Too much room or space equates with distance (the family has no room for the child). Too little room or space equates with excessive closeness (the family uses the child to fill a vacuum) (McGoldrick, 1980).

Parents sometimes are involved in so many activities that they do not have space or time for their child. Likewise, children who fill a vacuum in the couple's relationship may not be able adequately to develop a sense of autonomy. If a couple has already developed an intimate relationship that can resolve its own conflicts, then the couple will be able to provide a favorable environment for support and autonomy of the child.

The young child's development has a profound impact on the marital relationship. Women who have launched a career or have spent most of their time around adults, and now find their world made up of children, often experience a great deal of frustration. Husbands, however, are still able to maintain adult contacts on the job. Haley (1973) found that women at this stage often desire more involvement in the adult world and often feel "discontented and envious" of their husbands. Under such conditions, the marital relationship often deteriorates until the husband and wife can negotiate child rearing and adult activities outside the home. Take the following case, for example:

Jack, 32, and Wilma, 29, sought therapy for their 3-year-old son, Rob. Rob, who had frequent temper outbursts and cried when he did not get his way, had been born four months prematurely. He had been conceived shortly after Wilma had had a miscarriage. Both parents reported that Rob was often "ill and sickly." Jack reported that he had no difficulties with Rob, whereas Wilma stated that she could not handle Rob. Jack felt that Wilma should handle Rob more effectively. In the first session, Rob sat close to his mother. Wilma reported that she worried about Rob. He had few friends, and she was afraid to allow him to play outside because "he would get hurt." While Wilma agreed that she had difficulty controlling Rob, it also became clear to the therapist that she would not let her husband share in the parenting. Wilma reported that Jack didn't understand Rob. In subsequent sessions, both indicated that the marital relationship had deteriorated shortly after Rob's birth and the death of Jack's father. Jack reported that he then began spending time either at work or with his mother, who had never accepted his marriage to Wilma.

In this case, the mother became overinvested in the child while the father became overinvolved with his work and his own mother. The early phase of their marriage was characterized by a fragile bond. Jack would feel that he was betraying his mother when he became close to his wife. Also, the miscarriage and the death of Jack's father added further stress to their young relationship. With the birth of the baby, Jack responded by moving further away from his wife while Wilma moved closer to the needy infant. Jack and Wilma stayed connected through Rob's misbehavior, which eventually brought them to therapy.

School-Age Family

A couple may have difficulties with a small child; if these difficulties remain unresolved, they will escalate into a crisis when the child enters school. At this stage, problems often arise "partly because of what happens within the complex organization of the family, but also because [the child] is becoming more involved outside the family" (Haley, 1973, p. 55). The family system often becomes vulnerable to feedback from outside systems—neighborhood and school. The family must learn to relate to these new and competing systems. Rules, or **boundaries**, must permit contact with people outside the family in order for the child to experience relationships for himself or herself. New rules must be established: How will we help with school work? Who should help with school work? How will we deal with school evaluation? How much should we expect at school? at home? The extent to which these and countless other rules can be negotiated will often determine how a family manages this stage of the life cycle. Parents are also undergoing physical and emotional changes as they leave their youth and approach middle age. They experience stresses and pulls from their rising career responsibilities as well.

In this stage, the couple has already developed patterns of communication (Haley, 1973). In some cases, the patterns of communication may impede the child's success in the outside world. Difficulties often arise in this stage when the parental dyad is split. A typical difficulty is one parent's siding with the child against the other parent. Father may perceive mother as "too soft," whereas mother views father as "too hard." Such perceptions often result in each parent's trying to save the child from the other. The mother may become overinvolved and then frustrated with the child, while the father remains peripheral to avoid "spoiling the child." When the father attempts to control the child (from a distance), the mother may soften the blow (undermine him) by protecting the child (Haley, 1973). This cycle repeats itself, with neither parent being able to control the child and the parents being angry at each other. The child's misbehavior serves to bring the parents together (albeit in conflict) when such communication would not exist otherwise.

When the child enters school, parents are often making personal developmental changes, such as seeking a new career. Mothers who have stayed at home often go back to work or pursue avocational interests during this stage. Husbands may be faced with the recognition that they will not achieve their career goals. Now there needs to be more sharing and renegotiation of boundaries and responsibilities (for example, Dad may share some of his "breadwinning" prowess with Mom). As Mom's time becomes more budgeted, she may wish to share more chores with him. Both may need to share more emotional stress. When these changes cannot be negotiated, a crisis (for example, depression, ulcers, drinking, or problems with school) often arises that affects each member of the system.

When parents have not fulfilled their own goals, they often concentrate on the child. Those parents are denying their own problems and focusing on the child's problem (McGoldrick, 1980). In such cases it is not unusual for the child to have difficulty entering school. The child picks up the conflict and senses the need to be close to one of the parents. Somatic symptoms then develop in the child, sending a signal to the parents that the child must be kept home with them. Both parents unite to deal with this crisis and put their own disagreements on the back burner. Thus, symptoms often keep the focus on the child and help the parents to avoid their own personal issues and marital relationship. Therapy can help parents to ignore the child's symptomatic complaints (for example, headache or stomachache) and return the child to developmental normality (that is, back attending school).

Mr. and Mrs. Hall came to therapy because their 10-year-old son, Jerry, was afraid of school. Jerry insisted that he was afraid of the children: They called him names and threatened to beat him up. The mother appeared to fear for her son's safety; the father felt that his son was "putting one over on them." Reports from the school counselor and teacher, however, indicated that Jerry was withdrawn but did not appear to be threatened by the other children. Subsequent interviews with Mr. and Mrs. Hall indicated a very conflictual relationship for many years. Jerry was particularly involved as a third party through which they conducted their battle. He had been "school-phobic" in the first grade. When Jerry's mother would complain to his father that Jerry couldn't handle school, he would "lay down the law about Jerry going to school," which would then trigger Mrs. Hall's protectiveness toward her son. The parents would then begin an intense argument while Jerry withdrew to his room to cry. After the argument, Mrs. Hall would console Jerry and plead with him to go to school out of fear for what his father might do.

In this case, there was a two-generational conflict, the mother joining the child (and his school phobia) against the father. The mother was unnecessarily attempting to save the son from the father, and the father was unable to feel compassion for the mother's concerns. When the therapist can prevent developmental stalemates like this one, then families can return to more functional ways of relating, which will prepare them for the next developmental stage.

Adolescent Family

The adolescent family is the next stage of development, occurring between the time the first child reaches puberty and the time he or she leaves home. When adolescence occurs, the rules and roles of the family must change again. Parents must allow the adolescent more autonomy, and boundaries must become even more flexible. Parents can no longer maintain complete authority and must accommodate themselves to the adolescent's increasing competence. The way in which critical tasks of communication and negotiation have been resolved in previous stages will again affect resolution of challenges in this stage.

At the time of the child's adolescence, spouses are often going through their own life changes. Marital relationships are often reevaluated during this stage. The internal emotional turmoil of adolescents often triggers a struggle within the family system to maintain the previous familial arrangements (Haley, 1973). When the parental dyad is split, the child often allies with one parent or another in order to gain more freedom.

The adolescent often challenges and tests family rules and regulations concerning privacy, control, and responsibility. The adolescent challenges the family system with new values and behaviors. The adolescent acts like a child one minute and like an adult the next. Parents often do not know how to respond to the adolescent. Should parents set limits? What behaviors should be taken seriously? Should we let him or her try and fail? Should we ask about his or her friends? These questions become all the more difficult for parents who are themselves feeling rebellious in their work or relationships.

The challenges that the adolescent places on the family system also have reciprocal effects on the extended family (Ackerman, 1980). Parents may interact with their adolescents much as they once interacted with their own parents. Ackerman further notes:

> An overfunctioning parent, for example, is often simply repeating the early experience of having grown up with an underfunctioning parent. The parent may rationalize this behavior by saying that it is a deliberate attempt not to make the same mistakes as the grandparent, to spare the third generation the pain of the second, and to "prevent my children from having the same hangups as me." The result is that the third generation turns out to be like the first. The child of an underfunctioning parent rears an underfunctioning child. A mother used to an intense relationship with her mother and little interaction with her father may repeat this pattern with her daughter and husband. Moreover, the relationship between daughter and husband will tend to mimic the relationship between the grandparents in both quality and intensity. It is amazing how

often the relationships in the nuclear family tend to be mirror images of both extended families. This means that the child, particularly the adolescent, may often become a special kind of peer of a grandparent, either competing for nurturing or control, as in a sympathetic alliance. The rules of intensity also apply here. When the adolescent either makes demands on the parent (increasing intensity) or rejects the parent (decreasing intensity), there tends to be a reciprocal decrease or increase in the parent-grandparent relationship. This, in turn, affects the grandparents' marriage. Conversely, retirement, illness, migration, and, of course, death of a grandparent often have profound consequences for the parent-child relationship and the parents' marriage. (p. 150)

The key developmental task in adolescence is separation and individualization. However, this process begins in infancy. If mother has trouble separating from her mother, she will be likely to encourage dependency to maintain emotional equilibrium. A mother may be threatened as the child's individuality emerges. She will often project one of her own siblings or parents onto the child and see the child as an extension of herself. The parent is thus unable to recognize the child's individual needs. So the child learns early to disregard his or her own needs to get approval from mother. Support is withdrawn when the child is assertive or independent and provided when the child is dependent. In adolescence, then, there is low self-regulation and difficulty in expressing identity and relating to reality.

Adolescents who are not able to separate from their parents often experience depression. Depression often occurs when the adolescent is attempting to meet the parents' needs but is not meeting his or her own individual needs. Adolescents will not admit to having depression and will deny it if confronted, but they will plead for help through their behavior in school, excessive sexual activity, and antisocial behaviors. When these behaviors occur, parents become punitive, thereby reinforcing the depression. Thus, adolescents' behavior is labeled as unmotivated and incorrigible rather than being recognized as a plea for help in growing up.

Consider the case of a 14-year-old girl named Tina, who was hospitalized for attempted suicide and depression. Upon her leaving the hospital, an exit interview was conducted with the family. The therapist first met with Tina to learn more about her problem. The girl reported that she felt a lot of pressure from her parents. At times they treated her like an adult and at other times like a child. She would ask, "What do they expect of me?" The therapist noted that Tina appeared very depressed. After 10 minutes, the therapist asked the mother, father, and two younger brothers to join them. The therapist learned that the parents disagreed about rules for Tina. The father was particularly opposed to the daughter's seeing an older boy, whereas the mother felt that it was permissible. Subsequently, the therapist learned that the mother and father also argued frequently over money and whether or not it was appropriate for the wife to go out drinking with her girlfriends. As the interview went on, it became clear that the husband felt he had little or no control over his wife. "There isn't anything I can do when they gang up on me," he would say, referring to his wife and daughter

Tina. Although the husband couldn't control the wife's excursions, he could and would control the daughter. When the husband exercised control over Tina, his wife would undermine his efforts in order to get back at him.

Because the parents clearly were having trouble in their marriage, and because they could not resolve the issues alone as a couple, they were, unfortunately, fighting through their adolescent daughter. Thus, any healthy autonomous move by the daughter became a trigger for her parents' conflict. For Tina, to grow up was to grow into more conflict with her parents. Because growing up was her very obvious developmental need, she felt stalemated and depressed.

Launching Family

The launching family begins when the child is in late adolescence and ends when the child leaves home. In this stage, the young adult begins to separate from his or her parents. In some cultures, the separation process is marked by a ceremony acknowledging the adolescent as an adult (Haley, 1973). The ceremony provides the adolescent with status to relate to parents as an adult. Traditionally, ceremonies have marked such events as the young adult's entering college, military service, and even marriage. However, if the young adult is still receiving financial and emotional support from his or her parents, then these ceremonies do not signify clear separation and autonomy.

The way in which the young adult leaves determines whether he or she takes a responsive (choosing) position or a reactive (obligated) position in relation to the family. With an effective launching, young adults can return home by choice rather than feeling obligated to be there out of a sense of guilt. Likewise, even when problems in the family exist, the young adult does not feel an obligation to return to his or her previous role in the family to help solve the problem. The ability of the young adult to differentiate from his or her family of origin will lead to increased autonomy with future family members and friends.

The launching stage is also marked by the greatest change in membership in the family. Young adults marry and bring new spouses and children into the family. Parents then become grandparents, and new roles are established within the system. The family also loses members through the death of parents and grandparents. The effect that death has on the family system depends largely on the importance that the member who has died had with regard to that system (McCullough, 1980). In functional families, the addition and loss of members provide opportunities to explore new roles, whereas, in dysfunctional families, such changes produce disruption, which may lead to divorce or other related problems.

The launching phase presents still other problems. Because of the low birthrate and increased longevity, parents launch their last child on average nearly 20 years before their retirement (McGoldrick & Carter, 1982). Women who have been involved primarily with their children must adjust to new vocational or avocational activities. Spouses must also reexamine their marital relationship.

Parents may find that they have nothing to talk about because all their discussion has focused on the child or children. In some cases, couples will argue about old issues that were put aside when the children arrived (Haley, 1973). A couple will often hold onto a child who has been the focus of special concern and communication, particularly when the child holds a special position, has a diability, or is ill. In families that are not able to let go, conflict will lead to divorce or to severe problems in the adolescent (for example, running away, pregnancy, or suicide).

It is not terribly surprising that most serious behavioral disorders (for example, schizophrenia and anorexia nervosa) have their onset during this stage. In his book *Leaving Home* (1980), Jay Haley describes severely disturbed adults who have difficulty leaving home and supporting themselves. Stanton and Todd (1979) summarize Haley's approach in the following passage:

> There are certain assumptions that improve the chance of success with young adults who exhibit mad and bizarre behavior, or continually take illegal drugs, or who waste their lives and cause community concern. For therapy, it is best to assume that the problem is not the young person but a problem of a family and young person disengaging from one another. Ordinarily, an offspring leaves home by succeeding in work or school and forming intimate relations outside the family. In some families, when a son or daughter begins to leave home, the family becomes unstable and in distress. If at that point the young person fails by becoming incapacitated, the family stabilizes as if the offspring has not left home. This can happen even if the young person is living away from home, as long as he or she regularly lets the family know that failure continues. It can also exist even if the family is angry at the offspring and appears to have rejected him. Family stability continues as long as the young person is involved with the family by behaving in some abnormal way. (p. 58)

Thus, as long as the young adult remains incapacitated, parents can share their concerns about him or her without dealing with each other. Therapy at this stage should help to move the young adult out of the family and deal with the problems revolving around the separation.

The parent-adolescent separation process occurs across three generations (McCullough, 1980). The assumption underlying that assertion is that if parents have been successful in separating from their families of origin then they will be better able to help their own children separate and become autonomous. A mother who has difficulty separating from her mother may now have difficulty in separating from her daughter. The daughter's separation would be likely to produce changes in all three **subsystems**: that of child, that of parent, and that of grandparent.

In order for adequate separation to occur at this stage, all three generations must accomplish specific developmental tasks. McCullough (1980) notes that grandparents must learn how to spend more time together at a time when there may be a decrease in physical activity. There needs to be **intergenerational relatedness** to parents and grandchildren, and grandparents should be financially and emotionally independent of their children. Parents likewise should be less involved in taking care of their children. Parents should be involved in outside activities, such as volunteer work, school, or a career. At the same time, both spouses should recommit themselves to the marriage. They should explore new interests and activities. When children marry, parents must accept the in-laws and relatives. Children must be able to make their own decisions and relate to their parents as adults. The following case illustrates some of these issues.

> Bill and Stella had difficulties because of issues that had not been resolved in previous generations. Stella had always had trouble getting along with her mother. She met Bill at 15 and moved in with him secretly so as not to displease her parents. During the first year, Stella became pregnant and decided to marry Bill against her parents' wishes. Stella's parents felt that "Bill was not good enough for her." Stella's parents did not attend the wedding and broke off contact with her for 18 months. Later on, Bill and Stella were having financial problems and started accepting gifts (for example, furniture and household necessities) from Stella's parents. Stella's parents had just purchased a company in a neighboring state and offered Bill and Stella jobs. Bill and Stella accepted the job offers and moved in with Stella's parents until they could find an apartment. Shortly thereafter, Stella's sister accused Bill of stealing her ring. A fight ensued, and Bill left. Stella stayed with her parents, and soon afterward Bill and Stella filed for legal separation. Two months later, Bill and Stella sought therapy to decide whether they should get back together. The therapist learned that Stella's mother still treated Stella like a teenage daughter rather than like a 23-year-old mother. Stella's mother had run away from home at 14 and felt guilty about her relationship with her mother. Stella wanted to go back to Bill but felt it would be only a reaction to her parents. Although she had never thought of it before, Stella was not making enough money in her parents' business to support herself. Stella decided that she must first become financially and emotionally independent of her parents before deciding whether to continue her relationship with Bill.

This case illustrates how the difficulty in a separation process can affect more than one generation. In this case, Stella had had colitis when she was 8 years old, a circumstance that probably contributed to her mother's overinvolvement with Stella. Stella's choice of Bill and the fact that Stella's parents did not accept Bill are other instances of both generations' refusal to let go. Stella and Bill had never become financially independent, and Stella felt that her marriage to Bill was an act of disloyalty to her parents. Her primary loyalties remained with her parents at the time that she failed to support Bill when her sister accused him of stealing her ring.

Postparental Family

The postparental family, often referred to as the **empty nest**, begins when the last child leaves home. In this stage, a couple can be relatively happy if they have allowed their children both autonomy and intimacy. Many parents report the most happiness in this stage (Stinnett, Carter, & Montgomery, 1972). It appears, however, that couples who report satisfying relationships during the postparental stage have had harmonious relationships during previous stages. Where marital problems exist, they may be compounded by retirement. Couples who have little income or education are also more likely than others to experience marital dissatisfaction in old age (Duvall, 1977).

Adjustment to retirement is a major developmental task. Retirement appears to affect men and women differently. Those who retire, particularly men, experience a loss of productivity and social relationships. Women appear to have less difficulty with that problem, especially if they have maintained their role as homemakers (Walsh, 1980). Haley (1973) reports that a wife may become symptomatic at the time of her husband's retirement. The symptom serves to protect the husband by giving him responsibility for her recovery.

Adjustment to retirement can be broken down into five areas (Turner & Helms, 1983). First, retirement often means a significant loss of income. Approximately 65 percent of the retired population have incomes under $3000. Most retirees depend on Social Security as a primary source of income. Second, retirees often must deal with the loss of self-esteem. The retiree must find volunteer and avocational activities that are meaningful and provide a sense of self-worth. Third, retirement causes a loss of working relationships. New friendships must be established. Fourth, individuals often must adjust to the loss of meaningful work. It is now important to find other things that provide a sense of purpose. Finally, there is a loss of identity. Many people identify only with their work roles, and thus they must find other roles that provide new identities.

Problems of retirement can also be compounded by death of a spouse. In many cases, the dying are isolated in retirement homes or hospitals away from loved ones. Death is often difficult for the family to accept. The initial loss and loneliness that follow death often lead to depression, as evidenced by the increase in suicide rates, particularly for men (Walsh, 1980). The nuclear and extended families' response to the grief of loss affects each individual family member.

The major developmental task at the time of death is to grieve the loss of the loving relationship and reinvest oneself in other activities. Unless family members go through a process of grief, they will often experience guilt, anger, and depression. Colin Parkes (1970) identifies four stages of the grieving process. In the first stage, *numbness*, family members often experience general shock, with little emotional response. In stage two, *pining* is characterized by a preoccupation with the deceased. The grieving process is often facilitated by focusing on acquaintances and pictures of the deceased and memories of experiences with the deceased. In stage three, *dejection*, the intensity of grief subsides and the loss of the family member is accepted with some depression. In the final stage, *recovery*, family members begin to rearrange their lives. Remarriage is a reasonable option for many widowed spouses.

A critical role for the postparental family is grandparenthood. The grandchild establishes a common bond between the grandparents and their adult children. Grandparenting helps the postparental family adjust to retirement and the loss of a loved one. Newgartin and Weinstein (1968) studied 70 sets of middle-class grandparents and found that most expressed satisfaction with their role. Grandparenthood offers an opportunity to relive childhood experiences. Grandparents also learn to accept their accomplishments and failures as parents (Walsh, 1980). In some instances, however, grandparents may be drawn into intergenerational differences over child discipline (Lopata, 1973).

In every family, the tasks of the postparental families interact with the issues that concern the adult children and grandchildren, who are going through their own developmental phases (Walsh, 1980). Intergenerational conflict often arises when family members are unable to complete their own developmental tasks. For example, when parents become ill and dependent, a role reversal occurs, obligating adult children to take care of their parents. The adult child who is not autonomous or is confronting the pressures of his or her own aging, will have difficulty taking care of his or her parents' needs (Brody, 1974).

> Jerry was in his late twenties and was recently married. His mother was not supportive of Jerry's marriage. Jerry was an only child and had lived alone with his mother since the death of his father five years earlier. Jerry described his mother as being "strong-willed." Four months after the wedding, Jerry's mother was diagnosed with bone cancer. During the course of treatment, she was given drugs to treat the cancer. After six months, the prescribed drugs were no longer effective, and a decision had to be made whether to give Jerry's mother stronger medication, which had life-threatening consequences. Jerry avoided making the decision. At a joint conference with the doctor, Jerry indicated that he didn't want to be responsible. Jerry had felt guilty that he had left his mother and felt that his departure had triggered his mother's illness. The social worker at the hospital worked with Jerry to recognize that he had his own life to live and that his marriage was not the cause of his mother's cancer. The worker was able to convince Jerry that he was doing everything a "good son" could do for his mother.

This case illustrates how developmental issues occur across generations. Jerry had not separated from his mother and was not able to assume a new role and make a firm decision at the time of her illness. The fact that his marriage had been against his mother's wishes only exacerbated the problem.

Stages of Remarriage

The remarried or **blended family** goes through additional stages of development. Like the stages of the family life cycle, the stages of remarriage include developmental tasks and transitional periods. It is noteworthy, however, that remarried families must go through two sets of developmental processes simultaneously: those appropriate to the age and stage of family members and those related to the stage of the remarriage process (Whiteside, 1982). When

❀

TABLE 2.2
Developmental Phases and Tasks of Remarried Families

Phase	Developmental tasks
1. Separation/divorce	a. Dealing with loss of friends
	b. Developing new self-esteem and independence
	c. Allowing grief and mourning for the lost marriage
	d. Adjusting to the extended family's reaction to the divorce
2. Single parenthood	a. Reorganizing family to take care of child
	b. Resolving feelings of guilt and anger
	c. Creating new social support systems
3. Courtship	a. Establishing a willingness to reaccept intimacy
	b. Accepting conflict in the new relationship
	c. Developing a role for potential new members of the family
4. Remarriage	a. Giving up myths of remarried families
	b. Negotiating new traditions
	c. Developing new alliances
	d. Integrating boundaries between old and new families

treating the remarried family, the therapist must understand the integration of these two sets of developmental processes.

The remarried family goes through the following developmental stages: separation and divorce, single parenthood, courtship, and remarriage. A list of some of the developmental tasks for each phase appears in Table 2.2.

It may be more difficult for remarried families to complete developmental tasks than it is for the original nuclear family. Remarried families may have role models for parenthood but may lack such models for single parenthood or stepparenthood. In some cases, the developmental tasks for one stage may conflict with tasks at another stage (for example, courting and single parenthood). A discussion of each developmental phase of the remarried family follows.

Separation/Divorce

The basic developmental tasks of separation/divorce focus on establishing an emotional divorce (Kressel & Deutsch, 1977), establishing different relationships between the parent and child, and developing new levels of self-esteem and independence (Whiteside, 1982). Beal (1980, p. 248) suggests that the following conditions will increase the emotional loss in divorce:

1. A belief that the problem lies in the current relationship and is not likely to be found in subsequent relationships
2. A belief that a divorce will produce a long-term rather than a short-term serious loss of the sense of self or sense of identity
3. A high level of denial about the possibility of loss in the divorce process
4. A belief that the only important thing is to get away from the other person
5. A decision to divorce made solely on the basis of what "feels" right or what is legally possible for the purpose of revenge

By contrast, emotional loss will be reduced if a couple can maintain a cooperative relationship following the divorce. This is most likely to occur when the couple is flexible and can maintain a more or less functional parental relationship with the child.

Couples who have an intense emotional attachment have difficulty separating or divorcing emotionally. Couples who have lived together longer than two to four years have developed a significant attachment (Weiss, 1975). Intense relationships may have been a way for family members to leave their families of origin. In cases in which a strong attachment exists, a couple may be able to separate or divorce legally but not emotionally. If a person is unable to detach from his or her ex-spouse or family, he or she is likely to suffer negative consequences in the next marriage.

The major investigations of separation and divorce (Hetherington, Cox, & Cox, 1976; Wallerstein & Kelly, 1974; Weiss, 1975) emphasize the need for parental support for children. Indeed, children under 5 years old appear to have greater problems adjusting to divorce than older children (Wallerstein & Kelly, 1976). Moreover, the behavior of children from 2 to 4 years of age appears to regress at the time of the divorce. Children who have been pulled into the marital conflict experience "depression and developmental delays" when divorce occurs (Beal, 1980). Adolescents appear to experience fewer developmental problems than younger children (Wallerstein & Kelly, 1976).

There are several things parents can do to help children adjust to divorce. First, parents can reassure their children that they are not to blame for the divorce. Second, it is important for the couple to continue to agree on parental responsibilities during the divorce process. Third, parents should avoid suppressing the child's grief at the loss of the parent. Fourth, parents should help children understand that their painful feelings won't last forever, and, finally, children should have access to both parents and both sets of grandparents. When a spouse cuts off family contact with the ex-spouse, an imbalance is created that may be repeated in the children's marriages.

Single Parenthood

During the process of separation, the two-parent family becomes a one-parent family. In 1980, approximately one family in four was a one-parent family. Approximately 12 million children live in one-parent families. More than 90% of those families are headed by mothers. However, the number of children living in father-headed homes is increasing because of more liberal custody decisions. The alarming increase in one-parent families means that most children born in the United States in 1977 or later will spend some time in a one-parent family (Glick, 1977).

The term *one-parent family* is a misnomer because more than one parent is involved in the family (Whiteside, 1982). Instead, it is still a two-parent family, with both parents involved in rearing their children, although, in the typical arrangement, only one parent lives with the children. The one-parent family must reorganize itself to carry out the necessary functions of a family using fewer resources. New patterns of behavior must be established to maintain a household and earn a living. Two-parent families produce nearly twice the average income of a one-parent family. A single mother with young children may find herself seeking employment to maintain or retain the home (Beal, 1980). The family organization can be maintained as long as adequate child care is provided. However, when adequate child care cannot be provided, the parent often turns to grandparents and children for help in parenting.

When the parent is not able to maintain a household, he or she will often move back into the family of origin. Whereas such a move provides economic support, it also often re-creates old conflicts between the parent and grandparents. The grandparents may often relate to the parent as their daughter or son rather than as a mother or father. Because the parent lives in the grandparents' house, he or she often feels the lack of executive authority over the children. The parent's authority and competence disappears in the presence of the grandparents (Minuchin, 1974). The grandparents, in an attempt to protect the parent, will often intervene through communication with the ex-spouse. Thus, the parent is unable to become autonomous and function independently in his or her new role. Therapeutic intervention in such instances requires that functions be shared by grandparents and parents (for example, grandparent is in charge of children when parent is unavailable, and parent is in charge when available). This type of cooperation may be necessary when resources are limited.

In some cases, the parent who feels overloaded may turn to the *parental child*. The allocation of parental power to the eldest child often occurs in large families. The parental child may have responsibility for the younger children, as well as for other household tasks. Moreover, the parent who is socially isolated will often turn to the parental child for emotional support. Problems arise, however, if delegation of responsibilities is not explicit or if the child is given tasks inappropriate for his or her age (for example, asking a 7-year-old to cook dinner). In such instances, the parental boundaries between the parent and child break down. It is very difficult for a parent to discipline an older child on whom he or she relies for emotional and executive support. The parent may feel guilty and have difficulty setting limits. If the parent remarries, the child may have difficulty giving up this privileged relationship. Therapeutic intervention, in this case, should focus on delegation of clear responsibilities that are appropriate to the child's age. Efforts should be made to help parents to develop their own emotional support system so the parental child can meet his or her own developmental needs.

Courtship

The development of intimate relationships with others marks a new beginning for the single parent. Courtship or dating often means that the parent has given up emotional attachment to the ex-spouse. The development of new relationships helps to improve self-esteem and self-confidence. Courtship is a transitional period between the old family and the new, remarried family. The trust and intimacy that develop in courtship often serve as a foundation for remarriage.

In the courtship stage, however, the parent may often experience difficulties. First, the rules for courtship are not clearly defined for divorced spouses. Divorced people who had been married for some time often do not know how to act and may feel uncomfortable with new relationships. Second, single divorced people may experience in themselves feelings of approach and avoidance. They may often feel needy and overpursue their new acquaintances, yet the fear of closeness may scare them and produce distance in the relationship. They may be afraid of losing their new-found independence and of leaving themselves vulnerable to additional hurt and pain.

Unfortunately, in many cases, a third barrier to new relationships is children. Children often feel protective of the parent and complain about the new relationship. Children may see the new relationship as an act of disloyalty toward the ex-spouse. Moreover, children may not understand why the parent stays out late. When children see their parent embracing someone, they become aware of their own sexuality and may start acting out. A regular companion of the parent may want some share in the discipline of the children. Any one of or a combination of these factors may produce guilt feelings in the single parent, leading him or her to give up the new friendship. Therapeutic intervention should support parents in understanding their children and in reassuring them that they care for them.

Remarriage

The first marriage involves the joining of two families, but remarriage often means combining three or more families (Beal, 1980). Approximately 15% of the families in this country are remarried or blended families. Sixty percent of all remarriages involve at least one child from a previous marriage. Approximately 35 million adults are stepparents, and one child in five is a stepchild. Unfortunately, 40% of all remarriages end in divorce within the first five years, according to 1980 statistics from the U.S. Bureau of the Census.

One of the major problems in remarried families is that there are no traditions or norms. While society focuses on the joys of family living through advertising and television, the remarried family often has difficulty adjusting to this pattern. In fact, at the time of remarriage, spouses must deal with many of the issues unresolved in the previous marriage. Remarried spouses must blend together and achieve immediate intimacy at a time when roles and boundaries are often confused. In addition, remarried families carry the scars of the first marriage. Children often become upset at the time of the remarriage because their affections and loyalties are divided between the old and the new. Remarried family members need adequate time and space to adjust to their new situation.

The complex and conflicting roles in the remarried family produce emotional problems that are unique to this family system. All members come into the new family with feelings of guilt and loss. For example, a mother may feel guilty about the marriage and feel a need to make up to the children because of the loss. A father who has left the children of his first family may feel the need to develop intense relationships with his stepchildren. In both instances, parents feel that they should love their stepchildren as their own, yet that response is contrary to the effects of infant bonding and often produces intense relationships and dissatisfaction.

Formation of the remarried family often produces divided loyalties among the children (Beal, 1980). There is a remarriage for the parent, but the children often do not know where they belong. Children may feel loyal toward their natural parents and express dissatisfaction with their stepparent. Children often feel that if they are loyal to the stepparent, they will be disloyal to the noncustodial parent, and if they don't love the stepparent, they will offend the custodial parent. It is extremely important for children to express these feelings and have continued contact with the noncustodial parent.

The boundaries in a remarried family often remain unclear. Questions arise, such as "Who belongs to the family? What property belongs to me? What room is mine? Who is in charge of the children?" It is not uncommon for a mother to become angry when the stepfather disciplines her children. In addition, there are no rituals or traditions for maintaining boundaries. It can be unclear as to what role the stepparents should play. Children may have similar difficulties. How does a child explain why a brother has a different last name? How does a child learn to play the role of a middle child in the remarried family when he or she was the eldest child in the previous family?

The critical developmental task in a remarried family is to keep the boundaries open and permeable. Communication between ex-spouses and children should be open. The authority of the stepparent should be gradually strengthened. For example, it is important for the stepparent first to become a friend to the child or children and then move gradually toward disciplinary responsibilities. The major task is to establish clear boundaries around the remarried family in a way that allows strong continuing relationships with extended members outside the household while supporting the development of new relationships within the remarried family (Whiteside, 1982).

Case Illustration

The following case may be useful in illustrating the developmental issues we have been discussing.

Pam Notter called the counseling center requesting counseling for her 13-year-old daughter, Kathy. Kathy was throwing temper tantrums, and Pam said that no one could get along with her. Pam was divorced and lived with her two daughters (the second daughter was 8 years old) and her boy-friend, Donald. When Kathy became uncontrollable, Pam would call her ex-husband and send Kathy to his house. Often, the tantrums would occur when Donald was not around the house. Once Kathy had been over at her father's house for a while, she and her stepmother would start to fight about household chores. Those arguments frequently reached the point where the stepmother would threaten to leave, and Kathy's father would step in and send Kathy next door, to her grandparent's home. Her grandparents felt sorry for Kathy and thought that Pam shouldn't have a male friend living at her home.

Looking at this family developmentally, one can quickly grasp the com-plexity and interrelatedness of developmental tasks. Kathy was just entering adolescence. She was beginning to deal with herself as a sexual being and was trying to find a niche among her peers. She felt awkward, unliked, and mis-placed. She had not yet found any social roles or activities to make herself feel a part of the social system. She felt out of place at school and even more out of place at home. Kathy's mother, Pam, was having a particularly hard time with the developmental transitions of divorce and remarriage. Her first marriage occurred when she was quite young, before she had established an identity. Pam's divorce was an emotional one characterized by the struggle of two im-mature people desperately wanting to forge separate identities yet terrified of the pain that accompanies such a process. After the divorce, Pam was bitter, lonely, and extremely needy. She turned to her daughters for closeness, yet they also needed emotional security. Pam partially met the developmental tasks of divorce and single parenthood. Pam had difficulty developing a separate iden-tity and positive self-esteem. Life's events, however, do not await the resolu-tion of unresolved developmental tasks. In her needy state, Pam met and fell in love with Donald, a divorced man whose life's dream of having children had been slowly slipping away. Pam and her children represented a quick solution to his need for closeness and for a purpose in life.

Donald had achieved better resolution than Pam of the developmental tasks of divorce, but he was also experiencing the developmental issues of middle age. He was increasingly afraid that his life was going nowhere. His work was meaningless and he was fearful that he was now too old to start a family. Donald was beginning to feel that he had missed his chance at life and that life was passing him by. When he met Pam, it was as if his prayers and dreams had been answered. Although he didn't tell Pam immediately, on the first date, he had daydreams of the happy family life they could have together. Pam and her chil-dren had such strong emotional need that they absorbed Donald's interest and a vision of the future. Pam decided after only a month to move into Donald's house with her children.

The developmental tasks of courtship and remarriage were treated superficially in a rush to finally heal the pain of the past (without experiencing the pain of the present). A glaring developmental omission was Donald and Pam's blind refusal to see the myths about remarriage on which they were basing their future. Their untempered embrace of each other's needs precluded any possibility of the conflict inherent to any remarriage. Negotiation was not possible between themselves or with their former families because any sign of conflict threatened their fragile union. They were unconsciously afraid that their bubble would burst and that the pain held at bay would come crushing in upon them.

Kathy, however, was growing up. At first, she could participate in this family contract because it really didn't impede her own growth. She was not so old that her interests in the world outside her family conflicted too much with her role inside the family. Human growth cannot be checked for long, however, and her inevitable needs as an adolescent eventually came into harsh conflict with the family system. Her fear and the family contract kept her from fighting directly with Donald. Instead, she fought for autonomy with her mother. Such conflict, however, threatened Pam and her pseudomarriage, and Kathy was quickly moved to her father and stepmother's house.

Kathy's father, Joe, and his wife, Louann, were struggling to become a new family. Soon after they were married, they had one child and then another, and they had not taken the time to work through the developmental issues of remarriage. Particularly unresolved were their relationships with their families of origin and with Joe's ex-wife, Pam. When Kathy failed to get along at home and showed up at their door, she represented an additional stress on their life— a stress that they blamed on Pam and her live-in companion. They resented having this additional burden imposed on them because they had not developed adequate methods to negotiate shared parenting with Pam. Complicating the developmental problems was the fact that Joe and Louann lived next door to Joe's parents. Although that proximity was convenient for the financially struggling couple, it also reflected Joe's inability to separate from his parents. Always feeling that he was a failure in his parents' eyes, Joe kept trying unsuccessfully to please them.

Joe's parents were lonely people who had raised a large family on a farm and had then retired to the city. They were rootless and felt unproductive. They had not found new interests and, instead, grieved for their lost dreams. Their last child, Joe, was their only preoccupation. Helping Joe gave them something to do. It is not surprising that Kathy was soon passed off to Joe's parents to care for. Although at first Kathy appreciated their smothering closeness, she began to rebel against it. Too old to keep up with an angry, energetic teenager, Kathy's grandparents soon felt defeated and directed their anger at Pam for her "immoral" lifestyle. They threatened to take Pam to court for custody (their inability to tame Kathy notwithstanding). It was at that juncture, when developmental insufficiencies reached crisis proportions, that Pam decided to call for counseling.

We will not explore the treatment of this family until we take up integrative analysis in Chapter 9. The dynamics of this case can be viewed differently, depending on the theoretical perspective adopted. One can see clearly, however, that whether one approaches this family structurally, strategically, transgenerationally, experientially, or behaviorally, one will identify the same developmental deficits. Most important to note is that in each family, the developmental forces operate on many levels. Each individual progresses according to his or her own internal biological clock and in conjunction with his or her interactions with other individuals. Then all the individuals in the system develop as a family system according to their life cycle and their interaction with life events and other systems. This complex process of human growth is often difficult to describe in linear, progressive terms, yet knowledge of developmental issues and their degree of resolution can be vital to any sort of understanding of families.

In Part Two of this book, we present the predominant theoretical perspectives within the family therapy movement today. Once we have discussed each perspective separately (in Chapters 3 through 8), we will then turn in Chapter 9 to an integrative analysis of family development, family theory, and family practice. We will return to Kathy and her family at that time.

References

Ackerman, N. J. (1980). The family with adolescents. In E. A. Carter & M. McGoldrick (Eds.), *The family life cycle: A framework for family therapy*. New York: Gardner Press.

Bacon, L. (1974). Early motherhood, accelerated role transition, and social pathologies. *Social Forces, 52*, 333–341.

Beal, E. W. (1980). Separation, divorce, and single parent families. In E. A. Carter & M. McGoldrick (Eds.), *The family life cycle*. New York: Gardner Press.

Belsky, J. (1981). Early human experience: A family perspective. *Developmental Psychology, 17*, 3–23.

Berman, E., Leif, H., & Williams, A. M. (1981). A model of marital interaction. In G. P. Sholevar (Ed.), *The handbook of marriage and marital therapy*. Jamaica, NY: Spectrum.

Bowen, M. (1978). *Family therapy in clinical practice*. New York: Aronson.

Bradt, J. O. (1980). The family with young children. In E. A. Carter & M. McGoldrick (Eds.), *A framework for family therapy*. New York: Gardner Press.

Brody, E. M. (1974). Aging and family personality: A developmental view. *Family Process, 13*, 23–37.

Campbell, A. (1975). The American way of mating: Marriage, *si*, children only maybe. *Psychology Today, 8*, 37–43.

Carter, E. A., & McGoldrick, M. (Eds.). (1980). *The family life cycle: A framework for family therapy*. New York: Gardner Press.

Christensen, H. T. (1963). The timing of first pregnancy as a factor in divorce: A crosscultural analysis. *Eugenics Quarterly, 10*, 119–130.

Duvall, E. (1977). *Marriage and family development* (5th ed.). Philadelphia: Lippincott.

Glick, P. C. (1979). *The future of the American family*. Washington, D.C.: U.S. Government Printing Office.

Glick, P. C., & Norton, A. J. (1977). *Marrying, divorcing, and living together in the U.S. today.* Population Bulletin 32/5. Washington, D.C.: Population Reference Bureau.

Haley, J. (1973). *Uncommon therapy.* New York: Norton.

Haley, J. (1980). *Leaving home: The therapy of disturbed young people.* New York: McGraw-Hill.

Hetherington, E. M., Cox, M., & Cox, R. (1976). Divorced fathers. *The Family Coordinator, 25,* 417–428.

Kressel, K., & Deutsch, M. (1977). Divorce therapy: An in-depth survey of therapists' views. *Family Process, 16,* 413–443.

Lamb, M. E. (1977). Father-infant and mother-infant interaction in the first year of life. *Child Development, 48,* 167–181.

Lopata, H. (1973). *Widowhood in an American city.* Cambridge, MA: Schenkman.

McCullough, P. (1980). Launching children and moving on. In E. A. Carter & M. McGoldrick (Eds.), *The family life cycle: A framework for family therapy.* New York: Gardner Press.

McGoldrick, M. (1980). The joining of families through marriage: The new couple. In E. A. Carter & M. McGoldrick (Eds.), *The family life cycle: A framework for family therapy* (pp. 93–120). New York: Gardner Press.

McGoldrick, M., & Carter, E. A. (1982). The family life cycle. In F. Walsh (Ed.), *Normal family processes.* New York: Guilford Press.

Meyer, P. (1980). Between families: The unattached young adult. In E. A. Carter & M. McGoldrick (Eds.), *The family life cycle: A framework for family therapy* (pp. 71–92). New York: Gardner Press.

Minuchin, S. (1974). *Families and family therapy.* Cambridge, MA: Harvard University Press.

Newgartin, B., & Weinstein, K. (1968). The changing American grandparents. In B. Newgartin (Ed.), *Middle age and aging.* Chicago: University of Chicago Press.

Parke, R. D., & O'Leary, S. E. (1976). Father-mother-infant interaction in the newborn period: Some findings, some observations, and some unresolved issues. In K. Riegel & J. Meacham (Eds.), *The developing individual in a changing world: Vol. 2. Social and environmental issues.* The Hague: Mouton.

Parkes, C. M. (1970). Seeking and finding a lost object. *Social Science and Medicine, 5,* 175–208.

Schaffer, H. R., & Emerson, P. E. (1964). The development of social attachments in infancy. *Monographs of the Society for Research in Child Development, 29*(3, Serial No. 94).

Sroufe, L. A. (1978). Emotional development in infancy. In J. Osofsky (Ed.), *Handbook of infancy.* New York: Wiley.

Stanton, M. D., & Todd, T. C. (1979). Structural family therapy with drug addicts. In E. Kaufman & P. Kaufman (Eds.), *The family therapy of drug and alcohol abuse.* New York: Gardner.

Stinnett, N., Carter, L. M., & Montgomery, J. E. (1972). Older persons' perceptions of their marriages. *Journal of Marriage and the Family, 34,* 665–670.

Turner, J. S., & Helms, D. B. (1983). *Life span development.* New York: Holt, Rinehart & Winston.

Wallerstein, J. S., & Kelly, J. B. (1974). The effects of parental divorce: Experiences of the preschool child. *Journal of American Academy of Child Psychiatry, 14,* 606–616.

Wallerstein, J. S., & Kelly, J. B. (1976). The effects of parental divorce: Experiences of the preschool child in later latency. *American Journal of Orthopsychiatry, 46,* 256–269.

Walsh, F. (1980). The family in later life. In E. A. Carter & M. McGoldrick (Eds.), *The family life cycle: A framework for family therapy.* New York: Gardner Press.

Weiss, R. S. (1975). *Marital separation.* New York: Basic Books.

Whiteside, M. F. (1982). Remarriage: A family developmental process. *Journal of Marital and Family Therapy, 8,* 59–68.

Wolman, B. B. (1983). Marriage and parenthood: The changing scene. In B. B. Wolman & G. Strickler (Eds.), *Handbook of family and marital therapy.* New York: Plenum.

Yogman, M. J., Dixson, S., Tronick, E., Als, H., & Brazelton, T. B. (1977, March). *The goals and structure of face-to-face interaction between infants and fathers.* Paper presented at the Biennial Meeting of the Society for Research in Child Development, New Orleans.

PART TWO

MAJOR THEORETICAL APPROACHES TO FAMILY THERAPY

Chapter Three

Structural Family Therapy

Structural family therapy is a term that is used to encompass both a conceptual model of families and an applied model of intervention with families. It emphasizes the active and organized wholeness of the family system. Structural family therapists focus on the interactions and activities of family members to determine the *organization* or *structure* of the family. Emphasis is placed on how, when, and to whom family members currently relate in an effort to understand and then to change the family system's structure.

The theory and technique of structural family therapy are closely identified with the master therapist Salvador Minuchin. In the late 1960s, Minuchin and his colleagues developed their therapeutic approach at the Wiltwyck School, a residential institution for delinquent boys from New York City. The structural orientation was designed specifically to meet the problems of families at Wiltwyck—families who were more often than not single-parent families. The structural approach was also influenced by the problem-solving approach of Jay Haley (1976) and the network therapy of Ross Speck (Speck & Attneave, 1973), who were associated with Minuchin after he moved to the Philadelphia Child Guidance Clinic in the early 1970s. This chapter is based on the thinking of Salvador Minuchin and other theorists/clinicians who have contributed to the structural approach.

Theoretical Constructs and Philosophy

The practice of structural family therapy is grounded in some basic theoretical concepts that give meaning to the technique. Key concepts among them are (1) the family as a basic human system, (2) the function of subsystems within the family system, (3) the characteristics of system and subsystem boundaries, (4) the effects of **enmeshed behavior** between individual family members, and (5) the evolution of transaction patterns. A discussion of each concept follows.

The Family as a Basic Human System

Minuchin refers to the family as a "multibodied organism" (Minuchin, 1983). A strong systems therapist, Minuchin views the family not as a collection of individuals or a sum total of individual personalities, but as an entity, an organism, much like an amoeba or a human being. Just as the amoeba has various protoplasmic components and the h uman being is made up of organs, the family organism consists of individual family members.

In structural family therapy, then, the "patient" is the family, and the problem or symptom is seen as a function of the health of the whole family organism. Although the family may identify one family member as the patient, the structuralist will view that individual as merely the symptom bearer. The structuralist, viewing the family as an organism, assumes that the symptom is being created and/or maintained by interactional and structural problems within the system as a whole.

Subsystems

Structural family therapy focuses on the social organization of family organisms. Families carry out their functions through an internal organization of subsystems.

In the interior of a living cell, all the component parts contribute in their own way to the working of the whole. However, each part does not work its own free will uninfluenced by the other parts. On the contrary, there are certain parts that work together to manage or regulate the other components of the cell. For example, the nucleus of a single cell operates in an executive function in relation to other cell organelles. This organization of component parts to fulfill a particular, necessary function within a larger system is called a *subsystem*.

The family system contains three key subsystems within the total family organism (Minuchin, Montalvo, Guerney, Rosman, & Schumer, 1967). First, there is the **marital subsystem**. It is the first to form and is central to the functioning of the family. The marital subsystem's basic role is to provide mutual satisfaction of the couple's needs without compromising the emotional environment necessary for further growth and development of two maturing, changing individuals (Terkelsen, 1980). The marital subsystem is that part of a marriage that includes all the behavioral sequences that have evolved out of the partners' commitment to "love and cherish" each other. The marital subsystem does not include the roles each partner plays with other members of the nuclear and extended family. In other words, the marital subsystem would include transactional patterns related to giving attention to one another but would not include those transactional patterns concerning giving attention to their children. The latter patterns would be a function of the **parental subsystem**.

The parental subsystem includes those behavioral transactional patterns that have evolved in relation to raising children. This subsystem may consist of a father-mother team or may consist of one parent together with significant others who participate to varying degrees in the raising of the children.

The parental subsystem is sometimes confused with the marital subsystem because often the same two people make up both subsystems. Yet there are two distinct subsystems (or subsets of behavioral interactions), one subset consisting of husband-wife interactions and the other subset consisting of father-mother interactions. Each of us plays many roles at any given point in our lives, and each role is dependent on our interactions with others and the context of those interactions that have evolved within that group. Minuchin and Fishman (1981) find the term *holon* (derived from the Greek *holos* [whole] with suffix *on* [part]) particularly useful in referring to the various overlapping yet distinct roles in a family. As an example of subsystem roles (or holons), take the young woman who has returned to graduate school after giving birth to her first child. She is concurrently a wife to her husband, a mother to her child, a daughter to her parents, a sister to her siblings, a student to her teachers, a teacher to her students, and a colleague to her fellow graduate students. In each of these subsystems, relationships, or holons, she serves a different function, and she has developed transactional patterns for each of those functions. Some of these transactions undoubtedly overlap, and yet many more are patterns exclusive to a particular subsystem.

The parental or executive subsystem does not always consist of a father and mother as in the traditional family model. The parental subsystem may develop as a result of birth out of wedlock, adoption by a single parent, or divorce or death of a parent. Because parenting is a difficult task even for two people, the single parent often requires additional support systems to carry out this function. The parental support system may include members of the extended family (grandparents), or members of the community (church or social service agency), a boyfriend/girlfriend, or a separated or divorced spouse. The function of these supplements to the single parent's subsystem often varies with need and therefore varies in consistency. The single parent's need for help in raising children, combined with the stresses of sharing parental functions with inconsistent members of the parental subsystem, is often a source of difficulties within such families.

The children themselves are members of the **sibling subsystem**. Learning how to relate to peers, particularly with regard to authority, is the primary function of the sibling subsystem. This context provides a learning laboratory in which the child is able to explore and experiment with others. Sharing, standing up for oneself, building coalitions, and learning to negotiate with others are only a few of the lessons the child begins to learn about human relationships. The "only" child has the same needs to explore and experiment and will usually develop friendships with neighbors or relatives that serve as a surrogate sibling subsystem. Adequate functioning of the sibling subsystem requires the family to allow the child to develop relationships outside the family system.

Boundaries

The boundaries of a system or a subsystem are "the rules of who participates and how" (Minuchin, 1974, p. 53). Take, for instance, the Warner family, who came to therapy because their son Tommy would not stay in the backyard to play. The therapist chose to explore with the family members what their rules were about extrafamilial relationships as a way to put the presenting problem into the family context. The family rules that combined to form the family system's boundary were as follows:

1. Dad could make male friends at work and occasionally make social arrangements with them that revolved around sports. Any other social activities should include the spouse. Dad could not make female social friends unless they were much older.
2. Mom worked part-time and could make friends at work, but only on rather unusual occasions would she feel comfortable seeing them socially. Any such social occasions had to be announced well in advance.
3. The children in the family, Tommy (5) and his younger sister Cheryl (3), mostly played with each other in the backyard.
4. When another child did come over, the invitation to do so was extended by the mother, not the children. If Tommy went to someone else's home to play, it was because the other child's mother had called and made the arrangements.
5. Although Mr. Warner's sister and her family lived only a block away, they and other relatives were seen on a planned basis, the occasion always preceded by arrangements made over the phone or through the mail.
6. The Warners's social friends knew they were expected to call first rather than just dropping in unannounced.

These family rules formulated a system boundary that everyone in the family understood. The rules were sufficient until Tommy needed more autonomy to make friends outside the family. As Tommy grew more confident, he would wander into a neighbor's yard or call a friend across the fence to come and play. Before long, he would walk to his cousin's house to find something to do. Now Tommy's mother would be brought into contact with neighbors and relatives—not on her terms, but increasingly in response to Tommy's forays into the world outside the family. As family members' needs changed, the family had to evolve new rules to govern their system's boundary.

All families evolve such rules, and each family's boundaries vary in their degree of flexibility and permeability. Some families' boundaries may be too rigid (inflexible) and therefore make it difficult for the family members to adjust to new situations. **Permeability** of a system or subsystem boundary refers to the amount of access family members have across boundary lines. Some families' boundaries are too permeable in that the boundary becomes diffused or ill defined and allows too much access (or interference) by other family members or society. Other families may have boundaries around their system or their subsystems that are impermeable, limiting needed access to each other or the world outside the family. Why not take a moment and think about the spoken and unspoken rules in your own family? You might be surprised by such a list, particularly if you then compared it with your present values and attitudes about your current family's contact with people outside the family.

Boundaries (or well-established transactional patterns) do not exist just around the family system, as illustrated by the Warner family. There are interactional paths between or among individuals and subsystems that become so worn and well known that alternative paths are not chosen or possibly even noticed. The pattern of transactions between individuals of different subsystems is referred to by structuralists as *subsystem boundaries*. For example, when a mother and father argue about some issue of concern between them, a child will often experience some distress. Typically, the child will attempt to alleviate this internal stress by interrupting the parents' argument. The options available to the child are almost limitless. A child might seek attention by pulling on a skirt or pant leg and asking the parent for a cookie, begging to be played with, or summoning the parent to come and see the jar of jelly overturned in the kitchen. How the parents routinely respond to this kind of interruption contributes to the overall character of the marital subsystem boundary. On the one hand, the parents might ask the child not to interrupt, or they might say, "Mommy and Daddy are arguing, and we will be done in a minute." On the other hand, the parents might drop their disagreement and immediately attend to the child's request. In the latter instance, the boundary around the marital subsystem is weakened because the couple's disagreement goes unresolved and may be carried into other areas of their functioning. If we carry the scenario one step further, the husband might still be angry or upset and harshly criticize the child for spilling the jelly jar and then leave with a comment about his wife's carelessness in leaving the jar out where the child could reach it. Rather than disciplining the child, the wife may feel maligned and team up with the child by comforting herself and the child as victims of injustice.

The boundaries of the marital subsystem in this example will depend on how the parents typically handle the child's attempts to interrupt their interactions. A single transaction is not enough to establish an interactional rule. However, when similar interactions occur repeatedly, they form a pattern or rule or boundary that defines how the family members relate during times of marital conflict.

The concept of boundaries is closely related to the concept of enmeshed behavior in structural family therapy. Minuchin (1974) describes an axis at one end of which are families having extremely permeable or diffused boundaries between subsystems. For example, if a husband and wife allow a child to interfere with their marital disagreement, then the boundaries are too permeable and fail to protect the couple's subsystem. When boundaries are too permeable, family members are enmeshed in the family system at the cost of their own autonomy and personal mastery (that is, family members don't learn to work out their own problems). At the other end of this theoretical axis are families who have impermeable or rigid boundaries. Members of these families have only minimal contact with one another. The families appear to be collections of individuals who are very autonomous. However, they maintain their separateness at the expense of mutual support. Minuchin (1974) refers to such families as **disengaged families**.

To summarize, boundaries are interactional rules that tell each family member who participates in interactions under what conditions, and even how they should participate. The rules are patterned transactions that evolve over time and reflect the underlying structure of the family. Family systems vary in boundary permeability and flexibility, ranging from families whose subsystems are too diffuse and who exhibit enmeshed behavior to those families whose members function as isolated individuals and exhibit disengaged behavior.

Evolution of Transactional Patterns

We have discussed the basic theoretical concepts about families that serve as a core to structural family therapy. The family organism operates on many levels of organization. As a system, the family has evolved patterned rules and boundaries that regulate its functioning. At any given point on the developmental continuum of a family's life cycle, each member of the family has specific survival and growth needs (Terkelsen, 1980); that is, each has needs for such things as food, shelter, and safety (survival), as well as growth needs such as emotional caring, support, and nurturance (developmental).

The family must evolve methods of functioning that allow it to fulfill this complex set of often conflicting needs. Because each member is continually changing, the requests made of the family system continually change. Each stage of life brings with it a new set of needs for each family member. For example, the couple that is just starting out in adult life and that has small children has very different needs from the couple whose last child has just left for college. Without some patterns to guide them, the family would become overloaded with need-fulfillment decisions. Consequently, the family, like other systems, organizes its various functions into a structure that reflects the categories of its operation.

A young married couple without children needs a relatively uncomplex structure. The requests to meet a need come mainly from each other and from their families of origin. They begin to experiment with various operations to meet the existing needs of each other and their families of origin, trying to find ways that sufficiently satisfy often conflicting needs.

> A young couple, Mr. and Mrs. Babbs, want to spend time together when they are both off work. They are frustrated because every evening, the wife's mother calls because she is lonely and "just wants to talk." When the wife's mother doesn't call, they notice the omission and begin to worry, until eventually the wife calls her mother. This young family system has conflicting requests placed on it, and the members are dissatisfied with the situation. Out of their individual and collective dissatisfactions, they attempt different solutions (or compete for need attainment). These attempts include the

husband's chastising his wife for her dependency and complaining about her mother in a derogatory manner. In turn, the wife explains to her husband how lonely her mother is and how she is trying to be more supportive of her mother to help her become less lonely. Other attempts to change the situation include the husband's taking his evening meal into the den, the wife's trying to cut her telephone conversations short, and the husband's finding reasons to stay later at work.

This couple is trying to find a set of functional behaviors that protect their young relationship (boundary) and redefine the wife's relationship to her family of origin. The possibilities for finding a functional solution to this problem are extremely varied. For example, after considerable trial and error, this couple evolves a pattern of compromise whereby the husband and wife attend to each other's needs (though not to the extent either would like) at certain times of the day and on weekends, while at other times, the wife continues to attend to her mother. Also, the husband has more and more of his needs met at work and in the peace and solace of his den. All three parties have evolved a structure (patterned operations over time) that, although not perfect, is at least sufficient (Terkelsen, 1980). Terkelsen refers to these small developmental changes or adjustments that do not transform structure as **first-order** developmental **changes**. This early family structure is characterized by the husband's moving slightly toward his work (getting more needs satisfied there) while the wife and her mother are still involved in meeting each other's needs and the marital conflict over closeness is left unresolved, though less intense. Once this dominant structure (Aponte & Van Deusen, 1981) is in place, the family is able to operate and maintain a steady state, all else being equal.

The "all else being equal," of course, is a relatively temporary condition, one free of important stress events occurring either outside the family system (such as loss of job) or inside the family system (such as illness or birth of a child). Thus a structure may be sufficiently functional in one developmental phase, yet not be adequate in another, or function in one context and not another.

To aid further understanding of the evolution of family structure, let's see what happens to the structure of the Babbs family when they give birth to a baby girl. The wife is now also a mother, the husband becomes a father, and the wife's mother becomes a grandmother. Their new roles create new operational demands related not only to parenting but also to societal and intrapersonal expectations. That is, all family members carry needs with them in the form of cognitive sets (conscious and unconscious beliefs) about how they want and don't want to perform as parents; those are needs they have learned in their own families of origin and in their culture.

The structure that was sufficiently functional for the young couple without children is now stressed by the additional operational demands of meeting the infant's needs as well as the role needs of the parents. The Babbs family may help to illustrate how an old structure can become dysfunctional under new developmental stresses.

Mrs. Babbs spends most of her time satisfying the needs of her infant daughter. She in turn finds motherhood very satisfying. The already close relationship with the grandmother makes it easy to accept the grandmother's offer to help around the house by cooking, cleaning, and so forth. Mr. Babbs is also excited about the birth of his daughter but is irritated by the presence of his mother-in-law, and he soon begins to wish he had more time with his wife, because the little time he used to have alone with her is now taken up by either the baby or the grandmother. The existing family structure requires him to decrease his attempts to be with his wife and instead to focus more on his work. Because he spends less and less time with his wife, he often is irritable with both his mother-in-law and his wife. Because he is so irritable, his wife does not exactly yearn to be with him. Again the family goes through a period of stress and anxiety, experimenting with various ways of relating that will operationally provide for the increased complexity of the total system's needs.

The Babbs family is searching for a new structure, and small modifications of the old structure will not be adequate. **Second-order** developmental **change** (Terkelsen, 1980) requires a transformation not at the operational level but at the structural level. That is, the compromise that was learned in the previous stage of the family life cycle cannot simply be fine-tuned, as in first-order change; instead, new ways of relating must be forged out of the heat of their conflicting needs. Discovering alternatives in this reordering of the system takes some time.

After a month of having only a baby to take care of and of listening to grandmother's advice, Mrs. Babbs wants to move closer to her husband and reestablish her marital relationship (subsystem). Grandmother, too, is tiring of such closeness and the extra workload and is looking for ways to spend some quiet time at her own home. All parties are, in their separate ways, searching for some alternative. Yet it often takes a unique combination of events to trigger a new and more functional pattern of relationship, which, if sufficiently repeated over time, will develop into a workable structure. In the Babbs family, a wedding anniversary serves to trigger a new relationship pattern. Mr. Babbs makes special arrangements to go out for dinner, and Mrs. Babbs asks the grandmother to baby-sit. Grandmother agrees but requests that they bring the baby over to her home (a reflection of her own need for autonomy). Not consciously realizing that the evening has all the component operations indicative of a new structure, all the family members do find the evening particularly enjoyable. Mr. and Mrs. Babbs reestablish their connection, even mentioning over dinner how long it has been since they have had such an evening. On the way home, they stop at grandmother's house to pick up their child and hear grandmother tell how cute the little girl was and how she "seemed to enjoy being at grandma's house." Grandmother says she thinks she'll just stay home "and get caught up." Mr. Babbs, feeling freer, thanks the grandmother and has a pleasant conversation with her. Mr. and Mrs. Babbs then drive home and together put their child to bed. They linger at the child's bedside and watch their daughter sleep, further cementing the beginnings of the parental subsystem.

Although they didn't plan a dramatic shift, the new operation has a recognizable quality of fit to the family members; that is, it appears to meet everyone's needs. If this novel operation is generalized to other family functions, it will soon become patterned into a new structure. We would hope that this family's new structure will now be characterized by a less permeable boundary between generations, a rekindled marital subsystem, and the beginnings of a parental subsystem. This structure too is temporary and must provide the flexibility to meet the future needs of the family as it evolves.

The Babbs case example focused on a family that was able to evolve its structure in a more or less functional direction. Not all families succeed as well. Before we look at treatment techniques, we must first discuss the structural view of family dysfunction, the obvious focus of technique.

Dysfunctional Families

Structural family therapists consider a family system as functional if it provides both for mutual support and for autonomy of its individual members. The balancing of competing functions—support and autonomy—is always a compromise. To assess adequately the functional or dysfunctional aspect of a family, one must ask, "Does this family provide a context that supports the fulfillment of developmental needs for all its individual members?" The answer to this question depends in part on the social context and culture of the family. Structuralists do not propose an organizational paradigm to which all families, at all times, in all cultures, can be compared. Instead, the question of structure is one of sufficiency of fit: that is, does this family's structural organization, at this time, in this particular social context or culture, sufficiently meet the needs of all of the individual family members? If it does not, then the family system is considered to be dysfunctional. Aponte and Van Deusen (1981) propose a classification system that is useful in the assessment of families that do not have a structure for sufficient functioning. They categorize such structural dysfunction on the dimensions of boundary, alignment, and power.

Problems in Definition of Boundaries

If a functional family structure has well-defined and flexible boundaries, then it follows that a dysfunctional family has boundaries that are ill defined, inflexible, or both. Definition of boundaries refers to the degree of permeability of system and subsystem boundaries. If a boundary is too permeable, there is little differentiation among individual family members, among subsystems, or between the family and its social environment. This sort of extreme "stuck togetherness" we discussed earlier as enmeshed behavior. If a family relationship is characterized by poorly defined or enmeshed boundaries, the low tolerance for personal autonomy can impede individual developmental growth. Typical of such dysfunction would be a family in which one child becomes known as "Mommy's little boy" or "Daddy's girl." The relationship is so close that expressions of individual differences may be perceived as harmful acts. When the child becomes a young man or young woman, and his or her need for an autonomous identity becomes strong, closeness to parents can become suffocating to further development.

An ill-defined subsystem boundary can also cause the eldest child to function more as a parent than as a child. In such a family, the parental subsystem's boundary is too permeable. A child who carries out parental responsibilities is not necessarily a sign of dysfunction because many cultures or circumstances require such sharing of parental or executive functions. The term *parental child*, however, refers to the child who is locked into performing tasks for which the child is developmentally unprepared. Additional difficulties also occur in those cases because the siblings in the parental child's care usually have less access to their parent or parents.

At the other extreme are disengaged families, whose boundaries lack permeability. Members of those families are inaccessible to each other, like trains passing in the night. John Rosenberg (1982) spoke of the family of an upper-middle-class executive in whose household both parents and all four children ate different dinner meals in different parts of the house at different times. Obviously, such separateness among family members allows for independence, but what happens when someone becomes lonely or discouraged in his or her daily world? The rigidity of personal boundaries serves as a barrier in such families—a barrier to the benefits of reciprocal support, consolation, and nurturance.

Problems in Alignment

It is not unusual for members of a family to coalesce around a specific task. In functional families, there are shifting coalitions, depending on the particular issue. A stable coalition, however, is one in which two members join forces, with or without awareness, against a third; for example, father and daughter against mother. The stability of such a coalition forces other family interactions to contend with a team rather than an individual. Stable coalitions can sometimes become internally stressful, and their members may react by redirecting their conflict. They may either attack or show excessive concern for another member of the family. For example, a couple may detour conflict by agreeing only when they are discussing the misbehavior of their adolescent; the more the adolescent misbehaves, the more they agree.

Another dysfunction of alignment discussed by Minuchin (1974) is triangulation. Minuchin writes:

> In triangulation, each parent demands that the child side with him against the other parent. Whenever the child sides with one, he is automatically defined as attacking the other. In this highly dysfunctional structure, the child is paralyzed. Every movement he makes is defined by one parent as an attack. (p. 102)

Triangulation can also occur with other combinations of family members. Any two members in conflict can draw a third member into a triangle in an effort to compete for the third member's alliance. For an example on the macro scale, one need only view the diplomatic struggles of the superpower nations over the allegiance of the "nonaligned" countries of the Third World.

Aponte and Van Deusen (1981) point out that because of the interactional properties of a family system, a family's dysfunction may involve taxonomies in more than one category. That is, problems in alignment are often also problems in boundary definitions—for example, a cross-generational stable coalition, such as that of a wife and her mother coalescing against a husband, can be categorized as an alignment problem (wife and mother against husband) and a boundary problem (mother violating boundary of marital subsystem).

Problems in Power

In a family system, power always refers to the relative ability of an individual or a subsystem to carry out its functions. This ability is not an innate personal characteristic but is dependent on relationship characteristics. The ability of a family member to act is closely related to another person's willingness to be acted on. That willingness is often specific to time, role, and situation. A father may be able to get his teenage son to clean his room when the son is at home alone, but if the father were to order the son to clean his room when the son's friends were visiting, quite another event might occur.

Power relationships may also vary with time. Expressions of power that are agreed upon at one time may not be agreed upon at another. Problems with allocation of power are directly related to particular system functions (for example, parenting, problem solving, and bargaining for support). The accomplishment of any operation in a family requires force, in the sense of strength. If the force is inadequate, inappropriate for the function, or misdirected, the operation cannot be successfully carried out. Therapists often are presented with a parent or parents who say, "He won't do anything we say," or "I can't seem to get through to her." Dissatisfactions with power relationships are closely related to problems in boundary and alignment. For example, a **cross-generational coalition**, or alliance, between a parent and a parental child can often diminish the parent's power as an executive with the other children in the family. A **coalition** between a mother and daughter against the father reduces the power of the parents to control their daughter.

Another problem with dysfunctional allocation of power is its effect on individual family members' ability to reach their developmental potential. The family that is preoccupied with protecting its late adolescent from the vicissitudes of life is preventing the emerging adult from exercising his or her own personal power to gain mastery over his or her environment. This kind of situation can cause a 17-year-old to act like a 7-year-old, in turn eliciting even more use of parental power.

Therapeutic Practice
Assessment

Structural family therapists do not regard assessment as a distinct and separate process from treatment. Rather than using diagnostic instruments and interviews prior to treatment (Aponte & Van Deusen, 1981), they have integrated assessment into the therapeutic process. As the therapist begins to form the therapeutic system, he or she assesses the current interactional patterns of the family.

In assessing the family, the therapist attempts to expand the conceptualization of the problem. The family generally views the problem from an individual perspective, seeing it, for example, as alcoholism or an uncontrollable child. The family wishes the therapist to eliminate the problem of one member, the **identified patient,** without changing the transactional patterns of the family (Minuchin, 1974). The therapist, however, views the identified patient as a symptom of a dysfunctional family system. The therapist will need to attend to the identified patient's problem but at the same time must broaden the problem to include the family's current interactions.

Minuchin (1974, p. 130) outlines six major areas in which to assess family interactions. He says that the therapist

1. Considers the family structure, its preferred transactional patterns, and the alternatives available.
2. Evaluates the system's flexibility and its capacity for elaboration and restructuring, as revealed by the reshuffling of the system's alliances, coalitions, and subsystems in response to changing circumstances.
3. Examines the family system's resonance, its sensitivity to the individual members' actions. Families fall somewhere on the range between enmeshment, or such extreme sensitivity to individual members' inputs that the threshold for the activation of counterdeviation mechanisms is inappropriately low, and disengagement, or such extremely low sensitivity to individual members' inputs that the threshold for the activation of counterdeviation mechanisms is inappropriately high.
4. Reviews the family life context, analyzing the sources of support and stress in the family's ecology.
5. Examines the family's developmental stage and its performance of the tasks appropriate to that stage.
6. Explores ways in which the identified patient's symptoms are used for the maintenance of the family's preferred transactional patterns.

The therapist assesses family interaction by observing various kinds of behavior. The therapist may examine nonverbal clues such as tone of voice, facial expressions, or eye contact with other family members. The therapist is careful to note who speaks for whom and when. The therapist may also probe other family members to assess their view of the family problem. Using these data, the therapist formulates hypotheses about the family problem and the underlying structure of the system.

Goals

Setting goals in structural family therapy is based on forming hypotheses concerning the nature of the problem and its sustaining structure (Aponte & Van Deusen, 1981). The therapist attempts to intervene directly to change the transactional patterns and thereby alter the sequences surrounding the problem. The altered transactional patterns become the goals of structural family therapy. Goals are both immediate and long-range and determine the nature of therapeutic intervention.

The following example briefly illustrates how goals may be derived from a structural hypothesis. Consider a single-parent family consisting of a 36-year-old mother and six children. The identified client is a 16-year-old boy who has until recently been in a group-home foster placement for stealing tires. The family has been living with the maternal grandmother ever since the mother left her second husband two years ago. In the first session, the mother and the 16-year-old son struggle bitterly. The grandmother complains that the mother doesn't handle the children properly. Mother agrees that her son was a great deal of help to her before they moved in with her mother.

The therapist forms three hypotheses on the basis of the information gathered in the interview:

1. The mother needs to define her role as a mother.
2. The mother and grandmother need to work out executive responsibilities (boundaries) for parenting the children.
3. The mother and 16-year-old son need to be able to negotiate conflict as two adults.

The goals should be stated accordingly:

1. Mother should take responsibility for parenting the children.
2. Grandmother should become involved in some activities outside the home.
3. The mother and 16-year-old son will negotiate an agreement and end the conflict.

This overview of assessment and goals in structural family therapy is further expanded in the following discussion of structural technique.

Technique

From a systems perspective, and indeed from a structural perspective, the therapist cannot *not* intervene. From the first phone call to arrange for an appointment, the family enters into an interactional relationship with the therapist. Some operations are in the nature of a probe to elicit information about the problem, some are aimed at gaining acceptance by the family, and some are more directed at realigning the family structure. A structuralist's actions are like the individual brushstrokes that an artist creates on canvas. Some strokes are exploratory at first, yet, in combination with others, form the outline of a new image. As the new image begins to emerge, the finer touches of the brush help to change the vague outline into a recognizable image. The artist's finishing strokes give the form clarity, definition, and impact. Are any of the strokes more important than any other to the birth of a new image? Each stroke of the artist's brush contains within it both the tentativeness of exploration and the force of redefinition. Such is the case in structural technique. Because the techniques described by structuralists have components of both the tentativeness of problem identification and the force of structural change, the discussion of technique that follows includes both perspectives.

Creating the Therapeutic System

The technique of structural family therapy has at its core the therapist's efforts to become part of the family system. In doing so, the therapist and family combine to form a new and temporary system referred to as the *therapeutic system*. Technique therefore begins with the purposeful goal of joining (Minuchin, 1974) the family system, to become an "inside-the-system" agent of change. The importance of joining the family system early in therapy was stated this way by Minuchin (1974):

> The family moves only if the therapist has been able to enter the system in ways that are syntonic to it. He must accommodate to the family, and intervene in a manner that the particular family can accept. . . . But his goals, his tactics, and his stratagems are all dependent on the processes of joining. (p. 125)

The methods therapists use to join a family are often just beyond their conscious awareness and appear to be much like those used in ordinary human relationships. The past few decades of pop culture have produced several expressions to describe the phenomenon: the slang expressions *on the same wavelength, in the same groove,* and *on the same track* all refer to the operation of joining. Each family has a unique blend of characteristics that serve as interpersonal cues to family identity. Values, attitudes, history, life themes, culture, and language are but a few of the ingredients that combine uniquely to form family identity. Additionally, each family has a complex structure that provides rules for its interactions among members and with the outside world. Structuralists place a high priority on being attentive and responsive to family members. In writing about their technique, they have identified aspects of the process of joining the family. Key skills among them are **accommodation, tracking,** and **mimesis** (Minuchin, 1974).

Accommodation Accommodation is the technique of joining with the family by behaving in ways similar to the family's style, pace, and idiosyncrasies. It has two major components. The first is the therapist's efforts to modify his or her own behavior to conform to the style of the family system. This adaptation obviously requires a varied repertoire of therapeutic behavior. The therapist must be comfortable with listening to the family's use of metaphoric symbols and semantics while at the same time following the content of what is being said. It is particularly important for the therapist to be willing to experience personally the emotional impact of family transactions. The therapist must engage the family in a personal manner while conceptually organizing the experience. If accommodation has been successfully achieved, each member of the family should feel comfortable in sharing emotional issues with the therapist. The family may not be any closer to real change; however, members should feel, "This is someone we can work with. Let's come back."

The second component of the accommodation technique involves acknowledgment of and respect for the family's existing structure. Therapists must first play by the family's rules until such time as they can begin to interject any new rules. One way the therapist accommodates to the family's rules is to address the family through the family spokesperson. Each family has evolved its own unique methods for such interactions. A case of an Amish family offers an extreme example of acknowledging the family spokesperson. In this family's first interview, the therapist, unaccustomed to the family's rules, made the mistake of turning to the mother to ask her a direct question. The woman lowered her head and her gaze, as did the children, and silence followed. The husband then asked his wife the same question in German. She answered her husband in German, and then the husband related her answer to the therapist in English. However, the wife spoke perfect English, as the therapist later learned on a home visit. The family rules, strongly influenced by a rigid patriarchal structure, did not permit anyone but the father to address "strangers." The therapist accommodated to this family structure until he had joined the family, a process that took a rather long time in this case.

If the therapist attempts to intervene prior to creating the therapeutic system, the family will reject the therapist. Problems also occur when clinicians misinterpret accommodation to mean socializing. To join does not mean to be particularly friendly or agreeable; it means to be whatever the family is being.

Tracking   Tracking a family's communication is similar to the relationship techniques derived from client-centered therapy (Rogers, 1961). Asking open-ended questions, reflection of content and feelings, and attending behavior help to establish a supportive relationship between the therapist and family. More complex techniques of tracking center on the therapist's efforts to "listen with a third ear." The therapist responds to the thoughts and feelings that family members may not be able to respond to themselves. In some instances the therapist may use **metaphors** to represent patterns of communication. Minuchin is a master of such tracking skills, using metaphors for family functioning as diverse as "being wired to one another . . . you're his alarm clock," or "you're her memory bank." Often, he will derive a metaphor from a family member's occupation (for example, with an electrician he might say, "You are wired to each other," or with a mechanic, "You need a tune-up"), a point of family pride (for example, with a family whose policy is "never a late payment" he might say, "You are indebted to one another"), or a family rule (for example, with a family that has a strong work ethic he might say, "Play time should never be done slipshod!"). The therapeutic use of metaphor helps to reframe a family's reality by simply tracking the family's communication from the content to the process level. Tracking is a form of accommodation because it is effective only when therapists are able to tune themselves in to the family language rather than imposing their own.

Mimesis   *Mimesis* is a Greek word meaning "imitation" or "copy." Minuchin (1974) uses the term to help conceptualize those aspects of joining techniques that require the therapist to adopt the style, pace, mood, posture, physical appearance, and so forth, of the family. A therapist who intuitively takes off his tie and coat for a working-class family is using mimesis. The therapist can also convey personal stories or experiences that are similar to those of the family. Most acts of imitation by an experienced therapist are not purposeful steps but rather are a natural consequence of a structural family therapist's intention to fit into the family system.

The therapist may also practice mimesis with a particular member of the family (for example, by using the same body posture) as a way to align himself or herself with that particular family member. A typical goal of such an alignment is to team up temporarily with some member of the family for the purpose of shifting the balance of power. Mimesis can greatly ease such a teaming up by paving the way with the nonverbal message "We are very much alike."

Finally, it should be restated that the separation of joining/accommodation technique from interventional technique is largely for clarity in teaching. In structural family therapy, accommodation is an intervention, and interventions do not have impact without accommodation. All therapists attempt to be warm, caring, and interested in their clients, yet no other theory has placed this aspect of the therapeutic relationship under such study. By doing so, structural family therapy has promoted, particularly in training, an increased attention to the skills involved in creating a therapeutic system.

Focus

Focus refers to the therapist's selection of an area to explore from the vast amount of information presented by the family. The technique of focusing can be understood by analogy to its use in the field of photography. Imagine that two photographic reporters were requested to cover the same candidate during a political campaign. The photographers were asked to cover the candidate because the campaign was attracting large crowds and quickly building up support. The first photographer recorded each public appearance by capturing from a distance the candidate's speeches to various political constituencies. Comprehensive in approach, the photographer recorded each event with great proficiency and, by campaign's end, had a complete chronological history of the campaign trail.

The second photographer took a different approach. This photographer began by merely following the candidate through some speeches, taking pictures with a broad focus, as did the first photographer. But this second photographer began to notice in the pictures a particular relationship between the candidate and the audience during the speeches. The candidate often spoke with such oratorical passion that members of the audience would reflect its emotional impact in their faces. The photographer began to narrow the focus to capture just the politician and the face of someone in the audience. The photographer then began to follow the candidate in other situations, looking for more examples of this aspect of the candidate and finding the same theme echoing through diverse images. This second photographer narrowed the focus on the candidate by selecting one among many available themes.

In this analogy, the second photographer looked past the content of events to focus on a single theme that had the potential for saying the most about the relationship between the candidate and the voters. Similarly, the therapist avoids jumping from one area of content to another and instead focuses on a recurrent theme. The choice of theme often depends more on what the family presents at the process level than on what it presents at the content level. Both photographers captured the candidate's campaign, but only the second photographer saw the emotional electricity running between the candidate and the audience. The comparable process in therapy means a flexibility of focus that allows the therapist to track the content of what the family presents (wide focus) while concurrently tracking the family's interactional pattern for clues to the family structure (narrow focus). Focusing on a theme is one way the therapist is able to reframe a family's view of reality to open up alternative patterns of interaction.

A case example that illustrates this technique involves a family who had come to therapy because their daughter was so "disagreeable." The mother and father presented themselves as perfectly happy and compatible except for their daughter's behavior. The therapist tracked the family's description of the daughter's behavior. Early in the session, the therapist began to notice that each parent's description of how he or she responded to the girl's unpleasantness appeared to displease the other parent. Their expression of disagreement was a detail that did not fit with the content level of their report. The therapist slowly expanded the conversation about how they disagreed. As the session unfolded, the therapist developed a working theme: "This family doesn't know how to express disagreement." By focusing the therapy on this theme, the therapist could work to change the family structure by offering a perspective that would be necessary for the new structure to evolve; namely, that family disagreements are normal and even beneficial.

Enactment

Enactment occurs when the therapist decentralizes his or her participation and directs the family to enact rather than describe a situation. The therapist may ask the family to "talk to each other about the problem" or "continue last night's argument." The therapist's instructions must be specific, such as, "Tell your son what you want him to do." Enactments minimize the tendency to centralize the therapist and facilitate the interpersonal awareness of family members. The therapist is able to assess how family members resolve conflict, support each other, and enter coalitions and alliances (Minuchin, 1974).

Minuchin and Fishman (1981) present the technique of enactment as consisting of three movements:

> In the first movement, the therapist observes the spontaneous transactions of the family and decides which dysfunctional areas to highlight. In the second movement of enactment, the therapist organizes scenarios in which the family members dance their dysfunctional dance in his presence. And in the third movement of enactment, the therapist suggests alternative ways of transacting. (p. 81)

In the first movement, an enactment grows out of the therapist's experience of the family, often out of efforts at accommodation. As the therapist sits with the family and attempts to enter its system, he or she is pushed and pulled by the various forces that regulate family interaction. Sensitivity to those experiences serves as a clue to areas of possible dysfunction. In the second movement, the therapist focuses on an area that emerges from the first and formulates a hypothesis for testing. For example, the therapist might wish to explore the structure of the parental subsystem and so might focus on the misbehavior of one of the children by suggesting that the parents get the child to behave so that the discussion can continue. Instead of just talking about their problems, the therapist has them enact their problems in the session. This is very much an operation of diagnosis or problem identification for the therapist, but it is also a novel experience for the family and one that builds toward change. This latter potential advantage comes from the fact that, prior to an enactment, the family typically presents its problems as resulting from the behavior of only one of its members. Once family members begin to talk to each other rather than talking about each other, they gain a broader perspective on the problem. The advance toward eventual structural change is made clearer in the third movement discussed by Minuchin and Fishman (1981).

In the third movement, the therapist reenters the family's transactions by punctuating events with input, which takes many forms, depending on the therapist's goals. The therapist may wish to build **intensity** by lengthening the time of interaction or he might limit participation to specific members as a way of **boundary marking**. Other conditions might require the therapist to align with a family member, thus **unbalancing** an interaction. In still other circumstances the therapist may choose to emphasize the family's **complementarity** or relabel a family belief as a way to reconstruct their reality. All these techniques form the third movement of enactment in that they suggest alternative ways of relating to the family. A discussion of each in more depth follows.

Intensity

Intensity is a term used to describe the therapist's efforts to have a meaningful impact on the family. Family systems have built-in, self-sustaining mechanisms that evolve to reduce anxiety by absorbing or deflecting outside intrusions. Those protective mechanisms become dysfunctional only when the system's boundaries are so impenetrable that information necessary for change is deflected or when the family's boundaries are so permeable that individual boundaries must compensate for the lack of system security. Either way, the family has a low threshold for experiencing anxiety and will attempt to mollify the therapist's message by attempting to fit it into their preestablished patterns of response. (In this context, accommodation may be viewed as an attempt by the therapist to slip new information into the system in a form that can be easily processed by previously established response patterns.)

Structural therapists emphasize that the sending of a message to the family by the therapist does not mean that the family is ready to act on the message. They may have heard the message and responded to it in a positive manner but failed to make any change. Structural therapists, therefore, cultivate a personal style for achieving intensity by widening their range of potential responses beyond those that are deemed appropriate by cultural norms. Drama, timing, and intensity are not part of daily discourse, and a structural family therapist must be comfortable with the tension such behaviors can create.

Minuchin and Fishman (1981) discuss several techniques for building intensity, including (1) simple repetition of a message, (2) repetition of a message in dynamically equivalent situations, (3) changing the length of time of a particular interaction, (4) changing the distance between people interacting, and (5) avoiding induction into the family system. These techniques may be used either to probe the system or to facilitate change.

Simple repetition of the message creates intensity because the therapist locks onto the one theme, resisting the family's attempt to avoid the message. A structural therapist may continue to repeat a question until he or she receives an adequate response. The therapist may also accomplish repetition by highlighting the same message in a variety of ways. In such cases the therapist's power in immobility is like that of the Sitting Buddha; it creates tension that can be relieved only by the family's moving toward adaptation to the therapist's message. The therapist may also use repetition to create intensity by repeating messages that appear to be different yet focus on a single direction of structural change. For example, an overprotective parent of an immature teenager may be asked to (1) let the child wake himself up, (2) let him walk to school if he misses the bus, (3) stop bugging him about his homework, and (4) give him an allowance and not monitor his spending. The parent may also be asked to spend more time outside the home in social activities that the parent enjoys. These messages may be different on the surface, but all have the structurally equivalent message that the parent needs to encourage the teenager's responsibility.

The therapist can also produce intensity by encouraging the family, in session, to continue their interaction longer than the family would normally feel comfortable doing so. This technique pushes the family past its regulatory threshold that usually signals members that they are entering dangerous territory. Sometimes the extension of time may produce necessary conflict and at other times it provides for unavailable family resources such as nurturance or tenderness. Either way, the family breaks out of its predictable path and experiences new alternatives for relating.

Manipulating the physical space of the therapy setting can increase intensity. By moving closer to a person, or by moving two family members closer to each other, the therapist is able to take advantage of the emotional response inherent in a change in personal boundaries. Because family members grow up learning the "normal" distance to maintain with other members, a reduction in that distance creates momentary tension. If that tension is related to a therapeutic message, the therapist is able to maximize the drama and impact.

Finally, intensity may be achieved in therapy by simply not accepting the family's expectations of how the therapist should relate to them. This technique can be seen in many varied operations of the structuralist. For instance, the therapist may use the initial telephone contact with one family to insist that all members attend the sessions, even though the family has presented several reasons why all members can't come. In another family he may choose to increase intensity by appearing confused when the family is pressuring him to give an expert opinion. Take, for example, the family in which the young adults need to be leaving home but are having difficulty doing so successfully. The family's pattern for attempting a solution has been for the parents to seek expert help; they have seen their priest, they took free courses on parenting at the local high school, they even put charts on the refrigerator. All these normally useful actions failed because they were operations of a weak executive subsystem, which repeatedly sought outside help and then rejected the advice at the first difficulty. In order to build intensity, the therapist resisted their attempt to put him in the expert role.

Father: You are our last hope. We've heard you're the best, and believe me, we're ready to do exactly what you say. Just tell us what to do!

Therapist: [*Long pause*] Gosh, I don't have a single idea. The things you've tried usually work. [*Pause*] How about you? Any hunches?

The therapist's goal was to strengthen the parents' power to utilize their own internal resources. By resisting the family's desire to view him as another expert, the therapist increased the intensity of his message by forcefully pushing them to take responsibility for change.

The structuralist, then, has a wide range of behavior available to increase the drama, the impact, the crisis, or the intensity in therapy. Minuchin and Fishman (1981) say it this way: "The family must truly hear the therapist's message. If they are hard of hearing the therapist will have to shout" (p. 141).

Boundary Marking

Boundary marking is a series of operations that have the common goal of changing the family's structural boundaries. As the therapist begins to accommodate to the family system, he or she observes behavioral and transactional clues that aid in identifying the existing boundary structure of the family. The following case helps to illustrate how a therapist can change the family's structural boundaries.

A family visiting a community clinic consisted of a single mother, 20-year-old twin daughters who had just begun college, and a 15-year-old daughter who had been truant from school and was beyond parental control at home. At the beginning of the session, the therapist observed several clues about family boundaries. As the family entered, they shuffled for seats. The twin daughters sat next to each other, with their mother on one side of them and the 15-year-old on the other. The 15-year-old was told to move over a seat (further from the mother) by one of the twins. While agreeing to move, she pouted and slumped into the next chair. As the therapist first addressed the mother, he was answered by both the mother and the twins, each person embellishing the other's responses. As the discussion began to focus on problems in the morning hours, the therapist turned to the 15-year-old and inquired whether or not she had difficulty waking up in the morning. The therapist was answered by a barrage of complaints from the twins about how difficult it was to wake her up and how they had to use extreme measures to rout her from her bed.

At this point, the therapist could build a conceptual map of the family boundaries. He hypothesized that the twins served as parental children, thus indicating a rather weak parental subsystem boundary. The twins appeared to be a dysfunctional extension of the mother's parental authority, increasing the distance between the mother and the 15-year-old, between whom the boundary was too rigid. This misalignment also prevented the three daughters from learning to be sisters; that is, there was a weak sibling subsystem. These tentative hypotheses were enough to prompt several therapeutic boundary-making operations. First, the therapist changed the seating arrangement by putting the mother and the 15-year-old next to each other, with one twin next to the 15-year-old and the other, slightly more vocal, twin next to the therapist.

Because the mother worked in a personnel office, the therapist suggested (metaphorically) that the help she had hired—the twins—wanted to take over her job and, in the process, were neglecting their own duties. He advised her that strong leadership would be necessary to reroute them back to their primary responsibilities, that of getting an education and getting on with their careers. A few minutes later in the session, the therapist initiated an enactment between the mother and the 15-year-old daughter over some area of disagreement between them. One of the twins and then the other began to interrupt. At that occurrence, the therapist put a hand up to block the twin next to the mother and lightly touched the other twin's arm. The therapist then turned to the mother and said, "They're meddling in your department!" The mother, picking up the therapist's message, admonished them to not interfere.

In this case, the therapist marked boundaries by (1) rearranging the seating, (2) reframing the problem, and (3) blocking the twins' assumption of the mother's role. There are numerous ways in which therapists can mark boundaries between subsystems. Like techniques of intensity, techniques of boundary marking achieve greater impact with repetition in structurally similar situations.

Unbalancing

The term *unbalancing* is used in structural family therapy to describe those operations by which the therapist attempts to tip the balance of power within a subsystem or between subsystems. Specifically, the therapist uses unbalancing techniques purposefully to align or affiliate with a particular family member who is in a position of low power. By the act of asking for help, the family grants power (or influence) to the therapist, who then uses that power therapeutically. The only time that this power may not exist is when the family is externally commanded to therapy, as by a court referral. The family members often grant power under the assumption that the power will be exercised equally or that they personally will not feel its weight (that is, only the "sick" member will be asked to change). The structuralist would argue that if this were the therapist's position, little change would occur in therapy. On the contrary, in structural therapy, the therapist's power is often used to support one family member at the expense of others in an attempt to alter the family structure, thus creating new alternatives that will allow for greater complexity and flexibility in the family system.

An example of unbalancing can be found in the case of the single mother, twin daughters, and 15-year-old "troublemaker." The therapist used his power to unbalance the inappropriate parental subsystem. He empowered the mother to "fire" the twins from their parental role, even though the action and resulting loss of role placed temporary stress on the twins. He also did not let up on the pressure when the twins tried to reinvolve themselves. The structural therapist is able to maneuver in this manner because his treatment focuses on the whole family system or organism and not on its individual members.

Unbalancing may also take the simple form of the therapist's siding with a family member, saying, in effect, "I agree with you. You are right and they are wrong. They need to be convinced of your position." It is important to note that the content of the interaction matters less than the structural issues; that is, the therapist aligns with a family member not because he or she necessarily agrees with that member's position but because he or she wants to lend power to a family member to modify the structure. For instance, the therapist may align with a depressed wife in her complaints about her husband's work habits not because the therapist also objects to the work habits but because the therapist hopes to unbalance the marital subsystem.

The therapist may also choose to alternate affiliations, using his or her power to bolster competencies in different areas of family functioning. The same husband may feel powerless in the parental subsystem. Choosing to alternate affiliations, the therapist may decide to unbalance the relationship first by siding with the wife's objections to her husband's work habits and then by aligning with the husband's objections to being excluded from parenting. The therapist can unbalance by (1) affiliating, (2) alternating his affiliation, or (3) refusing to recognize a family member, thus excluding him or her from any affiliation with the therapist. This latter unbalancing technique is extremely powerful because it challenges the excluded family member's need to belong. A disengaged, oppositional, or controlling member of the family may begin to fight the therapist for a way back into the family. Because the therapist controls the interaction, he or she can influence how the family member comes back in; that is, the price of admission may be participation or tolerance or whatever would facilitate an improved structure.

Complementarity

The therapist often finds it useful to help the family members understand that they are all interconnected in ways that make one member's actions complementary to another's. Their interconnectedness is referred to by structuralists as *complementarity*. Consider the Smith family.

The husband begins the session with his head down, picking at the calluses on his hands. A butcher by trade, he has recently had bouts of depression, rage, and suicidal thoughts. He is particularly upset over the demands created by his wife's new job as an insurance agent. Moments into the session, Mr. Smith states the problem.

Husband: I guess it is me; I feel like two persons inside, and I'm all mixed up. One person inside me gets crazy jealous over my wife. I don't trust her. I think she is buying clothes to please someone else and then the other person inside me knows better and says I'm unreasonable and stupid, and it's driving me crazy. Sometimes I'm just all numb and can't figure anything out.

Therapist: How is your wife making you jealous?

Husband: Well, she is not, really. It's just that I'm so sensitive, I guess. I love my wife and I just don't want to lose her. I don't know.

Therapist: I think you do. Somehow your wife is doing things that make you jealous. How does she do that? I think that maybe she is overly sensitive and you are too careful with her. What happens if you get mad at her?

The husband has begun with the intrapersonal position that "it's all my fault." The therapist challenges this assessment by suggesting that the problem is interpersonal. Also evident in this exchange is the effort of the therapist to unbalance the marital system by implicitly aligning with the husband, at least momentarily. Later in the session, the husband is able to express his anger over his wife's behavior. The therapist then chooses another way to emphasize complementarity.

Therapist: [*To wife*] Congratulations. [*Shakes her hand*] You did something there, I'm not sure what it was, but you did something to help him say what he needed to say. Good. [*To husband*] What did she do? What is different?

Husband: I'm not sure. I think I've just been down lately and haven't felt strong enough to say what was happening.

Therapist: I understand that you have felt discouraged lately, but I think this thing, this way the two of you try to relate without talking, has been going on, building and building for years.

Here, the therapist underlines the couple's complementarity by congratulating the wife for the husband's change in behavior. The therapist is teaching them that they do in fact affect each other and that they have the potential to do so constructively. The intervention also allows the husband to reconnect with his wife by encouraging him to praise her for helping him express his anger. The therapist then follows with yet another variation on the theme of complementarity by suggesting that their individual behaviors are part of a much greater whole (that is, that this "thing" has been building over a long period). This change in temporal perspective may assist the couple in shifting from their focus on themselves at the moment to a focus on their relationship over time, thus increasing their awareness of their complementarity.

Reconstructing Reality

When a therapist relabels or reinterprets a family's world view he is reconstructing reality. Often a family is locked into a problem simply because it sees the problem only from one rigid perspective. An example from history may help to illustrate how reconstructing reality can be effective.

A young Sioux brave of the late 1800s found himself unhappy with life around him. He continued to carry out his responsibilities in the tribe in a listless manner. He pastured the horses, gathered large tree limbs for burning, and tended to odd duties around the camp. When there was nothing else for him to do, he took long walks and dreamed: dreams of killing a bison, or of sneaking into an enemy's camp, or of owning many horses and skins. At times, he felt like he had actually done such things. He told his family of his dreams and that he wanted to do such things. His parents told him a man did not spend his time dreaming and that he was not yet ready to be a man.

Eventually, his family became so concerned with his dreaming and listlessness that they decided to approach their tribe's wise man, a man of medicine and healing. The wise man listened to their fears and concerns and then asked them to leave while he thought about their problem. When the wise man emerged from his tepee he told the parents that he had had a vision, a vision that the spiritual world had chosen their boy to speak through. A great message for the tribe was about to be received by the boy, and much preparation was necessary. The medicine man instructed the parents to build a small hut, far from camp. The boy was to huddle and fast in the hut until his vision quest was accomplished. The medicine man instructed them to say good-bye to their former son because when the son next emerged from the hut he would be changed and be called by a different name. After discussions with the medicine man about being brave and about staying in the hut until he received the dream message from the Great Spirits, the boy entered the hut.

After two days, the parents were worried about their son. But the whole tribe was talking to them about their son, and about the vision that was coming, and the time passed quickly. Finally, the boy emerged, quite weak, and went immediately into the medicine man's tent to speak of his vision. When he and the medicine man emerged, the tribe was waiting to hear such important news. The parents held back as a hush settled over everyone. The medicine man interpreted the vision to the tribe: "The Spirits want us to perform a special dance, a dance that will ensure that our tribe will be protected and have prosperity."

In the days and weeks that followed, the boy, who now was referred to by his adult name Black Elk, instructed the tribe in how to perform the dance that he had seen in his dream. As the years passed, Black Elk went on to become a great spiritual leader of his people, using his gift of great vision for the benefit of the tribe. (Neihart, 1961)

The boy's family had originally constructed a view of reality that was keeping the young man a boy. They saw his dreams as a sign of weakness and tried to hold him close to them. Undoubtedly, there were structural elements of their family system that maintained their view of reality, and vice versa.

Structural family therapy has focused on techniques for reconstructing or reframing views of reality as a facet of challenging the underlying structure. In practice, structural change and construct change are intricately woven together as part of the structuralist's overall challenge to the family system. We will discuss several characteristics of reframing system constructs, illustrating their use through reference to the Black Elk story and to clinical examples.

In reframing a family system the therapist must first alter the family's view of reality. Using the technique of focus, the therapist must take bits and pieces of what the family supplies and provide information that forms a new perspective. As in accommodation, whereby the therapist creates a therapeutic system from a family system, the therapist must create a therapeutic reality from a family reality. In the story of Black Elk, the medicine man took the family's construct concerning their "dreamy son" and used his role as expert to create the reality of a son who received "great visions from the world beyond." Such a reconstruction is possible only because it is within the realm of alternate family constructs. That is, the family can accept this reality because they have a world view that includes such a possibility. A clinical example of creating a therapeutic construct would be to reframe a child's tantrums or runaway behavior as a signal that the parents have taught their child how to express independence.

The therapist can create a therapeutic construct by taking the symptom and giving it universal attributes. The medicine man in Black Elk's tribe redefined "dreaming" as a "vision." When the medicine man first stated that he had had a vision, he lent his own stature to the message that dreams could be viewed as part of a greater order. If a therapist is working with a family who belongs to a religious culture that emphasizes a dominant patriarchal order, the therapist might challenge the construct of a distant, emotionally controlled father by saying, "Surely you realize that it is only the courageous patriarch who is able to show his family his tenderness." By drawing on universal symbols, the structural therapist is able to pair a dysfunctional family construct with a universal construct that offers a new perspective for different thoughts and behaviors.

Another way that a therapist can reconstruct reality is to relabel deficits as strengths. In the story of Black Elk, the boy's family went from being a discouraged family whose son could not find his way into adulthood and spent his time dreaming life away to being the proud family of a son known throughout the tribe as a visionary. What changed? What changed was that deficits became strengths. Structuralists place a very high priority on reconstructing family deficits into family strengths. Discussing this priority, Minuchin and Fishman (1981) describe how the family's constructs about their own inabilities and deficits limit their exploration of alternatives: "In effect, their shared world view has narrowed and crystallized to a concentration on pathology. A challenge to that view which focuses on the healing capacities of the family may result in a transformation of the reality that the family apprehends" (p. 269).

The exploration of strengths in the family is not limited to any one therapeutic maneuver. Emphasizing strengths is a core technique of structural family therapy and is based on the assumption that, under the right conditions, the family has within itself the necessary ingredients for development. This optimistic assumption is part of all structural technique designed to create a "therapeutic reality." Whether finding and emphasizing competence in the identified patient or creating intensity by implying that a couple can work their conflict out if they just continue arguing, the structural therapist communicates an optimism based on the family's own unique strengths. Like the Sioux medicine man, a structural therapist believes that reality can be changed by how you describe it.

Case Illustration

The following case study will help to illustrate the principles of structural family therapy.

> Ethel, a 10-year-old, fifth-grade girl, was brought to the community mental health center by her parents, Leroy and Gloria Rodriguez, who were concerned about her frequent stomachaches and reluctance to go to school. Ethel had been seen by her family doctor, who administered various tests and reported that he could not determine any organic reasons for her pain. During the social part of the interview, the therapist learned that Mr. Rodriguez was a construction worker who worked long hours and was sometimes gone for a few days at a time. Mrs. Rodriguez was a homemaker who reported that her chief support system was her mother, who lived next door. A part of the interaction around the problem follows:

Mrs. Rodriguez: Well, my main concern is all this pain Ethel has. She Weems to feel so terrible that I feel guilty when I push her to go to school. I made her go yesterday, but she and my mother were both angry at me because of it and she does seem sick.

Therapist: Mr. Rodriguez, how do you see the problem?

Mr. Rodriguez: Actually, I don't know too much about it. They seem to argue a lot, but I just stay out of it because I have such a temper. I hate to see her go out when she's sick but I want to do what's best for her. I think she sort of fakes

	it sometimes.
Ethel:	[*Loudly and near tears*] They don't understand how much I hurt and how awful it is to stay at school feeling like that. I get headaches sometimes too! I don't see why I can't just study at home! Nobody listens to me!
Mrs. Rodriguez:	Honey, we do listen to you. All I know is, somebody's going to be unhappy, no matter what. The school is threatening that she has to come, my mother says I shouldn't make her go when she's sick, and Ethel won't cooperate. Leroy's usually gone when it's time for school.
Mr. Rodriguez:	Yeah, I have to go to work early. I can't take off from work every day just to make her go to school. Even today, I'm losing money by being here at this meeting.

From the interchanges up to that point, the therapist hypothesized some problems with boundaries. It appeared that there was interference in the parental subsystem by Mrs. Rodriguez' mother, and there was a diffused boundary between Mr. Rodriguez and other family members, probably due to conflict when there was involvement.

Focusing on the parental subsystem first, the therapist directed the parents to discuss what they planned to do to get Ethel to go to school the next day. Mr. Rodriguez began by saying, "I won't be there." When he was again instructed to talk to his wife, he tried talking to the therapist instead. Raising the intensity by extending the duration of their conversation, the therapist once more pressed them to continue. Mr. Rodriguez then turned to the therapist and said, "You know, we really don't talk much. It seems like our discussions sometimes turn out—" His wife interrupted to say, "it seems like you're not willing to do your part." At this point, Ethel loudly said, "You can't make me go to school when I'm sick."

The therapist marked boundaries by telling Ethel her parents were talking and not to interrupt and by asking the parents to face each other while they talked. As is typical in families with a psychosomatic child, conflict in the Rodriguez family was suppressed. When the couple again tried to talk to the therapist rather than to each other, she gestured for them to talk to each other and looked away. Although it took them a while, the parents agreed on a plan for getting Ethel to school the next day.

The therapist decided to work toward changing some of the family's transactional patterns by first getting the father more involved with his daughter. She did this by asking Ethel to keep a chart identifying when pain began and stopped, and she instructed Ethel to show the chart to her father each evening. They were to discuss what was going on prior to and during the pain, how she handled it, and so on. This discussion time forced the daughter and father to spend time together, creating healthier space between mother and daughter.

In subsequent sessions, the next stage of therapy was to work on the conflict in the marital subsystem. The parents discussed their other conflictual issues, and Mrs. Rodriguez related that she often got bored. With her husband's encouragement, she decided she would develop more activities outside the home. She obtained a part-time job, which further helped her to be less involved both with Ethel and with her own mother. With the improvement in her and her husband's ability to express and settle conflicts, they began spending more time together.

This family structure was one of a peripheral father and an overinvolved mother-daughter dyad. It was also a system in which conflict was avoided. A major goal, then, was to mark boundaries between the parents and child, making the father more accessible and the mother less so. A second goal was to get the suppressed conflict out into the open and help the parents deal with it. When the marital dyad became stronger, there was less need for triangulating either the child or members of the extended family.

Effectiveness of Structural Family Therapy

Structural family therapy has focused on four types of clinical families: families of low socioeconomic status (Minuchin, 1974), psychosomatic families (Minuchin, Rosman, & Baker, 1978), alcoholic families (Davis, Stern, & Van Deusen, 1977), and addict families (Stanton & Todd, 1979; Szapocznik, Kurtines, Foote, Perez-Vidal, & Hervis, 1983). These studies have focused on either the dysfunctional characteristics or outcome of treatment.

There seems to be strong evidence that structural family therapy is effective with psychosomatic children and adults who are addicted to drugs. Minuchin et al. (1978) report that conflictual patterns in families can trigger ketoacidosis in diabetic children who are psychosomatic. In an experimental study, the authors found that parents of psychosomatic children were more likely to detour conflict through their children than parents of behavior-disordered and normal children. This condition led to an increase in free fatty acid levels in children and provides strong evidence that psychosomatic children regulate stress between their parents.

The effects of structural family therapy with families of heroin addicts (Stanton & Todd, 1979) is an excellent example of theory, research, and practice (Piercy, Sprenkle, & Associates, 1986). In a well-controlled investigation, Duke Stanton and his associates found that structural family therapy was differentially effective to an individual therapy and placebo group in reducing symptomology in drug addicts and their families. Moreover, these changes maintained at 6 and 12 months.

Determining the effectiveness of structural family therapy on families of low socioeconomic class and families with psychosomatic, alcoholic, and addiction problems is made difficult by differences in sampling; in the identified patients' sex, age, and position in the family; and in status of treatment and by lack of controls in these and other variables (Aponte & Van Deusen, 1981). In addition, the use of nonstandardized rating scales and test batteries may not be an accurate measure of the dependent variables (for example, patterns of communication, overprotectiveness, and rigidity). It appears that patterns of enmeshment and disengagement may differ in each type of family, although those differences could be attributed to differences in research design or in other family characteristics.

Although there seem to be some limitations to these investigations, several patterns of family dysfunction are apparent across them. Families in therapy are operating under transactional rules and boundaries that are less productive and efficient than those of control families (Aponte & Van Deusen, 1981). Client families have more difficulties completing tasks, give fewer directives, and communicate less effectively than control families. Such characteristics warrant the use of instruments that measure interaction when assessing the effectiveness of structural family therapy (Stanton, Todd, Steier, Van Deusen, Marder, Rosoff, Seaman, & Schibinski, 1979).

More recently, Szapocznik, Kurtines, Santisteban, and Rio (1990) have developed the Structural Family Rating Scale (SFSR) to deal with these measurement problems. The SFSR is a theoretically based measure derived from Minuchin's theory of structural family therapy (Minuchin, 1974; Minuchin & Fishman, 1981). The SFSR uses standardized family tasks (Minuchin, Rosman, & Baker, 1978) to elicit family interactions. The SFSR is an important contribution to research on structural family therapy because in measuring the effects of treatment on family functioning, it is necessary to evaluate if in fact structural family therapy has had the desired effect on the structural dimensions of family interaction that are targeted in this therapy.

The SFSR is a promising instrument that has a number of advantages. First, the SFSR provides a psychometrically sound measure of family functioning that contributes to the integration of structural family theory, therapy, and assessment. Second, the SFSR can be easily administered in 20 minutes and scored in 30 minutes by a trained clinician. Third, in addition to evaluating the effects of treatment, the SFSR can be used as a diagnostic tool to assess maladaptive interaction patterns in families (Szapocznik, Rio, & Kurtines, 1989). Finally, the SFSR appears to discriminate among structural and nonstructural changes in families.

The effectiveness of structural family therapy on treatment outcomes is again difficult to determine because of the heterogeneity of methods and experimental designs. Aponte and Van Deusen (1981) state:

> As measured on indices of symptom and psychological change in the index patient, structural family therapy was described as effective with 73% of these cases, and ineffective for the remaining 27%. Effectiveness varied from study to study, however, ranging between 50% and 100%. Across these studies, therapy appears to have been deterioration-inducing in between 3% and 15% of the ineffective subsample. Attribution was marginal. (p. 357)

Structural therapeutic interventions have often been described as personal characteristics (for example, stage manager, director) rather than as behaviors that can be operationalized and measured. Consequently, it has often been difficult to detect therapeutic behaviors that have contributed to changes in families. In an effort to remedy this problem, Figley and Nelson (1990), as a part of their Basic Family Therapy Skills project, employed a panel of experts to identify a basic set of structural family therapy skills that can be operationalized and measured as behaviors in therapy rather than general personal characteristics. Such behaviors can be used to develop rating scales to measure the effectiveness of therapeutic behavior on changes in family interaction patterns. Although behaviors are not definitive, this appears to be a promising first step in developing a reliable measure of therapeutic behavior.

Upon further examination, it would appear that structural family therapy is most effective for psychosomatic families and marginally successful for families of low socioeconomic status, as well as for families in which alcoholism and addiction exist. However, the dropout rate for families in the low socioeconomic, alcoholic, and addict groups appears quite high. It may be that the structural approach must take into account external factors, such as unemployment or violence, which interfere with the successful treatment of these families.

More recently, an accumulating body of evidence documents the relationship between family structure and functioning and health-related outcomes for children (Patterson & Garwick, 1994). Patterson (1991) conducted a review of the literature and found eight factors associated with positive outcomes in children with chronic illness: (1) balancing childhood illness with the needs of the family, (2) maintaining clear family boundaries, (3) developing competent communication, (4) attributing positive meanings to an event, (5) maintaining flexibility, (6) engaging in active coping behaviors, (7) maintaining social support, and (8) developing collaborative relationships with others. These factors have been incorporated into treatment protocol for pediatric services.

An examination of the research on eating disorders reveals that structural family therapy is differentially effective with adolescents. In one investigation, structural family therapy was more effective than individual therapy for adolescent female anorectic clients (Russell, Szmukler, Dare, & Eisler, 1987). A second study found that adolescents with anorexia who received structural family therapy showed greater weight gains than those with individual therapy (Robin, Siegel, Koepke, Moye, & Tice, 1994).

Structural family therapy appears to be a promising treatment; nevertheless, its effectiveness must be further examined across a wider variety of families and presenting problems. Process studies should be conducted to measure the effectiveness of components of treatment (such as engagement, restructuring, and so on) of structural family therapy. A step in this direction is the work of Russell, Atilano, Anderson, Jurich, and Bergen (1984). They constructed a list of 21 separate intervention strategies of family therapy and used it to predict posttherapy happiness in life and marriage among the 31 husbands and wives in their study. Several component techniques of structural family therapy were included in their list of interventions. Specific to the structural approach, they found that boundary-marking interventions were associated with increases in husbands' reports of happiness in life and marriage. Such findings about components of treatment will be extremely useful in evaluating the effectiveness of structural family therapy and, in the field in general, may eventually lead to an empirically based model that integrates effective components.

References

Aponte, H., & Van Deusen, J. (1981). Structural family therapy. In A. S. Gurman & D. Kniskern (Eds.), *Handbook of family therapy* (pp. 310–360). New York: Brunner/Mazel.

Davis, P., Stern, D., & Van Deusen, J. (1977). Enmeshment-disengagement in the alcoholic family. In F. Seixas (Ed.), *Alcoholism: Clinical and experimental research.* New York: Grune & Stratton.

Figley, C. R., & Nelson, T. S. (1990). Basic family therapy skills, II: Structural family therapy. *Journal of Marital & Family Therapy, 16,* 225–239.

Haley, J. (1976). *Problem-solving therapy.* San Francisco: Jossey-Bass.

Minuchin, S. (1974). *Families and family therapy.* Cambridge, MA: Harvard University Press.

Minuchin, S. (1983, September). Structural family therapy. Workshop presented in Louisville, KY.

Minuchin, S., & Fishman, H. C. (1981). *Family therapy techniques.* Cambridge, MA: Harvard University Press.

Minuchin, S., Montalvo, B., Guerney, B., Rosman, B., & Shumer, F. (1967). *Families of the slums.* New York: Basic Books.

Minuchin, S., Rosman, B., & Baker, L. (1978). *Psychosomatic families.* Cambridge, MA: Harvard University Press.

Neihart, J. (1961). *Black Elk speaks: Being the life story of a holy man of the Oglala Sioux.* Lincoln: University of Nebraska Press.

Patterson, J. M. (1991). Family resilience to the challenge of a child's disability. *Pediatrics Annals, 20,* 491–499.

Patterson, J. M., & Garwick, A. W. (1994). The impact of chronic illness on families: A family systems perspective. *Annals of Behavioral Medicine, 16,* 131–142.

Piercy, F., & Sprenkle, D. (1986). *Family therapy sourcebook.* New York: Guilford Press.

Robin, A. L., Siegel, P. T., Koepke, T., Moye, A. W., & Tice, S. (1994). Family therapy versus individual therapy for adolescent females with anorexia nervosa. *Journal of Developmental and Behavioral Pediatrics, 15,* 111–116.

Rogers, C. (1961). *On becoming a person.* Boston: Houghton Mifflin.

Rosenberg, J. (1982, November). *Integrating art therapy with structural family therapy.* Paper presented at the meeting of the American Art Therapy Association, Philadelphia.

Russell, C., Atilano, R., Anderson, S., Jurich, A., & Bergen, L. (1984). Intervention strategies: Predicting family therapy outcomes. *Journal of Marital and Family Therapy, 10*(3), 241–252.

Russell, G. F. M., Szmukler, G. I., Dare, C., & Eisler, I. (1987). An evaluation of family therapy in anorexia nervosa and bulimia nervosa. *Archives of General Psychiatry, 44,* 1047–1056.

Speck, R., & Attneave, C. (1973). *Family networks.* New York: Vintage Books.

Stanton, M. D., & Todd, T. C. (1979). Structural family therapy with drug addicts. In E. Kaufmann & P. Kaufmann (Eds.), *The family therapy of drug and alcohol abuse.* New York: Gardner Press.

Stanton, M., Todd, T., Steier, F., Van Deusen, J., Marder, L., Rosoff, R., Seaman, S., & Schibinski, E. (1979). *Family characteristics and family therapy of heroin addicts: Final report, 1974–1978.* Philadelphia: Philadelphia Child Guidance Clinic.

Szapocznik, J., Kurtines, W., Foote, F., Perez-Vidal, A., & Hervis, O. (1983). Conjoint versus one-person family therapy: Some evidence for the effectiveness of conducting family therapy through one person. *Journal of Consulting and Clinical Psychology, 51*(6), 889–899.

Szapocznik, J., Kurtines, W., Santisteban, D. A., & Rio, A. T. (1990). Interplay of advances between theory, research, and application in treatment interventions aimed at behavior problem children and adolescents. *Journal of Consulting and Clinical Psychology, 58,* 696–703.

Szapocznik, J., Rio, A., & Kurtines, W. (1989). Brief strategic family therapy for Hispanic problem youth. In L. E. Beutler & C. Crags (Eds.), *Programs in psychotherapy research* (pp. 123–132). Washington, DC: American Psychological Association.

Terkelsen, K. (1980). Toward a theory of the family life cycle. In E. Carter & M. McGoldrick (Eds.), *The family life cycle: A framework for family therapy.* New York: Gardner Press.

Chapter Four

Strategic Family Therapy

Jay Haley (1973) defines strategic therapy as therapy in which the clinician *initiates* what happens during treatment and *designs* a particular approach for each problem. In other words, the therapist sets specific goals for solving each problem and designs a strategy to reach those goals. Strategic family therapy places the problem in a social context, and the therapist's task is to design a strategy for that context (Madanes, 1981).

The development of strategic family therapy by Haley and others was strongly influenced by Gregory Bateson and Milton Erickson. Bateson, a research anthropologist, was studying patterns of communication and cybernetic systems at the Palo Alto V. A. Hospital when he was joined by Jay Haley, John Weakland, and William Fry in the early 1950s. Concurrently, Don Jackson was beginning his work with people who have schizophrenia at the same institution. Jackson's collaborations with the Bateson project led to many significant contributions, including the double-bind theory of schizophrenia (Bateson, Jackson, Haley, & Weakland, 1956). This collaboration was significant because it provided the conceptual base for strategic therapy and led to the integration of **communications theory** and systems theory.

Another major figure who helped shape the development of strategic therapy was Milton Erickson. Haley and Weakland were strongly influenced by the hypnotic and paradoxical techniques of Erickson. Much of Haley's early therapeutic work is derived from Erickson and is outlined in Haley's (1973) book *Uncommon Therapy: The Psychiatric Techniques of Milton H. Erickson, M.D.* This text provides a comprehensive examination of Dr. Erickson's theories and techniques and their application to various cases at different stages of the family life cycle.

In 1967, Haley went to work with Salvador Minuchin at the Philadelphia Child Guidance Clinic and played an important role in the development of the structural approach. In 1975, they were joined by Lynn Hoffman. Much of the early work at the Philadelphia clinic focused on dysfunctional families characterized by confused hierarchies with cross-generational coalitions. These families often had difficulty making the transition from each stage of the developmental life cycle to the next (for example, the children's entering school or leaving home). From their work in Philadelphia, Haley and Hoffman developed a brief, problem-focused approach known as strategic family therapy.

Theoretical Constructs and Philosophy

Strategic family therapy shares similar constructs with structural family therapy. According to Stanton (1981), both approaches view the family in the following ways:

1. Family members interact within a context (that is, problems and their function must be considered within the interactional context in which they occur).

2. Problem families are seen as being "stuck" at a particular stage within the family life cycle (that is, family members have difficulty making the transition from each stage of the family life cycle to the next).

3. Symptoms are system-maintained and system-maintaining (that is, a family system works to maintain homeostasis in interactional patterns, and symptoms serve to maintain this system).

4. Emphasis is on the present rather than on the past. Family members' history is not as relevant as the present situation because dysfunctional behavior is maintained by current interactions.

5. Insight is not a necessary prerequisite for change. Problems cannot be alleviated through understanding alone because the problems are maintained by ongoing interactional processes.

Strategic family therapists are concerned principally with four interrelated elements: (1) symptoms, (2) metaphors, (3) hierarchy, and (4) power. They see symptoms as maintaining the homeostatic balance in the family system. Symptoms can be a way of communicating metaphorically within the family. (For example, a woman's depression may be a way of conveying her unhappiness in her marriage.) Symptoms can be conceptualized through hierarchically structured power ladders. The parent should have power over the child and thus be at the top of the hierarchy. However, in some cases children may develop a symptom (for example, using drugs or running away) to change the power relationship.

One family came for therapy with the presenting problem of a 15-year-old adolescent girl who was depressed. The girl refused to talk to members of her family and spent most of the time in her room. When the therapist met with the family, he noticed that when the father would try to set limits with his daughter, the mother would intervene. Both mother and daughter appeared depressed in the session. The therapist subsequently learned from the daughter that her father "had a girlfriend" and that the daughter felt that he didn't love her or her mother. It soon became clear that the child's symptom was an expression of her feelings about her father and a way of calling attention to the problem.

Symptoms

The basic difference between the structural and strategic approaches is the emphasis on the symptom. Strategic family therapists are much more symptom-focused than structural family therapists, and both are more symptom-oriented than the transgenerational therapists (Stanton, 1981). Strategic therapists assume that symptoms characterize the ways family members relate to each other. A symptom is a communicative act with a message that serves as a contract between two or more members and functions within the interpersonal network (Watzlawick, Weakland, & Fisch, 1974). It is a label for a nonlinear set of behaviors within a social organization (Haley, 1976). A symptom usually occurs when a person is stuck in a particular situation and cannot find a nonsymptomatic way of getting out of it.

Metaphors

The symptom may often be a metaphorical label for conceptualizing the problem. A metaphorical message usually contains an explicit element (for example, "I have a headache"), as well as an implicit element (for example, "I want more attention" or "I am unhappy"). Madanes (1981, pp. 225–226) discusses how symptomatic behaviors can be metaphorical in several ways:

1. A symptom may be both a report on an internal state and a metaphor for another internal state. For example, a child's headache may be expressing more than one kind of pain.

2. A symptom may be a report on an internal state and also an analogy and a metaphor for another person's symptoms or internal states. For example, a child who refuses to go to school may be expressing both his own fears and his mother's fears. The child's fear is analogical to the mother's fear (in that the child's fear symbolizes and represents the mother's fear).

3. The interaction between two people in a family can be both an analogy and a metaphor, replacing the interaction of another dyad in the family. For example, a husband may come home upset and worried, and his wife may try to reassure and comfort him. If a child develops a recurrent pain, the father may try to reassure and comfort the child in the same way that the wife was previously reassuring and comforting him. The father's involvement with the son in a helpful way will preclude his involvement with the wife in a helpless way, at least during the time in which the father is involved with the son. The interaction between father and son will have replaced the interaction between husband and wife.

4. The system of interaction around a symptom in one family member can be a metaphor for and replace another system of interaction around another issue in the family. Mother, father, and siblings may helpfully focus on a child's problem in a way that is analogical to the way they focused on the father's

problem before the child's problem developed. The focus on the child's problem precludes the interaction centered on the father's problems.

5. There may be a cyclical variation in the focus of interaction in families, sometimes centered on a symptomatic child, sometimes on the problem of a parent or on a marital difficulty; but the interaction remains the same, in that there is helplessness and incongruity.

Strategic family therapists often view symptoms as metaphors. Haley (1976) describes a man who entered therapy because of a heart attack. The man had been examined by several physicians, who found no organic basis for his complaint. Nevertheless, the man felt that his heart was failing and that he would die any minute. When one doctor reported, "Your heart is all right," the man proceeded to the next physician to support his complaint. However, if one accepts that the man's heart is functioning well, then one must assume that the man's complaints are a metaphor for something else. For example, the man's complaints might regulate his children's behavior—the children must be quiet in order to avoid upsetting father—or the man's complaints may help to avoid conflict or sexual intimacy with his wife.

Hierarchy

Symptoms can also reflect problems in the hierarchical structure and can be viewed as an effort to resolve the family's problem in the distribution of power. In most societies, parents are responsible for their children and therefore have the most power in a nuclear family; however, in many Asian cultures, grandparents are higher in the hierarchy than parents and may have more power than either the parents or the children in decision making. In functional families, members adhere to the generally accepted hierarchy, whereas in dysfunctional families, there is often a violation or confusion about the hierarchy; for example, a parent-child dyad sides against another parent. Symptomatic behavior in a family member may exist where such coalitions are present.

A cross-generational coalition, or a situation in which a parent sides with a child or grandparent against the other parent, often affects symptoms. When tension between two people (such as husband and wife) becomes intense, a third party is brought into the picture to decrease the tension. For example, after an intense conflict with her husband, a wife may become involved with a child in order to reduce the tension. Haley (1973) emphasizes that most of the problems parents have with children include a triangle consisting of an overinvolved parent-child dyad (a cross-generational coalition) and an underinvolved or peripheral parent. In a general case, such as Haley describes, the child's symptom seems to trigger a communicative sequence between the parents. The husband and wife may be forced to communicate about how to deal with the child's symptomatic behavior.

In a two-generational family coalition, one parent is often overinvolved with a child while the other parent remains peripheral. This type of family coalition can be mapped as follows:

father ⎫
⎬ mother   *or*
child ⎭

mother ⎫
⎬ father
child ⎭

Levant (1984, p. 128) describes the typical sequence of communication that often occurs with this type of organization:

1. Mother is overinvolved with child.
2. Child acts up, expressing the symptomatic behaviors.
3. Mother calls in father to assist.
4. Father deals with the problem ineffectively.
5. Mother criticizes father for not dealing with the problem appropriately.
6. Father withdraws.
7. Mother and child continue to be overinvolved until they reach another impasse.

An example of a three-generational coalition might involve a grandparent, mother, and child. Although such coalitions can take many forms, one typical configuration has the grandmother filling the executive role (that is, head of the family), with the mother's power and competence being undermined in the presence of her own mother (Minuchin, 1974). The mother's "incompetence" is often maintained because she is living with her mother (the grandmother) and is viewed by her mother more as a daughter than as a mother. This three-generation coalition may be mapped thus:

grandparent ⎫
⎬ parent   *or*
child ⎭

grandparent
——————————
child   parent

Levant (1984, p. 128) describes a sequence of communication that often occurs with this type of organization:

1. Grandmother is responsible for the child while complaining of mother's irresponsibility.
2. Mother withdraws, and grandmother continues to be responsible for child.
3. Child misbehaves.
4. Grandmother is angry with mother because she (the grandmother) should not have to discipline child.
5. Mother moves in to take care of child.
6. Grandmother criticizes mother for not being competent and moves in to rescue child from mother.
7. Mother withdraws, allowing grandmother to be responsible for child.
8. Child continues to misbehave.

More than one cross-generational triangle can occur at a given time. The likelihood of pathological behavior is increased in families in which a child's problem may be imbedded in several dysfunctional hierarchies.

Power

Haley (1976) believes that any relationship is a power struggle. As Haley describes it, the power struggle between two people is not a question of who controls whom, but rather, of who controls the definition of the relationship and by what maneuvers.

Haley notes that "when one person communicates a message to the other he is by that act making a maneuver to define the relationship" (Haley, 1963, p. 8). Any message has elements of both "command" and "report." When a mother says to her daughter, "It's raining. Your bicycle is outside," she is reporting on the weather and the location of the bicycle, and she is also commanding her daughter to get the bicycle out of the rain. If the daughter brings the bicycle inside, she is allowing the mother to remain in charge at the top of the hierarchy. If she refuses to bring the bicycle in or gets her brothers to bring in the bicycle, then she is engaging in a power struggle with the mother.

The major focus of strategic therapy has been to arrange the hierarchy so that parents are in a position superior to their children. Parents are encouraged to state rules concretely to increase the likelihood that they will be followed. Rules must be practical, and there should be consequences if the rules are not followed. When the child obeys rules, then he or she is placing the parents in a superior position in the hierarchy. However, when the child refuses to obey the rules, then he or she is in a position of superior power.

Madanes (1981) describes the difficulties parents experience in maintaining their superior position in the hierarchy:

> Parents typically use a series of communication maneuvers to avoid a definition of the hierarchy as one where they have power over the offspring. They do so because they are losing or have already lost their superior position in the hierarchy, because the youth is more powerful than they, because society has intervened to take power away from them, because they are afraid to do the wrong thing and harm the youth, or because they are afraid to lose their child. A parent can avoid a definition of the hierarchy as one where he has power over the youth by communicating (1) that he is not qualified to participate in the therapy because he cannot occupy an executive position in the hierarchy, or (2) that the other parent is not qualified, or (3) that the therapist is not qualified to be in charge of the therapy. It is these maneuvers that the therapist must counteract so that the proper hierarchy can be defined. (pp. 129–130)

Let's examine a case that illustrates the parents' inability to take an executive position in the hierarchy:

> The family has been referred to the therapist by a private school from which the 14-year-old son had recently been dismissed for absenteeism. The boy was currently residing in a group detention home for youngsters

with out-of-control behavior. A psychological staff evaluation at the home revealed that the boy had "emotional problems" and "chemical dependency." At the first meeting, the parents appeared exasperated. The parents reported that they had tried everything but that "he refused to do anything we said." When asked what they expected of their son, they said "some respect" and "a better attitude." When asked to state these expectations in the form of rules, both parents maintained that "it wouldn't do any good." The parents continued to resist setting rules, indicating that their son was "emotionally ill" and "chemically dependent."

In the second session, the therapist insisted that their son needed parental direction and that when he was under control he would be able to behave properly. Once the parents had agreed, the therapist asked them to discuss appropriate rules for their son. When the parents began to interact, the son attacked the mother saying, "You don't know what you're talking about." The wife then turned to the husband, who in turn looked at the therapist and said, "See what I mean?" The therapist encouraged the couple to continue their discussion and requested the son to "let them finish their discussion and [he] would have [his] chance to talk."

When the parents continued, it became quite apparent that they disagreed on how to handle their son. The father felt that he should be placed in a children's home. The mother, on the other hand, felt protective of him. At that point, the therapist removed the son from the room. The wife then accused her husband of being uncaring because this was not his real son. The husband denied her accusation and indicated that he was tired of fighting with the son and could not live in the same house with him. It soon became apparent that the son's behavior prevented the parents from agreement. In this case, the child was in a superior place in the hierarchy because he had the power to separate them.

The parents in this example were unable to take an executive position for several reasons. First, they accepted the label (that is, "emotionally ill" or "chemically dependent") that the school and the group home had placed on their son. Second, each parent felt that the other was incapable of controlling their son's behavior. Each parent viewed the other as "too hard" or "too soft"; the husband thought he must be tough because his wife was weak, and the wife felt she must be soft because her husband was too hard. The result was that neither parent could control their son's behavior.

Therapeutic Practice

Assessment

In assessing the family, the therapist gathers information in three categories: (1) demographic information, such as age, sex, occupation, and religion; (2) family history, such as previous treatment, medical information, physical violence, and sexual functioning; and (3) interactional data focusing on family rules, alignments, coalitions, subsystem functioning, and sequences of behavior around the problems (Bross & Benjamin, 1983).

Assessment begins when the family first enters therapy. Particular emphasis is given to the sequence of interactions. The therapist's initial inquiry is often general to elicit a description of the family's problem (for example, "What do you want to accomplish here?"). As family members describe the problem, it is critical not to confirm the family's perception that (1) the identified client is the problem, and (2) the identified client or symptom is unchangeable (Stanton, 1981). Accepting the family's definition of the problem is participating in the creation of a problem that the therapist must solve (Madanes, 1981). Instead, it is critical to redefine the presenting problem (for example, "emotional illness") in such a way that it can be alleviated (for example, coming home on time or holding a job).

Haley (1976) lists four things the therapist should and should not do when listening to the problem:

1. The therapist should not interpret a problem differently to a family member. Instead, he or she should accept what is said and rephrase any misunderstanding.
2. The therapist should not give advice at this stage, but instead ask for more information before saying what can be done.
3. The therapist should be concerned not about feelings but about how family members relate to each other.
4. The therapist should be helpful and not diverted from the family's reason for seeking therapy.

Each family member should have an opportunity to state the problem. When one person comments about someone else, the therapist should speak to that other person (Haley, 1976). The therapist must block any interruptions so that each member has a chance to describe the problem. Thus, the therapist's diagnostic statements have therapeutic value.

As the therapist listens to a member describe a problem, he or she tries to note the reactions of other family members. Do they appear angry? Do they try to interrupt? Do they look away? Do they seem concerned? The therapist should also pay particular attention to the reactions of the identified client. Does he or she seem depressed, upset, or otherwise affected? Regardless, the therapist should not share such observations with family members (Haley, 1976). Process comments during assessment only put family members on the defensive.

When assessing the problem, the therapist should begin to look for sequential patterns of behavior. For example, does one parent accuse the other of being too easy with the child? Does one parent feel that the other parent doesn't care what is going on? When one family member speaks, does another family member interrupt or reject what is being said? What is important is that the therapist be thinking about the sequence of interactions surrounding the presenting problem. By assessing the sequence of interactions around the presenting problem, the therapist gains information useful in developing a strategy to alleviate the problem.

Once family members have expressed their views on the problem, the therapist should get them to interact with each other about the problem. For example, the therapist may want to see whether the father and mother can discuss the problem in their child's presence. If the child interferes, the therapist has identified a problem area. The therapist should be careful not to be central to this interaction. Instead, he or she should get family members to talk to each other.

The therapist is always more interested in assessing how family members react to the problem than in what they say about the problem. Haley (1976) writes:

> There is less consequence and less result with talk. Rather than only have a conversation about a problem, he should try at this stage to bring the problem action into the room. For example, if a child deliberately bangs his head he can be asked to do so. The family will show how it responds. If a child sets fires, he can set one (in a metal ashtray) so that the knowledge he has of how to handle matches as well as the response of everyone is clarified. With toys in the room, problem situations can be performed. If a wife complains and is depressed she may be asked to behave that way and then everyone can show how they respond. However, these more active procedures should be attempted only when a therapist has learned to give directives effectively. (p. 38)

When the therapist requires family members to interact, the family structure and hierarchy begin to emerge. For example, one parent may be overinvolved with a child while the other parent is underinvolved. If the therapist asks the underinvolved parent to talk with the child, and the overinvolved parent interferes, then the interactional sequence around the presenting problem becomes clear. When the therapist can get the underinvolved parent and child to talk without interference from the overinvolved parent, then the intervention has both diagnostic and therapeutic value.

Goals

In discussing the problem, family members are asked what changes they would like to see in the family. The therapist may ask, "What do we need to work on?" or "What would need to happen for you to be successful here?" When the therapist selects a goal, he or she is making a therapeutic contract with the family. The therapist has the final responsibility for decisions about goals of treatment (Stanton, 1981).

Strategic family therapists place great emphasis on the clear statement of goals. Goals are stated objectively so that everyone can agree when the goal has been reached. This principle means that the goal should be an observed behavior that can be counted or measured. For example, if parents report that they want to improve their child's self-concept, then the therapist must get the parents to determine what the child will be doing when his self-concept is increased. Likewise, labels such as anxiety, unhappiness, mental retardation, hyperactivity, or school phobia must be stated in such a way that they can be solved (Haley,

1976). Like behavioral therapists, strategic therapists place a great deal of emphasis on measurable goals. The major difference, however, is that the strategic therapist has final responsibility for choosing the goal, whereas in behavioral therapy, family members bear that responsibility (Stanton, 1981).

The strategic family therapist often sets intermediate goals that lead to the final outcome goal. Each intermediate goal represents a step or stage toward the final goal. An illustrative goal concerned a mother who was overinvolved with the daughter and a father who was peripheral. The therapist set an intermediate goal (step) of having the daughter take all her requests to the father and exclude the mother. The next intermediate goal was to get mother and father to work out times at which each parent would be responsible for the child. Once these intermediate goals had been reached, the therapist got the couple to agree on times they would spend with each other without the children (final goal). The therapist will often set several intermediate goals before attempting a final goal or solution to the problem.

Technique

The principal focus of strategic family therapy is the symptom or the presenting problem; insight or understanding is of lesser importance. Strategic family therapists are concerned primarily with those techniques that change the sequence of interaction that is maintaining the problems. Techniques are tailored to alter repetitive sequences that lead to the presenting problems.

The strategic therapist maintains control of therapy through the use of tasks or directives. Tasks can be either explicit (for example, telling a family member what to do) or implicit (for example, verbal intonation or silence). Haley (1976) elaborates:

> Whatever a therapist does is a message for the other person to do something, and in that sense he is giving a directive. If someone says, "I feel unhappy," and the therapist replies, "I understand you feel unhappy," the reply does not look like a directive. But it can be defined as one since the therapist is indicating that he is interested in such statements and the person should say that sort of thing. Since the therapist may not have responded to something else the person said, but has responded to this statement, his response tells the person that this statement is important. The therapist's response also implies there should be more talk about such important things. Once a therapist faces the fact that whatever he says or does not say is telling a person to do something, or is telling him to stop doing something, then the therapist will find it easier to accept the idea of giving directives. In fact, even when a therapist tries to avoid giving directives by pointing out to the client that the client is trying to get the therapist to direct him what to do, the therapist is directing the client how to behave. (pp. 50–51)

Haley (1976) lists three reasons for giving tasks to family members. First, tasks are one way to get people to behave differently in therapy. Second, tasks increase the importance or value of the therapist. If a task or directive is given for the family to complete during the week, then the family members must decide whether they are going to comply with the therapist's directive and what they will say to the therapist when they return for the next interview. Third, tasks provide information about the family. If the family completes or fails to complete the task, the therapist has gathered useful information.

Each strategic technique involves three distinct components: task selection, task construction, and task delivery (Bross & Benjamin, 1983). The selection and construction of a therapeutic task is determined by the nature of the family and the therapeutic style. Before selecting a task, the therapist will often determine whether the family is resistant to change. If the family is not resistant, the therapist will choose **positive cooperative tasks** (also called **straightforward tasks**), which the therapist expects them to complete. When the family is resistant to change, the therapist will design **negative cooperative tasks (paradoxical directives),** which the family will fail to complete (Bross & Benjamin, 1983). Construction of these tasks is often determined by therapeutic style. For example, some therapists prefer to communicate through stories and fables rather than through direct advice.

The success of any task is dependent on its proper delivery. Tasks should be reasonable and stated in the family's own language. The task should be consistent with the family's belief system. The therapist states the task in an authoritative manner so the task seems possible.

Straightforward Tasks

Straightforward tasks are designed in expectation of family members' compliance. Straightforward tasks attempt to change the sequences of interaction in the family. They may help a family to become more organized, establish operational boundaries, set rules, or establish family goals (Madanes, 1981).

Straightforward tasks might include (1) advice, (2) explanations or suggestions, or (3) directives to change the interactional sequence in the family (Papp, 1980). For example, to a family with a mother and daughter who are overinvolved and a father who is peripheral, the therapist might give the following explanation: "Your daughter needs to treat you [mother] with respect. She will be able to do that when you have your husband's support. Right now he gets called on as the bad guy when you aren't able to deal with her. This is a critical time when your daughter needs to spend more time with her father." Unfortunately, advice may not be successful because family members often know what to do but don't know how to do it.

Encouraging compliance In many cases, the therapist must convince the family that it needs to follow the advice or directive. This may be difficult unless each family member sees that there is some payoff for following it. Persuading a family to perform a task will depend on the type of task, the family, and the kind of relationship the therapist has with the family (Haley, 1976). For example, there may not be a payoff for adolescents to talk in a session if they are uncertain that their parents care about them or if they can get their way without talking. In a case like this, the therapist's directive must provide some benefits (for example, more privileges or parental concern) for the adolescent as well as for other members of the family.

Haley (1976) offers several suggestions to therapists for getting families to follow their tasks or directives:

1. *Discuss all the things the family has done to try to solve the problem.* By this device, the therapist can avoid making suggestions that already have been tried before. The therapist should lead the family to the final conclusion that "everything has been tried and nothing has worked." At this point, the therapist is in a position to offer the family something different from what it has experienced before.

2. *Ask family members to discuss the negative consequences if their problem is not handled now* (that is, what is going to happen if this problem is not resolved?). Aversive consequences will probably be different for different members of the family. Nevertheless, examining the negative consequences of the problem for each family member emphasizes the intensity of the problem. A mother and her adolescent daughter, for instance, get into conflicts, cry, and feel unhappy, and neither one gets her way. The mother doesn't get the kind of respect she deserves, and the daughter doesn't get any privileges. It is important for the therapist to emphasize those consequences and to project what might happen if the problem is not resolved.

3. *Assign a task that is reasonable and easily accomplished.* To ensure that the family can complete the task at home, it is necessary to get the family to complete the task in the session. For example, the therapist may want an adolescent daughter to have conversations with her mother without interruptions from her father. Therefore, the therapist may ask the daughter to talk with her mother in session while the father reads a magazine. The therapist suggests an activity that the mother and daughter might enjoy doing together. If the father interrupts so that the mother and daughter do not complete the task, the therapist may wish to devise something else for the father to do, such as running an errand, so that when mother and daughter attempt to complete a conversation at home, the chances of noninterruption by the father will be improved. By directing the family to complete a trial run of the task in the session, the therapist can make the necessary adjustments so that the family can complete the task at home. The therapist can also ensure that the task will be accomplished by providing adequate instructions. In this instance, the therapist focuses attention on the relevant and essential aspects of each family member's performance. Before the family begins the task, the therapist might instruct the father that it will be difficult for him to "stay out of it" and that he needs to find something else to do instead. The therapist might also ask the daughter to "talk up" so that her mother will know what she wants to do. In some cases, the therapist might ask a parent to "listen to your daughter (or son)—she (or he) needs to know you care."

4. *Assign a task to fit the ability and performance level of the family members.* In the film *Family with a Little Fire* (Minuchin, 1974), the task is focused on the scapegoated child's fire setting. The therapist, Braulio Montalvo, asks the mother

to spend 5 minutes each day with her daughter teaching her how to light matches correctly. He also instructs the parental child who stands between mother and child to watch the other children while the mother is teaching the child. This task is suited to each family member's level of ability.

5. *Use your authority to get the family to follow the directive or task.* Sometimes the therapist must use his or her knowledge and expertise to get the family to comply. It is important for the therapist to accept the role of expert, rather than ask the family what they think they should do. The therapist might say, for example, "From my experience, I'd say that this is a critical time for your son, and he needs time with his father." The therapist is really saying, "On the basis of my experience (expertise), I believe that it is important for you to do this." Sometimes the therapist may ask whether the family or family member trusts him or her. If the family or family member says yes, the therapist might say, "Good; then I want you to do this because it is important. Trust me." Here the therapist uses trust to gain control of the interview.

6. *Give clear instructions.* Everyone should know what his or her responsibilities or role should be. If a therapist asks a father and daughter to do something together, then specific dates and times should be specified. By seeing that they decide in advance on a time, the therapist can determine if the father and daughter are committed to performing the task. By establishing a time, the therapist and family are also decreasing the likelihood that something else, such as TV or work, will interfere. Decisions should also be made about who will take care of the other children and what the mother will be doing during that time. The therapist might ask family members to describe what they will be doing so that everyone is clear about his or her part. Family members are encouraged to discuss anything that might interfere with the completion of the task.

Application The authors have used the following straightforward directives or tasks in their own clinical work:

1. A woman who had difficulty separating from her mother was asked to visit her mother unannounced and talk about something that would meet with her mother's disapproval.
2. A peripheral father was asked to handle all of his son's requests for one week while his wife did something she enjoyed, such as reading or playing tennis.
3. A peripheral father and his daughter were asked to do something that the mother would not be interested in, thus reducing the likelihood of the mother's interference.
4. In a psychosomatic family, a child with a stomachache was asked to record the amount of time he had the stomachache. He was to report it to his father, who was to pass the information on to the mother. The mother became less involved with the child, and the father was put in charge of the child's problems.
5. A conflictual couple was asked to return to a place, such as a restaurant or park, that had been pleasant during their courting period. The task

focused on positive experiences and changed the affect of the relationship.

6. A mother who was unemployed and overinvolved with her son was
   asked to apply for a job.
7. A 21-year-old who was unemployed and living at home was asked to
   spend 4 hours outside the house each day looking for a job.
8. A woman who had recently gone through a divorce was asked to join a
   group for divorced people.
9. A family who came to a group session without their teenage son was
   asked to bring him to the next session.
10. A couple living with their parents were having difficulty moving out.
    They were asked in the session to plan how they would move out and
    present the plan to the parents the next week.
11. A family whose members never talked with each other was asked to
    have a family meeting in which each member presented his or her view
    of the problem.
12. Parents who had concerns about a local mall frequented by their daugh-
    ter were asked to visit the mall and see for themselves what it was like.

The therapist discusses the task at the next session. If the family has completed the task, the therapist congratulates them. If the family has not completed the task, the therapist finds out why. The therapist may ask the family
either to complete the task in the session or to complete it during the coming
week. However, it is important for strategic therapists not to accept excuses; to
do so amounts to saying that the task is unimportant.

In some cases, the therapist will give a directive metaphorically, without
making explicit what he or she wants the family to do. Family members are
often more willing to follow this kind of directive because they really aren't
aware that they have received one. When therapists give a metaphorical directive, they are attempting to get family members to behave in a way that resembles or is similar to the way the therapist wants them to behave in the symptom area (Haley, 1976).

Take, for example, the case of a depressed 19-year-old who was brought
into treatment because she did nothing but sit around the house and cry. Learning that the girl had been sexually abused by her father several years earlier,
the therapist redefined the girl's depression as anger toward her mother. The
therapist believed that the anger was there because the mother had allowed (by
not stopping it) the abuse of the daughter. The anger (rage) was never expressed
because it was so volatile and explosive that the daughter feared losing her
mother completely. The daughter and mother were far too overinvolved with
each other. The mother admitted that she needed her daughter and did not
want her to leave home. The daughter resented her mother's wish but did nothing to change it because she was afraid that any disagreement would end in an
explosion of the relationship. Although neither would discuss these issues with
the other, the mother complained that her daughter would write bad checks on
the mother's account. While the therapist chose not to deal directly with the

problems of incest and leaving home, the issue of bad checks could be dealt with as a metaphor for the more serious issues because all the same dynamics were present. The therapist got the mother and daughter to argue about the checks as a metaphor for those other issues. At the end of the discussion, the therapist directed the daughter to get a separate account and directed the mother not to pay the daughter's bills. This task and other, similar ones became metaphorical steps in the mother and daughter's movement toward healthy conflict and increased autonomy.

In using metaphorical tasks, the therapist chooses an activity (for example, writing bad checks) that resembles the problem (for example, daughter's overinvolvement with mother). The activity must be one that family members can discuss and in which they can produce change. The therapist will typically assign tasks, such as having a heated discussion and obtaining separate checking accounts, that will produce a change—for instance, increasing autonomy in the desired area (Haley, 1976). If the mother and daughter are able to accomplish the task (that is, get separate checking accounts and pay their own bills), they will be more likely to accomplish separation around more sensitive issues later on.

Paradoxical Directives

Whereas straightforward directives are successful for family members who do what the therapist asks, paradoxical directives are more effective for members who resist completing tasks. The pattern of resistance is not uncommon. It appears in many families, particularly those with a member with schizophrenia or an addiction and those in which one or more members are characterized by a "personality disorder" (Stanton, 1981). These families are very effective in getting the therapist to work hard for improvement while they resist his or her efforts (Haley, 1976).

Resistance typically takes the form of failure to complete homework assignments. In most instances, the family remains stable because one family member continues to be the "problem." As long as one person is the problem, other, more serious issues can remain hidden: out of sight, out of mind. When therapists attempt to change the family member's problem, however, they are threatening the family's stability and thus will encounter the family's resistance to change (Haley, 1976). When meeting with such resistance, the experienced therapist may choose to give a paradoxical directive rather than a straightforward directive.

Anticipating noncompliance   Weeks and L'Abate (1982) list five types of family transactions that point to the appropriateness of paradoxical directives or tasks:

1. *Fighting and bickering.* Members of the family relate to one another primarily through fighting and bickering. Family members are at odds, regardless of the issue. Family members are highly volatile and reactive. Straightforward directives and tasks are ineffective with this type of family.

2. *Noncooperativeness and failure to complete assignments.* The family is not as expressive as the families whose members fight with each other. Members may cooperate verbally but undermine each other nonverbally. One or more members generally act out their aggression through other means, such as drinking, drugs, or work. Members will often agree to complete homework assignments but fail to take personal responsibility when they have left the session.

3. *Continuation of the problem regardless of the intervention.* The family fails to respond to any type of intervention. The therapist often feels discouraged with this type of family because he or she sees little change.

4. *Separation and polarization.* This pattern is characteristic of families whose children can easily separate them. Adolescents are especially effective in challenging or separating their parents.

5. *Disqualifying one another.* Family members contradict or disqualify each other's statements. Family members show no support of each other and fail to set limits for the children.

Peggy Papp (1980) describes three steps in giving a paradoxical directive:

1. Clearly explain the benefits the symptom provides to the family. The explanation comments directly on the interactional sequences that both are a benefit and create the symptom.

2. Prescribe the symptom: Encourage the family to continue what they have been doing because to change would result in the loss of benefits to the family (Stanton, 1981). If the family follows the therapist's directive, it is allowing the therapist to take control by continuing its symptomatic behavior. Compliance also implies that the symptomatic behavior is amenable to change (that is, the behavior can "be continued"). If the family defies the therapist's directive, however, it must discontinue the symptomatic behavior. Either compliance or defiance creates change.

3. Restrain the family when it begins to show improvement. The restraint of "growth" allows the therapist to take a position that keeps the paradox working. In essence, the therapist is saying, "I'm not sure this change is wise. I realize the symptoms have improved, but are you really sure you want to give up the benefits? I'm concerned." The therapist is careful not to change posture or take credit for the change. This sort of "reverse psychology" must be genuine and avoid sarcasm. In other words, the therapist must have some empathy for the family's need to develop the symptoms to preserve their collective stability.

This three-step process can be illustrated by the case of a recovering alcoholic and his wife.

> The wife had taken care of her alcoholic husband for five years. The husband had been sober for six months and now wished to take control of the family finances and other matters. The wife reported that she wanted her husband to "take control" but resented helping him do such things as balancing the checkbook. The husband felt that the wife was unsupportive and often became angry with her attempts to help him.

The symptomatic husband appeared to be in an inferior position to his wife, who was trying to help him. Yet, in reality, the symptomatic spouse was in a superior position because he refused to be helped, even though he requested his wife's help. The wife offered help, but did so in a way that was not helpful.

The therapist discussed the benefits of their relationship. If the husband gave up his symptomatic behavior—that is, anger, complaints, and threats to resume drinking—then he would lose his superior position in the relationship because he no longer would frustrate his wife. If the wife were able to help her husband take charge of the household, then she would lose her superior position. If they were to change, each might lose his or her imagined preferred position.

In an attempt to change the family, the therapist directed the couple to continue arguing over the checkbook and other household responsibilities because any change might be too threatening for their relationship. The therapist was communicating several things with that directive. He was saying, "It would be nice if you could share responsibilities, but I'm not sure you are ready to change." When the couple reported that they were fighting less, the therapist celebrated their change but cautioned the couple to slow down—otherwise, each might panic over losing a preferred position in the family. When giving those directives, the therapist was careful to communicate that he was concerned about the couple and somewhat surprised, but a little more hopeful for change.

Application   Jay Haley (1976, pp. 72–74) outlines eight stages he considers important when giving paradoxical directives:

1. *Defining a therapeutic relationship.* The therapist must join with family members to establish a trusting relationship. The trust between the therapist and family allows the therapist to give a paradoxical directive in a way that still shows concern for the family.

2. *Defining the problem clearly.* The problem should be clearly and concretely defined. Weeks and L'Abate (1982, p. 75) ask the following questions, which are useful in defining the problem: "Who is involved in the problem? Where does the problem occur? How frequently does the problem occur? What happens when you experience this problem?" It is important to identify the sequence of events that maintain the problem.

3. *Setting goals.* Goals should be stated in concrete terms so everyone will know whether the goals have been achieved. Goals can be established by asking family members how they would like things to be after treatment ("What would you be doing after we have finished?"). The therapist must make sure that the goals are reasonable and set an appropriate time period for their accomplishment.

4. *Designing a plan.* All tasks should be provided at the end of the session. A directive to any member should be stated clearly and connected to other family members in the system. The therapist should make sure the client has under-

stood the directive. The therapist should present the task with an authoritative voice if he wants the family member or members to resist him (Rohrbaugh, Tennen, Press, White, Raskin, & Pickering, 1977). If the therapist wishes the client to perform the task, he or she will need to encourage the client to complete the task.

5. *Disqualifying the current authority on the problem.* The authority is generally a spouse or other family member who is trying to help solve the problem (Haley, 1976). In some cases, the authority may be people outside who have influence on the family. Unfortunately, family members often attempt to do more of the same to solve the problem. Thus, those who attempt to solve the problem may be an obstacle to its resolution. Consequently, the person who is attempting to solve the problem is actually maintaining it and must be disqualified.

6. *Giving a paradoxical directive.* Paradoxical directives or tasks should be designed to fit the client's special interest (Weeks & L'Abate, 1982). The directives should play to the client's style, values, and abilities if possible. The authors have found that written directives can be phrased in language that appeals to special types of clients, such as lawyers or doctors. The directive or task should be tailored to the family members' schedules so that the task does not occur spontaneously.

7. *Encouraging symptomatic behavior to occur.* When improvement occurs, the therapist should restate the rationale and encourage the client to continue to follow the directive. If the client fails to comply, the therapist should be solemn and suggest that the client is not cooperating. The therapist should avoid behaving in a way that the family might view as insincere or sarcastic (Stanton, 1981). The therapist should then request that the client continue the symptomatic behavior. The therapist should not back off if the family is resistant, or he or she will lose credibility.

8. *Avoiding taking credit for change.* If improvement occurs, the therapist should avoid taking credit for it. If a task does not produce the desired result, the therapist should accept responsibility for the failure. If the therapist accepts credit for change, he or she risks a relapse for the client, who is acting to please the therapist.

Weeks and L'Abate (1982) suggest that the therapist have a firm grounding in systems theory and the principles of paradoxical intervention before working paradoxically. They also recommend that the beginning therapist have supervision to prevent isolation and self-doubt. As with all other techniques, the therapist must have confidence in the intervention and understand the changes that are likely to occur. This is sometimes difficult because each task is created anew for each unique family and situation. With supervision and experience with a wide range of uses, therapists progressively sharpen their skill, and with increased skill, their confidence increases. The authors have used the following paradoxical tasks in their own clinical work:

1. A fiercely independent single parent who was reluctant to give her son more autonomy was asked to do even more for him lest she experience the anxiety of being on her own.

2. A boy who threw frequent "out-of-control" temper tantrums was asked to continue having his tantrums but to have them in a special place at home and only after school, when he could really have ample time to throw one.

3. A wife who tried to leave her husband but couldn't was urged to stay with her husband because he needed someone to take care of him.

4. A woman who was often depressed was asked to set 1 hour aside each day to be depressed. The woman was told that if she was to be in control of her depression, she would have to learn to turn it on as well as turn it off.

5. A couple whose only contact occurred when they argued were told to increase their bickering so they would be closer to each other.

6. A teenage girl who was having trouble separating from her mother was told that she was noble and that her sacrifice, though very sad, did protect her mother from the realities of life.

7. A depressed girl was asked to pretend she was depressed, and her parents were told to encourage her to give a better performance of her depression.

8. A mother who worried constantly about her son was asked to set aside 1 hour each day to worry so she could be more effective at it. She was to do nothing else during this hour.

Positive Labeling and Connotation

Strategic family therapists generally attribute "positive motives to clients" (Stanton, 1981, p. 376). Problem behaviors are often relabeled to have more positive meaning. For example, a **positive label** for "jealousy" could be "caring," and "anger" could be relabeled as "desiring attention." New labels often provide family members with a new way of thinking about the problem so that it can be resolved. For example, Madanes (1981) cites a case in which a woman's "hysterical paralysis" was relabeled as "muscular cramp" and another in which a man's "depression" was labeled as "irresponsibility." In both cases, the problem was relabeled to make it amenable to change.

DeShazer (1975) suggests that symptoms are adaptive and that families do what is necessary at the time. This idea is shared by Haley (1976), Minuchin and Fishman (1981), and Boszormenyi-Nagy and Spark (1973). Stanton (1981) labels this concept as "ascribing noble intention." Stanton and his co-workers found that in working with addict families, they needed to attribute positive motives to extremely destructive behaviors exhibited by these families. Although Stanton credits Boszormenyi-Nagy for the idea that symptoms are adaptive across generations, he differs from Boszormenyi-Nagy in that he will use this approach to produce a desired effect.

Relabeling has also been used by Palazzoli-Selvini and associates (Palazzoli-Selvini, Boscolo, Cecchin, & Prata, 1978) in Milan. They refer to their technique as "positive connotation." They write that "all the observable behaviors of the group as a whole appeared to be inspired by the common goal of preserving the cohesion of the family group" (p. 56). For example, Palazzoli-Selvini et al.

(1978) describe a 10-year-old boy who exhibited psychotic symptoms following the death of his grandfather. At the end of the first session, the therapist told the boy that he was "doing a good thing" (p. 81). The therapist further noted that the grandfather was a "central pillar of the family" and kept the family together. The boy was told that he had assumed his grandfather's role to maintain balance in the family and that he should continue this role until the next session. Here, the therapist used "positive connotation" to maintain the homeostasis in the family. The boy had taken the grandfather's place to maintain a heterosexual balance in a family that, following the grandfather's death, had been dominated by women. The use of positive connotation allows the therapist to join with the family at a time of crisis and shift the problem to a systemic level.

Recent Applications of Strategic Family Therapy

Several variations of the strategic approach to family therapy have evolved over time, but the most prominent contributions have been made by the Mental Research Institute Brief Therapy Center and the Milan Center for Family Studies.

Mental Research Institute Brief Therapy Center

Brief family therapy was first associated with Watzlawick, Weakland, and Fisch and is best described in the book *Change: Principles of Problem Formation and Problem Resolution* (Watzlawick, Weakland, & Fisch, 1974). Brief family therapy is a step-by-step approach that lasts from five to ten sessions. Clear procedures are developed for each interview. The therapist can ask the following questions: What is the problem? Who did what the last time the problem occurred? When is the problem likely to occur? When did the problem first occur? (Hoffman, 1981). After getting a definition of the problem, the next step is to explore what solutions have been tried to resolve the problem (Weakland, Fisch, Watzlawick, & Bodin, 1974). Often, the family's attempt to solve its problems has created a worse situation than the original problem (Watzlawick et al., 1974).

In the second session, goals for treatment are established. Goals are formulated by asking clients to specify what behaviors they need to change to resolve the problem. Clients are encouraged to make small initial changes that will be likely to lead to greater changes in the system later (Weakland et al., 1974). Paradoxical suggestions and therapeutic influence help clients reach their goals. Session three often focuses on treatment of the problem-maintaining behaviors. Succeeding sessions are designed to maintain the desired changes in behavior.

In an article in *Family Process*, John J. O'Connor (1983) describes brief family therapy with a 10-year-old boy, Mike, who obsessively feared that he would vomit. The treatment lasted five sessions over three months, with a two-year follow-up. Treatment was focused on the problem and was designed to eliminate Mike's obsessive behavior. A brief description of the case follows:

Mike was preoccupied with the fear of vomiting. The fear of vomiting would produce intense stomachaches, cold sweat, and incapacitation from 1 to 3 hours. The typical sequence would begin with Mike's seeking reassurance in the morning from his parents that he would not vomit. Mike's request for reassurance would result in the parents' increasing their comforting statements without mentioning the word *vomit*. Mike felt that if his parents told him he would not vomit, he would not. At school, when Mike felt he would vomit, his mother would come to pick him up. Mike would also be frightened when his parents attempted to leave the house because he feared they would die. The parents would stay out no longer than two hours and would promise they would be home at a designated hour. A medical examination revealed nothing significant about Mike's digestive system. Mike's parents described him as "fragile" and "plagued with allergies."

In the interview, Mike was "anxious and fidgety" and "obsessed about his obsessions." His mother did most of the talking throughout the interview, while Mike and his father nodded in agreement. Whenever Mike became angry, his parents would deny it. The mother agreed that she had been "overprotective" when he was younger and was now willing to give Mike more autonomy, but "now he doesn't want to." The father seemed passive and showed affection toward Mike during the interview. The therapist viewed Mike's fear of vomiting as the problem. Mike's fears were "self-perpetuating." When he would think about vomiting, he felt he would have no control and thus would vomit. The solution was the problem (that is, "Mike's reporting of his obsessions to his parents precipitated a circular homeostatic parent-child loop of reassurances"). The parents' attempts to find a solution helped to maintain the problem.

In the first session, the therapist indicated that Mike was indeed in a great deal of pain and that the parents' reassurances were not enough. Mike needed to do some difficult tasks to gain control over the fears. Mike was told that the first step was to decide when and where he would vomit or think about vomiting. Mike was told to have those thoughts only at the designated time and place. The therapist had noticed that Mike's father was wearing a slogan button of some sort. At the therapist's suggestion, Mike's father removed the button and pinned it to Mike's sweater. The button was to represent the father's reassurance that Mike would not vomit; his father was not to give him verbal reassurance. The parents were told to go out one evening a week for at least 3 hours. The parents were also to agree on responsibilities around the house that were appropriate for Mike's age level.

In the second session (two weeks later), Mike reported that he could not maintain his thoughts at the designated time. Mike was encouraged to think about vomiting during the session. The therapist told the father to give Mike a penny, saying that "the penny was just like the button and represented his father's strength." The parents were encouraged to continue going out together in the evening. At the third session, Mike had forgotten to bring the penny but indicated that his thoughts of vomiting were "fleeting." The therapist then instructed the father to give Mike a nickel with the same description as the penny. In the fourth and fifth sessions, Mike was asymptomatic.

The treatment consisted of three parts to alter Mike's obsessive behavior and the homeostatic interaction between Mike and his parents (O'Connor, 1983). The first part of the treatment focused on Mike's fear of vomiting. The paradoxical prescription changed the time and place at which Mike was to think about vomiting and gave him control over the behavior/symptom. The second part of the treatment was designed to block the problem-maintaining solutions of Mike's parents. When Mike's parents did not verbally reassure him, other solutions (that is, buttons and coins used as symbols of the father's reassurance) became available. The third set of directives encouraged the parents to go out and Mike to assume age-appropriate responsibilities so he could no longer be viewed as "fragile" and "dependent."

The paradoxical directives in Mike's case helped to reframe the problem/symptom and give it a different meaning. When Mike was put in charge of his problem/symptom (vomiting), the family could no longer view the problem/symptom in the same way. Thus, the parents were able to accept new solutions to the problem/symptom. The small change in Mike's behavior (control over his vomiting) led to adaptive changes in the family system. Mike remained asymptomatic and had progressed developmentally at the two-year follow-up.

The Milan Center for Family Studies

In 1967, Mara Palazzoli-Selvini organized the Milan Center for Family Studies. Palazzoli-Selvini was joined by Luigi Boscolo, Giuliana Prata, and Gianfranco Cecchin. This group developed a systemic approach for treating people with anorexia, people with encopresis, and families of children with emotional disturbances. Their book *Paradox and Counterparadox* (1978) provides the most comprehensive description of their therapy.

Cases treated at the Milan Center last from 3 to 20 sessions. Treatment generally lasts for 10 sessions. Families are normally seen only once each month because they must travel a long way for treatment (Palazzoli-Selvini et al., 1978). The Milan Associates believe that one-month intervals are often necessary for families to process information (Palazzoli-Selvini, 1980). Requests by the family to be seen more frequently are an indication that the intervention is producing desired change. Thus, the Milan Associates often refer to their treatment as "long, brief therapy" because the number of hours in treatment is brief, but the total amount of time for change in the family system is long (Palazzoli-Selvini et al., 1978).

The standard format for a session includes (1) observation of the family's transactional style without comments by the team, (2) consultation with the team at the end of the session, (3) prescription of the therapeutic task or ritual to the family following the team meeting, and (4) a team meeting following the interview to discuss the family's acceptance of the prescription and to write a summary of the session (Stanton, 1981).

The Milan Associates often present the prescription in the form of a letter, in which case each family member receives a copy. Weeks and L'Abate (1982) list four advantages of using written messages as opposed to spoken messages. First, unlike spoken messages, written messages cannot be ignored or distorted. Second, written messages can be repeated and can have a greater impact on the family. Third, written instructions may be more "binding" than spoken instructions. Finally, written messages often are clearer and help to break the family's patterns of "denial" and "avoidance."

Written paradoxical instructions may be presented in the form of a "family ritual" (Palazzoli-Selvini et al., 1978). Ritualized prescriptions are designed for "breaking up those behaviors through which each parent disqualifies and sabotages the initiatives and directions of the other parent in his relation with the children" (Palazzoli-Selvini et al., 1978, p. 3). The prescription can be repeated with the same format to any type of family. The prescription is used instead of interpretation, which is often effective in altering the rules of the system. At the end of the session, the prescription is dictated to a family member, who records it. Here is the essential text of a sample prescription:

> On even days of the week—Tuesdays, Thursdays, and Saturdays—beginning from tomorrow onwards until the date of the next session and fixing the time between X o'clock and Y o'clock (making sure that the whole family will be at home during this time), whatever Z does [name of patient, followed by a list of his or her symptomatic behaviors], father will decide alone, at his absolute discretion, what to do with Z. Mother will have to behave as if she were not there. On odd days of the week—Mondays, Wednesdays and Fridays—at the same time, whatever Z may do, mother will have full power to decide what course of action to follow regarding Z. Father will have to behave as if he were not there. On Sundays, everyone must behave spontaneously. Each parent, on the days assigned to him or her, must record in a diary any infringement by the partner of the prescription according to which he is expected to behave as if he were not there. (In some cases, the job of recording the possible mistakes of one of the parents has been entrusted to a child acting as a recorder or to the patient himself if he is fit for the task.) (p. 5)

Palazzoli-Selvini et al. (1978) note that the ritualized prescription operates at several levels. First, the "rules of the game" are changed to prevent interferences from occurring. Second, parents are blocked from competing for the therapist's approval. These efforts only serve to deflect attention from the problem (relationship). Finally, the therapist gains information, regardless of whether the family follows the prescription. This information can be used to design subsequent interventions.

With families that fail to follow the prescription, the Milan Associates often write paradoxical letters that admit defeat or helplessness (for example, "Your family has special power. . . ." or "I feel a sense of helplessness. . . ."). When the therapist admits defeat, the family will continue in therapy and discuss its influence on the therapist when it is united (Weeks & L'Abate, 1982). Furthermore, paradoxical letters allow the therapist to be more homeostatic than the family. The family in turn often "rebounds" to prove the therapist wrong. Thus, the Milan Associates use the family's resistance to produce change in the system. The use of paradoxical letters "allows the therapist or team to stay in a position from which maximum change can be achieved" (Hoffman, 1981, p. 303).

Case Illustration

Sara and Joe had been married for 17 years. They had met in college and had married immediately upon graduation. Although each was career-oriented, Sara soon become pregnant with Ann, and Joe was accepted into law school. Their early years were a struggle but also were full of hope for the future. When Ann was 2 years old, her brother, Billy, was born. Billy was born somewhat prematurely and was unhealthy in his first few months of life. Looking back, both Sara and Joe considered the early years of their marriage the best. They characterized the last decade as a lot of work, a lot of stress, and little time to spend together. Joe was very aggressive in his career, and, although he felt driven, he also said he enjoyed it. His job did require him to be out of town a lot, a circumstance that Sara had never liked and had recently begun to complain about. Sara found motherhood very satisfying, particularly when the children were young. Although she had never made a formal decision not to work, she had let events take their course, which meant that she had never acted on her career plans. At the time, she thought she didn't care, but recently she had found herself daydreaming about what it would have been like.

The family had been in counseling before, or at least its members had been in treatment. Joe, at the request of his family doctor, had seen a psychiatrist about his drinking. This psychoanalytically based treatment lasted about 18 months and ended two years before the start of family therapy. Sara had also become very depressed during that same period and had been placed in outpatient group therapy for a year. Neither Sara nor Joe had ever participated in each other's therapy, nor had they met each other's therapist.

What brought them into therapy this time was a crisis with their children, Ann (now 15) and Billy (now 13). The therapist received a call from Joe, who said that Billy was out of control and had threatened his sister Ann with a kitchen knife. Joe also noted that Ann was doing poorly in school and was constantly "mouthing off" to her mother. The entire family was seen by a strategic family therapist for a period of five weeks. From what the therapist learned during those five weeks, he hypothesized that crossgenerational power coalitions were keeping a dysfunctional hierarchy operative. The parents were clearly not at the top of the hierarchy. The therapist also conjectured that the symptom of fighting between the children was a metaphor for unresolved marital conflict. The therapist used several straightforward tasks aimed at realigning the hierarchical boundary, but they were of little or no avail. With each new directive, the family found new ways to resist change. The therapist then decided to call in a team of therapists to work behind an observation mirror. Because straightforward tasks had been ineffective, the team decided to work with a paradoxical approach.

What follows is a session-by-session discussion of what occurred in therapy. Included are the verbatim written messages (Turner, Rickert, Brown, & Christensen, 1985) that were sent in to the therapy sessions, together with brief rationales for each.

From Session 1

During the session, the group began to note the submerged marital conflict and the rapidity with which it would be interrupted by the children's behavior. Once, when Joe and Sara were discussing their disagreement over what to do about discipline, Billy tipped backwards in his chair and sent furniture flying. Ann responded by stomping out of the room to go to the bathroom. Once everyone was back in the room, the group sent in the following message:

> *Message 1.* The group is impressed with both Billy's and Ann's efforts to protect their parents from too much conflict between them. Evidently, if Mom and Dad were to exclude their children from their disagreements, one or the other spouse might not be able to handle direct contact, draw back into themselves, even get depressed. We caution both parents against limiting the children too much. It appears safer and possibly more advisable for each parent to continue to team up with each child as a way to avoid the marital conflict. Mom with son, dad with daughter.

The session was about over, but there was time for the children to say, "That's dumb." Sara and Joe said they would think about it and were given a copy of the note to take with them. To extend their therapeutic reach, the team decided to mail a second copy to the family between sessions.

From Session 2

Again, the session began with the therapist's attempt to put the parents in charge of their children's behavior. According to the agreed-on plan, the therapist was continuing, in a straightforward manner, to change the power hierarchy. At one point in the session, Sara harshly criticized her daughter, Ann, for something while Joe looked on passively with a wry smile. This interaction immediately followed one in which Joe scolded Billy for rock-ing and spinning in his chair (Billy had been using his mother's chair as a foothold for bigger and bigger spins). The team behind the mirror sent in the following message:

Message 2. We see Dad's efforts to discipline Billy as very helpful and gen-erous to Mother. By saving her from such necessary dirty work, Mother can maintain her protective relationship with the son. We realize that this is at great cost to Dad (i.e., it keeps him from being close to his son), but the sacrifice is remarkable.

Similarly, we notice Mother's selfless efforts at shouldering the disci-plinary role with Ann. It too is a sacrifice, as it would be nice for Mom to feel closer to her daughter, but maybe such sacrifice is needed.

This message was designed to commend the uncommendable. Sara and Joe, when hearing the message read, just frowned for a while and then asked to hear the message again. Again, the family was quiet. The therapist sug-gested they think about it over the coming week and then ended the session.

From Session 3

This session began with the parents working together to keep the kids be-having and not interrupting. The team felt that change was occurring and therefore moved to restrain the change very early in the session.

Message 3. The group is sensing a change in the family today. The parents appear to be trying to keep the kids from splitting them up and are show-ing some signs of wanting not to undermine each other. We seriously ques-tion the wisdom of this. If they keep going in this direction, the parents will soon be confronting the conflicts between them, which may be dan-gerous at this time. We see occasional signs of both kids attempting to rescue their parents and are concerned the kids are not distracting them enough to ensure the team arrangement (mom with son, dad with daugh-ter).

The family asked the therapist what he thought about the team's mes-sage. The therapist purposely expressed mixed feelings, though he thought that maybe he was a little more optimistic than the team behind the mirror. During this discussion, the children again started to act inappropriately and became even more disruptive when the conversation between Joe and Sara turned more argumentative. The team then sent in the following mes-sage right at the end of the session:

Message 4. We agree that it is safer to focus on the kids at this point than risk the consequences of facing their marital issues, even though that could help them. Part of the group is particularly concerned that the couple is not ready to discuss the husband's drinking and the wife's difficulty with sharing of self.

From Session 4

Between sessions, Joe and Sara called the therapist and requested that they meet next time without the kids present. The therapist expressed concern about the behavior problems at home, but they reassured him that it had been a good week, and they thought they could handle anything that might come up. The therapist agreed to meet with just the couple on the understanding that should something terrible happen at home, the parents would bring the kids.

The session began at a high level of involvement for both Joe and Sara. They spent the first 30 minutes "unloading" on each other the issues that had been buried. The group waited until near the end of the session to send in a message because they did not wish to interrupt the process. At one point, the therapist elicited a little more emotion from Joe than had been seen earlier, and the group chose to support that therapeutic direction with the following message.

> *Message 5.* We as a group are impressed today with the tender, romantic side of Joe. Sara must have seen this quality in him when she fell in love with him. We are curious what little things she does to bring this tender, sweet side out of him.

From Session 5

Joe and Sara had made the shift in hierarchy that was needed. Although tentative and frightened about facing their marital conflict, they were buoyed by the success of the newfound teamwork. This session was basically marital therapy, and the group decided to echo and complement whatever direction the therapist headed. The team behind the mirror sent in several short messages that dovetailed with the therapist's efforts. First, when Sara was being open and sharing but Joe was continuing to spar, the team sent in the following message:

> *Message 6.* We are impressed with Sara's growing openness. We are increasingly coming to the view that she will be able to develop a team with Joe if only he will do his part to make the team a pleasant place to be.

Then, when Sara and Joe later became bitter, angry, and discouraged, the team sent in the following:

> *Message 7.* The group sees two people who think they are full of resentment. The group disagrees. The group sees two people who are very good at hurting each other when they themselves are hurting the most. It is very sad that they won't let themselves feel the other's hurt.

Later, when the therapist was discussing a possible signal or code they could use to let each other know when they were vulnerable, the team sent in this message:

Message 8. The group thinks that the code is already established. Any time either person sounds resentful, they are saying, "I am hurting, comfort me." Joe just sent his code.

From Session 6

The therapist chose to see Joe and Sara together a few times without the team observing. The sessions between Team Sessions 5 and 6 centered on marital issues, with only short references to how the children were now behaving. Team Session 6 became a review of what had occurred over the preceding several months of therapy. The team decided to send in one final message toward the end of that session:

Message 9. The group particularly notices the change that Joe and Sara have made in the nurturing part of their relationship. We are tempted to even be optimistic that they will continue to build their relationship rather than tear it down. However, the group is aware of the danger that a crisis will occur concerning the kids, or daily stresses, that will again split their team.

The group wished to make a final important point: We may have made an error. Joe and Sara may be capable of far more intimacy than we first thought.

After reading the messages and getting up to leave, Joe turned to Sara and said quietly, "I guess we showed them."

At the six-month follow-up, no problems were reported to the therapist.

Effectiveness of Strategic Family Therapy

Investigations of strategic family therapy have demonstrated more scientific rigor than is found in other approaches to family therapy. In 1978, Gurman and Kniskern reviewed 27 studies that compared families in one type of family therapy with a control group or with families in another type of therapy. Six of those comparative investigations included strategic therapy (Alexander & Parsons, 1973; Langsley, Fairbairn, & DeYoung, 1968; Langsley & Kaplan, 1968; Langsley, Machotka, & Flomenhaft, 1971; Pittman, Flomenhaft, DeYoung, Kaplan, & Langsley, 1966; Pittman, Langsley, Flomenhaft, DeYoung, Machotka, & Kaplan, 1971). Gurman and Kniskern further note that the investigations of strategic family therapy apply tighter research designs than do investigations of other types of family therapy. Stanton (1981) compared the quality of research designs for strategic and nonstrategic investigations. Stanton found that investigations of strategic family therapy were significantly greater in quality of research design than other types of family therapy studies (Stanton, 1981).

Since 1978, the effectiveness of strategic family therapy has received mixed reviews. Garrigan and Bambrick (1979) investigated 24 families in which the oldest male sibling was the identified patient (IP). One-third (8) of these families were led by a single parent. Of the 24 families, half were randomly assigned to a brief family therapy condition and half to a control condition. There appeared to be no significant differences in the IP's perceptions of family adjustment in the brief family therapy and control groups. However, mothers of intact families who received brief family therapy reported a decrease in symptomatic behaviors of the IP, whereas single-parent families reported an increase in symptomatic behavior of the IP. This study appears to be experimentally sound, but it is unclear whether the control groups received an alternative treatment (Stanton, 1981).

Scully (1982) studied how effective strategic family therapy was in decreasing the frequency of maladaptive behaviors in conduct-disordered clients and their families. Scully reports that in his study strategic family therapy was not shown to be effective in curtailing client or family problems. The researcher points out that, due to small sample size and related design issues, the results should be considered tentative.

One promising investigation has been conducted by Wagner, Weeks, and L'Abate (1980) to determine the effectiveness of written linear and paradoxical letters with couples. Fifty-six couples participating in a marital enrichment program were randomly assigned to one of four groups: (1) enrichment plus a paradoxical letter, (2) enrichment plus a direct linear letter, (3) enrichment, and (4) control. The results indicated that the experimental groups showed significant gains in marital functioning compared with the control group. The group receiving the paradoxical letter plus enrichment was not significantly different from the other two experimental groups. Wagner, Weeks, and L'Abate believe that more sensitive instruments may be necessary to measure the direct effects of paradoxical messages.

More recent study has been given to the Milan model (Palazzoli-Selvini et al., 1978, 1980). In contrast to earlier reports (Palazzoli-Selvini, 1986), Machal, Feldman, and Sigal (1989) cite clients' negative reactions to the therapist and the reflecting team. Families reported that the therapists appeared distant, and the team seemed impersonal. This is consistent with a study by Sells, Smith, Coe, Yoshioka, and Roblins (1994) in which clients reported that therapists were ineffective in establishing "trust" and "rapport." Moreover, clients and therapists shared different perspectives of the effectiveness of this approach.

These two investigations raise questions about the effectiveness of the Milan model. There appears to be a need for outcome studies of this model before confirming earlier assumptions. Ethnographic research, which examines conversations between therapists and clients, appears to be a promising method for examining the effectiveness of this model (Smith, Sells, & Clevenger, 1994). Engaging in such efforts will permit clinicians to benefit from research findings and will allow researchers to better understand therapist-client relationships.

Strategic family therapy, when combined with structural family therapy, appears effective for treating adolescent drug abuse. Two investigations (Santisteban, Szapocznik, Perez-Vidal, Kurtines, Murray, & LaPerriere, in press; Szapocznik, Perez-Vidal, Brickman, Foote, Santisteban, Hervis, & Kurtines, 1988) tested the effectiveness of an enhanced engagement program (structural strategic systems engagement (SSSE) versus traditional engagement interventions (EAU) to engage and retain adolescent families in treatment. SSSE attempts to assess, join, and restructure the family with the first contact. The traditional engagement approach is limited to expressing polite concern and asking questions related to the problem. The results from both studies indicate that SSSE is effective in engaging and maintaining adolescent drug users and the families in treatment. For example, 9,390 of the participants were engaged, and over 75% completed treatment, as opposed to the traditional approach, with engagement and completion rates of 42% and 35% (Liddle & Dakof, 1996).

In summary, strategic family therapy appears to be an effective treatment that shows promise when combined with other types of treatment (such as structural family therapy). Research on strategic family therapy appears more experimentally sound than investigations of other types of family therapy. However, further efforts and new initiatives must be made to investigate the critical components of strategic family therapy and their long-term outcomes (Stanton, 1981). The documentation of related treatment effects (for example, family interaction) beyond improvement of symptoms is crucial.

References

Alexander, J. F., & Parsons, B. V. (1973). Short-term behavioral intervention with delinquent families: Impact on family process and recidivism. *Journal of Abnormal Psychology, 81,* 219–225.

Bateson, G., Jackson, D. D., Haley, J., & Weakland, J. H. (1956). Toward a theory of schizophrenia. *Behavioral Science, 1,* 251–261.

Boszormenyi-Nagy, I., & Spark, G. M. (1973). *Invisible loyalties.* Hagerstown, MD: Harper & Row.

Bross, A., & Benjamin, M. (1983). Family therapy: A recursive model of strategic practice. In A. Bross (Ed.), *Family therapy: Principles of strategic practice.* New York: Guilford Press.

deShazer, S. (1975). Brief therapy: Two's company. *Family Process, 14,* 79–83.

Garrigan, J. J., & Bambrick, A. F. (1979). New findings in research on go-between process. *International Journal of Family Therapy, 1,* 76–85.

Gurman, A. S., & Kniskern, D. P. (1978). Research on marital and family therapy: Progress, perspective, and prospect. In S. L. Garfield & A. E. Bergin (Eds.), *Handbook of psychotherapy and behavior change: An empirical analysis* (2nd ed.). New York: Wiley.

Haley, J. (1963). *Strategies of psychotherapy.* New York: Grune & Stratton.

Haley, J. (1973). *Uncommon therapy: The psychiatric techniques of Milton H. Erickson, M.D.* New York: Norton.

Haley, J. (1976). *Problem-solving therapy.* San Francisco: Jossey-Bass.

Hoffman, L. (1981). *Foundations of family therapy: A conceptual framework for systems change.* New York: Basic Books.

Langsley, D. G., Fairbairn, R. H., & DeYoung, C. D. (1968). Adolescence and family crises. *Canadian Psychiatric Association Journal, 13,* 125–133.

Langsley, D. G., & Kaplan, D. M. (1968). *The treatment of families in crisis.* New York: Grune & Stratton.

Langsley, D. G., Machotka, P., & Flomenhaft, K. (1971). Avoiding mental hospital admission: A follow-up study. *American Journal of Psychiatry, 127,* 1391–1394.

Levant, R. F. (1984). *Family therapy: A comprehensive overview.* Englewood Cliffs, NJ: Prentice Hall.

Liddle, H. A., & Dakof, G. A. (1995). Efficacy of family therapy for drug abuse: Promising but not definitive. *Journal of Marital & Family Therapy, 21,* 511–543.

Machal, M., Feldman, R., & Sigal, J. (1989). The unraveling of a treatment program: A follow-up study of the Milan approach to family therapy. *Family Process, 28,* 457–470.

Madanes, C. (1981). *Strategic family therapy.* San Francisco: Jossey-Bass.

Minuchin, S. (1974). *Families and family therapy.* Cambridge, MA: Harvard University Press.

Minuchin, S., & Fishman, H. C. (1981). *Family therapy techniques.* Cambridge, MA: Harvard University Press.

O'Connor, J. J. (1983). Why I can't get hives: Brief strategic intervention with an obsessional child. *Family Process, 22,* 201–209.

Palazzoli-Selvini, M. (1980). Why a long interval between sessions? In M. Andolfi and I. Zwerling (Eds.), *Dimensions of family therapy.* New York: Guilford Press.

Palazzoli-Selvini, M. (1986). Towards a general model of psychotic games. *Journal of Marital and Family Therapy, 12,* 339–349.

Palazzoli-Selvini, M., Boscolo, L., Cecchin, G., & Prata, G. (1978). *Paradox and counterparadox.* New York: Aronson.

Papp, P. (1980). The Greek chorus and other techniques of paradoxical therapy. *Family Process, 19,* 45–57.

Pittman, F. S., Flomenhaft, K., DeYoung, C., Kaplan, D., & Langsley, D. G. (1966). Techniques of family crisis therapy. In J. Masserman (Ed.), *Current psychiatric therapies.* New York: Grune & Stratton.

Pittman, F. S., Langsley, D. G., Flomenhaft, K., DeYoung, C., Machotka, P., & Kaplan, D. M. (1971). Therapy techniques of the family treatment unit. In J. Haley (Ed.), *Changing families.* New York: Grune & Stratton.

Rohrbaugh, M., Tennen, H., Press, S., White, L., Raskin, P., & Pickering, M. (1977, August). *Paradoxical strategies in psychotherapy.* Paper presented at meeting of the American Psychological Association, San Francisco.

Santisteban, D. A., Szapocznik, J., Perez-Vidal, A., Kurtines, W. M., Murray, E. J., & LaPerriere, A. (in press). Engaging behavior problem drug abusing youth and their families into treatment: An investigation of the efficacy of specialized engagement interventions and factors that contribute to differential effectiveness. *Journal of Family Psychology.*

Scully, T. (1982). Strategic family therapy with conduct disordered children and adolescents: An outcome study (Doctoral dissertation. University of Toledo). *Dissertation Abstracts International,* DA8227817.

Sells, S. P., Smith, T. E., Coe, M. J., Yoshioka, M., & Roblins, J. (1994). An ethnography of couple and therapist experiences in reflecting team practice. *Journal of Marital and Family Therapy, 20,* 247–266.

Smith, T. E., Sells, S. P., & Clevenger, T. (1994). Ethnographic content analysis of couple and therapist perceptions in a reflecting team setting. *Journal of Marital and Family Therapy, 20,* 267–286.

Stanton, M. D. (1981). An integrated structural/strategic approach to family therapy. *Journal of Marital and Family Therapy, 1,* 427–439.

Szapocznik, J., Perez-Vidal, A., Brickman, A. L., Foote, F. H., Santisteban, D., Hervis, O.,

& Kurtines, W. (1988). Engaging adolescent drug abusers and their families in treatment: A strategic structural systems approach. *Journal of Consulting and Clinical Psychology, 56,* 552–557.

Turner, J., Rickert, V., Brown, J., & Christensen, D. (1985, April). *The bicameral model. Team therapy through the mirror.* Paper presented at the meeting of the Kentucky Division, American Association for Marital and Family Therapy, Louisville.

Wagner, V., Weeks, G., & L'Abate, L. (1980). Enrichment and written messages with couples. *American Journal of Family Therapy, 8,* 36–44.

Watzlawick, P., Weakland, J., & Fisch, R. (1974). *Change: Principles of problem formation and problem resolution.* New York: Norton.

Weakland, J. B., Fisch, R., Watzlawick, P., & Bodin, A. M. (1974). Brief therapy: Focused problem resolution. *Family Process, 13,* 141–168.

Weeks, G. R., & L'Abate, L. (1982). *Paradoxical psychotherapy: Theory and practice with individuals, couples, and families.* New York: Brunner/Mazel.

Chapter Five

Transgenerational Family Therapy

The term *transgenerational family therapy* categorizes several theoretical and practical approaches that share both an attention to family dynamics across three or more generations and a history in psychodynamic theory. This categorization, however, does not imply that other schools of therapy do not concern themselves with generational issues or that transgenerational therapists do not make eclectic choices of both theory and technique from other approaches.

Transgenerational family therapy encompasses the work of several theorist/practitioners who not only routinely see more than two generations in their sessions, but also conceptualize families and their problems in terms of the psychological dynamics that are passed from generation to generation. Transgenerational family therapists are concerned with current family relationships; however, they are particularly interested in how the current transactional patterns have evolved through the generations. They see the past as operating in the present and therefore have evolved theories that help them chart a therapeutic course "across time."

This chapter is not meant to be exhaustive in scope; rather, it has been written to give the reader an integrative understanding of the transgenerational approach. Particularly in the area of technique, the various theorist/clinicians approach many of the same issues in different ways. Their diversity will be represented as much as possible.

Theoretical Constructs and Philosophy

Transgenerational family therapy has evolved through the merging of two great philosophical and theoretical schools of thought: psychodynamic and systems theory. Each school of thought has well-developed theoretical concepts that serve as the core theory for transgenerational family therapy. For instance, there have been volumes written on the psychodynamic object-relations theory alone. What is offered here is only a synopsis of theoretical confluence; readers interested in the approach should research the literature to achieve a comprehensive knowledge.

There are some basic concepts of transgenerational family therapy that form the significant structure out of which technique has grown. Among them, key concepts are that (1) the past is active in the present, and (2) evolution has left us with a primitive emotional system and a more recently evolved reasoning system. A discussion of each concept follows.

The Past Is Active in the Present

The concept that past family relationships are actively influencing how we view our current relationships is often a difficult one for people living in contemporary culture to accept or understand. Modern American culture idealizes the independent, free-from-ties individual who is concerned primarily with self-development. The seeming ease with which families of one generation pick up and move across the country, far away from generational ties, gives the impression that individuals can literally leave everything behind them. Everyday life offers many examples of how many people would prefer to ignore the past. However, understanding the past is basic to transgenerational family therapy.

Given this cultural context, it is remarkable that Freud's basic theory of emotional illness as the product of past disturbed relationships has had such enduring influence on our thinking. Freud (1923/1961) theorized that early life experiences molded the personality through adaptations of the ego. The ego was conceptualized as something of a regulator that would try to satisfy the deep instinctual demands of the psyche without inviting more tension from the external world. Thus, the ego would balance the satisfaction of needs with the natural consequences of obtaining satisfaction in a civilized world.

Object Relations

Fairbairn (1954), elaborating on Freud's thinking, postulated that the ego focused outwardly on objects in reality rather than inwardly on somatic instincts. For Fairbairn, the human being was an object-seeking organism; that is, from birth, a person attempts to establish relationships with external objects that can satisfy needs. In a sense, the person (the **ego**) tries to hook up with someone or something outside itself that will meet its needs.

Fairbairn further suggested that the personality developed as a result of the ego's drive for object relationships. In short, Fairbairn postulated that when the object does not completely satisfy the ego, the person experiences anxiety. Because the needs left unsatisfied early in life are basic to survival and because the person has few resources for establishing alternative object relationships, the anxiety that results is often expressed in strong feelings such as abandonment or rejection. Because the child can't simply give up or change the external object (for example, mother), the child copes with the anxiety by internalizing the object into the inner psychic world where the child can more adequately control it. Internalization is a difficult concept for many people to understand or accept. It goes beyond feelings or memories to become something more like incorporated subidentities or parts of the personality. We often recognize the process of internalization in our daily speech with phrases like "a part of me wants to just . . . ," "I have an inner war going on," or "I have to watch myself constantly on that issue." These everyday sayings refer to our sense that the personality is not a unified entity but a mixture of current and past relationships that have been deeply incorporated, some of them repressed, in our psyche.

Two additional key points should be made about those of Fairbairn's concepts that have directly influenced transgenerational family therapy. First, Fairbairn theorized that external life events were perceived through the filter of internalized relationships. For example, someone who has a persecutory introject (that is, a persecutory relationship that has been internalized) tends to see current close relationships as persecuting; that is, present relationships would be seen through the lens of the past relationships. Again, this is not an unfamiliar notion because it is a recurring theme in everything from everyday comments, such as a wife's saying to her husband, "I'm not your mother, you know," to themes in popular culture. One example of the latter can be found in the lyrics of the musical group The Police. In a song entitled "Mother," they sing of the frustration a young man feels when the girls he goes out with end up behaving too much like his mother.

The second key concept of Fairbairn's that has direct application to transgenerational family therapy is that we unconsciously attempt to influence, change, and coerce our intimate relationships into ones that better reflect what we are used to—our internalized models; that is, not only do we perceive others who are close to us in terms of the past but we unknowingly attempt to change those present relationships to fit our internal mold. For example, a wife may say to her mother, "That husband of mine makes me so angry. He has a preconceived notion about what a wife is 'supposed' to be like!" The speaker is complaining that her husband's internal model for "wife" does not fit with her own behaviors. Her anger may also be saying that his notions or values do not fit her internal model of a husband either. Or perhaps the opposite is occurring: She may have a rigid, critical introject that she is both perceiving in her spouse (projection) and creating in her spouse's reactive behavior to her own insistence and complaints. This example could be explored further within its own context. Because she is complaining to her mother about her husband, the wife may be both fulfilling some object need of her mother's (for example, a daughter who loves her more than anyone else) and eliciting a comment from her mother that fits the daughter's internal model of "mother" (such as, "Honey, he sounds just like your father.").

Henry Dicks (1967) was an early pioneer in conceptualizing the interactional implications of Fairbairn's object-relations theory in marital interaction. Dicks outlined the process by which marital partners complement one another in complex object relationships. Stated simply, each partner represents an object ideal to the other in the sense that each is seen as possessing qualities or characteristics that were missing in past object relationships. People often introduce a spouse as "my better half" or express the import of their wedding vows as "We were half, now we are whole." Dicks postulated that this reciprocal object assignment leads people to treat aspects of their spouses as if they were aspects of themselves, and indeed treat their spouse in a similar manner to the way they treat aspects of themselves.

Framo (1981) summarized object-relations theory as follows:

1. Human beings are fundamentally an object-seeking species.
2. Human beings can't really change objects in reality, so they create internal psychological substitutes.
3. These internal substitutes undergo transformation over the years as people develop new relationships.
4. People use their current relationships as symbolic pawns to heal previous conflicts in the original family.
5. A person's choice of mate and treatment of children is based on a projective process by which spouses and children become stand-ins for past primary object relationships.

Family Loyalty

The past also impinges on the present in the form of family loyalty (Boszormenyi-Nagy & Spark, 1973). The loyalty a person feels toward his or her family is more than the overt feeling of "owing" parents something for raising him or her. The debt also has to do with the complex web of covert loyalties, generational legacies, and unhealed wounds in the multigenerational history of the family. The following example elaborates on this concept.

A young insurance salesman, John, sought therapy because he was depressed and suicidal. He had recently been divorced and had taken a new job in a new profession outside his hometown, leaving the banking business behind. Although he had managed to get through the difficult first year after his divorce, he felt no relief from his grief and reported that his emotions were even more uncontrollable than before. When asked about his continued depression, he could only respond vaguely that "he had let everyone down." Although he did not consider the divorce a failure, he described himself as a "profound failure." The feeling of failing was so strong he could not imagine being able to "make it up" to everyone. The "everyone" included his family of origin, his extended family, and his young son.

John's predicament became clearer as the therapist learned more about his family's binding loyalties. His grandfather had come from very poor social standing and was poorly educated, but he had built an insurance business on hard work and ruthless competition. Nevertheless, John's grandfather's success was not enough to gain him acceptance in the upper social strata he desired. He was a hard drinker, brutal in public, and cruel to his wife and two sons at home. The elder of the two sons was the favorite of John's grandfather; the younger son (John's father, Walter) was closer to his mother. Walter envied his older brother and secretly longed for his father's acceptance and love. The older brother was killed at war, leaving Walter the sole inheritor of the family's legacy—a legacy that included his father's reputation, the family business, and the grieving family emotional system.

The death of the older son was a severe blow to Walter's father, and he soon retired to his home, his wife, and the bottle. That was a very difficult time for Walter, who was extremely busy trying to save the business, keep his father out of public view, protect his mother from his father, and, at the same time, court the daughter of a well-respected and socially established family. Walter drove himself to fill the void created by his brother's death and to cover up the family's grief and deeper problems. Walter paid a great personal cost, a cost that his son, John, would someday feel he had to repay. With the death of his alcoholic father, Walter embarked on a life mission to make up for his father, to become a cultured person, to make his mother proud, to achieve the social success that his father was unable to reach, and to give his newborn son, John, what he felt he had never had—respectability and a close father-son relationship.

As John matured, he received the fruits of affluence, the ties of loyalty. Unlike his own father, Walter wanted to pamper his wife and give John the best. Therefore, at an early age, John was placed in well-respected boarding schools. John had all the material goods he wanted but lacked real emotional closeness with his parents. He felt obligated simultaneously to (1) keep the family name untarnished, (2) be grateful for the enormous sacrifices his father had made, (3) act as though his mother were a very warm and affectionate person, (4) enjoy life in ways his father had never allowed for himself, and (5) never criticize the father-son relationship or his grandfather's darker side. John grew up with a very polished surface but experienced deep feelings of inadequacy. He drove himself to live up to the expectations his father placed on him. He was the sole product of his father's "sacrificial" life, and he felt enormous pressure to live up to that dream. Beneath the surface, however, he felt the conflicting sacrifices of the whole family across the generations. He felt rage for his lonely childhood, and he felt unworthy because he felt the rage. He was hurt by his mother's preoccupation with herself, yet he felt obliged not to express his hurt to anyone.

As a young adult, John adopted the solution of achievement in his father's eyes, a fulfillment of the family ideal, and a living repayment of past generations' sacrifices. He went to the right college, he married the right girl, chose the right profession (banking), even painted his house the right color. He drove the correct car and wore the correct clothes. He even had his shirts starched the same way his father had. The obligation of loyalty to his generational legacy extended into every aspect of his life. Unfortunately, his wife left him and took their son with her. John's indebtedness to respectability was so critically demanding and all-encompassing that she simply felt she no longer had any sense of herself in the marriage. Unable to face his social friends and to accept his family's sympathies, John had exiled himself to another city, where he took a job selling insurance. He chose that profession because, in his words, "That's all that was available, and it seemed right." Not only did John have his own divorce to work through emotionally, but he had the inherited legacy of balancing previous generations' lives. Boszormenyi-Nagy (Boszormenyi-Nagy & Spark, 1973) calls this process *ledger balancing*. John was depressed not only because of his divorce, but also because the losses of generations past were active in his present loss.

John's story illustrates some of the more dysfunctional potentials of family loyalty. However, family loyalty is also the glue that holds families together, helps people make sacrifices for altruistic goals, and provides hope for the future. The formula of "giving to get" applies directly to family life across the generations. The immediate rewards for the young parents when they walk the floor with their infant are few, yet those events are recorded in the family's loyalty system. The young couple with the infant are concomitantly "paying back" their parents for their sacrifices while building their own future credit of merit. It is in the family that people learn about giving and about the debt of loyalty that the gift creates for the receiver. In some families, the debt is small, and the payments in autonomy are also small. In other families, like John's, the debt created out of the giving of one generation to another is high, and the repayment cuts deeply into an individual's autonomy.

What accounts for the differences between the extremes on the family continuum? Why should the giving in one family have such high costs, and why should those costs be greater for one family member than for another? Transgenerational family therapists, Murray Bowen (1978) in particular, have asked similar questions. The following section explores some of their theoretical answers.

Evolved Systems of Emotion and Reason

On one end of the continuum we are discussing, emotional giving or caring is offered without the receiver's feeling trapped by the gift. At the other end of the continuum, however, the receiver feels his or her sense of self suffocated by the burden of the gift. What is reflected in the continuum is the tension between individuality and togetherness (Kerr, 1981) in families. Other approaches to family therapy have identified this concept similarly; for instance, Minuchin (1974) has referred to the concept as the "matrix of identity." In order to understand this concept from a transgenerational point of view, it may be helpful to discuss some of the interlocking concepts of Murray Bowen (1966, 1978), such as (1) **differentiation**, (2) **triangulation**, and (3) the **family projection process**.

Differentiation

Although trained in psychodynamic psychiatry, Murray Bowen worked to evolve a theory of emotional illness that was syntonic with the other sciences, particularly biology. Bowen merged diverse concepts such as Freud's unconscious id, Darwin's theory of evolution, and his own observational research of families of people with schizophrenia at NIMH (Bowen, Dysinger, Brodey, & Basmania, 1957). Bowen suggested that emotional illness was a by-product of our evolution. He developed the idea that human beings have two systems of functioning: an emotional system, which they share with lower forms of life, and an intellectual/rational system (cerebral cortex), which is a more recent evolutionary development. The greater the degree that these two systems are fused, or undifferentiated, the more the individual responds to the impulses of his or her emotional system. When an individual is anxious, the systems are also much more likely to fuse and lose their ability to function separately. Phrases such as "his thoughts are overwhelmed with emotion" or "she is not thinking clearly" speak to our common perception of a person who is using emotional rather than objective reasoning.

The extent to which individuals have differentiated their thinking system from their feeling system will determine how able they are to maintain a sense of self in a relationship (Kerr, 1981). The more their thinking can be differentiated from their feelings, the more they will sense a separate "self" in an intimate relationship. Each person enters a marriage with a certain similar amount of internal differentiation in ability to reason versus emotional reactiveness.

Although partners may appear to differ in their levels of differentiation, Bowen (1978) points out that that appearance is based on differences in styles of coping with emotion. One partner may appear to be less emotionally reactive than the other simply because of a tendency to intellectualize his or her emotions. Also, each spouse has a basic level of differentiation of self; that is, a sense of where the spouse's values and attitudes end and his or her own values and attitudes begin. Hypothetically, couples could range from having no selves (emotionally reactive) to having complete selves (able to reason). Because most couples certainly fall somewhere in between the two extremes, it follows that all couples experience some emotional reactiveness and tension. There is inherent conflict in dyadic relationships as each partner reacts to the other's reaction until at some point the relationship (or the individual) feels threatened. At that point, a third person or entity (for example, alcohol or work) is brought into the dyadic struggle to reduce tension, thus creating a triangle.

Triangulation

A classic example of triangulation was the plight of poor Ethel Mertz of the old *I Love Lucy* show. In every episode, her standard line was, "Oh, no, Lucy, you're not going to get me involved in one of your harebrained schemes again just because Ricky won't let you do something!" Well, of course, she did get "triangled in." The results are not always so humorous in real life for those families who have low differentiation and the chronic need to dissipate stress through others. Triangles are the natural consequence of two less than differentiated people who need to dissipate some of their conflict and tension through a third party. Triangles are not necessarily pathological—all human relationships can be thought of as possessing this characteristic.

In families in which the differentiation is high and the stress and anxiety low, the dissipation of stress has very low costs in terms of sacrifices of individuality. Family members shift positions, depending on what the issue is and who is most uncomfortable. However, in families in which the differentiation is low and tension high, the emotional reactivity reverberates through many interconnected triangles. For example, triangulation automatically occurs when a baby is born into the family system. This new triangle (father-mother-child) creates effects on existing triangles. Suppose that before the child's birth, the couple's conflict would increase until it reached a level at which the wife would usually triangle in her mother (that is, talk to her about the problem). Although the mother's involvement reduced the stress, the husband felt left outside the family. The triangle fulfilled the mother's needs because she was using her daughter to dissipate stress in her own relationship. One can also appreciate how active previous family loyalties might be in such an example. At the time of the birth, the husband's desire for closeness to the child motivates him to get back to an inside position. One way to get inside is to attempt to get his mother-in-law into an outside position. As the mother-in-law becomes more of an outsider, the stress is redirected to her marital relationship. If there is enough differentiation across the generations, then the older generational triangle may find an alternative object to absorb stress. If an object is not available, one possible outcome could be a "triangle showdown"—that is, the husband and his mother-in-law may struggle for the inside position with the wife/daughter. This conflict will probably triangle in more people and things such as work and health.

The preceding example illustrates that levels of differentiation travel across generational boundaries. How they do so will be discussed in the next section.

Family Projection Process

The term *family projection process* (Bowen, 1966) refers to the observation that children's level of differentiation generally approximates that of their parents. However, this process often distributes differentiation unevenly among the children. One child may grow up with a high level of differentiation (that is, well-defined sense of self and low emotional reactivity), whereas a brother or sister may grow up with a low level of differentiation (that is, poorly defined sense of self and high emotional reactivity). Such variability often occurs when parents attempt to diffuse their emotional conflicts through a particular child. In a sense, the parents project their own emotional conflicts onto a child and attempt to control them there. A brief chronological summary of a case that illustrates the process may clarify how the conflicts of object relations, loyalty, indebtedness, differentiation, triangulation, and the family projection process all describe different characteristics of the same multigenerational process. We will use the case example of John discussed earlier in this chapter and take John's father (Walter) as a starting point, working back into the past to see its effect on the present.

> Walter was the younger son of a father whose love and esteem he couldn't seem to earn and a mother who used him far too often to absorb the stress of her marriage (family projection process). Unable to change these objects, Walter internalized them and created subidentities within himself (object relations). Walter resisted the need in himself for love and nurturance and instead sought respectability. His mother's chief complaint against her husband was his disreputable nature. She often told Walter of the suffering she

endured because his father lacked respectability. Walter felt indebted to his mother but at the same time felt suffocated by her and wished to push away some of the emotional togetherness that grew out of such a rigid triangular alliance.

In a wife, Walter sought a mate who had good character, social status, manners, and emotional control. He found the woman who represented the object relationships that were missing in his life and he married her. Of course, his bride (Helen), by marrying Walter, was also meeting her needs in selecting her ego ideal. She had grown up an only child in an affluent family, with her parents' focus on her rather than on themselves. Helen's own object relationships left her longing for both intimacy and autonomy. Her ambivalence was expressed in her need to be the center of attention and her paradoxical refusal to let anyone get close to her.

The marriage of Walter and Helen worked well on the surface. Helen demanded, Walter provided, and both achieved part of their needs. Yet with intimacy came the pain of past relationships, in which closeness had meant hurt feelings and loss of self. Because both partners were the focus of intense emotional triangles in their original families, neither had developed a very stable sense of self—that is, differentiation. Under stress, each partner would lose reason and become dominated by emotion. They developed a relationship that was outwardly successful but inwardly contained a great deal of unresolved conflict.

Walter and his older brother became triangulated into their parents' emotional reactivity partially on the basis of their birth order. The couple focused on the older son as a sign of success and an homage to the previous generation, symbolizing that the family had made good. The second son, Walter, was triangulated as a projected target of their suppressed marital strife. With the death of the older son came not only the significant grief any parent would feel, but also the loss of the family dream to achieve full social status. Generations had worked to produce a full-fledged upper-class person, and there had been considerable sacrifice. This debt then fell to Walter. Although the debt was not communicated directly, Walter felt the need to repay it. Family loyalties are often experienced without conscious recognition. Walter and Helen's son, John, was the next inheritor of unmet needs. Because he was the primary focus of triangulated conflict between his parents, he had developed very little differentiation of self. That is, when something occurred outside himself in his parents' relationship, he learned over the years to experience it internally. He had little ability to apply reason to his emotions, not always knowing whether it was his emotions he was experiencing or a reaction to his parents' emotions. He had internalized a critical object and appeased it with overachievement. John was sensitive to criticism and tried to behave in a way that would please his parents. John felt that to be different was to be disloyal.

John chose his wife, Susan, because she reminded him of his mother but was kind and sweet and came from a less affluent socioeconomic background. John hoped subconsciously that this would put distance between himself and his parents. Susan chose John because he seemed to need her, and she had hoped he wouldn't be as critical as her own father. In the early years of marriage, however, Susan had a very difficult time. She missed her family and felt a great deal of social pressure. Moreover, John was increasingly critical of her. They were trapped in a vicious cycle that had no real beginning in their own generation. John would push hard to impress someone in the family or business, and Susan would feel pressure to perform and would accuse him of being critical of her efforts. John would react to the conflict by criticizing her harshly, and she would retaliate by embarrassing him in some small but public way (for example, not dressing appropriately). John's panic reaction would increase because of the perceived threat to the generations of sacrifice that had gone into the cultivation of the family image. He would rage against her until she would retreat to her parents' home, returning only when things had calmed down. This tension escalated until Susan decided one day not to return at all. For her, leaving was a symbolic victory over her critical father; for John, it was the crumbling of a house of cards. Lost love is a tragic loss, but, as is the case in many divorces, the loss is often a culmination of family dynamics spread across many generations.

This example is, of course, just a fragmentary slice of the total family history. One could go back to Walter's father's early life or forward to John's great-grandchildren. John's divorce becomes the historical context for his son's object relations, and of course, his son will eventually meet someone from another family with another dynamic history.

Transgenerational family therapists view past relationships as influencing present family dynamics. They theorize that the past affects our thinking so strongly because, as a species, we have only recently acquired our ability to reason through our emotions. Thus it is often the emotional experiences of our past that dictate to us, rather than what seems reasonable in the present. Current intimate relationships become an arena for both partners to work through past relationships. This complementary process can be easily upset by conflict, tension, and stress. When conflict or tension occurs, other people are triangled into this process to absorb the excess tension. The projected family stress becomes the context for future object relationships across generational lines, thus creating an emotional dowry or inheritance.

We have briefly described the theoretical concepts of transgenerational family therapy and are now ready to examine their application in therapeutic practice.

Therapeutic Practice

Transgenerational family therapy differs from other approaches to family therapy in that its proponents do not emphasize moment-by-moment process technique. Whereas the structural and strategic therapists are very much concerned with the details of communication between therapist and family, even offering verbatim transcripts for study, the transgenerational practitioners discuss technique in a broader context. Transgenerational family therapists are more concerned with the therapist's grasp of theory and with the therapist's examination of his or her own family of origin. They believe that if therapists have prepared conceptually and have resolved their own generational family conflicts, then they will naturally produce their own style and method when applying the theory to practice. For example, the therapist needs to achieve a certain level of differentiation so that he or she will not be triangulated into the family's emotional conflict (Bowen, 1978). Avoiding that risk requires genuine differentiation, rather than merely the copying of technique.

This section will focus on the technical guidelines offered by the transgenerational family therapists, again with the understanding that these therapists are a coalition of unique individuals. The discussion will primarily emphasize points of confluence in approaches to assessment, therapeutic goals, and technique.

Assessment

The clinical interview is the primary mode of assessment for transgenerational family therapists. Rather than using paper-and-pencil questionnaires or objective tests, these clinicians rely on the theory and clinical experience to assess relationships. Whereas Framo (1981), Bowen (1978), and Williamson (1982b) all stress the need for more than one interview, Boszormenyi-Nagy (Boszormenyi-Nagy & Spark, 1973) does not address assessment as a separate phase of treatment. Rather, Boszormenyi-Nagy describes assessment as a part of the total process of relating to the family in a trustworthy manner. Thus assessment of family relationships by clinical interview varies slightly, depending on the clinician's personal approach. However, Kerr (1981) offers the following assessment outline, which is consistent with a wide range of transgenerational approaches:

1. Focus on the history of the symptomology (physical, emotional, or behavioral) in terms of its etiology. Give specific attention to identifying significant life events in the chronology of the family.

2. Collect information, beginning with how the parents met and continuing chronologically to the present. The nature of the courtship and marriage is of particular interest. Information about the family life cycle, geographical relocations, and educational and vocational history are also a part of the evaluation.

3. Explore the extended families of each spouse. Information regarding sibling position, emotional life of the siblings' current families, and the history of emotional functioning of the parents are all basic areas to be assessed. In addition, data on births, deaths, health, physical proximity, and significant life events are important facets of family dynamics to assess in each spouse's family of origin.

The clinician listens throughout these stages to help identify how the presenting problem fits into the family's historical context. If the presenting problem is depression, for instance, the clinician will start to make some initial hypotheses based on clinical experience and theories of depression. For example, the therapist might assume that the patient has an internalized critical voice that keeps telling him he is incapable of changing his problem or his perception of the problem. The transgenerational therapist asks questions to track the source of the critical voice. The therapist will want to identify current situations that elicit this response. What do those situations have in common with past experiences? Who were involved in those past experiences and why were they involved? This line of inquiry is just the first venture into the family's emotional history. Other issues will have to be explored before the complex historical map of the family is re-created in the therapist's mind. To illustrate, we will use the core theoretical concepts presented earlier in this chapter as an outline for pertinent areas of inquiry needed to set appropriate therapeutic goals.

I. How is the past active in the present?
   A. What were the person's early object relationships like?
   B. What relationship strata have been layered over those early relationships?
   C. How is this history expressed in recent intimate relationships?
   D. What are the emotional debts in the family?
   E. What are the issues of loyalty?
   F. How is intergenerational balance disturbed?
II. What is the history of emotional and rational processes in the family?
   A. What is the potential for rational functioning and how does it vary from family member to family member?
   B. What are the major triangles in the family, and how did they evolve?
   C. How has the family projection process worked in this family? For the client?

As this outline illustrates, the assessment process in transgenerational family therapy is often slow and methodical.

Goals

Transgenerational family therapy views the presenting problem as the result of intergenerational issues; thus, the goals of therapy encompass more than the alleviation of the presenting problem. The presenting problem is important, but the symptom is not given primary focus, as it is in strategic therapy.

Goals for transgenerational therapy are derived from the theoretical constructs and are then individualized to the specific case. At the theoretical level, the clinician attempts to reduce the influence the past has on the present and increase the influence the rational process has over the emotional process throughout the family. Client goals are formulated, depending on the presenting symptom, the dynamics, and the temporal circumstances (for example, geographical location, finances, and health). The following section discusses how the technique of transgenerational family therapy is applied to meeting those goals.

Technique

The literature on the transgenerational approach is focused predominantly on theory versus technique. This emphasis on cognition and understanding is in fact the primary characteristic of transgenerational technique; that is, the therapist works to maintain an objective (emotionally uninvolved) position from which rational processes can be reinforced and emotional reactivity in the family can be reduced. The therapist stays objective by using techniques such as interpretation, transference analysis, education, and assignments involving family of origin to minimize influences of the past on the present. Although these techniques are used concurrently by the therapist, we will treat them separately.

Objectivity

Objectivity needs to be discussed first because it is basic to a transgenerationalist approach. The emphasis on objectivity has been consistent since the early days of psychoanalysis. Psychoanalysis evolved during a time of great interest in the objective inquiry. To maintain objectivity, the therapeutic relationship was strictly controlled so that any feelings the patient had for the therapist were considered to be feelings from the patient's past relationships, transferred to the analyst (transference will be discussed later in this section).

The importance of objectivity was restated by Bowen (1978), though for different conceptual reasons. Objectivity, for Bowen and the clinicians he has influenced, means an ability to remain rational during emotional turbulence. Bowen found that to be objective one must achieve differentiation through work with one's family of origin. The family-of-origin work required of the therapist is basically the same process that the client must accomplish (the process will be discussed later in this section). A therapist who is differentiated and objective will (1) ask "thinking" questions rather than "feeling" questions and (2) avoid triangulation by having each family member speak to the therapist rather than speaking to each other. "Thinking" questions help to maintain objectivity by using the rational system to process information, instead of focusing on emotional reactions to a situation. If the family members "think" rather than "feel," therapists are also less likely to become emotionally entangled because they will have to react to less emotion.

Avoiding triangulation also helps the therapist maintain objectivity. Resistance to triangulation helps the therapist avoid being absorbed into the stress of the conflictual dyad. There are two basic transgenerational approaches to avoiding triangulation. First, Boszormenyi-Nagy (1965) and Framo (1965) suggest that the therapist alternate who he or she aligns with in the family. Second, Bowen (1978) keeps the conversation directed through him. Bowen's approach runs counter to structural and communications approaches, in which the therapist typically works to get family members talking to each other. The transgenerationalist takes the view that for lasting change to occur, the family members must learn not to react emotionally to what other family members are saying. By interacting calmly with the therapist, each family member learns to tolerate emotional discussions without reacting to another family member. By remaining an objective third party to whom all family members address their feelings, the therapist is able to help the family become less emotionally reactive.

Boszormenyi-Nagy (1965), in contrast, advocates a shifting therapeutic allegiance that prevents triangular relationships from forming. Boszormenyi-Nagy's suggestion that the therapist side with a family member is very close to what Minuchin refers to as "unbalancing" in structural family therapy. By shifting alliances, therapists are able to shift the power in the relationship and keep themselves from being absorbed in the emotional conflict. It should be noted, however, that when Minuchin is unbalancing, he is attempting to change the family structure. When Boszormenyi-Nagy sides with a family member, he is trying to tip the balance of the relationship toward increased fairness. These interventions are similar but are used for different reasons.

Interpretation

Another technique by which the transgenerationalist can support rational thinking is interpretation. When therapists use interpretation, they are providing the family with a rationale for its emotional conflicts. The explanation is based on the collective theory of psychodynamics, family systems, and the clinician's experience.

An interpretation has several effects on the therapy. It has the immediate effect of calming a person's emotions because in order for the person to understand the interpretation he or she must shift toward analytical thinking and away from feelings. An interpretation often will reduce acute fear in a family member because it can explain away something that was unknown and mysterious. Childlike fears of the "dark unknown" can be assuaged by "shedding light" on a subject, thus removing some of the powerful impact the mysterious can have on a person.

Interpretation is also a behavior of the therapist that is observed by the family and can therefore be modeled. In other words, the family observes someone it respects responding to an emotional conflict with a rational thought aimed at trying to understand the emotional dilemma. The action underlines the therapist's overall message about thinking versus emotional reactivity as a way to solve problems.

Interpretation helps to reframe present symbolic conflict as the result of unresolved relationships in the past, giving the family member some perspective and emotional distance from the turbulence of current situations. For example, the angry and hurt husband in a conflicted marriage currently can muster only contempt for his wife's "mothering" qualities. Through interpretation, he can be shown that his real anger is aimed not at his wife but at his mother, who was too protective when he was a child. Rather than feeling contempt for his wife, he can now feel compassion. Oftentimes interpretation will be directed at some aspect of the family member's past object relations in an attempt to help the person sort out what is real in his or her relationships and what is projection from old relationships. This process will be discussed further in the following section.

Transference Analysis

Transference is the psychodynamic term for the sum total of emotional relationships between the therapist and client. The term was chosen because it conveys the concept that past relationships serve as models for current relationships; that is, the old model for a close relationship is transferred to the new circumstance. In transgenerational family therapy, the therapist is thought of as a symbolic screen upon which complex *relationships* from the past are projected. This view of transference not only includes the one-to-one type of transference (for example, the mother of the family may see her critical father in the therapist) but also the whole family system's collective projection onto the therapist. Boszormenyi-Nagy (Boszormenyi-Nagy & Spark, 1973) discusses a case in which the therapist has helped the family to forgive an elderly parent, only to find that he—the therapist—is now the target of the family's scapegoating anger. This type of transference goes beyond the dyadic relationship between the therapist and an individual family member and becomes the total family system's transference. Both forms of transference are most likely to occur when there is a male-female co-therapy team, which gives rise to potential associations with parents.

Transference analysis is an important technique in transgenerational family therapy because it permits family members to experience the past in the present. Through the interpretation of the therapeutic relationship as something similar to a past relationship, family members become aware of how the past relationship was incomplete and how they continue to work on past relationships through present ones. Interpretation of the transference relationship also enables family members to gain control by shifting the conflict from the unconscious emotional system to the conscious rational system.

This shift into awareness can often be uncomfortable for family members. Past relationships have been pushed out of awareness because of the emotional pain connected with them. The pain must be reencountered, assimilated, and resolved in order to reduce the influence of those past relationships. Resistance to such psychic reorganization often occurs and often takes the form of increased transference. For example, a male therapist might attempt to interpret a female family member's dependency on him as a transference from the person's relationship with her father. If she has deeply repressed the pain from that past relationship, the therapist's interpretation is likely to feel threatening (that is, if it is correct, she will have to reexperience some of that repressed pain). The family member will probably resist this interpretation and, still in the transference mode, respond as if her father had criticized and rejected her. She may then become depressed and accuse the therapist of not caring about her (as she also accuses her father). Such resistance can shake a therapist's objectivity. If the therapist has been drawn into this projective drama, he may overreact to the person's accusation with either stern denial or overcompensating compassion rather than with a rational strategy to help the person face the pain of the past relationship.

The technique of transference analysis involves interpretation of both dyadic and system-wide transferences. The analysis must include strategies for dealing with resistance and demands a high level of emotional integration in the therapist's own life.

Education

We have been talking about various types of interpretations as being key techniques of the transgenerational therapists. Another aspect of interpretation is that, over time, the family members start to gain more information about themselves. That knowledge base serves to offer explanations for human behavior. The family progressively adopts a new conceptualization of its experience, a new map of its life's territory. Thus, a focal technique of transgenerational family therapy is *education*.

Educational technique takes three basic forms. First, there is the subtle transmission of values. This category of educational technique includes all of the explicit and implicit behaviors of the therapist that combine to create a paradigm for the family members to emulate. The family comes to therapy in a crisis of conflict, their predominant interaction one of emotion, tension, and blaming. Transgenerational therapists respond with reason and calm, and, rather than judging who is at fault for the present crisis, they expand the discussion to the history of the family. What does this initial step communicate to the family? Some of the values that may be transmitted to the family are that (1) the family is not going to fall apart—there is even time to take a history, (2) this problem didn't just arise today but has a background, (3) everyone seems to play some part in it, (4) rational discussion of the problem may be better than emotional outbursts, (5) there is hope in that alternatives may be found, and (6) maybe some order could be applied to life's chaos. The therapist begins the educational process by the way he or she responds to the family.

Second, the educational process continues to develop with therapeutic interpretation and analysis. The therapist's knowledge of human behavior is made available point by point as the family members discuss their lives. Therapeutic knowledge is offered when necessary and is adapted to the family's situations. Like a good teacher, the therapist stimulates awareness by asking strategic questions. For example, rather than teaching a family about adolescent psychology because the 16-year-old son now needs new relationships with his parents, the therapist might instead ask the father and mother to reminisce about their own adolescent lives. Or the therapist may stress the generational legacy even more by inviting the parents' parents into the session to talk about how their kids handled adolescence. By strategic questioning, the therapist teaches the family about important issues, using the family's own life experience as examples.

A third way the transgenerationalist educates is to assign related readings or special academic coursework. Kerr (1981) discusses the benefits of assigning readings and coursework outside the emotional environment of therapy. He suggests that families often assimilate theory more quickly in an educational setting. These educational efforts range from subtle modeling to direct, didactic minilectures. Teaching psychological concepts is an important step in understanding past relationships. The following section discusses how the transgenerational therapist works to change family dynamics across generations.

Work with the Family of Origin

Quite possibly, the greatest contribution to transgenerational family therapy has been the idea that people can go back to their original families to work out some of their problems. This idea is remarkable because psychoanalysis has operated on the functional premise that a person's context does not cause the illness but that people make themselves sick in reaction to their context. Given such an operational definition, "feeling better" means to work out these reactions intrapsychically (within the person's own psyche). Trips home, or intergenerational meetings, would only complicate the situation with unnecessary stress, according to common psychoanalytic practice. It was Murray Bowen who took the then-radical step of describing his own family-of-origin work to an audience of national family therapy professionals in March, 1967 (Anonymous, 1972). This section will discuss Bowen's pioneering use of the technique in therapy and training, as well as covering the significant contributions and elaborations on that technique by Framo, Boszormenyi-Nagy, Paul, and Williamson.

Bowen (1978) describes his role in helping individuals define themselves in their family of origin as that of a "coach." Like the coach of an athlete, Bowen helps the person prepare, analyze the situation, and plan strategies for every contingency. Moreover, like the athlete's coach, Bowen provides encouragement from the sidelines. He encourages his clients and students, or trainees, to develop specific strategies for visiting their family of origin and then meets with them again when they return. Bowen's coaching technique involves many strategies, but three are most prominent. First, he encourages the person to build "person-to-person" relationships. What he means by this is that a daughter, for instance, would be able to have a relationship with her father that is separate (or increasingly separate) from her relationship with her mother. Practically, having separate relationships means being able to talk with one parent without the other's being triangled in. For most families, this sort of change is very difficult to accept. When an adult child moves toward one parent to establish such a relationship, the other parent often feels neglected, hurt, or suspicious. The adult child may also feel guilty because of past injunctions to balance affection and loyalty. One student, for example, couldn't bring himself to write separate letters to his father and his mother. He first wrote them the triangular way ("Dear Mom and Dad") and informed them together that the next time he was going to write them separate letters as "part of a school course requirement." He wanted to prepare them because of the guilt he felt about excluding one of them. Such feelings of guilt are often associated with childish fantasies of physical harm, such as heart attack, that might come to a parent if the triangular relationship were to change.

As a second assignment, Bowen suggests having the person start to observe his or her emotional reactiveness. Bowen believes that if people are able to observe their own emotional reactiveness, they will be able to control it. Bowen helps his clients and trainees study their families. The process involves analyzing what is already known prior to the person's visit to his or her family of origin. Bowen helps his clients to speculate on family dynamics and to identify areas of particular study for the visit. When the client returns, Bowen assists the person in the difficult task of processing the information that has been gathered.

The third part of the coaching process focuses on the person's efforts to avoid triangulation during emotional situations. The client or trainee is encouraged to go home during times of emotional stress in the family (which is when triangling of relationships is most acute). Bowen coaches the person to be in constant contact with an emotional issue involving two other family members and to remain emotionally neutral. This means that the person doesn't take sides, become defensive, or counterattack. Avoiding triangulation is possible only after one learns to control one's own emotional reactiveness successfully.

Bowen uses this three-part technique with both his clients and his family therapy trainees. The major emphasis he places on work with family of origin has had a dramatic impact on the entire profession of family therapy. Other transgenerational therapists have also made significant contributions to approaching family-of-origin work.

Framo (1981) introduces work with family of origin into couples' group sessions. He places a conflicted couple in a group for couples and informs them that he often has each individual meet with his or her own family of origin toward the end of therapy. Then, throughout the life of the couples' group, he progressively encourages them to examine their relationships with their families of origin. When the time comes for the meeting, Framo has the individual organize the meeting. This approach is different from that of Bowen, who "coaches from the sideline." Framo is an active participant and prefers to include a female co-therapist. These family-of-origin sessions are audiotaped and typically involve two 2-hour sessions with a short break between sessions.

Boszormenyi-Nagy (Boszormenyi-Nagy & Spark, 1973) approaches family-of-origin work similarly, yet in a somewhat less structured manner. He weighs fairness and ethical considerations in his decisions about whether to include parents and grandparents. In a progressive fashion, he attempts to help the nuclear family consider intergenerational issues. If that approach is not adequate, then the older generations might be invited for a session or more.

Norman Paul (Paul & Paul, 1975) brings yet another slant to the family-of-origin field of technique by using intergenerational sessions to increase empathy through mourning. Paul, through his writings and filmed therapy sessions, has illustrated how real and imagined object loss can account for many of the unresolved relational conflicts in a family's history. Briefly stated, Paul helps a family go back to a point in time at which loss occurred or was perceived to have occurred (such as a death or feared abandonment) and helps a family member complete the process of mourning and grieving in the presence of other members. This cathartic response will typically also elicit empathy from other family members, thus changing a repressed, fixated, incomplete, and painful memory into a moment of grief shared by the whole family. This latter result allows the healing process to occur and can serve as a base for further improvement in family relationships.

Don Williamson (1981, 1982a, 1982b) has offered a dramatic approach to family-of-origin work that includes a developmental reordering of the family hierarchy. Williamson has proposed the identification of a stage in the family life cycle that marks the elimination of hierarchical boundaries between generations. In essence, he suggests that there is a stage, yet to be described, at which parents are no longer "parents," adult children are no longer "children," and the generational boundary is replaced with peerhood. As a part of the process, the emotional conflicts and mysteries of the past—including issues of power, sexuality, values, attitudes, secrets, and fears—are first discussed and then declared to be over. Williamson gives a detailed description of his technique elsewhere (Williamson, 1982a, 1982b), but we will outline it briefly here.

Williamson begins with careful selection of clients, paying particular attention to their life experiences and level of maturity. Like Framo, he then assigns them to a small supportive group in which they undergo a fairly long period of preparation. The preparation involves them in writing autobiographies, analyzing their family's patterns of communication, audiotaping letters to the parents (used in therapy only), having conversations with the parents, and much strategizing with the therapist. If the preparation has been adequate and the therapist judges them ready to meet, a three-day, in-office consultation is organized between the adult child and the parents. Williamson then orchestrates a discussion of personal family issues that is designed to shift the vertical power in the family. The discussion is punctuated by dramatic moments in which the adult child declares that he or she no longer needs parenting or protecting and that one-to-one relationships will now be different. Although Williamson's technique is very different from, for instance, Bowen's, one can see commonalities in the emphasis on freeing oneself from past triangular relationships and on developing dyadic relationships. Williamson has stressed the additional and very significant variable of power.

Case Illustration

Earlier in this chapter, we presented the case of John, who had entered treatment because he was extremely depressed and suicidal. We have discussed his case from the perspectives of family loyalty and indebtedness and have seen how the family projection process operated through the generations. The dynamics in John's family have been presented from a transgenerational point of view. In this section, we will discuss how John was successfully treated using many of the techniques covered in this chapter.

When John first came to treatment, his emotional system was completely overwhelming his reasoning system. He could make only vague connections between his feelings and real-life events. If someone in his family phoned him, he was so undifferentiated that he would start to cry and have to cut the conversation short. The first step in treatment was to offer John an objective relationship in which he could slowly recover his ability to function. Because John was so overwhelmed with emotion, the therapist, through education, explained to John some of the reasons for his feelings and assured him that with time and discussion, John could work his way out of his emotional turmoil. This initial conceptual structuring helped to calm John as he modeled his behavior on the therapist's attitude that he could work out his problems with reason.

The second step in therapy was a long process of assessment. Although the therapist was working with only one member of the family, the transgenerational theory guided him through the family history. Many sessions were spent exploring John's family history in increasing depth. As information was added, the therapist could begin to conceptualize how the struggles of generations had affected John, as well as how John's current relationships had become an outlet for issues of the past. As the therapist increased his understanding of the family's dynamics over the generations, he educated John through explanation and interpretation. Early in therapy, John became angry with the therapist and accused him of expecting too much of him too early. The therapist let John vent his feelings and then showed John how his angry feelings were most likely meant for John's father. Through transference analysis, the therapist was able to assist John in further exploring his relational history.

Increasingly, John was gaining perspective on his life and his family and was now depressed only when he returned home for a visit or received an emotional letter from his family. At that point in therapy, the therapist decided to begin a third phase of treatment. The third phase focused on coaching John to help him stay differentiated when he returned to his family of origin.

Although John had learned a great deal about himself and his family as they had been in the past, he had yet to develop new ways of relating in the present. The therapist, following Bowen's three-step process, encouraged John to build person-to-person relationships. John began with his father. After considerable preparation (that is, writing make-believe letters, rehearsing, and making tapes), John scheduled a visit with his father on neutral ground. They went fishing together for the first time in 20 years. During the trip, John found many opportunities to ask about his father's past. By the end of the trip, they had a different relationship. John felt "emotionally reactive" only once on the entire trip. This success was followed by similar trips to be with his mother and grandparents. Some of those trips went better than others, but each became a testing ground for John and was then later discussed with the therapist. Often, John would not see the therapist for several months between these exercises. Although the treatment did not last more than 30 sessions, it covered almost three years.

After making inroads into his family of origin and feeling able to be more himself even when family relationships became turbulent, John scheduled a session with his ex-wife, Susan, to discuss issues related to co-parenting. In this meeting, the therapist assisted John and Susan in a rational discussion about what each would like to do about raising their son. Both parents were able to share how they felt, what they thought, and what they hoped for in the future. A side benefit of this meeting was that, for the first time in years, each parent felt the success of their teamwork when each was less emotionally reactive.

Treatment was ended about a month after John went home for his grandmother's funeral. It was an extremely disruptive time in the family, when estate issues were complicated with issues of loyalty and indebtedness. However, John was able to be home and be close to his family but not be consumed in reverberating emotional triangles. Transgenerational therapy ended on a successful note, with an invitation for John to return at a later date if he ever desired.

Effectiveness of Transgenerational Family Therapy

There is little empirical evidence that supports the effectiveness of transgenerational family therapy This lack may, in fact, be due to psychoanalytic therapists' opposition to empirical evaluation of therapy. Nichols (1984) notes that reduction of symptoms cannot be considered a standard for success for the psychoanalytic therapist. Likewise, unconscious conflict is not open to reliable observation. Thus, studies to evaluate the effectiveness of transgenerational family therapy are based largely on the patient's satisfaction with treatment or on the therapist's self-report. Those studies are uncontrolled and fail to consider changes in the client's life or the therapist's lack of objectivity.

The evaluation of Murray Bowen's contributions, however, shows promise. Although Bowen provides no empirical evidence to support his theory, Winer (1971) has evaluated Bowen's theory of differentiation. Winer found that Bowen's therapy increased the number of differentiated "I" statements and decreased the number of "we" and "us" statements in a group of four families over three and one-half years. Although this study did not evaluate the effectiveness of therapeutic outcome, it demonstrates that a major therapeutic construct (differentiation) can be made operational and systematically evaluated. It is important that Winer's pilot data be followed by more rigorous investigation testing the reliability of these results and assessing the relationship of differentiation to therapeutic outcome (Pinsoff, 1981).

Frances Baker (1982) offered the field the first investigation of James Framo's theory and practice. Through follow-up study, Baker gathered information on clients' experiences in therapy, outcome of treatment, marital adjustment, and relationships with family of origin. Of particular interest was her attempt to determine whether those clients who received a family-of-origin session in addition to couples therapy had more successful therapeutic outcomes than those who had received only the couples therapy. Baker's study did not support the differential effectiveness of the family-of-origin session; however, the study did find an 84% overall success rate of Framo's therapy as measured by clients' ratings of outcome of therapy. Although these are promising findings, conclusions are drawn about effectiveness without reference to specificity of treatment, and the study has inherent design problems relating to external validity.

More recently, Turgay (1990) found that psychodynamic, problem-centered family therapy was highly effective for children with conversion disorders (such as pseudoseizures, muscle contractions, and so on). Unfortunately, as in earlier investigations, it is not possible to determine what contributed to the outcome because there was no comparison group, and there were no standardized outcome measures or long-term follow-up. Confidence in the results of this study and earlier studies is limited because of inadequate instruments to measure the effects of transgenerational family therapy.

The use of instruments designed specifically to measure transgenerational concepts may improve the research on effectiveness of this theoretical approach. One promising instrument is the Family of Origin Scale (FOS) being studied by Hovestadt, Anderson, Piercy, Cochran, and Fine (1985). The 40-item, standardized, self-report measure is designed to measure an individual's perceptions of autonomy and intimacy within their family of origin. Although subjective, this self-report instrument has received some empirical validation (Canfield, 1983; Fine & Hovestadt, 1984; Holter, 1982). Hovestadt et al. (1985) suggest several uses of the FOS as a clinical tool, but, more important to this discussion, they also suggest that the instrument may be useful in measuring change in clients whose therapy incorporates family-of-origin experiences.

Gavin & Wamboldt (1992) report that the FOS has a limited research history but endorsed the use of the scale as a measure of "the individual's satisfaction with his/her family-of-origin" (p.187). One recent investigation (Kline & Newman, 1994) suggests the FOS should incorporate other family-of-origin concepts, such as the Personal Authority in the Family System Questionnaire and the Differentiation in the Family Systems Scale. The development of this instrument may lead to establishing the effectiveness of transgenerational family therapy.

There appears to be potential for expanding our understanding of the effectiveness of transgenerational family therapy. Fine and Norris (1989) conclude:

> . . . Researchers in the sociological and psycho-sociological disciplines have conducted research in inter-generational relations. While family therapy researchers can and should learn from those studies, much more research needs to be conducted specifically for the needs of the family therapy field. Although intergenerational family relations is a complex and difficult area to investigate, the effort would help unlock information that will be of great value to family therapy research and the families they treat. (p. 311)

References

Anonymous. (1972). On the differentiation of self. In J. Framo (Ed.), *Family interactions, a dialogue between family researchers and family therapists*. New York: Springer.

Baker, F. (1982). Framo's method of integration of family of origin with couples therapy: A follow-up study of intergenerational approach (Doctoral dissertation, Temple University). *Dissertation Abstracts International, 44*, DA8311581.

Boszormenyi-Nagy, I. (1965). A theory of relationships: Experience and transaction. In I. Boszormenyi-Nagy & J. Framo (Eds.), *Intensive family therapy: Theoretical and practical aspects*. New York: Harper & Row.

Boszormenyi-Nagy, I., & Spark, G. (1973). *Invisible loyalties: Reciprocity in intergenerational family therapy*. New York: Harper & Row.

Bowen, M. (1966). The use of family theory in clinical practice. *Comprehensive Psychiatry, 7*, 345–374.

Bowen, M. (1978). *Family therapy in clinical practice*. New York: Aronson.

Bowen, M., Dysinger, R., Brodey, W., & Basmania, B. (1957, March). *Study and treatment of five hospitalized families each with a psychotic member*. Paper presented at the meeting of the American Orthopsychiatric Association, Chicago.

Canfield, B. (1983). *Family of origin experiences with selected demographic factors as predictors of current family functioning*. Unpublished doctoral dissertation, East Texas State University.

Dicks, H. (1967). *Marital tensions*. New York: Basic Books.

Fairbairn, W. (1954). *An object-relations theory of the personality*. New York: Basic Books.

Fine, M., & Hovestadt, A. (1984). Perceptions of marriage and rationality by levels of perceived health in the family of origin. *Journal of Marital and Family Therapy, 10*, 193–195.

Fine, M., & Norris, J. E. (1989). Intergenerational relations and family therapy research: What we can learn from other disciplines. *Family Process, 28*, 301–315.

Framo, J. (1965). Rationale and technique of intensive family therapy. In I. Boszormenyi-Nagy and J. Framo (Eds.), *Intensive family therapy: Theoretical and practical aspects*. New York: Harper & Row.

Framo, J. (1981). The integration of marital therapy with sessions with family of origin. In A. Gurman & D. Kniskern (Eds.), *Handbook of family therapy*. New York: Brunner/ Mazel.

Freud, S. (1961). The ego and the id. In J. Strachey (Ed. and Trans.), *The standard edition of the complete psychological works of Sigmund Freud* (Vol. 19, pp. 3–66). London: Hogarth Press. (Original work published 1923).

Gavin, L., & Wamboldt, F. S. (1992). A reconsideration of the family of origin scale. *Journal of Marital and Family Therapy, 18*, 179–188.

Holter, J. (1982). *A comparison of selected family-of-origin perceptions within the alcohol-distressed marital dyad and the non-alcohol-distressed marital dyad*. Unpublished doctoral dissertation, East Texas State University.

Hovestadt, A., Anderson, W., Piercy, F., Cochran, S., & Fine, M. (1985). A family of origin scale. *Journal of Marital and Family Therapy, 11*(3), 287–297.

Kerr, M. (1981). Family systems theory and therapy. In A. Gurman & D. Kniskern (Eds.), *Handbook of family therapy*. New York: Brunner/Mazel.

Minuchin, S. (1974). *Families and family therapy*. Cambridge, MA: Harvard University Press.

Nichols, M. (1984). *Family therapy: Concepts and methods.* New York: Gardner Press.

Paul, N., & Paul, B. (1975). *A marital puzzle.* New York: Norton.

Pinsoff, W. (1981). Family therapy process search. In A. Gurman & D. Kniskern (Eds.), *Handbook of family therapy.* New York: Brunner/Mazel.

Turgay, A. (1990). Treatment outcome for children and adolescents with conversion disorder. *Canadian Journal of Psychiatry, 35,* 585–588.

Williamson, D. (1981). Termination of the intergenerational hierarchical boundary between the first and second generations: A new stage in the family. *Journal of Marital and Family Therapy, 7*(4), 441–452.

Williamson, D. (1982a). Personal authority in family experience via termination of the intergenerational hierarchical boundary: Part II. The consultation process and the therapeutic method. *Journal of Marital and Family Therapy, 8*(2), 23–38.

Williamson, D. (1982b). Personal authority in family experience via termination of the intergenerational hierarchical boundary: Part III. Personal authority defined, and the power of play in the change process. *Journal of Marital and Family Therapy, 8*(3), 309–324.

Winer, L. (1971). The qualified pronoun count as a measure of change in family psychotherapy. *Family Process, 10,* 243–247.

Chapter Six

Experiential Family Therapy

The experiential approach to family therapy evolved from existential-humanistic psychotherapy. Like the structural and strategic approaches, it emphasizes the present rather than the past. However, unlike the structural or strategic approach and like the psychodynamic approach, experiential family therapy focuses primarily on individual members. Individual members are encouraged to share personal experiences with each other.

Although the experiential approach focuses on the individual, the therapy is still considered a systems therapy. However, the systems orientation is derived more from the Gestalt psychology of Fritz Perls than from the general systems theory of Bertalanffy. Perls had studied the writing of Gestalt psychologists Wertheimer and Kohler and had worked with Goldstein, who used the organismic, holistic principles of Gestalt psychology to treat neurological problems (Levant, 1984). Concepts such as Gestalt and intrapsychic-interpersonal boundaries are loosely related to systems thinking (in that they are context-related) and have had a major impact on experiential family therapies.

The practice of experiential family therapy is led by Carl Whitaker, Virginia Satir, and others. Whitaker and Satir both place great emphasis on personal growth rather than on altering dysfunctional interactions or removing symptoms. Growth may include autonomy and freedom of choice. Growth occurs when each member of the family is able to experience the present moment and, furthermore, share that moment with other members. The therapist uses himself or herself to help family members express things as openly and honestly as possible. Family members are encouraged to share their problems rather than focusing on one person as the problem or symptom.

Theoretical Constructs and Philosophy

Experiential family therapy does not rely primarily on theory. Carl Whitaker suggests that therapists are more effective when they are being themselves. Whereas theory may be necessary for the beginner, the creative therapist is open and spontaneous (Whitaker, 1976b). Moreover, Virginia Satir suggests that much of the therapist's language is sterile and technical and often keeps distance between the therapist and client (Satir, 1972). Experiential family therapists focus on being fully with the family to help them handle problems. With theory deemphasized in experiential family therapy, the conceptual focus is on individuality, freedom of choice, and personal growth.

Individuality

Experiential family therapists are concerned primarily with the perceptions, meanings, and values of individual family members. Experiential therapists emphasize the subjective experience of the individual rather than observable behavior; thus, they focus more on the deterministic forces encountered in behavioralism and psychoanalysis.

An emphasis on individuality is in part derived from the existential writings of Martin Heidegger (1963), Jean-Paul Sartre (1964), Paul Tillich (1952), and Martin Buber (1958). Heidegger notes that one becomes aware of one's existence by recognizing that we could not exist. Since one's individuality is discovered only through personal meaning (Sartre, 1964), when one does not find personal meaning, one's individuality is threatened and one experiences a fear of nothingness or nonbeing (Tillich, 1952).

Martin Buber also emphasized individuality in focusing on personal relationships. Buber argued for the "I-thou" relationship, in which both parties can be together yet maintain their individuality. Whitaker and Keith (1981) note that one can be intimate only when individuality (separateness) can be maintained in the relationship:

> Increases in intimacy and separateness must go hand-in-hand. Neither can increase without an increase in the other. One can only be as separate as one can be close. Family rules define the degree of pressure tolerated, and the unspoken family barometer is very accurate. In a healthy family, a wide range of intimacy and separateness levels are found. . . . Real dependency is linked to real autonomy in the same way that intimacy and separateness are linked. A symbiotic relationship is one in which there is a fixed emotional distance. Each member is dependent upon the other to not alter the distance. The relationship controls the two persons. Thus, two married persons may appear to be quite autonomous, but, if the relationship heats up in some way, such as having a child or one member's becoming ill, it may cause quite a bit of stress in the other member because they are dependent upon this relationship remaining distant. In a marriage, the wife may appear dependent, while the husband appears autonomous and independent. However, on the covert side, it may appear quite different: the wife carries a lot of power, while the husband is really a little boy and his power is in his tantrums and/or his good behavior. (p. 193)

Thus, one's individuality or separateness is intrinsically related to one's togetherness with others. There is an existential need to feel both separate and to-gether with members of one's family.

Freedom of Choice

The existential philosophers emphasized freedom of choice as well. Experiential family therapists have echoed their beliefs that because we live in an absurd world our choice must be significant and give us meaning. Existential anxiety occurs when our choices lack meaning to ourselves and to other family members. The family gives meaning to its individual members by supporting the choices they make.

The writings of existential theorists, such as Carl Rogers, are grounded on freedom of choice. Rogers emphasized that the individual must be aware of his or her own existential processes when making choices. Rogers noted that one's freedom to fulfill one's potential is limited by others. Problems occur when the family fails to allow individual members to reach their potential (Rogers, 1951).

In healthy families, individual members are more or less encouraged to express themselves freely. Family members tend to listen to one another and accept one another's feelings. In this way, family members may develop appropriate ways for expressing their emotions. Satir (1967) suggests that when family members are free to express themselves, they feel valued and loved. Moreover, such freedom of expression allows family members the important opportunity to nurture each other.

Whitaker (Whitaker & Keith, 1981) observes that "freedom of choice is each individual's right to be himself." Individual family members are encouraged to develop their own unique roles. Whitaker (Whitaker & Keith, 1981) describes the freedom to play such roles:

> A basic characteristic of all healthy families is the availability of this "as if" structure. Play characterizes all metacommunication. For example, the 6-year-old son says to daddy, "Can I serve the meat tonight?" and daddy says, "Sure, you sit over on this chair and serve the meat and the potatoes and I'll sit over in your place and complain." Daddy does this and probably gets more out of making believe he's 6 than the son gets out of the great experience of making believe he's mother's husband, father of the family, and an adult man. Metacommunication is considered to be an experiential process, and an offer of participation that implies the clear freedom to return to an established role security rather than be caught in the "as if" tongue-in-cheek micro-theater. That trap is the context that pushes the son into stealing cars or the daughter into incest with her father while mother plays the madame. The whims and creativity of the family can even be exaggerated to the point that family subgroups or individuals are free to be non-rational or crazy. (p. 190)

Experiential family therapy assists family members in finding roles that are self-fulfilling and promote personal growth and individuality.

Personal Growth

Experiential family therapists focus on personal growth rather than the removal of symptomatic behaviors. To the experiential family therapist, growth is a continuous process. Change requires that family members continue to challenge their beliefs and open themselves to new experiences. The therapist often grows and changes as family members change. Thus, experience in therapy can mean personal growth for all participants.

The healthy family continues to grow under stress (Whitaker & Keith, 1981). In healthy families, problems are used to increase family experience and growth. When problems arise, family members are free to play various roles and thereby expand their experience. In dysfunctional families, roles are bound by myths and customs, and change is not permitted. In such families, problems become symptoms.

In functional families, open communication allows growth. Overt rules are clearly understood and flexible, depending on what is needed in a given situation. Family members are allowed to move in and out of the system as they mature (Satir, 1972). "In open systems, the individual can say what he feels and thinks and can negotiate for reality and personal growth without destroying himself or the others in the system" (Satir, 1967). Experiential family therapy encourages open self-expression and negotiation to develop personal growth and healthy family functioning.

Therapeutic Practice

Assessment

Dysfunctional families are characterized by interactional rigidity and emotional deadness. These conditions often produce symptoms in one or more family members. The specific symptom is often related to the preestablished roles and triangles of the family members. Whitaker (Whitaker & Keith, 1981) refers to some of these roles as "the lonely father syndrome," "the battle-fatigued mother syndrome," and "the parentified child syndrome." Each of these rigid roles (symptoms) serves to maintain the status quo.

In dysfunctional families, communication is often vague, and role expectations are unclear (Satir, 1972). Rules are rigid and are not altered to fit the demands of a given situation. When a problem arises, the family adheres to the same old rules and customs. Satir (1967) writes of the **closed system:**

> Dysfunctional families constitute a "closed system": closed systems are those in which every participatory member must be very cautious about what he or she says. The principal rule seems to be that everyone is supposed to have the same feelings, opinions, and desires, whether or not this is true. In closed systems honest self-expression is impossible, and if it does occur, the expression is viewed as deviant, or "sick" or "crazy" by the . . . family. Differences are treated

as dangerous; a situation that results in one or more members having to figuratively "be mad at themselves" if they are to remain in the system. The limitations placed on individual growth and health in such a group are obvious, and I have found that emotional or behavioral disturbance is a certain sign that the disturbed person is a member of a closed family system. (p. 185)

In families of this type, differences or conflict are often perceived as personal rejection. Thus, to maintain "sameness," members must adhere to complementary roles. If one member wishes to be "strict," another member must remain "soft." The way in which family members avoid conflict reinforces those roles and prevents the family from discussing alternative solutions when a problem arises.

Dysfunctional families who adhere to fixed roles often reach an impasse during a transition in the family's life cycle. The birth of a baby, the oldest child's leaving home, or the death of a family member can often call for alternatives that are rejected or blocked from the family's awareness. When change and flexibility are required, transactions become more firmly fixed, or rigidified and symptomatic behavior may develop.

When assessing family dysfunction, experiential therapy, like other approaches within the systemic perspective, examines the family of origin, the developmental stage of the family, and the emotional age of each child. However, experiential family therapists are noted for their focus on the experiential aspects of the interview itself. The therapist pays close attention to his or her own responses to the family. Whitaker and Keith (1981) write:

We always read our own responses in the assessment. What is our anxiety level? Do we gain access to our own primary process as we talk with this family? Do we experience physical sensations: muscle tightness, beginning erection, depersonalization of feelings, absence of anxiety? We listen for voice tone, changes in posture, changes in subject matter, facial set, and special metaphorical words. (p. 198)

Like Whitaker, Satir also uses herself actively to assess family functioning. Both use metaphor, exaggeration, and fantasy to assess family communication.

Goals

The goal of experiential family therapy is growth rather than reduction of symptoms. Therapists believe that individual growth will reduce the need for the symptom. Family members are therefore encouraged to express their uniqueness and to make independent and creative choices. Individual family members are encouraged to experience a deeper meaning when communicating with other family members. Virginia Satir (1972) describes the goals of family therapy in the following manner:

We attempt to make three changes in the family system. First, each member of the family should be able to report congruently, completely, and obviously on what he sees and hears, feels and thinks about himself and others in the presence of others. Second, each person should be addressed and related to in terms of his uniqueness so that decisions are made in terms of exploration and negotiation rather than in terms of power. Third, differentness must be openly acknowledged and used for growth. (p. 120)

Whitaker (Whitaker & Keith, 1981) adds creativity as a primary goal of therapy. When family members can be creative and playful, they will be more aware of their emotions and those areas that have been repressed. The freedom to be creative or "crazy" allows family members to be close and at the same time to be separate. These conditions are considered necessary for proper family functioning and integration.

In experiential family therapy, goals are established by both the therapist and the family. Whitaker (Whitaker & Keith, 1981) notes that the therapist's early goals may be simply to keep the family in treatment. The family, on the other hand, often comes to therapy to alleviate the symptomatic behavior. The experiential therapists focus on ways of increasing the family's creative solutions to problems. Such goals are often stated in metaphorical language to expand their meaning. The metaphor may have both verbal and nonverbal components. As we will discuss shortly, Satir often uses a family sculpture to portray the way family members want things to be. Whitaker (Whitaker & Keith, 1981) notes that metaphorical goals are incomplete and thereby allow the family to experience new levels of personal awareness and growth. In experiential family therapy, goals are not as overt as in other forms of family therapy.

Technique

The experiential family therapists do not have a well-defined set of techniques. They are not uninterested in technique; they just haven't defined to other therapists what it is they do. Most experiential therapists use techniques that are an extension of their own personalities. The personal encounter between the therapist and the family allows the therapist to become an important member of the family. When the therapist becomes a member of the family, he or she experiences the same joy, sadness, and helplessness that other members of the family experience (Whitaker, 1976a). Experiential family therapists argue that technique evolves naturally out of each unique family relationship.

Like Whitaker, Satir (Satir, Stachowiak, & Taschman, 1975) states that she cannot teach specific techniques of family therapy. Instead, she prefers to teach therapists to become aware of their own responses and to use them to produce change in the family. Satir (Satir, Stachowiak, & Taschman, 1975) notes that whereas therapists do need interventional techniques such as interviewing, confronting, and supporting, it is more important to be self-actualized, congruent, and genuine in the therapeutic process.

Both Whitaker (1976a) and Satir (Satir, Stachowiak, & Taschman, 1975) believe that the therapist is a teacher and a model of good communication to the family. When the therapist is open and spontaneous, then family members will learn to behave in the same way. Satir describes the therapist as a "resource person" and a "model of congruent communication." The therapist helps family members to clarify and alter their values so that they can communicate openly with one another. The therapist teaches family members how to observe discrepancies between the "intent" and the "impact" of their messages (Satir, 1967). The therapist becomes a standard by which family members can evaluate themselves and the effectiveness of their communication.

In addition to the teaching/modeling role, the experiential family therapist becomes a facilitator in the therapeutic process. Although experiential family therapists refrain from emphasizing their use of specific therapeutic techniques, their use of questions, empathic responses, clarification, and directives facilitate effective communication in the family. Family members learn to solve their own problems without overt expert guidance. The therapist trusts that the family will find a creative solution to its problems within the therapeutic relationship.

Thus, the effectiveness of experiential family therapy depends not on therapeutic technique but on the therapist. The personhood of the therapist is the crucial variable in the treatment of the family. Therapists must be genuine, open, and trusting before they can expect family members to be the same with each other (Keith & Whitaker, 1983). Although experiential family therapists refrain from espousing therapeutic technique, it is still possible to describe from observation of leading proponents what the therapist does in therapy.

Experiential therapists are not systematic; nonetheless, a careful examination of their technique suggests that the concept of therapeutic strategies may be useful in discussing it. The strategies use a range of devices from unstructured techniques such as fantasy, affective confrontation, and absurdity (Whitaker & Keith, 1981) to structured techniques such as family sculpting and choreography (Satir, 1972). The remainder of this section will discuss the therapeutic strategies (techniques) of Carl Whitaker and Virginia Satir because of their influential contributions.

The Techniques of Carl Whitaker

Use of a co-therapist The therapy of Carl Whitaker is one of personal involvement. Because the treatment is so involved, Whitaker typically employs a co-therapist to share the emotional involvement of the therapeutic process. The personal involvement of the treatment process often produces **countertransference** reactions in the therapist. Countertransference reactions operate at an unconscious level. The co-therapist is able to observe and help to extract the therapist from the emotional entanglements of countertransference. The co-therapist can also provide an opportunity for each therapist to reflect on the relationship and focus on specific members or subsystems of the family.

According to Whitaker (Whitaker & Keith, 1981), therapy occurs in three phases. In the *beginning* phase, therapy is quite structured. The co-therapy team must battle for "structure" and "initiative." In the battle for structure, the therapists want the family to know who is in charge of therapy. Although the battle for initiative involves getting the family to take responsibility for its decisions, the therapists try to gain therapeutic leverage by first insisting that all family members attend the first session. Grandparents and other extended family members may be asked to attend, and, if they refuse therapy, the team may terminate therapy.

In the first interview, Whitaker (Whitaker & Keith, 1981) tells the family that he will speak with each member individually to get all the views of the family. Whitaker normally begins with the family member who seems to be furthest removed from the family and finishes with the member who seems to be most aware of the problem. This type of interview helps the co-therapy team to gather important data and restructure family interactions (Napier & Whitaker, 1978).

In the *middle* phase, the therapists become more involved with the family. The family begins to work on those issues that most concern it. In some cases, the family reaches an impasse when its members are unable or unwilling to take responsibility for their own lives. The therapists then attempt to involve grandparents and other extended family members through consultation with grandparents and reunion of the extended family. The grandparents become assistants to the therapists rather than clients. The therapists act helpless to get the parents to take more responsibility for themselves and resolve the therapeutic impasse (Whitaker, 1976b).

In the *end* phase, the family becomes more independent and the therapist begins to disengage himself or herself from the family. The family members become less dependent on the therapist and more involved with each other. Family members begin to complain that therapy is interfering with their outside activities and work (Whitaker & Keith, 1981). This is often an indication that the time for termination has come.

The techniques of each phase are unstructured and evolve out of the therapist's own creativity. The therapist makes spontaneous use of fantasy, absurdity, and paradoxical intention in order to disrupt the family dynamics.

Whitaker and Keith (1981) have delineated several techniques that are important to disrupting family dynamics. Among them are redefining the symptom, suggesting fantasy alternatives, and affective confrontation.

Redefining the symptom   Experiential family therapists challenge the family's narrow definition of the problem. A family's attempt to define all the pathology as existing in one person restricts the members' individuality, freedom of choice, and personal growth. The therapeutic team seeks to counter this effect by implicating other family members in the pathology. Whitaker and Keith (1981) write about it this way:

> We then increase the pathology and implicate the whole family. The family scene is converted into an absurd one. Our effort is to depathologize human experience. [One woman] was complaining that her husband was trying to get rid of her. "He's never loved me, you know," she said. "He said once that he

would cut me up. Another time he threatened me with a gun." The therapist replies, "How can you say he doesn't love you? Why else would he want to kill you?" Psychosis in one of the family members can be defined as an effort to be Christlike: "I'll be a nobody so that you and father will be saved," or the desperation felt by one member of the family can be redefined as a hopeful sign since it means the family cares enough. Just a mild degree of tongue-in-cheek quality must be included with this technical play so that the confrontation will not be too painful. (p. 211)

Many therapists would find it difficult to say such things to family members. However, experiential family therapists accept absurdity as a necessary tool in challenging the family's definition of the symptom. This capacity to say and do the unconventional can be seen in the experientialist's use of fantasy as technique.

Suggesting fantasy alternatives There are at least two ways that the therapeutic team employs the technique of fantasy. First, stressful real-life situations are treated as if they weren't dreadful to discuss: A therapist might ask a series of "what if" questions about a subject the family would prefer not to discuss. Whitaker and Keith (1981) give the following examples:

A woman who has attempted suicide can be pushed to a fantasy. "If you were going to murder your husband, how would you do it?" Or, "Suppose when you got suicidal you decided you were going to kill me. How would you do it? Would you use a gun or a knife or cyanide?" In a family with a schizophrenic son, the daughter's conversation with her father was understood by the therapist as a sexual pass. The family was embarrassed and perplexed by that. At the end of the hour, however, the father tenderly held his daughter and rocked her in his arms. (p. 212)

And further:

The patient who has attempted suicide can be encouraged to talk with the group about whom her husband would marry if she killed herself, how soon he would marry, how long he would be sad, how long the children would be sad, who would get the insurance, how her mother-in-law would feel, what they would do with her personal belongings, etc. (p. 212)

By suggesting that the family can tolerate the fantasy discussion, the therapists expand the family's emotional life without real violence or acting out. The consideration of fantasy alternatives offers the family a new freedom to communicate about frightening ideas.

In addition to deemphasizing stressful real-life situations by suggesting fantasy alternatives, the therapist may make absurd suggestions directly. Whitaker and Keith (1981) put it this way:

Technically, once the relationship is established and the supra-unit team is operational, the therapist can add many practical bits of intervention which in one-to-one therapy would seem like inappropriate moves, but in the context of the family are safe since the family will utilize what it wants and is perfectly competent in discarding what is not useful. For example, the husband whose wife is having headaches can be offhandedly offered the possibility that if he should spank her, the headaches might go away. Or the wife who is "driven" up the wall by her children's nagging or dad's aloofness can casually be offered, in the presence of the whole family, the idea that she could run away to her mother's for a week and let the family make its own meals. (p. 212)

The experiential therapist uses his or her own creative perceptions, admittedly subjective, to challenge the family system with absurd suggestions of alternatives. Families are forced to struggle with the resulting confusion and therefore find it difficult to operate in their usual way.

Affective confrontation   The therapist confronts the family with his or her subjective emotional experience of them. If a therapist is experiencing boredom, he or she might yawn and tell the family to "spice things up." A therapist who feels angry might choose to express his or her anger at a family member. Such emotional expressions are short-lived and often have dramatic impact. Whitaker and Keith (1981) describe the therapist's confrontational technique in the following:

This is the kind of event that takes place vis-à-vis the parents, most often in defense of the children. It is the change in tone that occurs when the child in play therapy goes from knocking over a pile of blocks to throwing a block at a windowpane. An 8-year-old boy and the therapist were mock-fighting during a family interview. The parents viewed it as a distraction and continually interrupted as though the boy were initiator, although it was clearly the therapist. After several minutes of the parents' complaining to the boy, the therapist got angry and told them to bug off. He said he was playing with their son and he did not want to be interrupted by them. (p. 212)

They continue:

Younger children, at times, like to tease us or to fight us physically. We enjoy taking them on and always overpower them. We are willing to be supportive and understanding of teenagers, but we also set strong limits with them. Despite our usual openness and acceptance, we can be very moralistic when chewing out a teenager for pushing us around. (p. 213)

Openness to subjective experience is a unique feature of the experientialists. Other forms of family therapy will purposely create intense encounters among family members, but none gives therapists as much license to trust their emotional reactions to family members.

Carl Whitaker and his students contribute significantly to the body of technique in experiential family therapy. Their use of absurdity and spontaneity are at the heart of their techniques of redefining the symptom, suggesting fantasy alternatives, and affective confrontation. All these techniques speak of the high degree of personal involvement practiced by the experiential family therapist. Virginia Satir is also intensely involved with her client families, but her style is very different.

The Techniques of Virginia Satir

The therapy of Virginia Satir requires a high degree of personal involvement by the therapist in order to create a supportive environment. The empathic context constructed in therapy allows each member of the family the opportunity to develop to his or her fullest potential. The therapist, as a model of personal growth, is a resource person for developing congruent communication in the family. Satir will focus on various patterns of interaction in the family with the intent to improve communication. She will use techniques drawn from psychodrama (Moreno, 1952), Gestalt therapy (Perls, 1969), and her own creative genius to change the rules and functions of family interaction. Chief among her contributions to technique are first, her use of herself as a model, and second, **family sculpting.**

Modeling communication In watching Satir, one is impressed with how she models and teaches effective communication. Perhaps Satir's greatest contribution to the field of family therapy is her ability to take the most negative situation and turn it into a positive one. Hoffman (1981) notes that Satir is able to "join with people not in terms of anger, blaming, hostility, but in terms of disappointment, pain, and hope" (p. 221). When a family member sends a message that is unclear, Satir clarifies the message and establishes rules for good communication. In *Peoplemaking* (1972), Satir outlines three simple rules for effective communication:

1. Family members should speak in the first person and express what they think or feel. Consider the following interaction:

Wife: We don't like to go to his mother's house.
Therapist: I want to know how you feel about that. Your husband can speak for himself.

2. Each family member is asked to take the "I-position." "I" statements indicate that family members are taking responsibility for themselves. Likewise, "I" statements also encourage others to express their feelings and disclose differences of opinion (Miller, Nunnally, & Wackman, 1976). Consider the following dialogue:

Wife: Every time we go over there it's trouble.
Therapist: Tell me how you feel when you go to her house.
Wife: Well, it makes me—
Therapist: No, "I feel . . ."
Wife: I feel helpless. I feel she has an answer for everything.

Only when the wife states "I feel helpless" does she communicate her own feelings and take responsibility for the accuracy of the message.

3. Each family member must "level" with the others. "In this response, all parts of the message are going in the same direction—the voice says words that match facial expression, the body position and the voice tone" (Satir, 1972). For example:

Father: My son doesn't do anything around the house, but that's
            OK, I guess.
Therapist: Let's level with him and be specific. Describe the things
            you want him to do.
Father: He needs to clean his room. He needs to get his home-
            work done after school and. . . .

Satir (1972) notes that when family members level with one another, then they are communicating acceptance of each other, thus improving self-esteem.

Family sculpting   In addition to establishing new rules for effective communication, Satir has popularized the technique of sculpting the family structure. Family sculpture or choreography (Papp, 1976) was developed by David Kantor and Fred and Bunny Duhl (Duhl, Kantor, & Duhl, 1973) at the Boston Family Institute. Sculpture is similar to the psychodrama of Joseph Moreno (1946, 1952), wherein family members are asked to act out roles they take in the current family.

Family sculpture may be used throughout the therapeutic process to increase family members' awareness of perceptions and thereby alter family relationships (Satir, 1972). In implementing the technique, Satir physically positions each family member in a composite living sculpture as other family members can see him or her. Each family member's position is spatially related to the role he or she occupies in the family. It is very common for Satir to have a dependent member on his or her knees holding another member, or a peripheral parent standing in the corner. Space then becomes a metaphor for closeness or distance, symbolizing the boundaries of the system. Satir also asks family members to express emotions through exaggerated facial expressions such as extreme smiling or frowning at each other. In *Peoplemaking* (1972), Satir gives a hypothetical example of how one might sculpt a family in which everyone wanted the attention of the father (John):

> Let's start with "John." He should stand in the middle of the floor, straight and
> balanced. Then "Alice" is asked to take his right hand. The firstborn is asked
> to take his left hand. The secondborn, "Bob," then grasps "John" around the
> waist from the front. "Trudy" should put her arms around his waist from the
> back. If there is a fourth, he should grasp the right knee, and, if there is a fifth,
> he should grab the left knee. They keep going until all members of the family
> have their hands on "John." Now everyone is asked to pull gently but firmly
> toward themselves until everyone feels the pull. Then they freeze. After a very
> few seconds, John will begin to feel stretched, uneasy, uncomfortable, and mis-
> erable. He may even fear he will lose his balance. (p. 155)

In such a sculpture, members of the family can express the way things are or the way they would like them to be. With reference to the above example, Satir notes that John cannot stay in that position for long and must decide what changes he would like to see in the family sculpture. John may be asked to role-play his choices (for example, pulling away or crying for help) and to tell other members of his family how he felt at the time. The sculpture technique allows family members to express in actions what they are unable to express in words.

Case Illustration

The following case example illustrates the use of experiential family therapy.

Background

Mike and Teri entered therapy to end their marital conflict. Both spouses were in their mid-thirties and had been married for 19 years. The couple had one child. Mike was a realtor, and Teri was a teacher. Teri had had an unhappy childhood and had married after she became pregnant at the age of 16. Her mother blamed her for the pregnancy and consequently made her feel guilty. Teri felt "grateful" to Mike for marrying her and taking care of her. She reported that most of her life was devoted to making things easy for him. However, shortly after they were married, she realized that Mike often placed his own needs over hers. Mike spent a great deal of time at work and was unavailable to help her with the baby.

Relationship

Their relationship soured early in their history and settled into a compromise of roles for each that kept conflict from surfacing. The compromise was characterized by low tolerance of differences. Teri subjugated her personal individuality, freedom of choice, and potential growth to Mike's needs. It was not done without bitterness, however, which of course leaked into her feelings toward Mike. She begrudged his requests, but instead of dealing with them directly, she would make herself a martyr to his needs. Mike, in his own way, started the relationship by "doing the honorable thing." He wasn't straight with Teri about where he stood and instead punished her for "tying him down." Each had a fear that if they were themselves, either they or the other would get hurt.

Because Teri felt powerless, she would use crying to get Mike's attention. Although crying did get Mike's attention, it did not lead to intimacy. Mike would often ignore his wife by suggesting that her problems were "insignificant" and that she "was acting like a child." Her crying frightened him, but he wouldn't admit it. Teri would then become frustrated and scream, scaring Mike even more. Mike would withdraw and shortly thereafter return and make sexual advances as his way of "making up." Teri responded to those advances while still resenting them.

The pattern slowly began to affect their sexual relationship. Mike accused Teri of being uninterested in sex, and each blamed the other for this unhappiness in the relationship.

In the first session, the therapist attempted to get each spouse to take an "I" position. Each spouse was asked to directly express what he or she wanted from the other. At first, Teri began to cry when she tried to express what she needed from her husband. At that point, the therapist affirmed the importance of what she had to say and asked her to try again when she was ready. Mike was told "to listen because her concerns were important." Shortly thereafter, the following dialogue took place:

Teri: You're so insensitive, you never listen, you just—
Therapist: Talk about yourself, Teri. How do you feel during these times?
Teri: Well, he just—
Therapist: How about starting, "I feel . . . "
Teri: I feel OK. I can take it. [*She starts to sob*]
Therapist: Teri, you need to be straight with Mike; he deserves that. What are your tears saying? Give them a voice.
Teri: It's hard. [*More tears*]
Therapist: [*Leaning next to Teri*] You have some legitimate concerns, but I have a feeling that every time you begin to tell him what you want . . . you feel stupid. [*Teri nods.*] You tell him something that bothers you, and he says, "That's silly," or says it in a way that you doubt yourself. Then you feel like a fool and fall apart . . . and the issue never gets resolved. For instance, he promised he would help Kim with her homework, and then he left for an appointment? But the way you handled it, he never got the message, and the issue never got settled. The same thing happens in here when I ask you to go with an issue and you back off and don't get heard. Did the issue with Kim's homework ever get settled? [*Therapist moves next to Teri*] OK, let's tell Mike how that makes you feel when he said he would help Kim and then left for the appointment. How about saying, "I feel really angry when you say you are going to do something and don't do it"?
Teri: I do feel angry—I am angry at you, I'm still angry, I guess.

The technique helped Mike and Teri to begin to communicate more effectively and to begin the long-overdue process of negotiating their differences. Each spouse felt increasingly that they could both speak for themselves and be taken seriously in the relationship. Not because of this one intervention did new openness and alternatives enter their relationship, but because it was repeated over and over with each partner. The therapist served as a model for good communication, stressing the need for each spouse to be direct, to speak for himself or herself, and to check out his or her perceptions with the other. One by one, areas of conflict were discussed. The therapist created a supportive environment in which each partner could express his or her needs and move toward personal growth.

Effectiveness of
Experiential Family Therapy

Unfortunately, the clinician interested in knowing whether or not experiential family therapy is effective cannot turn to outcome studies for guidance. Carl Whitaker and Virginia Satir, the leading proponents of this major theoretical approach, have not conducted scientific studies of their treatment, perhaps in part because they see their work as based as much in philosophy as in science. The reluctance of the leaders to delineate theoretical concepts and then empirically test them may explain why second- and third-generation researchers have not evaluated the approach. Experiential family therapists have preferred to cite self-report measures as evidence of effectiveness of treatment. Success in experiential family therapy is measured by personal growth, individuality, and autonomy. Experiential family therapists argue that these variables are very subjective and that to assign objective criteria to them would arbitrarily depersonalize their meaning. Whitaker points to his own satisfaction as evidence of success (Napier & Whitaker, 1978). Whitaker argues that if he weren't successful, he wouldn't be happy, and therefore that since he is happy, he must be successful.

Although experiential family therapy awaits outcome evaluation, a few studies have been conducted that assess a single concept or technique typically associated with the approach. For example, Russell, Atilano, Anderson, Jurich, and Bergen (1984) included in their study of 21 intervention strategies several techniques that experiential family therapy has contributed to the field. Russell et al. assessed therapy outcome through instruments that measure the client's perceived life and marital happiness. These data were then linked to the specific family therapy interventions that had been used in treatment. Of importance to this discussion, the researchers reported that favorable response among the wives of their study was associated with interventions in which the therapist disengaged from the in-session interaction or in which the therapist reframed the symptom as an effort toward growth. Both of these techniques are used in experiential family therapy, although they are not its exclusive domain.

Another study, by Johnson and Greenberg (1985), offers an assessment of what the authors call "emotionally focused couples therapy." This approach to couples therapy focuses on the emotional experience of each partner in relation to the spouse. Its attention to affective awareness is an element it shares with experiential family therapy, and therefore the results of this study may have implications for evaluating the effectiveness of experiential family therapy. Johnson and Greenberg (1985) used a within-subjects design in which couples acted as their own controls. Participants (14 couples) were assessed at initial contact, after an eight-week waiting period, after an eight-session treatment, and at an eight-week follow-up. The researchers used instruments that measured dyadic adjustment, intimacy, specific complaints, and desired goals. To summarize the results, Johnson and Greenberg found significant differences in expected directions between the waiting period (control) and the treatment period (experimental) on all the variables tested. At follow-up, they found that the couples still had significantly fewer specific complaints than when they were in the waiting period. Because of the similarities in approach, these findings may have implications for future outcome studies in experiential family therapy.

In a review of the literature on the effectiveness of marital therapy, Bray and Jouriles (1995) found that emotionally focused couples therapy was effective in increasing marital satisfaction when compared with no-treatment controls. Shadish, Ragsdale, Glaser, and Montgomery (1995), in conducting a meta-analysis of the research, found that emotionally focused couples therapy was no more effective than other approaches (for example, behavior marital therapy and insight-oriented marital therapy) in treating marital conflict. Researchers who wish to study the effects of the experiential approach must find qualitative methods for assessing personal experience within the family system—an often-neglected dimension of family therapy.

References

Bray, J. H., & Jouriles, E. N. (1995). Treatment of marital conflict and prevention of divorce. *Journal of Marital and Family Therapy, 21,* 461–473.

Buber, M. (1958). *I and thou.* New York: Scribner's.

Duhl, F. J., Kantor, D., & Duhl, B. S. (1973). Learning, space, and action in family therapy: A primer of sculpture. In D. A. Block (Ed.), *Techniques of family psychotherapy: A primer.* New York: Grune & Stratton.

Heidegger, M. (1963). *Being and time.* New York: Harper & Row.

Hoffman, L. (1981). *Foundations of family therapy.* New York: Basic Books.

Johnson, S., & Greenberg, L. (1985). Emotionally focused couples therapy: An outcome study. *Journal of Marital and Family Therapy, 14*(3), 313–317.

Keith, D. V., & Whitaker, C. (1983). Co-therapy with families. In B. B. Wolman & G. Stricker (Eds.), *Handbook of family and marital therapy.* New York: Plenum.

Levant, R. F. (1984). *Family therapy: A comprehensive overview.* Englewood Cliffs, NJ: Prentice Hall.

Miller, S., Nunnally, E. W., & Wackman, D. B. (1976). A communication training program for couples. *Social Casework, 57,* 9–18.

Moreno, J. L. (1946). *Psychodrama.* Beacon, NY: Beacon House.

Moreno, J. L. (1952). Psychodrama of a family conflict. *Group Psychotherapy, 5,* 20–37.

Napier, A. Y., & Whitaker, C. A. (1978). *The family crucible.* New York: Harper & Row.

Papp, D. (1976). Family choreography. In P. J. Guerin, Jr. (Ed.), *Family therapy: Theory and practice.* New York: Gardner Press.

Perls, F. S. (1969). *Gestalt therapy verbatim.* Lafayette, CA: Real People Press.

Rogers, C. R. (1951). *Client-centered therapy.* Boston: Houghton Mifflin.

Russell, C., Atilano, R., Anderson, S., Jurich, A., & Bergen, L. (1984). Intervention strategies: Predicting family therapy outcome. *Journal of Marital and Family Therapy, 10*(3), 241–252.

Sartre, J.-P. (1964). *Being and nothingness.* New York: Citadel Press.

Satir, V. (1967). *Conjoint family therapy.* Palo Alto, CA: Science and Behavior Books.

Satir, V. (1972). *Peoplemaking.* Palo Alto, CA: Science and Behavior Books.

Satir, V., Stachowiak, J., & Taschman, H. A. (1975). *Helping families to change.* New York: Aronson.

Shadish, W. R., Ragsdale, K., Glaser, R. R., & Montgomery, L. M. (1995). The efficiency and effectiveness of marital and family therapy: A perspective from meta-analysis. *Journal of Marital and Family Therapy, 21,* 345–360.

Tillich, P. (1952). *The courage to be.* New Haven: Yale University Press.

Whitaker, C. A. (1976a). A family is a four dimensional relationship. In P. J. Guerin, Jr. (Ed.), *Family therapy: Theory and practice.* New York: Gardner Press.

Whitaker, C. A. (1976b). The hindrance of theory in clinical work. In P. J. Guerin, Jr. (Ed.), *Family therapy: Theory and practice.* New York: Gardner Press.

Whitaker, C. A., & Keith, D. V. (1981). Symbolic-experiential family therapy. In A. S. Gurman & D. P. Kniskern (Eds.), *Handbook of family therapy.* New York: Brunner/Mazel.

Chapter Seven

Behavioral Family Therapy

Behavioral family therapy is derived from **social learning theory** (Bandura, 1969), which combines **operant conditioning** with social modeling. These procedures have been effective for treating individuals rather than families as systems. Behavioral family therapists have incorporated principles of systems theory (Birchler & Spinks, 1980), but they have done so within a linear structure. Family problems are seen as being caused by ineffective patterns of **reinforcement** between parents and children or between marital partners. Behavioral family therapists give little attention to the circular interactional patterns in the family system that may be maintaining the problem.

Behavioral family therapy and systems family therapy do, however, have many properties in common. First, both approaches share a functional view of problem behaviors and interactional sequences. Problems are seen by both theories as serving some function within the family and as being maintained by a family member's behavior (Levant, 1980). Both theories focus on the present interaction of family members rather than on past history. The goal of therapy in both orientations is to restructure family interactions through behavioral or cognitive change in order to alleviate the presenting problem (Levant, 1980). Finally, both approaches employ cognitive restructuring or reframing and both assign tasks to facilitate behavior change at home.

Despite their commonalities, the systems and behavioral approaches diverge in their analysis of family interaction as well as in their targets of intervention. Behavioral approaches focus on observable behavior (that is, behaviors you can see and hear). A systems approach, in contrast, views behaviors as clues to the underlying family organization and is characterized by constructs such as enmeshment and disengagement. Those constructs are viewed by the behavioral family therapist as too global and unspecific. Behavioral family therapists concentrate on dyadic interactions (parent-child or spouse-spouse), whereas systems family therapists focus on triadic interactions (mother-father-child) (Nichols, 1984). Thus, behavioral family therapists focus primarily on the family member or members who administer consequences for the problem behavior (for example, a mother who rewards a child's problem behavior), while systems family therapists center their attention on patterns of behavior within the entire family system (Foster & Hoier, 1982).

Behavioral and family systems approaches also differ in their views of resistance to change. Behavior theorists, on the one hand, view failure to change as a result of either (1) the client's feeling that the short-term cost of change outweighs the perceived long-range benefits (Jacobson & Margolin, 1979) or (2) the therapist's failure to select the correct behavior or contingencies for change (Birchler & Spinks, 1980). Systems theorists, on the other hand, view resistance as a consequence of disrupting the homeostatic balance. They see resistance as the family's efforts to preserve its equilibrium or, in cybernetic terms, as negative feedback (Steinglass, 1978). Behavioral theorists view resistance as an obstacle to behavior change, whereas systems theorists often view resistance as a necessary step toward change.

Despite the differences between the approaches, there have been a number of recent articles that discuss their commonalities, pointing to areas of conceptual integration (Foster & Hoier, 1982; Levant, 1980). Furthermore, behavioral family investigators such as Wahler (1980) have been examining family social systems. And systems theorists, such as Haley (1976), are emphasizing the family's presenting problem when assessing treatment outcome. Both approaches appear to examine a general description of behavior (pleasure, displeasure, coercion, and so forth). Regardless of how the therapist describes behavior, then, it seems that observation of behavior is common to both approaches. In this respect, behavioral family therapy appears to offer a workable methodology for assessing family interaction and change.

Theoretical Constructs and Philosophy

The behavioral approach has traditionally focused on the behavior of individual subjects and the environmental events that trigger, shape, and maintain their behavior. The emphasis on the individual has continued into family therapy, which has concentrated on how individual family members exercise stimulus control over those behaviors rather than on the organizational dynamics of the family system (Foster & Hoier, 1982).

Based on principles of operant conditioning, the social learning approach views family dysfunction as the result of infrequent **positive reinforcement** between family members (that is, not enough "strokes" for things appreciated). Often, an aversive **stimulus**, or **punishment**, is used by one family member to control the behavior of another family member. For example, a wife's nagging may trigger a husband's drinking and vice versa. Social learning theory views family conflict as resulting from the use of aversive control tactics rather than the use of positive reinforcement. The eventual outcome of a low rate of positive reinforcers exchanged over an extended period of time is that each person feels less attracted to the other (Stuart, 1969).

The most obvious influence in the early development of behavioral family therapy was the social learning approach used to modify the behavior of children (Patterson, 1976). As behavior therapists began to consider the cost-effectiveness of their treatment of children, they paid increased attention to employing the child's parents as the agents of change (O'Dell, 1974). The training of parents centers in the predictable relationships of parent-child interactions (that is, one member's impact on another). Typically, treatment involved parent training in which parents were instructed to identify and record inappropriate behaviors of the child and then systematically intervene, using social learning principles (for example, reinforcement, **modeling, time out**, and **extinction**) to eliminate the problem.

As behavior therapists began to train parents to change the behavior of their children, they also observed and noted with interest the interactional patterns of other family members (Jacobson, 1981). Research then began to shift from investigating the child's inappropriate behavior to studying patterns of bidirectional interaction between family members (that is, two family members' influence on each other) that maintained that behavior (Patterson & Hops, 1972). When parent training was ineffective, parents often reported marital difficulties that contributed to the child's problem (Reisinger, Frangia, & Hoffman, 1976). Moreover, investigators increasingly reported the limitations of parent training with dysfunctional families who dropped out of treatment or sabotaged efforts at treatment (O'Dell, 1974). Thus, marital discord and other outside factors, such as peer relations and illness, began to be seen as contributing to the child's behavior.

The same operant principles used to modify children's behaviors were also applied to couples' behavioral problems. Whereas operant control could be easily applied to children, however, the behavior therapist had no such control when treating married couples (Jacobson, 1981). Jacobson further states:

> Instead, the therapist had to induce couples to collaborate in producing an environment which was supportive of desirable relationship behavior. This required that the couple learn to negotiate with one another. Hence, the purely operant approach first suggested by Stuart (1969) was augmented by programs designed to teach couples communication and problem solving skills (Patterson & Hops, 1972; Jacobson & Weiss, 1978). In a marital dyad, behavior of each member serves as both antecedent and consequence for the behavior of the partner. As a result, any attempt to establish functional relationships between behavior and environment by applying a unidirectional cause-effect model was unsatisfactory. Thus, early investigators read and borrowed from theorists who had attempted to grapple with complexities of understanding ongoing systems of two or more individuals (Homans, 1961; Steinglass, 1978; Thibaut & Kelly, 1959). (pp. 556–557)

Despite its efforts to extrapolate from systems theory, behavioral family therapy is typically not categorized with other family systems approaches, such as interactional, structural, and strategic. The rationale for considering behavioral family therapy approaches separately may be best understood by reference to Gurman and Knudson's (1978) critique of behavioral marital therapy, which appeared in *Family Process*. Briefly, their concerns can be summarized in two main points. First, behavioral family therapists focus on the decrease of negative behaviors and increase of positive behaviors among family members without regard to structural or perceptual context. This is an example of first-order change (Watzlawick, Weakland, & Fisch, 1974). However, a systems-oriented therapist believes that one can change the conceptual and/or emotional meaning of the behavior without first changing the behavior itself, an example of second-order change. Second, Gurman and Knudson write that behavior-oriented therapists may view interaction as being unidirectional: X causes Y; for example, a wife feels rejected and punishes her husband. From the systems therapist's perspective, causality is seen as circular. Systems theory views causality as "chains of interactions such that a stimulus X triggers a response Y that, in turn, becomes the stimulus X_2, for another response Y_2, etc." (Olson, 1970); for example, the wife scowls, the husband makes a crude remark, the wife demands an apology, and the husband storms off. Thus, a behavioral family therapist may intervene specifically when one family member's behavior is or appears to be triggering another family member's behavior, whereas the systems-oriented therapist may intervene in a more indirect fashion because he or she believes that the primary discriminative stimulus of another person's behavior does not exist unto itself.

In a rejoinder, Jacobson and Weiss (1978) summarized Gurman and Knudson's misconceptions about behavioral family therapy:

> Our corrections can be summarized as follows: (a) the essence of the concept *reciprocity*, which is a central concept in a behavioral formulation, is circular causality in which spouse behaviors reciprocally affect and influence one another, a position that seems to be in accord with that of our critics; (b) positive and negative communication is defined largely in terms of what is reinforcing or punishing to a particular couple, despite standardized assessment that admittedly compromises this treatment principle; (c) in behavioral marriage therapy, the relationship, rather than any one partner, is always the identified patient. (p. 160)

Jacobson and Weiss further note that to accept Gurman and Knudson's criticism is to deny the importance of the contingent relationship between the behavior of spouses and its importance in treating marital dysfunction.

Although these issues cannot be easily resolved, the effectiveness of behavioral family therapy is receiving strong support. Partially on account of the theoretical emphasis on observable, measurable behavior, the behaviorists appear to be more committed to empirical investigation of their therapy than do proponents of other approaches. However, given the brief number of controlled studies, the conclusions that can be drawn are extremely limited. Nevertheless, early investigations show great promise for behavioral approaches to problem solving (Jacobson & Weiss, 1978) and couples communication (Stuart, 1969).

We have been discussing both the theoretical evolution of behavioral therapies and their relationship to systems therapies. As can be seen from this discussion, behavioral treatment of relationship problems can be categorized into two basic approaches: the treatment of inappropriate child behavior and the treatment of marital dissatisfaction. Behavioral family therapists give no consideration to the function of marital problems in the treatment of children or the role of children in marital problems (Nichols, 1984); they work with only the subsystem—couple or parent—that is directly related to the problem. Treatment strategies are designed to train parents to obtain more appropriate behavior from each of their children and assist couples in obtaining increased satisfaction in their marriage. Because the methodology of each branch of treatment is somewhat different, the treatments will be discussed separately, beginning with behavioral parent training and concluding with behavioral marital therapy.

Therapeutic Practice: Behavioral Parent Training

There is a massive body of literature demonstrating that parents can be trained to change their children's maladaptive behaviors. Such changes are often brought about when parents encourage (that is, reinforce) the occurrence of appropriate child behaviors and correspondingly discourage (for example, ignore or mildly punish) inappropriate child behaviors.

Children are often referred to therapy by parents who are upset by their behavior. Initially, the therapist generally gathers information regarding the problem behavior, as well as the social and medical history of the child. Information obtained from the parents is also important to see how the child's problem relates to other family members. Thus, the parental interview is an important part of the assessment process.

Assessment

The Parental Interview

The parental interview has a number of purposes, primarily the identification of the problem behavior, as well as the assessment of the parents' role in the present maintenance and future alleviation of the problem behavior (Evans & Nelson, 1977). Regarding the second point, the therapist must often reframe the child's problems to a parent. In the interview it is often best to gather information in the child's absence. The child's attention-getting behaviors, the parents' reluctance to discuss private events, or both, may inhibit information gathering in the interview (Gordon & Davidson, 1981).

In the beginning stages of the interview, parents often use labels to describe a problem. For example, a parent may refer to a child as "rude" or "lazy." Although such labels offer a general indication of the problem area, they have different meanings for different people. Consequently, it is more beneficial to avoid labels and deal with specific, observable behaviors whose presence can easily be confirmed by two or more people.

In guiding the parents from use of labels to identification of specific behavior, the therapist directs the parent to give concrete examples of behavior that led him or her to choose the particular labels. If the parent says the child is "disruptive," the therapist may ask exactly what "disruptive" means, saying, for instance, "Give me an example of what you mean by 'disruptive' or describe a situation in which she was too 'disruptive.'" This interaction proceeds until the therapist knows what a parent means by "disruptive."

Here is an example of a behavioral translation in a therapist-parent interchange:

Parent: Gene just seems to keep things disrupted all the time.
Therapist: When you say he is disruptive, what do you mean?
Parent: When we are at dinner, he is always bugging his sister.
Therapist: What does he do to bug her?
Parent: He kicks her.
Therapist: How else does Gene act disruptive?

This interchange is continued until all the problems are defined in behavioral terms.

Once the parent has defined the problem in behavioral terms, the therapist must isolate those stimuli that precede and follow the problem behavior and serve to control its occurrence; that is, the therapist attempts to identify those stimuli that elicit the problem behavior and specify the reinforcing and punishing stimuli that follow it. Often, controlling conditions evident in the stimuli directly preceding or following behavior either maintain the problem behavior or, by some deficit in their operation, fail to maintain the desirable behavior. When a child has a tantrum, for example, a parent may plead with the child to stop crying, but the pleading only provokes further crying. Information about what triggers the problem may be difficult to gather in the interview. Detailed observations are often necessary to determine what might be triggering the problem.

In some cases, the therapist can determine what precedes the problem by knowing when the problem occurs. For example, a child may be known to have tantrums only when mother is talking on the telephone. The time when the child has temper tantrums can be a key to understanding what elicits or sets off the problem. Questions such as "When does he start crying?" or "What time does he do this?" often pinpoint the antecedents to the problem.

For operant behavior such as thinking, talking, and many motor reactions of the musculoskeletal system, the controlling conditions are reinforcing or punishing stimuli. For example, a child's crying is often positively reinforced by a parent's attention. Aversive or punishing consequences might occur when a parent requires a child to stay in his or her room on a sunny day. Sometimes, there can be both reinforcing and punishing consequences for the same behavior. The child may receive verbal attention for crying (positive consequence) and be sent to his or her room for bothering others (negative consequence).

The behavior therapist might gather information concerning what is maintaining the child's problem behavior with the following questions: "When is the problem most severe?" "When do these situations occur?" "How do other children respond to him or her after it happens?" "What happens after the problem occurs?" "What do you do after he or she does this?" Such questions often prompt the parent to examine what he or she is doing after the problem occurs. For example, a parent could be maintaining a child's aggressive behavior by criticizing it when it occurs. When the child hits or kicks another child, the parent might yell, "Stop it!" or make idle threats, such as "You know what will happen if you do that again." In most cases, a number of factors may be maintaining the problem. The behavior therapist can listen to the following narrative and transform it into a three-column table.

> Mrs. Reims complained of Jimmy's noncompliant behavior. Whenever Mrs. Reims asked Jimmy to clean his room, he would say, "OK" and then would not do it. Mrs. Reims would ask him to clean his room again. Jimmy would still fail to clean his room. Mrs. Reims would then threaten to take his television privileges away. Jimmy would clean his room then, but Mrs. Reims would not say anything. The next day, Mrs. Reims would ask Jimmy to clean his room again. When he refused repeatedly, she would remove his TV privileges. This scenario recurred frequently.

Using this case, the behavior therapist can record the narrative in terms of antecedent (stimulus) events, behaviors, and consequent events. (See Table 7.1.)

It is important to note that the consequent event (for example, Mrs. Reims's asking Jimmy to clean his room) may also serve as the antecedent for Jimmy's

※

TABLE 7.1
Identifying Patterns That Maintain the Undesirable Behavior

Antecedent event	Behavior	Consequent event
(First day)		
1. Mrs. Reims asks Jimmy to clean his room.	2. Jimmy doesn't clean his room.	3. Mrs. Reims asks Jimmy to clean his room.
3. Mrs. Reims asks Jimmy to clean his room.	4. Jimmy doesn't clean his room.	5. Mrs. Reims threatens to take TV privileges away.
5. Mrs. Reims threatens to take TV privileges away if he doesn't clean his room.	6. Jimmy cleans his room.	7. Mrs. Reims ignores Jimmy.
(Second day)		
7. Mrs. Reims asks Jimmy to clean his room.	8. Jimmy doesn't clean his room.	9. Mrs. Reims threatens to take TV privileges away.
9. Mrs. Reims threatens to take TV privileges away.	10. Jimmy doesn't clean his room.	11. Mrs. Reims removes TV privileges.

next response (for example, Jimmy doesn't clean his room). When Mrs. Reims threatened Jimmy the first time, he cleaned his room. But when Jimmy cleaned his room, Mrs. Reims ignored him, and the positive behavior (that is, room cleaning) was extinguished. When Mrs. Reims threatened Jimmy the second time, he ignored her and lost his TV time. A pattern of events that occurs repeatedly will be likely to produce conditions that are maintaining the undesired behavior.

Making a Functional Analysis

Researchers perform a **functional analysis** when they want to determine what stimulus conditions control the target behavior. Each hypothesis is based on behavioral observations of those stimuli that control the client's positive and negative behavior. If a behavior occurs in response to a stimulus and we begin to see a pattern emerge, then we hypothesize that that stimulus is maintaining the behavior; for example, Mrs. Reims reinforces Jimmy's noncompliant behavior (not cleaning his room) and ignores his compliant behavior (cleaning his room).

When a functional analysis has been made on the basis of the interview or preliminary observations, additional observations should be made to evaluate the validity of the hypothesis. It is possible that more than one type of antecedent or consequence is acting to maintain the behavior (for example, the other parent may be reinforcing the child's noncompliant behavior). The next step is to gather further observational data to determine whether the hypothesis is adequate.

Goals

The goals of behavioral parent training are to eliminate undesirable behavior and substitute desirable behavior as defined by the parent or parents. Identifying the desired behaviors for the child, however, can often be difficult for the parent. A parent may request help from the therapist in eliminating a problem behavior, such as temper tantrums or fighting, but may have given less thought to an alternative to fighting or tantrums. If parents wish to eliminate an undesirable attention-getting behavior, they must replace it with a desirable behavior that provides the child with an equal or greater amount of attention.

The process of identifying desired behaviors or goals provides a standard by which the therapist can measure progress. Specific points along the way can be stated in the form of objectives to help the therapist and parents measure progress toward the goal. The effectiveness of therapy is measured by whether or not the parent reaches the goal with the child.

Desired behaviors or goals are often stated in vague or imprecise terms by the parent. The therapist may have to assist the parent in changing vague goals into specific, measurable goals. That is, the therapist must work closely with the parent to determine what behaviors the child will be performing in order to reach his or her goal.

It is sometimes difficult for parents to describe what they want the child to do. The following transcript illustrates some of the problems of identifying goal behaviors:

Parent: He just bugs me all the time.
Therapist: Tell me what he does to bug you.
Parent: Well, last night he sprayed shaving cream all over the bathroom.
Therapist: What did you do?
Parent: I told him to clean it up or he was getting a spanking.
Therapist: What did you want him to be doing?
Parent: I just want him to stay out of the cabinet.
Therapist: You mean the shaving cream.
Parent: Just play without getting into things.
Therapist: What do you want him to be playing?
Parent: Playing games in his room.

In this example, a description of what the child will be doing is known as *terminal behavior*. Vague descriptions of terminal behaviors, such as "staying out of things," are not acceptable because there is no way to measure them reliably. If the parent wants the child to stay out of things, what will the child be doing? Playing a game? Painting?

Once the therapist and parents have agreed on the goal, the next step is to specify the conditions under which the goal behavior will occur and where it will occur. For example, it may be easier for a child to clean his room than clean the kitchen. The conditions under which the problem occurs also help to identify where the specified behavior is to occur. If a particular problem occurs in a certain room in the house, then that is where the desired behavior should also occur. For example, if a child fights with his younger brother in the family room, then the goal behavior—watching television, reading, or the like—should also occur in the family room. Parents may want some kinds of desired behavior to occur across situations (for example, whenever they make a request). Knowing where the desired behavior should occur allows the parent to monitor the child's behavior.

Once the goal has been stated in performance terms and the setting has been identified, a criterion level of performance must be established. The criterion level refers to the frequency and/or quantity of behaviors. For example, the goal "complying with parental requests" does not tell us if the child should comply with all requests, 90% of them, or 75% of them. It is preferable to specify the desired level of the behavior, such as "complying with parental requests 80% of the time." The therapist, parent, and child will then know when the behavioral goal has been reached.

Achievable goals should be set for parents as well. A parent who makes requests of a child 15 times each day may need to make no more than 5 requests each day. Likewise, a parent who never praises his or her child might set a goal to praise 80% of the instances of the child's compliance with parental requests. "Achievable" or "reasonable" criterion levels mean those that correspond to what can currently be accomplished. Once a goal is accomplished, it is possible to specify new criterion levels of behavior.

Technique

Selecting the Appropriate Treatment

When the goal has been specified and a criterion level set, a strategy must be selected to reach the goal. Blechman (1981, pp. 227–230) suggests that ten questions must be answered before selecting a desired strategy for change. The questions are always asked in the same order, beginning with Question 1. These questions are discussed in the following list and are also presented in flowchart format in Figure 7.1.

    1. *Can the target child be involved in treatments?* A hostile child may refuse to enter treatment. Similarly, a child who is hospitalized or institutionalized may not be able to participate directly in treatment. When a child cannot participate in treatment, parent contingency management is recommended.

    2. *Is the child's behavior life-threatening or uncontrollable?* When the answer to this question is "yes," parent contingency management is again recommended.

    3. *Is the child preverbal or nonverbal?* If the answer is "yes," contingency contracts and problem-solving training are ruled out, and contingency management is recommended.

    4. *Is parental behavior poorly controlled?* Parents may inflict punishment on both themselves and their children; they may exhibit the same poorly controlled behavior that they find objectionable in their children. When the answer to this question is "yes," parents must learn to control their own behavior before they learn to control their children's behavior. Thus, for these parents, parent self-control training is recommended.

    5. *Is marital conflict severe?* Parents may strongly disagree about how to handle their child's behavior. Thus, when parents are conflictual, marital cooperation training is recommended.

    6. *Are basic life-maintenance problems unresolved?* Parents may not only be having difficulty with their child but may also have other life-maintenance problems. Parents will have difficulty controlling their child or children if the parents are ill or lack money to purchase clothes, food, or adequate child care. When these conditions exist, parent self-sufficiency training is preferred.

    7. *Are time or resources for treatment very limited?* When parents lack resources, family skill training approaches (for example, problem solving) are inappropriate. Rather, contingency contracting or management is the recommended strategy.

    8. *Does the family want to change its style of interaction?* A family may not want to change the way its members relate to each other but may simply want to change the child's behavior. If families do want to change their pattern of interaction, family problem solving is recommended.

    9. *Has marital conflict interfered with training?* If an intervention has been unsuccessful, the therapist should determine if marital conflict exists. If marital conflict exists, marital cooperation training is preferred.

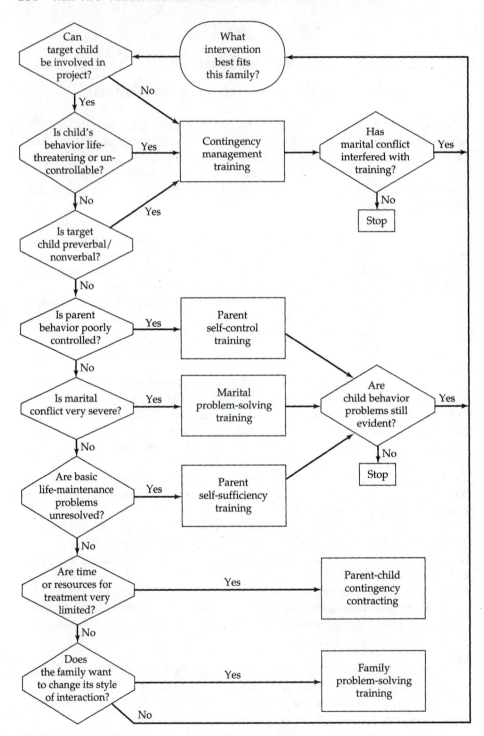

FIGURE 7.1
An array of behavioral family interventions

10. *Are child behavior problems still evident?* This question should be posed if parent self-control training, marital cooperation training, or parent self-sufficiency training has been successfully implemented. If the child's behavior problem still exists, then the search for a new strategy begins again.

Strategies for Treatment

Four approaches to parent training are mentioned in the preceding list of questions. A brief overview of each and the settings in which they have been used is presented so as to clarify their unique advantages and disadvantages.

Contingency management/contracting   Contingency management is a written contract between the parent or parents and child (Stuart, 1971). Contracting is an effective instrument when the parent is trying to get the child to take more responsibility for his or her behavior; that is, contracting is particularly useful for clients who are aware of the negative consequences of their behavior and would like to do something about it. The contract is the parent's and child's commitment to change (Hackney & Nye, 1973).

Contracting is a form of structured bargaining that specifies clearly what is expected. The therapist is a mediator who facilitates mutual agreements between opposing parties about reciprocal exchanges of mutual behaviors, reinforcers, and punishers. This approach has been highly successful with parent-youth conflicts (Stuart, 1971). Contracts usually specify that the child can engage in a high-preference activity, such as watching television, when he or she has completed a low-preference activity, such as taking the trash out.

The following guidelines (Homme, Csanyi, Gonzales, & Rechs, 1974) should assist the therapist in negotiating a contract between parent and child.

1. *Contracts should be stated in a positive way.* For example, a parent may request that a child "interact positively with his brother" rather than "not fight."

2. *The contract should make explicit the responsibilities of all parties.* Each member of the family may have a responsibility. Parents may alternate in spending time alone with their child. Each party agrees to the role responsibilities of the contract and signs it.

3. *A time line should be included in each contract.* This time line should specify the amount of time within which the child can complete the contract (for example, a child must clean the bedroom, take out the trash each day, and so on) This makes it clear when the contract has been fulfilled and signals when the reinforcer is to be delivered. The contract should also state when the agreement begins, ends, and is to be renegotiated.

4. *A bonus or penalty clause may be built into the contract.* For example, for each additional chore, the child may receive 10 minutes of television time up to 1 hour. Similarly, a penalty clause may be included. In using penalties, the therapist should be careful that the child has enough points accumulated to absorb the penalty, because it becomes punishing if the child loses more points than he or she is able to accumulate.

5. *Each contract should contain a provision for renegotiation.* A contract should be revised when one or more of the following occurs: (a) failing to complete

two progress checks, (b) making excuses for not fulfilling the contract, and (c) complaining about the contract. In many cases, the therapist, parent, and child may have misjudged what the child could do in the given period of time. In other cases, the child may wish to renegotiate to change the reward, the amount of the reward, or both.

Parent self-control training Parent self-control training is most appropriate for parents who exhibit high levels of aggressive behaviors themselves. Such parents must first learn to control their own behaviors before they can control those of their children. Blechman (1981) outlines the parent self-control training objectives as follows: (1) identify instances of parents' aggressive behaviors while viewing videotapes of the parents interacting with their child, (2) identify antecedent events to the aggressive behaviors on the videotape, (3) have the parents stop the videotape as soon as the antecedent events appear and relax for 5 minutes, (4) record each instance of aggressive behavior at home, and (5) have the parent leave home or go to another room as soon as the antecedent behavior occurs and relax for 5 minutes.

Marital problem-solving training Marital problem-solving training is appropriate for parents who disagree about how to handle their child's behavior. Such couples are inconsistent and have difficulty in setting rules and providing reinforcement to the child for following the rules. Problem-solving training focuses on ways parents can work cooperatively to control their child's behavior. Problem-solving training is discussed in a wider context within the section on behavioral marital therapy.

Parent self-sufficiency training Parent self-sufficiency training is appropriate for parents who lack basic resources, such as money and education. For example, parents with less than seven years of formal education who have reading problems often require more training than do parents with more education. O'Dell (1974) believes that such differences may be due to the fact that parent training programs rely on written handouts and books, and thus, parents with reading problems have difficulty understanding the concepts being presented in the program. Likewise, Goldstein (1973) found that clients of low socioeconomic status were more likely to progress in therapy when specific behaviors, rather than verbal concepts, were emphasized.

In addition to education, Patterson, Cobb, and Ray (1972) found that both specificity of training and availability of reinforcers and resources are critical areas in training parents. Even when parents have basic parenting skills, they may have difficulty because they lack the reinforcers (for example, resources for games and activities) necessary to increase the desired behaviors in children. In addition, if parents are single or live alone, they may be less consistent in applying child management skills without someone else, such as a spouse or a relative, in the home to support their efforts. Patterson et al. (1972) suggest that these problems might be overcome through additional individual training support from the therapist.

Parent self-sufficiency training is predicated on parents' meeting their personal needs (for example, financial, educational, and emotional) before meeting the needs of their children. Objectives of training include (1) identification of parent-child problem areas, (2) selection of problem for remediation, (3) identification of contingencies controlling the problem, (4) identification of goals, (5) identification of an interventional plan to reach the goal, (6) implementation of the plan, and (7) evaluation of the plan.

Content of Parent Training

Parent training programs vary widely in their content, ranging from those that emphasize teaching parents behavioral concepts such as reinforcement to those that focus on specific techniques, such as time out, designed to modify specific target behaviors (Gordon & Davidson, 1981). There is striking evidence to support the efficacy of training in specific skills (O'Dell, 1978); however, evidence about the effectiveness of teaching general principles of behavior analysis has been inconsistent. Currently, most behavioral parent training programs provide a combination of principles and skills.

Although programs vary in content and method of teaching, their basic content is summarized in the following outline:

1. *Introduction to social learning theory.* Basic principles of reinforcement are generally covered in this phase.

2. *Identification of the problem behaviors and controlling conditions.* Parents are taught to define problems in specific behavioral terms so that they can be objectively measured. Parents are then taught to identify the antecedents and consequences of the problem behavior.

3. *Gathering baseline of problem behavior.* Parents are taught to record the frequency or duration (or both) of the problem behavior. Once parents have collected baseline data, they are taught to graph the behavior to assess progress.

4. *Stating rules or directions.* Parents are taught how to state rules. Rules should be specific and positive and should include a time (for example, today, end of the week) when the rule should be followed.

5. *Positive reinforcement.* Teaching the use of positive reinforcement generally focuses on increasing the frequency and range of reinforcers used by parents. Parents are taught to praise their child, thus reinforcing desired behavior. Parents are also taught to selectively reinforce behaviors (for example, playing quietly) that are incompatible with an undesirable target behavior (for example, fighting).

6. *Ignoring undesirable behaviors.* Parents are taught to ignore behaviors that they can tolerate and that are not harmful to the child. If parents cannot ignore undesirable behaviors, they are taught to give verbal reprimands. Verbal reprimands are effective in decreasing noncompliance, whereas simple repetition of a command may be ineffective (Forehand et al., 1979).

7. *Teaching new behaviors.* When certain behaviors do not exist in the child's repertoire, parents often use shaping, modeling, instructions, and prompting to assist the child in developing new behaviors.

8. *Time out or isolation.* If children are behaving in ways that are harmful to themselves or others (for example, fighting), then time out is most effective. Time out involves isolating the child in a neutral area devoid of reinforcing persons or objects. Time out is effective only when used in conjunction with reinforcement techniques (that is, a child must lose the opportunity to earn reinforcement when sent to take time out). In teaching the use of time out, therapists encourage parents to give a warning to the child before administering time out.

It should be noted that the content and method of presentation (for example, lecture, videotape, handouts) often depends on the sophistication of the parents, the time available for training, age of the children, and the target behaviors to be remediated. Regardless, it is important that therapists encourage parents to set goals for their children that are developmentally appropriate.

Effectiveness of Behavioral Parent Training

A number of reviews of the literature (Berkowitz & Graziano, 1972; Johnson & Katz, 1973; Moreland, Schwebel, Beck, & Wells, 1982) have reported on a broad range of studies demonstrating the effectiveness of parent training programs in the reduction of children's problem behaviors. Evaluating what is producing these effects is difficult because of the variability of content and training methods and the lack of generality across settings and time.

Content

Parents have been taught to alter a wide range of children's behaviors through a variety of behavioral procedures. They have been taught to decrease stealing (Stumphauser, 1976), improve eating habits (Israel, Stolmaker, & Andrian, 1985), decrease noncompliant behavior (Forehand, Sturgis, McMahon, Aguar, Green, Wells, & Breiner, 1979), increase compliance during shopping trips (Clark, Green, MacRae, McNees, Davis, & Risley, 1977), and decrease oppositional behavior in children (Strain, Steele, Ellis, & Timm, 1982). These studies have basically used a behavioral treatment package of contingent positive reinforcement, contingent withdrawal/time out, and response cost. Further research is warranted to determine the differential effectiveness of each of these procedures.

Training Methods

Several studies have examined methods of teaching parents to apply behavioral procedures. O'Dell, Krug, Patterson, and Faustman (1980) and O'Dell, Mahoney, Horton, and Turner (1979) found that modeling and role playing were more effective than a traditional lecture-discussion format in training parents to use time out. Hudson (1982) found that modeling and role playing were more effective than teaching behavioral principles in helping mothers to modify inappropriate behavior of their developmentally handicapped children. O'Dell, O'Quin, Alford, O'Briant, Bradlyn, and Giebenhain (1982) found that videotaped modeling seemed particularly effective in training a wide variety of parents in child management skills. Modeling, shaping, and role playing appear to be the most effective methods for teaching parents behavioral methodology; nevertheless, further research is warranted.

Generalization

Although overall the evidence concerning behavioral parent training appears positive for a specific setting (for instance, home, clinic, or restaurant), the generalization of treatment effects across settings appears to have mixed results. Some investigators (Forehand et al., 1979) report successful generalization from clinic to home. Other studies (Embry, Kelly, Jackson, & Baer, 1979; Wulburt, Barach, Perry, Straughan, Sulzbacher, Turner, & Wiltz, 1974) report no transfer effects. In several investigations (Mindell & Budd, 1977; Peed, Roberts, & Forehand, 1977), generalization effects were produced by the therapist's instructing parents to follow the procedures in the home.

Studies that investigate generalization of treatment effects over time have been minimal. Nevertheless, it is difficult to know what variables (for example, socioeconomic status, target problem, method of training, or relationship between spouses) contribute to generalization. Studies conducted with more scientific rigor are needed; meanwhile, it would appear that conditions favoring generalization must be created rather than assumed (Sanders & Dadds, 1982; Sanders & James, 1983). Similarly, there seems to be some question regarding the maintenance of treatment effects over time. It appears that maintenance effects, like generalization effects, must be programmed. Patterson has demonstrated that treatment effects can be maintained over two years through the use of "booster shots" and "refresher courses" (Patterson, 1974; Patterson, Chamberlain, & Reid, 1982).

More recently, there has been increasing evidence that training parents to treat children's behaviors may not always be desirable (Griest & Wells, 1983). Indeed, parents' cognitive, psychological, and marital/social adjustment may be related to the behavioral problems of children (Wells, 1981). New and expanding technologies must be designed to account for those variables. For example, Rabin, Blechman, Kahn, and Carel (1985) developed a marriage contract game to help distressed couples to refocus their attention away from their children and toward their marriages.

In summary, behavioral parent training is effective in producing short-term treatment effects for situation-specific behaviors. Treatment effects generalize across settings and time when programmed into the treatment. Further research is warranted to determine what training variables (content and methods) are producing these effects. Moreover, new technologies are needed to account for those variables (such as marital distress) that might impede the effectiveness of parent training.

Often the issue of parenting skills and their treatment is a first step in therapy that eventually leads to marital therapy. Behavioral marital therapy has evolved as a somewhat separate discipline; its theory, technique, and issues will be discussed in the following section.

Therapeutic Practice: Behavioral Marital Therapy

The theoretical core of behavior therapy for marital conflict is best represented by **social exchange theory** (Thibaut & Kelly, 1959). In social exchange theory, the individual is seen as attempting to maximize "rewards" while minimizing "costs." A couple's relationship is viewed as satisfying to the degree that the partners provide one another with a high ratio of benefits to costs and that alternative relationships offer fewer comparative rewards and more costs (Thibaut & Kelly, 1959). Any married couple has a minimum reward/cost ratio that determines the success of the relationship; the ratio is unique to each couple.

Social learning theory also asserts that the rate of rewards one receives from a partner determines the number of rewards one is likely to transmit in return. When two people reward one another at an equitable rate, we refer to the nature of the exchange as **reciprocity**. Family members often reinforce each other at an equitable rate that maintains the behavior of both parties (Patterson & Reid, 1970). It is important to note that reciprocity is conditional on other aspects of the relationship and does not mean that one will immediately reciprocate. Unfortunately, the expectation that one's spouse will immediately reciprocate often leads to frustration and conflict in a relationship (Stuart, 1980).

Marital conflict may also occur when either spouse attempts to control the partner's behavior with aversive stimuli. This attempt to control another person's behavior with negative reinforcement is referred to as coercion. Coercion often sets off a string of sequential interactions that, although unpleasant for both partners, becomes self-perpetuating. For example, a wife may try to control her husband's behavior by complaining that he never spends any time with her. When the husband ignores her request, possibly because her complaining is aversive to him, her complaints become amplified. As the wife becomes more demanding, the husband may grudgingly agree to do something with her in order to end the unpleasant interaction. Thus, the husband's behavior is negatively reinforced because it terminates an unpleasant interaction, and the wife's unpleasant demands are positively reinforced because at least he has agreed to do something with her. It is interesting to note that avoidance of anxiety-arousing stimuli such as intimacy may be negatively reinforced by withdrawing from an anxiety-provoking situation (Jacobson, 1981); for example, a husband withdraws to the basement and watches TV to avoid being with his wife. In short, marital conflict may be the result of the use of aversive control, and thus partners exchange a low rate of positive reinforcers so that each spouse becomes less satisfied with the relationship (Gurman & Knudson, 1978).

It would appear that the concepts of coercion and reciprocity would enable us to predict satisfaction in a marriage. That is, the more reciprocity present and the fewer coercive exchanges, the higher the level of satisfaction we might predict in the marriage. Unfortunately, spouses may not characterize their marriages by the exchange of rewards at a high rate or of punishment at a low rate. They may "feel" happily married because of some outside factor (for example, protection) in their marriage. However, it would be difficult to characterize a marriage as being satisfying without some degree of reciprocity.

Regardless of the rate of exchange of rewards and costs, a certain amount of conflict will arise that interferes with the ratio. For instance, the unrealistic expectations that newlyweds have for their relationship will eventually create conflict. Jacobson (1981) says:

> Maintaining a high ratio (rewards/cost) is not much of a problem for couples during the early stages of a relationship, particularly given a large degree of initial attraction. Reinforcing value is at its peak, fueled by the novelty inherent in the exchanges and shared activities. Couples insure during these periods that the contacts are as positive as possible. None of the costs inherent in a long-term commitment has been realized as yet. (p. 559)

However, the probability of conflict increases as spouses begin to share the burdens of daily living, rearing children, and adjusting to shifting role responsibilities. The failure to resolve such conflict is the single most prominent cause of marital failure (Mace, 1979).

According to behavior theorists, distressed couples fail to resolve their disagreements because they lack the necessary skills for problem solving or conflict resolution. The skills and the practice of behavioral marital therapy will be the focus of the next section.

Assessment

Assessment in behavioral marital therapy is a prerequisite for designing an effective strategy for change. The assessment procedures are designed to evaluate (1) the strengths and weaknesses of a couple's interactional behavior, (2) the variety of ways that rewards and punishment are exchanged by the spouses, and (3) each spouse's subjective appraisal of the relationship (Jacobson, 1981). In addition, behavioral therapists assess those deficits in skills such as problem solving, communication, and child rearing that may be influencing dysfunctional family interaction. The therapist also conducts a behavioral assessment of the time that the partners spend together, as well as how they spend that time.

It is important to understand that assessment is often indistinguishable from treatment intervention in behavioral therapy (Jacob, 1976). The couple typically arrives at the therapist's office armed with a wide array of global complaints and dissatisfactions. It is not unusual for a spouse to report dissatisfaction without knowing the reason or even to be unable to give any immediate examples of his or her partner's displeasing behavior. Instead, the therapist hears general complaints such as, "He doesn't respect me enough," or "I just don't feel as much love as I used to," or even, "I don't know, maybe it is just me."

The behavioral therapist is interested in narrowing down such statements of dissatisfaction into more specific and objectively verifiable ones. The partners must slowly adapt to the therapist's conceptual language if they are to use his or her professional expertise. As the therapist begins to ask questions that are designed to collect the information for assessment, intervention, in the form of modeling, has also begun.

As each question is asked, the therapist begins to convey values and attitudes about the behavioral perspective. As each question is answered, the partners, out of the necessity of answering the question, move closer to adopting the perspective of viewing their problem within a behavioral framework. Assessment and intervention are therefore interrelated; it is only for the purposes of explanation that they are separated here.

Two major areas of inquiry must be answered during the assessment process: (1) What are the problematic behaviors that each partner would like to change? and (2) How are these problematic behaviors currently reinforced in the relationship? Behavioral therapists attempt to answer these questions through a multidimensional assessment of verbal, psychological, and behavioral variables (Goldfried & Spratkin, 1974). Let's now look at some of the techniques that are used to conduct the assessment. In particular, we will focus on the use of interviews, observation, and a variety of self-report measures that are typically used in behavioral assessment.

Interviews

The conjoint interview is important for determining what leads up to a problem interaction **(antecedent behavior),** as well as what happens as a *consequence* of the interactions. Certain types of information can be more easily obtained through the free exchange that is offered in an interview format. The important subtleties of *time* and *setting* in which the problem occurs (for example, the husband asks for attention while the wife is trying to sleep) may be more easily obtained through an interview than by any other means. Likewise, the therapist may be aided in determining what is maintaining the problem by knowing when the problem is both most severe and least severe and why those situations differ.

The direction and content of the interview are suggested by the following outline:

   I. Relationship in time and place
     A. Trajectory: moving toward past, future, nowhere
     B. Degree of dyadic involvement: more, less, no change
     C. Other viable relationship alternatives, such as separation
  II. Lifestyle and tempo
     A. In space: home
     B. With others as individuals: animals, children, and so on
     C. With others as collectives: community and so on
     D. Role of pleasures: work-to-pleasure ratio
     E. Responsibilities: kinfolk, legal, and so on
 III. Factors impeding attainment of relationship goals
     A. Structural

    1. Limitations of individual resources
    2. Limitations of joint resources
    3. Individual versus dyadic energy imbalance
  B. Functional
    1. Communication skills deficits (specify)
    2. Deficient rewards (amount versus contingency)
    3. Failures of stimulus control (specify)
IV. The couple's aptitudes for intervention
  A. Background factors
    1. Seeking relationship goals defined as reciprocity or otherwise consistent with behavioral exchange model
    2. Physical gratification important to both
    3. Common investment, such as children, social status, business
    4. Clear statement of objectives
  B. Process factors
    1. Clients' in-session behaviors
      a. Follow therapist
      b. Adopt therapist's model for viewing problems
      c. Progress in focusing issues
      d. Relevant questioning of program
    2. Therapist's estimate of movement
      a. Aversive behaviors brought under control
      b. On average, problem solving greater than name calling
      c. Ability to understand clients' complaints
      d. The therapist can define three goals of intervention for these clients
V. Obstacles to intervention progress
  A. Client expectations
    1. Attachment to previous therapist
    2. Model of behavior antagonistic to therapist's
    3. Extra therapeutic agents
  B. Intellectual/educational limitations
    1. Verbal skills (including reading and writing)
    2. Undeveloped "work habits"
  C. Resource limitations
    1. Time, money for intervention
    2. Medical and health-related conditions, such as addictions
VI. Treatment planning
  A. Alternative treatment options
  B. Therapist-client match
  C. Menus of treatment options within system

Observation

Several types of recording systems have been developed to gather baseline information and monitor treatment. The most popular of these instruments have been developed by the Oregon Marital Studies Program (Weiss & Perry, 1979). Its ten-session assessment/intervention package begins with a two-session assessment phase in which spouses are phoned each night for observational data (Gurman & Knudson, 1978). Weiss and Perry have developed another mechanism called the Spouse Observation Checklist (SOC) to aid couples in their collection of observational data in the home. The Spouse Observation Checklist contains a checklist of "pleases" (*p*'s) and "displeases" (*d*'s), defined as behaviors of the spouse that the respondent finds pleasing or displeasing. Both instrumental and affectional *p*'s and *d*'s are recorded from 12 categories: affection, companionship, consideration, sex, communication process, coupling activities, child care and parenting, household responsibilities, financial management, work, personal habits, and self- and spouse independence. The SOC provides for recording daily frequencies of spouse behavior, which can be useful in the identification of critical roadblocks to change. The SOC can also be useful in monitoring changes during therapy. Several research investigations support the validity of the SOC instrument (for example, Weiss, Hops, & Patterson, 1973; Wills, Weiss, & Patterson, 1974). The SOC appears at the end of this chapter (pp. 199–221).

The Oregon group has also developed the Marital Interaction Coding System (MICS) (Hops, Wills, Patterson, & Weiss, 1972). The MICS is a behavioral coding system useful for describing the content and process of a couple's interaction, usually while attempting to negotiate a marital conflict. The videotaped (or audiotaped) interaction is coded by trained coders, and the stream of ongoing coded behaviors is then subjected to a computer analysis, the results of which include rate per minute of problem solving, positive behaviors, negative behaviors, frequency and content of interruptions, and successful and unsuccessful interruptions. For example, what does a spouse do to take over the floor? Does it work? Is this characteristic of their interaction?

The MICS differs from other forms of laboratory observation in that observational codes are designed to examine the couple's interactional patterns as they actually occur (Ciminero, Calhoun, & Adams, 1977). The MICS can be used to assess the couple's problem-solving and communication abilities. It consists of 30 codes that account for most responses in a problem-solving situation (Patterson, Hops, & Weiss, 1974). These codes were derived from videotapes of couples' interactions. The relationship among code categories is illustrated in Figure 7.2; an abbreviated description of the codes themselves follows:

AG Agree. Statement of agreement with spouse's opinion.

AP Approve. Respondent favors spouse's attributes, actions, or statements.

AR Accept responsibility. A statement that conveys "'I' or 'We' are responsible for this problem."

AS Assent. Listener says, "yeah," nods head, and so on, to indicate "I'm listening" or to facilitate conversation.

AT Attention. Listener maintains eye contact for at least 3 seconds.

CH Command. Direct request for immediate action (for example, "Listen to me!" or "Please put out your cigarette").

CO Compliance. Fulfills command within 30 seconds of command (for example, spouse puts out cigarette).

CP Complain. Whining or bitter expression of one's own suffering without explicitly blaming the spouse (for example, expressing dissatisfaction with world at large, job, health, other people, and so on).

CR Criticize. Hostile statement of unambiguous dislike or disapproval of a specific behavior in spouse.

CS Compromise. A negotiation of mutually exchanged behaviors, such as "I'll do this if you'll do that."

DG Disagree. A statement of disagreement with spouse's opinion.

DR Deny responsibility. A statement that conveys I (we) are not responsible for this problem.

EX Excuse. Personal denial of responsibility based on an implausible or weak rationale (often characterized by embarrassment, nervous laughter, and so on).

HM Humor. Lighthearted humor; no sarcasm.

IN Interrupt. Listener breaks in and disrupts the flow of the other person's speech.

MR Mindreading. Statement that infers or assumes an attitude or feeling on the part of the other.

NC Noncompliance. Failure to fulfill command within 30 seconds of a command.

NO Normative. Broad category for silence resulting from behaviors that compete with the conversation, such as lighting a cigarette, writing, coughing, and so on.

NR No response. Verbal response is explicitly required, but none is given within 3 seconds (for example, failure to answer a question).

NS Negative solution. A solution proposing termination or a decrease in the frequency of some behavior.

NT Not tracking. Listener does not make eye contact within 3 seconds.

PD Problem description. Any statement, said in a neutral or friendly tone of voice, describing a problem.

PP Positive physical contact. Affectionate touch, hug, and so on.

PR Paraphrase/Reflection. A statement that mirrors or restates an immediately preceding statement of the other person.

PS Positive solution. A solution proposing initiation or increase in the frequency of some behavior.

PU Putdown. A comment intended to demean or embarrass the spouse.

QU Question. Any interrogative statement.

SL Smile/Laugh. Smile or laughter.

TA Talk. Catch-all category that includes inaudible speech, irrelevent comments, noninformational responses, and so on (for example, "I don't know.").

TO Turn-off. Nonverbal gestures that communicate displeasure, disgust, disapproval, or disagreement (for example, sighing, turning one's head away).

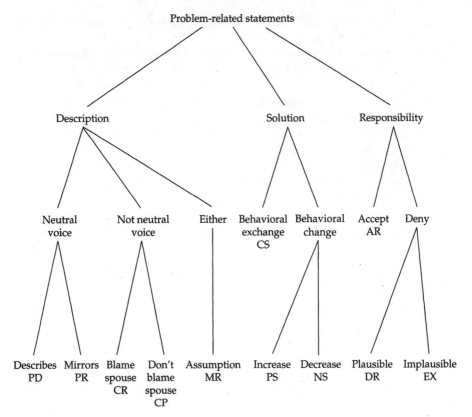

FIGURE 7.2
Hierarchy for distinguishing selected MICS codes

The 30 codes are often condensed into three summary scores: positive social reinforcement, negative social reinforcement, and problem solving. One disadvantage of the MICS is that it requires trained observers to score the data. The MICS has been used widely in the United States and other countries.

Self-Report Measures

Self-report measures are those for which clients keep records of their own behaviors. There are several self-report instruments that are commonly used. We will discuss three of them: the Locke-Wallace Marital Status Inventory (L-W), the Dyadic Adjustment Scale (DAS), and the Marital Precounseling Inventory (MPI).

The Locke-Wallace Marital Status Inventory contains a set of true/false items to assess steps toward dissolution of the marriage. According to Weiss and Perry (1979), the test was designed to provide "an intensity scale (e.g., Guttman scale) such that any given step would necessarily include all preceding steps. Thus before one sought legal aid for a divorce it would be reasonable to assume that one had thoughts about divorce and engaged in behaviors preparatory to that of seeking legal advice" (p. 17).

The Dyadic Adjustment Scale (Spanier, 1976) includes many items from the Locke-Wallace inventory (Locke & Wallace, 1959). Weiss and Perry (1979) altered the items omitted by Spanier so that both measures are incorporated into one questionnaire, called the Dyadic Adjustment Scale. The DAS is somewhat more modern in its wording than the Locke-Wallace inventory and provides four factor scales: dyadic consensus (for example, problem solving), dyadic satisfaction (for example, "good feelings" and "sentiment" in the relationship), dyadic cohesion (for example, outside interests, exchange of ideas, cooperation), and affectional expression (for example, sexual and emotional expression). The DAS is easy to score and can be very useful to the behavioral family therapist.

The Marital Precounseling Inventory (Stuart & Stuart, 1972) is administered before treatment in order to aid in treatment planning. The 11-page inventory provides assessment information in the following areas: daily activities of both spouses, general goals and resources for change, spouse satisfaction and targets for change in 12 areas of marital and family functioning, rationale for decision making, and level of commitment to the marriage (Stuart, 1976).

The data from the MPI serves several purposes. It provides the therapist with data for planning a treatment program. It also helps to orient the couple to treatment. Each spouse can often anticipate those issues that will be discussed. At the end of treatment, the inventory can be completed to evaluate therapy.

These self-report instruments serve a variety of assessment functions. First, they provide objective measures of behaviors important to the satisfaction of both spouses.

Second, these instruments often reveal information that spouses might be reluctant to provide in an interview. (For example, a spouse may find it embarrassing to discuss sexual issues in the interview.) The therapist can often use this information to help spouses to focus on critical issues that might otherwise be avoided. Finally, instruments often provide an ongoing measure of subjective satisfaction that cannot be obtained through direct observation.

Jacobson (1981) suggests that the combined contributions of the interview, self-report questionnaires, spouse observation, and observation of spouse interaction should yield answers to the following questions:

A. *Strengths and skills of the relationship*
   - What are the major strengths of this relationship
   - What specific resources do these spouses have that explain their current level of commitment to the relationship?
   - What is each spouse's current capacity to reinforce the other?
   - What behaviors on the part of each spouse are highly valued by the other?
   - What shared activities do the couple currently engage in?
   - What common interests do they share?
   - What are the couple's competencies and skills in meeting the essential tasks of a relationship: problem solving, provision of support and understanding, ability to provide social reinforcement effectively, sexual capabilities, child-rearing and parenting skills, ability to manage fi-

nances, household responsibilities, and interpersonal skills regarding interaction with people outside the relationship?

B. *Presenting problems*
   - What are the major complaints, and how do they translate into explicitly behavioral terms?
   - What behaviors occur too frequently or at inappropriate times from the standpoint of each spouse?
   - Under what conditions do these behaviors occur?
   - What are the reinforcers that are maintaining these behaviors?
   - What behaviors occur at less than the desired frequency or fail to occur at appropriate times from the standpoint of each spouse?
   - Under what conditions would each spouse like to see these behaviors occur?
   - What are the consequences of these behaviors currently, when they occur?
   - How did the current problems develop over time?
   - How are current lines of decision-making authority drawn?
   - Is there a consensus on who makes important decisions in regard to various areas of the relationship?
   - What kinds of decisions are made collectively as opposed to unilaterally?

C. *Sex and affection*
   - Are the spouses physically attracted to one another?
   - Is either currently dissatisfied with rate, quality, or diversity of sex life together?
   - If sex is currently a problem, was there a time when it was mutually satisfying?
   - What are the sexual behaviors that seem to be associated with current dissatisfaction?
   - Are either or both partners dissatisfied with the amount or quality of nonsexual physical affection?
   - Are either or both partners currently engaged in an extramarital sexual relationship?
   - If so, is the uninvolved partner aware of the affair?
   - What is the couple's history regarding extramarital affairs?

D. *Future prospects*
   - Are the partners seeking therapy to improve their relationship, to separate, or to decide whether the relationship is worth working on?
   - What are each spouse's reasons for continuing the relationship despite current problems?
   - What steps has each spouse taken in the direction of divorce?

E. *Assessment of social environment*
   - What are each person's alternatives to the present relationship?
   - How attractive are these alternatives to each person?
   - Is the environment (parents, relatives, friends, work associates, children) supportive of either continuance or dissolution of the present relationship?

- Are any of the children suffering from psychological problems of their own?
- What would the probable consequences of relationship dissolution be for the children?

F. *Individual functioning of each spouse*
- Does either spouse exhibit any severe emotional or behavioral problems?
- Does either spouse present a psychiatric history of his or her own? Specify.
- Have they been in therapy before, either alone or together? What kind of therapy? Outcome?
- What is each spouse's past experience with intimate relationships?
- How is the present relationship different?

At the end of the assessment phase, the couple meets with the therapist to examine the information and design a treatment program with specific goals. Periodic assessment is made to evaluate the progress of treatment and to modify the program as needed. The goals of the treatment program and the strategies for behavior change that flow directly out of the assessment will be discussed in the next two sections.

Goals

The process of formulating behavioral goals not only specifies "where we are going" but also provides standards by which the therapist can demonstrate his or her effectiveness in getting there. Subgoals and objectives, which are specifically defined, can be used to measure the couple's progress from week to week. Measurable goals provide direction in therapy and prevent the therapist from claiming effectiveness without demonstrating it.

Goals in behavioral marital therapy, having evolved directly from the assessment, refer to the specific behaviors each spouse desires in the other and to the increase in frequency of those behaviors. There are basic reasons underlying the specification of reciprocal goals: (1) because the feelings one spouse has toward the other are a direct function of the other's behavior, if specific behaviors change, the spouse's feelings will also change; and (2) marital problems arise from interactional, not intrapsychic, problems (Gurman & Knudson, 1978). On the basis of these assumptions, spouses are encouraged to communicate their desires in terms of what they would like their spouse to do differently— that is, the therapist must ask each partner what behaviors the other will be performing to demonstrate that he or she has reached the goal.

In therapy, the specific behavioral goals describe what each spouse will be doing as a result of treatment. Vague goal descriptions such as, "I want you to care about me," and "You have to think about someone besides yourself" are not acceptable because there is no way to measure them reliably. Instead, a spouse might be asked to communicate his or her desires or complaints in specific terms (for example, "I want you to ask me about my job at least once each day").

It is interesting to note that while goal setting in behavioral marital therapy is often discussed from the therapist's technical point of view (that is, the need for specificity, measurability, observability, quantifiability, and so forth), the systems therapist might argue that the very structure and process of goal setting serve to homeostatically organize the tension in the couple's previous runaway style of conflict negotiation. Through the therapist's insistence on clarity in the transmission of information, as well as his or her desire that the information be phrased in a particular way (that is, stated as a positive request and detailing what is desired), the therapist positions himself or herself as a potent model of attitudes and skills that are so necessary to the negotiation process. (See the discussion of modeling later in this chapter.)

Technique

Creating an Atmosphere of Change

Seldom, if ever, does a couple come for marital therapy in a positive, optimistic, confident, and forgiving posture, eager to hear what the therapist has to say and then ready to rush home and put it into practice. On the contrary, all too often, marital therapy begins when one spouse, who "can't take it anymore," insists that the other one "go to counseling or else." The emotional climate between them is, of course, unique to each couple but often includes bitterness, mistrust, hurt feelings, envy, grief, fear, and vulnerability. The therapist is often not seen with a clear focus; rather, he or she may be seen as an intruder, an ally of the other spouse, a judge and jury, or an insensitive manipulator. This combination of factors hardly produces an atmosphere conducive to positive expectancies and collaborative feelings. Thus, as an initial strategy, creating an environment that will facilitate future treatment goals becomes paramount for the therapist.

The behavioral marital therapist handles this threatening climate by defining it as one in which positive changes are necessary to increase satisfaction in the marriage (and marriage counseling) with as few costs as possible. Rather than focusing immediately on the presenting problems, the therapist may initially discuss the history of the couple's relationship as part of the ongoing process of assessment (Jacobson & Margolin, 1979). By reviewing the period of the couple's early courtship, the therapist evokes cognitive images of pleasant interactions between them, which momentarily replace the bitter, conflicted images of the present relationship. This effect gives the therapist an opportunity to reinforce those images socially and to present himself or herself as sensitive to the complexity of their relationship. The couple who had entered the office expecting the worst in their relationship to be displayed for full view to a total stranger instead find themselves reminiscing about better times with someone who appreciates the fact that they did not set out to create a marriage full of pain and dissatisfaction. By focusing on the positive behaviors, each spouse can view the couple's current problems with greater perspective and move closer to accepting responsibility in and for their relationship.

Another strategy for establishing the proper atmosphere for couples to work together is to obtain from them an agreement that they will follow the therapist's advice and counsel—in short, that the couple expresses its commitment to do what the therapist instructs. This agreement then establishes the framework within which the therapist instructs the couple to collaborate (Jacobson, 1981). Rather than doing something to please the other in response to the other's request, each does something because he or she has told the therapist he or she would, and it happens to please the other spouse. This expedient allows them both to save face, an experience necessary to every embittered adversary.

How does the therapist obtain the couple's commitment to follow his or her instructions? Not by simply demanding it, although without it, the behavioral marital therapist sees little likelihood for success. The commitment is instead gradually built through the pretreatment assessment process by verbal and nonverbal cues that the therapist has something to offer them, that the therapist sees their problems as not insurmountable, and that the therapist is a reasonable and sensitive professional who can be trusted. After summarizing the results of pretreatment assessment and after outlining the goals, procedure, and rationale of treatment, the therapist then asks for the couple's commitment to follow his or her instructions.

By considering the emotional anxiety and confusion that couples bring to therapy, and by being sensitive to it, the behavioral marital therapist begins to create an atmosphere conducive to change. The process is continued and extended through a "commitment to collaborate" in which the therapist progressively builds a bridge between the spouses, across which they can begin to work on their marriage.

Once the behavioral marital therapist has worked to create an atmosphere for change in the couple, he or she can then turn to focusing on the more salient treatment goals and procedures that emerged in the assessment process. Although the treatment protocols vary from therapist to therapist, these procedures can be discussed under two primary categories: behavioral exchange techniques and communication/problem-solving training. In treatment, these two generic techniques may dovetail or overlap; however, for the purpose of discussion they will be approached separately.

Behavioral Exchange Practice

The behavioral exchange model relies on the principle of social exchange (reciprocity). Within this model, each spouse "gives" in order to "get" an increase in desired behaviors from the other. Behavioral exchange appears to work best when both parties possess resources (that is, reinforcement potential valuable to each other). When both partners have equal or nearly equal resources (for example, friends, skills, and so on), then a willingness to compromise appears likely. But when one spouse has more resources than the other, negotiation and compromise appear unlikely.

Behavioral exchange consists of two basic procedures. First, desirable behaviors are pinpointed by one or both spouses. Spouses are encouraged to request change by directly identifying the specific behaviors they wish to see more frequently. For example, "I want you to pay more attention to me" might mean "I want you to talk to me when you come home." Second, there is an attempt to increase the frequency of the desired behaviors (Jacobson, 1981). The goal is to eliminate undesirable behaviors, replacing them with desirable behaviors. Behavioral exchange attempts to extinguish undesirable behaviors and increase desirable behaviors that are more rewarding to both partners in the relationship.

The principle of pinpointing desirable target behaviors in which each spouse would like the other to engage more often is derived from the reinforcement model of marital exchange. A wife may, for instance, make three requests of the husband: (1) that he assume responsibility for the children on Saturday afternoon, (2) that he put his clothes in the hamper each night, and (3) that he ask her each night how her day went. The husband might make three requests of his wife: (1) that she compliment him when he does something for her, (2) that she ask him about his work once a week, and (3) that she tell him when something is bothering her. Jacobson (1981) notes that it is not the place of the behavioral therapist to determine the desired behavior for each spouse.

Behavior exchange procedures are derived from principles of operant reinforcement. Spouses may, for example, make deals about joint activities, exchanging something she wants them to do for something he wants them to do. When spouses substitute desired behaviors for undesired behaviors, then reciprocal behaviors will serve to reinforce both spouses positively and thus lead to a more satisfying relationship.

Cost/benefit analysis There are various ways to enact the behavioral exchange. Weiss and Perry (1979) ask couples to conduct a cost/benefit analysis; the purpose of this procedure is to help partners see how much effort they expend for each other and to determine what behaviors each considers important in the other. Couples are given "Benefit Exchange Sheets" (Weiss, 1978), which contain a list of potentially pleasing behaviors taken from the Spouse Observation Checklist. The Benefit Exchange Sheet is divided into 12 categories:

1. Companionship (for example, "listening to music," "going out to eat")
2. Affection (for example, "holding hands")
3. Consideration (for example, "talking about personal feelings")
4. Sex (for example, "We were both sexually responsive to each other")
5. Coupling activities (for example, "visiting relatives")
6. Communication process (for example, "We agreed about something")
7. Child care and parenting (for example, "disciplining the children")
8. Household management (for example, "running errands")
9. Financial decision making (for example, "working on a budget")
10. Employment and education (for example, "showing interest in work")
11. Personal habits and appearance (for example, "dressing nicely")
12. Self- and spouse independence (for example, "engaging in independent activities")

Each spouse is requested to rate each item as being "beneficial" or "costly" on a 5-point scale. In some cases, spouses may focus only on a particular area, such as parenting or communication. Benefit exchange works best when there is a balance of benefits and costs for both spouses. The exercise provides an opportunity for compromise and negotiation.

Once both spouses have completed the cost/benefit exercise, they complete a weekly client assignment sheet that lists (1) what each spouse will do and (2) when the spouse will complete it. Thus, the client assignment sheet becomes a contingency contract whereby each spouse's change is contingent on the other spouse's change. For example, if one partner agrees to pay the bills, the other agrees to clean the house. If one spouse fails to keep his or her end of the bargain, the other spouse is free of his or her obligation. Thus, if the exchange is successful, each spouse is maximizing his or her benefits while minimizing the costs (that is, having the bills paid is more rewarding to one partner than cleaning the house is costly, and vice versa).

Caring days   Another variation of the behavioral exchange procedure is the use of "caring days" (Stuart, 1980). On caring days, each spouse makes a special effort to please the other by engaging in a significantly greater number of caring behaviors than the other spouse expects (Paolino & McCrady, 1978). Stuart asks spouses to request specific behaviors that they would like to receive from one another and to increase the number of requests they make each day. For example, a spouse may request a back rub or a special meal. Spouses often use written notes and poems to communicate messages. The assumption is that caring behaviors will increase positive feelings between the two partners. Spouses also learn the importance of making requests rather than assuming that their partner knows what is wanted.

According to Stuart (1980), requests should be specific and stated in positive terms. Requests should avoid major conflictual issues and focus on "small" behaviors that can be emitted each day. For example, a negative request ("You don't care about me") could be stated in positive and specific terms ("Ask me how my day went"). Responses to this request can be emitted frequently, and it provides opportunities for positive interactions. Stuart emphasizes conflict-free requests on caring days because spouses will not be able to resolve conflict until there has been initial improvement in the relationship: "Therefore, if the couple have been having arguments over when to turn off the television set and go to bed—one wishing to watch the late show through to the end, while the other wishes to retire much earlier—this would not be an acceptable item to include on the list" (Stuart, 1980, p. 201).

The therapist can facilitate the use of caring days by modeling appropriate request lists, which might include such items as "Rub my back," "Go for a walk," "Look at me when we talk," "Call me at work." Stuart suggests that each list contain 18 items. Lists should be open-ended so that spouses can add and delete items as their interests shift. Every item on the list should be clarified and discussed so that both spouses understand the request. Once the list has been finalized, each spouse is asked to perform five behaviors each day. In addition, each spouse is requested to perform the caring behaviors regardless of whether the other reciprocates. This unconditionality is critical because otherwise each spouse would perform a caring behavior only when the partner responds in a positive manner, in which case neither partner would be taking responsibility for the relationship. Therefore, each spouse is asked to "change before the other" (Stuart, 1980). The caring days of intervention are helpful for rebuilding trust, as well as for improving the quality of interaction in the relationship.

Reactivation of symbols   Stuart (1975) also encourages closeness in couples by evoking symbolic events, places, objects, or rituals that hold special meaning to the couple. These symbols help connect the couple to more pleasant times in their marriage. When using this procedure, the therapist will often ask a couple to return to a special place (for example, a restaurant or park) and suggest that each wear special clothing that is attractive to the other partner. In some cases, couples take a second honeymoon or celebrate a special anniversary. Regardless of the activity, the importance lies in the symbolic meaning it holds for the couple.

In cases of couples who lack important symbols, the therapist must help them create new ones. One couple in therapy had not had a courtship or honeymoon. Thus, there were no important symbols to reactivate from the past. The couple planned the honeymoon they had never taken and created new activities, including square dancing and candlelight dinners. The couple also developed new friendships, thereby discovering additional activities that were both pleasurable and incompatible with old conflicts.

These procedures help couples establish "reinforcement reciprocity," whereby rewarding behavior replaces coercive behavior (Nichols, 1984). The structured exchange of caring behaviors provides an opportunity for trust. Trust is established through the daily exchange of caring behaviors. Trust is the foundation for intimacy and long-term commitments to one another.

Limitations   There are three major limitations to reciprocal reinforcement and caring days. First, although exchange of caring behaviors increases positive feelings in spouses, some spouses react negatively because they perceive the behaviors as preplanned rather than spontaneous and therefore discount them. Second, Nichols (1984) notes that the concept of reciprocal reinforcement suggests a symmetrical relationship in which couples play a continuous game of "tit for tat." However, many couples are complementary but unequal in their relationship. These couples do not respond well to reciprocal reinforcement procedures.

Third, many couples complain of the mechanical nature of the exchange procedures. Gurman and Kniskern (1978) agree that because exchange procedures focus only on behavior change rather than expression there is little opportunity for expression of emotions and feelings. Thus in some cases the artificial nature of reciprocal reinforcement procedures inhibits their effectiveness.

Conflict Resolution and Communication

Skills in conflict resolution and problem solving are a set of well-developed strategies for dealing with disagreements when they arise (Stuart, 1980). Problem solving/conflict resolution has proven effective in treating marital conflict (Jacobson & Margolin, 1979). Problem solving/conflict resolution has two distinct phases: problem definition and problem solution. The phase of problem definition is designed to define operationally the critical issue or problem. For example, "You don't come home after work" provides a clearer definition of a problem than "You don't care about me." The important advantage of defining a problem in operational terms is that it is more likely to lead to an effective response to the problem.

Once the issue or problem has been defined operationally, then efforts are directed toward resolving the problem. The resolution phase emphasizes behavior change rather than insight. Couples are given a set of instructions or cues for the acquisition of more effective problem-solving behaviors. To ensure focus on the solution, couples are taught to generate alternative solutions through brainstorming (Goldfried & Davison, 1976). Couples are asked to brainstorm as many solutions as possible, without criticism. In addition to contributing his or her own ideas, each spouse is encouraged to suggest how the ideas of the other spouse can be turned into better ideas and how two or more ideas can be combined into still another idea (Osborn, 1963). When all alternatives have been proposed, then the advantages and disadvantages of each alternative can be considered.

In the process of determining the best course of action, couples are encouraged to (1) predict the likely consequences of each course of action and (2) consider the utility of these consequences in dealing with the problem (D'Zurilla & Goldfried, 1971). Couples are taught that the solution should be equitable and involve some change on the part of each spouse. Couples should also be assisted in selecting behaviors for exchange that require equal time and effort.

Once a solution has been selected, then an agreement should be made that specifies the selected behavior. The agreement should help to verify the behaviors of each spouse and should include the specific conditions of their exchange. It should include who will do what, when, how often, and in what location, the consequences, and what happens when a spouse does not follow through on an exchange (Harrell & Guerney, 1976). The actual exchange of behaviors should be sufficiently reinforcing to ensure maintenance of the desired behaviors.

Problem-solving/conflict-resolution skills are facilitated by communication skills training. Although communication training is common to systems (Satir, 1967), relationship (Rogers, 1951), and psychoanalytic approaches (Ables & Brandsma, 1977), the behavioral approach to communication training is unusual. Jacobson (1981) states:

> First, it utilizes a systematic method of training adapted from other skill training paradigms in behavior therapy. . . . Second, the communication training tends to be change-oriented rather than expression-oriented. That is, whereas most approaches to communication training focus on communication per se

(i.e., the expression and reception of feelings), behavior therapy teaches couples how to communicate in order to facilitate the resolution of conflict. (p. 574)

One of the most effective communication skills programs is the Relationship Enhancement program developed by Bernard Guerney at Pennsylvania State University. This training program is based largely on social learning theory. The Relationship Enhancement program teaches six sets of skills or modes:

1. The express mode, in which individuals learn self-awareness and self-expression
2. The empathic response mode, which focuses on listening and reflective responding skills
3. Mode switching, which focuses on changing modes to improve communication
4. The facilitator mode, in which individuals assist others in developing the first three sets of skills
5. Problem-solving and conflict-resolution skills, which use the first three skills in a six-step process
6. Maintenance and generalization skills, which help individuals to apply the other skills in the home setting

The Relationship Enhancement program has been developed for couples (Conjugal Relationship Enhancement) (Rappaport, 1976) and for parents and adolescents (Parent Adolescent Relationship Development) (Grando & Ginsberg, 1976). Similar programs have been developed for premarital couples (Program for Relationship Improvement by Maximizing Empathy and Self-Disclosure) (Ginsberg & Vogelsong, 1977), children of divorced parents (Children of Divorce) (Guerney & Jordan, 1979), and divorced persons (Avery & Thiessen, 1982). These programs usually last between 10 and 15 weeks, although timetables do vary. Relationship Enhancement is typical of most behavioral communication training programs, which focus on modeling, instruction, practice, and feedback.

Modeling   The first step in helping a couple communicate more effectively is to demonstrate, or model, the appropriate communication skill to be learned. That is, the behavior therapist shows each spouse what the response looks like or how it sounds. Modeling has been effective in teaching clients information-seeking behavior (Krumboltz, Varenhorst, & Thoresen, 1967), reducing feelings of alienation (Warner & Hansen, 1970), and improving attitudes toward drug abuse (Warner, Swisher, & Horan, 1973).

The process of modeling or demonstration often consists of the therapist's providing live or symbolic models, on audiotapes or videotapes, for example, who show in sequential steps the specific behaviors necessary to solve the problem (Hosford & deVisser, 1974). Taped or filmed models have been successfully used for problem solving (Hansen, Pound, & Warner, 1976). Since the models are being used only to demonstrate the desired behaviors, there is no opportunity for interaction between the models and the spouses. The taped models, however, may help to stimulate discussion in the desired direction. Such discussion may prevent rote imitation by the spouses. If new behaviors are to be effective, spouses need to learn a variety of responses for a particular problem situation.

The therapist may also wish to develop models for each of several sessions. For example, the therapist could develop tapes that teach each spouse to (1) listen, (2) express a compliment, (3) express appreciation, (4) ask for help, (5) give feedback, and (6) express affection (Goldstein, 1973). Each skill could be modeled and practiced during a session, if the spouses' skill level allowed. Each modeling sequence could thus represent a closer approximation of the final behavior.

Instruction Once the couple has attended to and understood the model's behavior, the therapist should provide instructions before the couple begins practicing the new behavior. The therapist can focus attention on the relevant and essential aspects of the model's performance. The instruction may be spoken or written by the therapist, or it can be provided through an audiotape or videotape recorder. If each spouse knows how to follow instructions, the therapist need not go through a lengthy shaping process (Gelfand & Hartmann, 1975). The therapist might say, "Watch how I show appreciation to your husband," and then model the appropriate behavior, adding, "Now I want you to show appreciation for something your husband has done recently."

The therapist is now essentially serving as a coach who prompts specific behavior for the couple to try out. Instructions generally are broken down into *do* and *don't do*, and the therapist gives numerous specific examples. Instructing a wife to give feedback to her husband, the therapist might say, "Look directly at your husband and tell him how it makes you feel when he doesn't call to say he won't be home. Don't just accuse him of being inconsiderate."

The therapist might discuss when to give feedback—for example, "when you have time to sit down" or "when you are not so angry"—because a spouse may know what to say but not know when to say it. By going over the demonstration, the therapist can pinpoint behaviors performed by the model spouses and discuss why such behaviors can serve as a cue to the spouse to perform a specific behavior.

Practice Having received instructions on what to say and do, the couple is ready to practice the behavior. Practice is an essential part of the learning process because we learn by doing. By practicing or role-playing the behavior, the couple is able to try out new behavior without the risk of failure. In addition, practice allows each spouse to anticipate difficult encounters and ways of handling them.

Before practicing or role-playing a new behavior, the couple must be prepared. Both partners must accept the idea that practice would be an appropriate way to develop new relationships or problem-solving behaviors. If either spouse shows resistance to this idea, the therapist can provide examples of the usefulness of practice. The crucial point is that each spouse must feel that he or she is not just learning a role that is artificial and unusable. Consequently, the role-playing situations should be as realistic as possible and should include verbal responses with which each spouse feels comfortable.

Feedback   When each partner has practiced the sequence of skills, both must receive feedback on their performances. Knowledge of one's performance provides an incentive for improvement. Information received about poor performance can be as potentially helpful for improving performance as knowledge regarding positive performance.

There are several factors that influence the effects of feedback on learning. Feedback is more effective when it is solicited or agreed upon prior to practice. When a spouse denies or disagrees with feedback from the therapist, then feedback was probably not solicited or agreed upon prior to practice. Feedback should also describe rather than evaluate the spouse's response. The therapist's statements of feedback should avoid judgment or blame. Finally, in some cases the therapist may wish to reinforce a spouse's response and at the same time prompt similar responses. By prompting similar responses, the therapist is encouraging the generalization of the behavior to other situations.

Termination

Two criteria should be used in determining whether to continue therapy. First, the couple's objective should have been met or the presenting problem alleviated. Some couples may report that they feel the problem no longer exists, whereas the data (for instance, observed frequency of behaviors or scores on posttests of marital satisfaction) indicate otherwise. In those cases, therapy should continue until the desired behavior is occurring.

Second, the desired behaviors may be occurring and be recognized by the spouse, but the couple may not be satisfied with the change produced. When this happens, new behaviors need to be targeted that are likely to produce satisfaction in the marriage.

Termination of therapy occurs for various reasons, but the process can be made much easier if the therapist and couple have reached their goals. If the goals have been reached and no new goals have been set, then the therapist and couple can focus on maintenance and generalization of behavior change.

Case Illustration

The following case study will help to illustrate the principles of behavioral parent training and behavioral marital therapy.

> Mrs. Heath came to the clinic seeking assistance for her 7-year-old son, Andy. Andy was the second oldest of five children. At the time of the referral, Mrs. Heath reported that she was seriously depressed over Andy's behavior. She felt that she had no control over him and that she had little support from her husband. Mrs. Heath reported that Mr. Heath worked the night shift at a factory. She said that her husband was distant and critical of her housecleaning and personal appearance. She further stated that he was always negative and never noticed what she did well.
>
> Mrs. Heath's main concern at the first session was her lack of control over Andy. He refused to clean his room, come home on time, or change his

clothes when he came home from school. When Mrs. Heath tried to get him to do something, he would often swear and throw a temper tantrum. In addition, when provoked, he would often strike his siblings or other neighborhood children. After the initial intake session, the therapist requested that Mrs. Heath bring Mr. Heath and Andy to the next session.

The therapist met with Mr. and Mrs. Heath for the first part of the second session. Mr. Heath reported that his wife was "too easy on Andy" and that he had to do most of the disciplining. For her part, Mrs. Heath felt that her husband was "too hard on Andy." She reported that occasionally he would "slap him" and use a belt when necessary. Both parents admitted that there was little cooperation or agreement on how to handle Andy's behavior. Mrs. Heath also reported that when her husband criticized Andy, she felt he was criticizing her, particularly when he commented on Andy's appearance and his "messy room." Thus, Mrs. Heath would often confuse her husband's criticism of Andy with his criticism of her. Although there were other marital problems, that particular matter seemed most related to their problems with Andy. At the end of the second session the therapist made an initial contract with Mr. and Mrs. Heath to work on Andy's failure to comply with their requests. Each parent was then asked to record (1) each time they made a request and (2) each time Andy complied with the request. These baseline records were to be brought to the next session.

Mr. and Mrs. Heath brought their records to the third session. The therapist noted that Mrs. Heath was making an average of 12 requests per day and Mr. Heath was making two requests per day. Andy's mean level of compliances with his mother's requests was 25%, and he complied with both of his father's requests. She also noted that the parents disagreed on Andy's daily responsibilities. In the third session, therefore, the therapist first got Mr. and Mrs. Heath to agree on Andy's daily responsibilities. Second, she asked that the parents make a combined total of no more than five requests per day. Finally, both parents agreed that for each time Andy complied with their requests they would praise him and award him one point. Each point was worth five minutes of TV time or could be counted toward a trip to the Rollerdrome, which required five points. Both parents were encouraged to continue recording requests and Andy's compliance or noncompliance with requests.

At the fourth session Mr. and Mrs. Heath reported that Andy complied with 80% of their requests, of which they were making no more than five each day. The therapist asked them to continue the same procedures for the next two weeks.

Once Andy's behavior had stabilized, the therapist suggested that maintenance of Andy's change in behavior was most likely if both parents agreed to work on their marital issues. Both spouses reported that they received little attention and affection from each other. Their reports were confirmed by responses to the Dyadic Adjustment Scale and the Marital Precounseling Inventory, on which each spouse recorded his or her daily activities. On the basis of the accumulated data, both parties agreed to reciprocally exchange behaviors that were pleasing to each other. Mrs. Heath agreed (1) to cook

Mr. Heath's meals on time and (2) to go bowling with him on Friday nights, and Mr. Heath agreed (1) to hug Mrs. Heath each day and (2) to talk with her at dinner time. Both spouses were to record whether the exchange was made. Once the behaviors were being exchanged satisfactorily, the exchange procedure was applied to other areas of the relationship: sexual, financial, and so on.

A successful treatment program was established when Mr. and Mrs. Heath agreed on Andy's responsibilities and reinforcing consequences for his compliant behavior. Both parents were able to carry out the treatment program with minimal instruction, a unique advantage of behavioral parent training. The self-recording procedure that the parents used to monitor their behavior and the behavior of their son probably made them more aware of their requests and Andy's reaction to their requests. In working together to solve Andy's behavior problems, Mr. and Mrs. Heath set the foundation for working on their marital relationship. Working on the marital relationship made both partners less likely to confuse marital and parental issues. For example, Mrs. Heath no longer felt that when her husband commented on Andy's appearance he was commenting on her. This case study illustrates the direct relationship between behavioral parent training and behavioral marital therapy.

Effectiveness of Behavioral Marital Therapy

There are a number of controlled investigations illustrating the effectiveness of behavioral marital therapy. Five of these investigations evaluated the effectiveness of a behavioral marital therapy treatment package, which included both behavior exchange and communication procedures (Hahlweg, Revenstorf, & Schindler, 1982; Jacobson, 1977, 1978, 1984; Liberman, Levine, Wheeler, Sanders, & Wallace, 1976). Behavioral marital therapy was significantly effective in producing more reinforcing communications and marital satisfaction than were found among waiting list and control groups. Improved communication was maintained at six-month and one-year follow-ups.

Communication training appears to be effective in changing verbal interaction patterns between spouses. However, there have been few controlled studies that examined its effectiveness (O'Leary & Turkowitz, 1978). One investigation (O'Leary & Turkowitz, 1981) found that behavioral exchange procedures were no more effective with one group than communication training was with another, although both groups had more success than a waiting-list control group in decreasing marital problems and improving general communication. No differences were found between the treatment and control groups in changing feelings toward spouse or in communication during conflict-resolution discussions.

Behavioral marital therapy has also demonstrated its effectiveness employing several components of reciprocity counseling, such as contracting, problem solving, and feedback. Mead (1981) reviewed the findings in this area and concluded that contracting was able to increase the couple's reciprocal reinforcement significantly (Rappaport & Harrell, 1972; Tsoi-Hoshmand, 1976; Wieman, Shoulders, & Farr, 1974). Problem solving has proven effective with a limited number of cases (Jacobson, 1979). The use of feedback alone has had mixed results and in some cases may have a negative effect (Jacobson, 1979).

In a more recent investigation, Baucom (1982) studied a behavioral marital therapy treatment program that examined problem solving and contingency contracting in isolation. A waiting-list group of families served as a control group. The results indicated that the treatment groups showed greater improvement than the control group; however, there were no significant differences between contracting and problem solving.

Whereas these investigations examined the effects of behavioral marital therapy *between* spouses, other investigations have examined the effects of behavioral marital therapy *within* spouses (Gurman & Kniskern, 1978). Margolin and Weiss (1978) found that a couple's communication was more effective when each spouse altered his or her cognitions about the other. Barlow, O'Brien, and Last (1984) found that cognitive restructuring and self-initiated exposure were more effective in decreasing agoraphobia in women treated with their spouses than in women treated without their spouses. However, practice between sessions may have affected the outcome of this study.

The abovementioned studies have reported on the statistical significance of behavioral marital therapy, but there has been little discussion of its clinical significance. One investigation (Jacobson, Follette, Revenstorf, Hahlweg, Baucom, & Margolin, 1984) reanalyzed the data from four previous investigations of behavioral marital therapy (Baucom, 1982; Hahlweg, Revenstorf, & Schindler, 1982; Jacobson, 1984; Margolin & Weiss, 1978). Jacobson et al. (1984) classified 148 couples from these four studies into categories of improved, unimproved, and deteriorated. The results indicated that more than half the couples improved, ranging from 39.4% in one investigation to 72.1% in another, and that deterioration occurred infrequently. In 40% of the improved couples there was a positive change in marital satisfaction, and slightly more than one-third changed from distressed to nondistressed by the end of therapy. Six percent of the couples maintained their improvement at six-month follow-up; improvement was rare for those couples that did not receive treatment.

More recently, Jacobson (in press) reports that conflict-solving interventions (for example, communication and problem solving) are effective if both spouses agree they need to change for things to improve. Otherwise, acceptance interventions are the preferred method of treatment. Acceptance interventions require spouses to view the problem as something they must face together rather than as something one does to the other. Acceptance therapy helps each spouse to express pain without blaming the other. Jacobson combines conflict-oriented interventions with acceptance. Treatment averages 20 sessions. Traditional therapy is effective for two-thirds of couples, however 30% of those relapse into old patterns. Only 5%, however, of the couples in Jacobson's two-year pilot project have relapsed.

Conflict management and communication skills can also be taught in a group format. Markman, Renick, Floyd, Stanley, and Clemons (1993) taught 33 couples effective communication and conflict management skills through the Prevention and Relationship Enhancement Program (PREP). The PREP program utilized techniques of cognitive-behavioral marital therapy (Jacobson & Margolin, 1979) and communication-oriented marital enhancement programs (Guerney, 1977). Couples were taught active listening and expressive speaking skills as well as how to problem solve from problem discussion interactions. Training included instruction, videotape feedback, and role-playing. At the five-year follow-up, the behavioral intervention compared with the control had higher levels of positive and lower levels of negative communication skills, and lower levels of marital violence. Programs such as PREP offer couples the opportunity to manage conflicts before serious problems arise.

In summary, behavioral marital therapy appears to be an effective approach. However, BMT may not work for all couples. Bray and Jouriles (1995) state the following:

> Although the general efficacy of marital therapy, particularly BMT, has been established, marital therapy does not work for all couples. This may be due to a variety of factors, including different goals of therapy, that is, some people may enter therapy to get out of the relationship, as well as the possibility that the versions of marital therapy that have been empirically validated may not be of sufficient potency and duration to be effective. Prominent marital therapy researchers suggest that booster sessions may be necessary to maintain the gains established during the initial treatments (Jacobson & Addis, 1993). A reasonable question is whether it is realistic to expect that one round of therapy is enough to last a lifetime, particularly for some individuals who may bring significant and unresolved psychological and family-of-origin issues into their marriages. It is clear from longitudinal studies of other mental disorders, for example, depression, and physical disorders, for example, hypertension, that there are repeated relapses and that monitoring and ongoing treatment may be necessary through the life cycle. A family life cycle approach may be a useful framework within which to conceptualize the long-term process of marital relations.

More investigations are warranted that assess levels of distress and compatibility among couples (Jacobson & Addis, 1993), diversity of couples (Bray & Hetherington, 1993), and external validity questions to increase the likelihood that outcome research is relevant to clinical practice (Bray & Jouriles, 1995).

References

Ables, B. S., & Brandsma, J. M. (1977). *Therapy for couples*. San Francisco: Jossey-Bass.

Avery, A. W., & Thiessen, J. D. (1982). Communication skills training for divorces. *Journal of Counseling Psychology, 29,* 203–205.

Bandura A. (1969). *Principles of behavior modification*. New York: Holt, Rinehart & Winston.

Bandura, A. (1974). *Social learning theory*. Englewood Cliffs, NJ: Prentice Hall.

Barlow, D., O'Brien, G., & Last, C. (1984). Couples treatment of agoraphobia. *Behavior Therapy, 15,* 41–58.

Baucom, D. H. (1982). A comparison of behavioral contracting and problem-solving/ communications training in behavioral marital therapy. *Behavior Therapy, 13,* 162–174.

Berkowitz, B. P., & Graziano, A. M. (1972). Training parents as behavior therapists: A review. *Behavior Research and Therapy, 10,* 297–317.

Beutler, L. E. (1971). Attitude similarity in marital therapy. *Journal of Consulting and Clinical Psychology, 37,* 298–301.

Birchler, G. R., & Spinks, S. H. (1980). Behavioral systems marital and family therapy integration and clinical application. *American Journal of Family Therapy, 8,* 6–28.

Blechman, E. A. (1980). Family problem-solving training. *American Journal of Family Therapy, 8,* 3–21.

Blechman, E. A. (1981). Toward comprehensive behavioral family intervention: An algorithm for matching families and interactions. *Behavior Modification, 5,* 221–236.

Bray, J. H., & Hetherington, E. M. (1993). Families in transition: Introduction and overview. *Journal of Family Psychology, 7,* 3–8.

Bray, J. H., & Jouriles, E. N. (1995). Treatment of marital conflict and prevention of divorce. *Journal of Marital and Family Therapy, 21,* 461–473.

Ciminero, A. R., Calhoun, K. S., & Adams, H. E. (1977). *Handbook of behavioral assessment.* New York: Wiley.

Clark, H. B., Greene, B. F., MacRae, J. W., McNees, M. P., Davis, J. L., & Risley, T. R. (1977). A parent advice package for family shopping trips: Development and evaluation. *Journal of Applied Behavior Analysis, 10,* 605–624.

D'Zurilla, T. J., & Goldfried, M. R. (1971). Problem-solving and behavior modification. *Journal of American Psychology, 78,* 107–126.

Embry, L. H., Kelly, M. L., Jackson, E., & Baer, D. M. (1979). *Group parent training: An analysis of generalization from classroom to home.* Research brief, Kansas Research Institute.

Evans, I. M., & Nelson, R. O. (1977). Assessment of child behavior problems. In A. R. Ciminero, K. S. Calhoun, & H. E. Adams (Eds.), *Handbook of behavioral assessment* (pp. 603–681). New York: Wiley.

Forehand, R., Sturgis, E. T., McMahon, R. J., Aguar, D., Green, K., Wells, K. C., & Breiner, J. (1979). Parent behavioral training to modify child noncompliance: Treatment generalization across time and from home to school. *Behavioral Modification, 3,* 3–25.

Foster, S. L., & Hoier, T. S. (1982). Behavioral and systems family therapies: A comparison of theoretical assumptions. *American Journal of Family Therapy, 10,* 13–22.

Gelfand, D. M., & Hartmann, D. P. (1975). *Child behavior: Analysis and therapy.* Elmsford, NJ: Pergamon Press.

Ginsberg, B., & Vogelsong, E. L. (1977). Premarital relationship improvement by maximizing empathy and self-disclosure: The PRIMES program. In B. G. Guerney, Jr. (Ed.), *Relationship enhancement.* San Francisco: Jossey-Bass.

Goldfried, M. R., & Davison, G. C. (1976). *Clinical behaviors therapy.* New York: Holt, Rinehart & Winston.

Goldfried, M. R., & Sprafkin, J. (1974). *Behavioral personality assessment.* Morristown, NJ: General Learning Press.

Goldstein, A. P. (1973). *Structured learning therapy.* New York: Academic Press.

Gordon, S. B., & Davidson, N. (1981). Behavior parent training. In A. S. Gurman & D. P. Kniskern (Eds.), *Handbook of family therapy.* New York: Brunner/Mazel.

Grando, R., & Ginsberg, B. G. (1976). Communication in the father-son relationship: The parent adolescent relationship development program. *The Family Coordinator, 4,* 465–473.

Griest, P. L., & Wells, K. C. (1983). Behavioral family therapy with conduct disorders in children. *Behavior Therapy, 14,* 37–53.

Guerney, B. G. (1977). *Relationship enhancement.* San Francisco: Jossey-Bass.

Guerney, L., & Jordan, L. (1979). Children of divorce—a community support group. *Journal of Divorce, 2*(2), 283–294.

Gurman, A. S., & Kniskern, D. P. (1978). Research on marital and family therapy: Progress, perspective, and prospect. In S. L. Garfield & A. E. Bergin (Eds.), *Handbook of psychotherapy and behavior change: An empirical analysis* (2nd ed.). New York: Wiley.

Gurman, A. S., & Kniskern, D. P. (Eds.). (1981). *Handbook of family therapy.* New York: Brunner/Mazel.

Gurman, A. S., & Knudson, R. M. (1978). Behavioral marriage therapy: I. A psychodynamic systems analysis and critique. *Family Process, 17,* 121–138.

Hackney, H., & Nye, S. (1973). *Counseling strategies and objectives.* Englewood Cliffs, NJ: Prentice Hall.

Hahlweg, K., Revenstorf, D., & Schindler, L. (1982). Treatment of marital distress: Comparing formats and modalities. *Advances in Behavior Research and Therapy, 4,* 57–74.

Haley, J. (1976). *Problem-solving therapy.* San Francisco: Jossey-Bass.

Hansen, J. C., Pound, R. E., & Warner, R. W. (1976). Use of modeling procedures. *Personnel and Guidance Journal, 54,* 242–245.

Harrell, J., & Guerney, B. (1976). Training married couples in conflict negotiation skills. In D. H. L. Olson (Ed.), *Treating relationships.* Lake Mills, IA: Graphic.

Herbert, E. W., Pinkston, E. M., Hayden, M. L., Sajwaj, T. E., Pinkston, J., Cardva, G., & Jackson, D. (1973). Adverse effects of differential parental attention. *Journal of Applied Behavior Analysis, 6,* 15–30.

Homans, G. C. (1961). *Social behavior: Its elementary forms.* New York: Harcourt Brace Jovanovich.

Homme, L., Csanyi, A. P., Gonzales, M. A., & Rechs, J. R. (1974). *How to use contingency contracting in the classroom.* Champaign, IL: Research Press.

Hops, H., Wills, T. A., Patterson, G. R., & Weiss, R. L. (1972). *Marital interaction coding system.* Eugene: University of Oregon and Oregon Research.

Hosford, R. E., & deVisser, C. A. (1974). *Behavioral counseling: An introduction.* Washington, DC: American Personnel and Guidance Press.

Hudson, A. M. (1982). Training parents of developmentally handicapped children: A component analysis. *Behavior Therapy, 13,* 325–333.

Israel, A. C., Stolmaker, L., & Andrian, C. A. G. (1985). The effects of training parents in general child management skills on a behavioral weight loss program for children. *Behavior Therapy, 16,* 169–180.

Jacob, T. (1976). Assessment of marital dysfunction. In M. Hensen & A. S. Bellack (Eds.), *Behavioral assessment: A practical handbook.* New York: Pergamon Press.

Jacobson, N. S. (in press). Couple therapy: Integrating change and acceptance. *Behavior Therapy.*

Jacobson, N. S. (1977). Problem solving and contingency contracting in the treatment of marital discord. *Journal of Consulting and Clinical Psychology, 45,* 92–100.

Jacobson, N. S. (1978). Specific and nonspecific factors in the effectiveness of a behavioral approach to the treatment of marital discord. *Journal of Consulting and Clinical Psychology, 46,* 442–452.

Jacobson, N. S. (1979). Increasing positive behavior in severely distressed marital relationships: The effects of problem-solving training. *Behavior Therapy, 10,* 311–326.

Jacobson, N. S. (1981). Behavioral marital therapy. In A. S. Gurman & D. P. Kniskern (Eds.), *Handbook of family therapy.* New York: Brunner/Mazel.

Jacobson, N. S. (1984). A component analysis of behavioral marital therapy: The relative effectiveness of behavior exchange and communication/problem-solving training. *Journal of Consulting and Clinical Psychology, 52*, 295–305.

Jacobson, N. S., & Addis, M. E. (1993). Research on couples and couple therapy: What do we know? Where are we going? *Journal of Consulting and Clinical Psychology, 61*, 85–93.

Jacobson, N., Follette, W., Revenstorf, D., Hahlweg, K., Baucom, D., & Margolin, G. (1984). Variability in outcome and clinical significance of behavioral marital therapy: A reanalysis of outcome data. *Journal of Consulting and Clinical Psychology, 52*(4), 497–504.

Jacobson, N. S., & Margolin, G. (1979). *Marital therapy: Strategies based on social learning and behavior exchange principles.* New York: Brunner/Mazel.

Jacobson, N. S., & Weiss, R. L. (1978). Behavioral marriage therapy: III. The contents of Gurman et al. may be hazardous to our health. *Family Process, 17*, 149–164.

Johnson, C. A., & Katz, R. C. (1973). Using parents as change agents for their children: A review. *Journal of Child Psychology and Psychiatry, 14*, 181–200.

Karoly, P., & Rosenthal, M. (1977). Training parents in behavior modification: Effects on perceptions of family interaction and deviant behaviors. *Behavior Therapy, 8*, 406–410.

Krumboltz, J. D., Varenhorst, B. B., & Thoresen, C. E. (1967). Nonverbal factors in effectiveness of models in counseling. *Journal of Counseling Psychology, 14*, 412–418.

Levant, R. F. (1980). A classification of the field of family therapy: A review of prior attempts and a new paradigmatic model. *American Journal of Family Therapy, 8*, 3–16.

Liberman, R. P., Levine, J., Wheeler, E., Sanders, N., & Wallace, C. (1976). *Experimental evaluation of marital group therapy: Behavioral versus interaction-insight formats.* Acta Psychiatrica Scandinavia (supplement).

Locke, H., & Wallace, K. (1959). Short marital-adjustment and prediction tests: The reliability and validity. *Marriage and Family Living, 21*, 251–255.

Mace, D. R. (1979). Marriage and family enrichment—a new field. *Family Coordinator, 28*, 409–419.

Margolin, G., & Weiss, R. L. (1978). A comparative evaluation of therapeutic components associated with behavioral marital treatment. *Journal of Consulting and Clinical Psychology, 46*, 1476–1486.

Markman, H. J., Renick, M. J., Floyd, F. J., Stanley, S. M., & Clemons, M. (1993). Preventing marital distress through communication and conflict management training: A 4 and 5 year follow up. *Journal of Consulting and Clinical Psychology, 6*, 70–77.

Mead, D. E. (1981). Reciprocity counseling: Practice and research. *Journal of Marital and Family Therapy, 7*, 189–200.

Meichenbaum, D. H. (1977). *Cognitive behavior modification.* New York: Plenum.

Mindell, C., & Budd, K. S. (1977, September). *Issues in the generalization of parent training across settings.* Paper presented at the 85th Annual Convention of the American Psychological Association, San Francisco.

Moreland, J. R., Schwebel, A. I., Beck, S., & Wells, R. (1982). Parents as therapists: A review of behavior therapy parent training literature—1975–1981. *Behavior Modification, 6*, 250–276.

Nichols, M. P. (1984). *Family therapy: Concepts and methods.* New York: Gardner Press.

O'Dell, S. (1974). Training parents in behavior modification: A review. *Psychological Bulletin, 81*, 418–433.

O'Dell, S. L. (1978, November). *A comparison and evaluation of methods for producing be-*

havior change in parents. Paper presented at the Association for the Advancement of Behavior Therapy, Chicago.

O'Dell, S. L., Krug, W. W., Patterson, J. N., & Faustman, W. O. (1980). An assessment of methods for training parents in the use of time out. *Journal of Behavior Therapy and Experimental Psychiatry, 11,* 21–25.

O'Dell, S. L., Mahoney, N. D., Horton, W. G., & Turner, P. E. (1979). Media-assisted parent training: Alternative models. *Behavior Therapy, 10,* 103–110.

O'Dell, S., O'Quin, J., Alford, B., O'Briant, A., Bradlyn, J., & Giebenhain, J. (1982). Predicting the acquisition of parenting skills via four training methods. *Behavior Therapy, 13,* 194–208.

O'Leary, K. D., & Turkowitz, H. (1978). The treatment of marital disorders from a behavioral perspective. In T. J. Paolino, Jr., & B. S. McCrady (Eds.), *Marriage and marital therapy: Psychoanalytic, behavioral, and systems theory perspectives.* New York: Brunner/Mazel.

O'Leary, K. D., & Turkowitz, H. (1981). A comparative outcome study of behavioral marital therapy and communication therapy. *Journal of Marital and Family Therapy, 7,* 159–169.

Olson, D. H. (1970). Marital and family therapy: Integrative review and critique. *Journal of Marriage and the Family, 33,* 501–538.

Osborn, A. F. (1963). *Applied imagination* (3rd ed.). New York: Scribner's.

Paolino, T., & McCrady, B. (1978). *Marriage and marital therapy.* New York: Brunner/Mazel.

Patterson, G. R. (1974). Interventions for boys with conduct problems: Multiple settings, treatments, and criteria. *Journal of Consulting and Clinical Psychology, 42,* 471–481.

Patterson, G. R. (1976). Some procedures for assessing changes in marital interaction patterns. *Oregon Research Institute Bulletin, 16*(7).

Patterson, G. R., Chamberline, P., & Reid, J. B. (1982). A comparative evaluation of a parent training program. *Behavior Therapy, 13,* 638–650.

Patterson, G. R., Cobb, J. A., & Ray, R. S. (1972). A social engineering technology for retraining the families of aggressive boys. In H. E. Adams & I. P. Unikel (Eds.), *Issues and trends in behavior therapy.* Springfield, IL: Charles C Thomas.

Patterson, G. R., & Hops, H. (1972). Coercion, a game for two: Intervention techniques for marital conflict. In K. E. Ulrich & P. Mountjoy (Eds.), *The experimental analysis of social behavior.* New York: Appleton.

Patterson, G. R., Hops, H., & Weiss, R. L. (1974). A social learning approach to reducing rates of marital conflict. In R. Stuart, R. Liberman, & S. Wilder (Eds.), *Advances in behavior therapy.* New York: Academic Press.

Patterson, G. R., & Reid, J. B. (1970). Reciprocity and coercion: Two facets of social systems. In C. Neuringer & J. L. Michael (Eds.), *Behavior modification in clinical psychology.* New York: Appleton.

Peed, S., Roberts, M., & Forehand, R. (1977). Evaluation of the effectiveness of a standardized parent training program in altering the interaction of mothers and their noncompliant children. *Behavior Modification, 1,* 323–350.

Rabin, C., Blechman, E. A., Kahn, D., & Carel, C. A. (1985). Refocusing from child to marital problems using the marriage contract game. *Journal of Marital and Family Therapy, 11,* 75–85.

Rappaport, A. F. (1976). Conjugal relationship enhancement program. In D. H. L. Olson (Ed.), *Treating relationships.* Lake Mills, IA: Graphic.

Rappaport, A. F., & Harrell, J. (1972). A behavioral-exchange model for marital counseling. *The Family Coordinator, 21,* 203–212.

Reisinger, J. J., Frangia, G. W., & Hoffman, E. H. (1976). Toddler management training: Generalization and marital status. *Journal of Behavior Therapy and Experiential Psychiatry, 7*, 335–340.

Rogers, C. R. (1951). *Client-centered therapy.* Boston: Houghton Mifflin.

Sanders, M., & Dadds, M. (1982). The effects of planned activities and child management procedures in parent training: An analysis of setting generality. *Behavior Therapy, 13*, 452–461.

Sanders, M. R., & James, J. E. (1983). The modification of parent behaviors: A review of generalization and maintenance. *Behavior Modification, 7*, 3–27.

Satir, V. (1967). Conjoint family therapy. Palo Alto, CA: Science and Behavior Books.

Spanier, G. B. (1976). Measuring dyadic adjustment: New scales for assessing the quality of marriage and similar dyads. *Journal of Marriage and the Family, 38*, 15–28.

Steinglass, P. (1978). Conceptualization of marriage from a systems theory perspective. In T. J. Paolino, Jr., & B. S. McCrady (Eds.), *Marriage and marital therapy: Psychoanalytic, behavioral, and systems theory perspectives.* New York: Brunner/Mazel.

Stokes, T., & Baer, D. (1977). An implicit technology of generalization. *Journal of Applied Behavior Analysis, 15*, 349–367.

Strain, P., Steele, P., Ellis, T., & Timm, M. (1982). Long-term effects of oppositional child treatment with mothers as therapists and therapist trainers. *Journal of Applied Behavior Analysis, 15*, 163–169.

Stuart, R. B. (1969). Operant-interpersonal treatment for marital discord. *Journal of Consulting and Clinical Psychology, 33*, 675–682.

Stuart, R. B. (1971). Behavioral contracting within the families of delinquents. *Journal of Behavioral Therapy and Experimental Psychiatry, 2*, 1–11.

Stuart, R. B. (1975). Behavioral remedies for marital ills: A guide to the use of operant-interpersonal techniques. In A. S. Gurman & D. G. Rice (Eds.), *Couples in conflict: New directions in marital therapy.* New York: Aronson.

Stuart, R. B. (1976). Operant interpersonal treatment for marital discord. In D. H. L. Olson (Ed.), *Treating relationships.* Lake Mills, IA: Graphic.

Stuart, R. B. (1980). *Helping couples change: A social learning approach for marital therapy.* New York: Guilford Press.

Stuart, R. B., & Stuart, F. (1972). *Marital pre-counseling inventory.* Champaign, IL: Research Press.

Stumphauser, J. S. (1976). Elimination of stealing by self-reinforcement of alternative behavior and family contracting. *Journal of Behavior Therapy & Experimental Psychiatry, 7*, 265–268.

Thibaut, J. W., & Kelly, H. H. (1959). *The social psychology of groups.* New York: Wiley.

Tsoi-Hoshmand, L. (1976). Marital therapy: An integrative behavioral-learning model. *Journal of Marriage and Family Counseling, 2*(2), 179–191.

Wahler, R. G. (1980). The insular mother: Her problems in parent-child treatment. *Journal of Applied Analysis, 13*, 207–219.

Warner, R. W., & Hansen, J. C. (1970). Verbal-reinforcement and model-reinforcement group counseling with alienated students. *Journal of Counseling Psychology, 17*, 168–172.

Warner, R. W., Swisher, J. D., & Horan, J. J. (1973). Drug abuse prevention: A behavioral approach. *NAASP Bulletin, 372*, 49–54.

Watzlawick, P., Weakland, J., & Fisch, R. (1974). *Change: Principles and problem resolution.* New York: Norton.

Weiss, R. L. (1978). The conceptualization of marriage and marriage disorders from a behavioral perspective. In T. J. Paolino, Jr., & B. S. McCrady (Eds.), *Marriage and marital therapy: Psychoanalytic, behavioral, and systems theory perspectives.* New York: Brunner/Mazel.

Weiss, R. L., Hops, H., & Patterson, G. R. (1973). A framework for conceptualizing marital conflict, technology for altering it, some data for evaluating it. In L. A. Hamerlynck, L. C. Handy, & E. J. Mash (Eds.), *Behavior change: Methodology, concepts and practice.* Champaign, IL: Research Press.

Weiss, R. L., & Perry, B. A. (1979). *Assessment and treatment of marital dysfunction.* Eugene: Oregon Marital Studies Program.

Wells, K. C. (1981). Assessment of children in outpatient settings. In M. Hersen & A. S. Bellack (Eds.), *Behavioral assessment: A practical handbook.* New York: Pergamon Press.

Wieman, R. J., Shoulders, D. K., & Farr, J. H. (1974). Reciprocal reinforcement in marital therapy. *Behavior Therapy & Experimental Psychiatry, 5,* 291–295.

Wills, T. A., Weiss, R. L., & Patterson, G. R. (1974). A behavioral analysis of the determinants of marital satisfaction. *Journal of Consulting and Clinical Psychology, 42,* 802–811.

Wulbert, M., Barach, R., Perry, M., Straughan, J., Sulzbacher, S., Turner, K., & Wiltz, N. (1974). The generalization of newly acquired behaviors by parents and child across three different settings: A study of an autistic child. *Journal of Abnormal Child Psychology, 2,* 87–98.

Spouse Observation Checklist

Spouse initials
Male _____   Female _____

Date	1		2		3		4		5		6		7	
	p	d	p	d	p	d	p	d	p	d	p	d	p	d

AFFECTION

We held each other ....
We took a shower or bath together ....
We warmed each other in bed ....
We tickled and rough-housed together ....
We held hands ....
Spouse hugged or kissed me ....
Spouse gave me a massage, rubbed lotion on my back, etc. ....
Spouse cuddled close to me in bed ....
Spouse warmed my cold feet ....
Spouse greeted me affectionately when I came home ......
Spouse touched me affectionately ....

Affection total

COMPANIONSHIP

We listened to music on the radio or stereo ....
We sat and read together ....
We watched TV (1/2 hour or more) ....
We read aloud to each other ....
We worked together on decorating our home ....
We played musical instruments together (sang together) ....
We read the newspaper together ....
We gardened ....
We played with our pets ....

Companionship subtotal

COMPANIONSHIP *(continued)*

	1		2		3		4		5		6		7	
	p	d	p	d	p	d	p	d	p	d	p	d	p	d
We baked bread or pastries														
We played chess, Monopoly, Scrabble, etc. (any board game)														
We played cards														
We got high on drugs or alcohol														
We hunted for interesting things to photograph														
We took a walk														
We went for a ride														
We did exercises together														
We sunbathed together														
We played volleyball, basketball, etc. together														
We went bowling, skating, or played pool														
We went swimming or diving														
We played Frisbee														
We attended a sporting event														
We went jogging or bicycle riding														
We played golf, tennis, badminton, or ping-pong														
We went shopping for new clothes														
We went to a dance or party														
We had a fancy "candlelight" dinner at home														
We went out for a nice meal or dinner														
We went out for coffee, soda, or ice cream														
We ate at an inexpensive restaurant or drive-in														
We went to a museum														
We went to a bar or tavern														
We went to a movie (play, concert, ballet, etc.)														
We went to a club or organizational meeting														
We worked on a community project														
We went to a class or lecture														
Companionship subtotal														

COMPANIONSHIP (continued)

	1		2		3		4		5		6		7	
	p	d	p	d	p	d	p	d	p	d	p	d	p	d
We went to the library together.														
We went folk dancing or square dancing														
We worked together on an art or craft project														
We discussed or worked on a project that one of us is responsible for														
We worked together on a hobby (stamp collecting, etc.)														
We participated in religious activities														
We went to a church service														
We took a nap together														
We exchanged a gift														
We watched the sunset (sunrise)														
We laughed together														
We had a pillow fight														
Companionship total														

CONSIDERATION

	1		2		3		4		5		6		7	
	p	d	p	d	p	d	p	d	p	d	p	d	p	d
We talked affectionately														
Spouse thanked me for doing something														
Spouse said he/she loved me														
Spouse asked me how my day was														
Spouse complimented me on my appearance														
Spouse said he/she likes me														
Spouse acted patient when I was cross														
Spouse showed he/she was glad to see me														
Spouse listened sympathetically to my problems														
Spouse skillfully calmed me down when I was being unreasonable														
Consideration subtotal														

CONSIDERATION (*continued*)

	1		2		3		4		5		6		7	
	p	d	p	d	p	d	p	d	p	d	p	d	p	d
Spouse agreed strongly with something I said														
Spouse complimented something I made														
Spouse talked to me when I asked for some attention														
Spouse tried to cheer me up														
Spouse apologized to me														
Spouse forgave me for something														
Spouse expressed approval of me or something I did														
Spouse was tolerant when I made a mistake														
Spouse comforted me when I was upset														
Spouse complied in a friendly manner to a request														
Spouse called to tell me where he/she was														
Spouse called me just to say hello														
Spouse waved goodbye to me when I left and/or wished me a good day														
Spouse smiled at me or laughed with me														
Spouse laughed at my jokes														
Spouse answered my questions with respect														
Spouse was tolerant of me when I was late														
Spouse was tolerant of my friends														
Spouse was careful not to wake me when I was asleep														
Spouse met me on time														
Spouse answered the phone while I was busy														
Spouse cut my hair														
Spouse patched my clothes														
Spouse packed a lunch for me														
Spouse prepared a favorite food or dessert														
Spouse got up and made breakfast for me														
Spouse brought me a cup of coffee, tea, etc.														
Spouse prepared a snack for me														
Consideration subtotal														

CONSIDERATION (*continued*)

	1		2		3		4		5		6		7	
	p	d	p	d	p	d	p	d	p	d	p	d	p	d
Spouse prepared breakfast-in-bed														
Spouse prepared a food or dessert I especially like														
Spouse bought some food item especially for me														
Spouse did some of "my" chores so I could finish a rush job														
Spouse asked me if I needed anything at the store														
Spouse brought me home something to read														
Spouse went to bed when I did														
Spouse showed interest in my hobby														
Spouse told me he/she sees my work as important														
Spouse said something unkind to me														
Spouse failed to call when he/she was coming home late														
Spouse talked while I was trying to sleep														
Spouse woke me up when I was sleeping														
Spouse fell asleep while I was talking to him/her														
Spouse wouldn't accept my apology														
Spouse was sarcastic with me														
Spouse commanded me to do something														
Spouse lectured me rather than listened to me														
Spouse ignored me when I asked for some attention														
Spouse told me how to do something I already know how to do														
Spouse did something for me instead of showing me how														
Spouse said my jokes are stupid														
Spouse did not respect my opinion														
Spouse disapproved of me or something I did														
Spouse refused my apology														
Spouse did not give me the attention I asked for														
Consideration subtotal														

CONSIDERATION (continued)

	1 p	1 d	2 p	2 d	3 p	3 d	4 p	4 d	5 p	5 d	6 p	6 d	7 p	7 d
Spouse did not pay attention when I was talking about something that interests me: he/she looked away or had a bored expression														
Spouse complained about something I did														
Spouse criticized me in front of others														
Spouse criticized something I made														
Spouse criticized my body														
Spouse called me just to complain about something I did														
Spouse came home late when I needed the car														
Spouse was late when I went to pick him/her up														
Spouse bothered me when I was concentrating														
Spouse bothered me when I was on the phone														
Spouse mimicked me														
Spouse did not come to a meal when asked														
Spouse read the paper (or watched TV) rather than attending to me														
Spouse criticized me for smoking														
Spouse insisted we go somewhere I didn't want to go														
Spouse showed no interest in my hobby														
Consideration total														

SEX

	1 p	1 d	2 p	2 d	3 p	3 d	4 p	4 d	5 p	5 d	6 p	6 d	7 p	7 d
We engaged in sexual intercourse														
We enjoyed petting and other sex play														
We hugged and kissed passionately														
We tried some new sexual behaviors that we liked														
We had oral-genital sex														
We both were sexually responsive to each other														
We were both sexually satisfied														
Sex subtotal														

SEX (*continued*)

	1		2		3		4		5		6		7	
	p	d	p	d	p	d	p	d	p	d	p	d	p	d
Spouse admired my body														
Spouse helped me to reach orgasm														
Spouse set mood for sexual experience (music, wine, candles)														
Spouse wrote something that was provocative, enticing, etc. for me														
Spouse caressed me with hands														
Spouse caressed me with mouth														
Spouse wore clothing I found sexually stimulating														
Spouse read something pornographic aloud														
Spouse engaged in other sexual behaviors that I especially like														
Spouse let me know that he/she enjoyed intercourse with me														
Spouse initiated sexual advances														
Spouse was pleasantly responsive to my sexual advances														
Spouse petted me														
Spouse participated in a sexual fantasy														
Spouse presented him/herself in the nude														
Spouse was uncommunicative during sexual activity														
Spouse left me frustrated at end of sexual session														
Spouse rushed into intercourse without foreplay														
Spouse complained about my sexual behaviors														
Spouse rejected my sexual advances														
Spouse turned off in the middle of making love														
Spouse fell asleep immediately after making love														
Spouse insisted on sexual practices that I dislike														
Spouse hurt me or made me uncomfortable during sexual activities														
Sex subtotal														

	1		2		3		4		5		6		7	
	p	d	p	d	p	d	p	d	p	d	p	d	p	d

SEX (*continued*)

Sex total

COMMUNICATION PROCESS

We talked about something troubling, outside of our relationship ....

We were able to work successfully on a problem ....

We had a good talk about our relationship ....

We agreed about something ....

We talked about personal feelings ....

We talked about personal day-to-day happenings ....

We had a constructive conversation about family management ....

We talked about a vacation ....

We had an intellectual, philosophical, or political discussion ....

We talked about a show we had seen ....

We had a humorous conversation ....

Spouse asked about my feelings ....

Spouse expressed feelings and thoughts to me ....

Spouse confided in me ....

Spouse consulted me about an important decision ....

Spouse asked for my opinion ....

Spouse showed particular interest in what I said by agreeing or asking relevant questions ....

Spouse helped in planning an outing or social event ....

Communication subtotal

	1		2		3		4		5		6		7	
	p	*d*	*p*	*d*	*p*	*d*	*p*	*d*	*p*	*d*	*p*	*d*	*p*	*d*

COMMUNICATION PROCESS *(continued)*

Spouse suggested something fun or interesting that we could do for the evening ....

Spouse refused to make a decision on a significant issue ....

Spouse refused to talk about a problem we share ....

Spouse brought up bad times from the past ....

Spouse dominated the conversation ....

Spouse interrupted me ....

Spouse offered unsolicited advice ....

Spouse responded "I don't know" without considering the question ....

Spouse disagreed harshly with something I said ....

Spouse didn't want to talk about his/her problem with me ....

Communication total

COUPLING ACTIVITIES

Spouse got angry and wouldn't tell me why ....

Spouse refused to listen to my feelings ....

Spouse made an important decision without consulting me ....

Spouse complained ....

Spouse read a book or watched TV and wouldn't talk to me ....

Spouse wouldn't talk to me about an outing or social event ....

Coupling subtotal

COUPLING ACTIVITIES (continued)	1		2		3		4		5		6		7	
	p	d	p	d	p	d	p	d	p	d	p	d	p	d
Spouse planned an outing or social event without consulting me														
Spouse refused to help in planning an outing or social event														
Spouse wouldn't talk to me about his/her special interest														
We went out for an evening with friends														
We invited a couple of our friends over to visit														
We visited with relatives														
We met new people														
We wrote letters to friends or relatives														
We telephoned friends or relatives														
We went to a party														
We entertained a business/work associate														
We made plans for entertaining friends, associates, relatives, etc.														
We talked about friends or relatives														
Spouse arranged to get together with relatives or in-laws														
Spouse invited friends over to visit														
Spouse invited company for dinner														
Spouse arranged for us to go to a party														
Spouse made a good impression on my friends														
Spouse was unpleasant to people we had over for company														
Spouse went to bed early while we had company														
Spouse criticized my parents or relatives														
Spouse made a bad impression on my friends														
Spouse embarrassed me in front of friends or relatives														
Coupling total														

CHILD CARE AND PARENTING

	1		2		3		4		5		6		7	
	p	d	p	d	p	d	p	d	p	d	p	d	p	d
We discussed the children														
We took the children on a family outing														
We cared for child when sick														
We played with the children														
We disciplined the children														
Spouse read a story to the children														
Spouse played with the children														
Spouse disciplined children appropriately														
Spouse answered child's question														
Spouse took the children to school or elsewhere														
Spouse taught the children something														
Spouse helped child with homework														
Spouse gave the children responsibility for a job														
Spouse helped resolve a fight between the children														
Spouse comforted a baby, made him/her stop crying														
Spouse watched the children for a few minutes while I was busy														
Spouse took care of children while I did some work														
Spouse helped feed the children														
Spouse gave child a bath														
Spouse got up in the night to take care of child														
Spouse changed baby's diapers														
Spouse helped put the children to bed														
Spouse arranged for babysitting														
Spouse cleaned out dirty diaper														
Spouse criticized the way I handled children in front of them														
Spouse refused to help with the children														
Spouse punished child too severely														
Child care subtotal														

CHILD CARE AND PARENTING (continued)

	1		2		3		4		5		6		7	
	p	d	p	d	p	d	p	d	p	d	p	d	p	d
Spouse refused to answer child's question														
Spouse was unkind to children by criticizing or humiliating them														
Spouse yelled at the children														
Spouse was too permissive with child														
Spouse was too protective toward child														
Spouse hit child														
Spouse told child to leave him/her alone														
Spouse conspired with children to break rules														
Spouse contradicted me in front of child														
Spouse favored one child over another														
Spouse refused to help in babysitting arrangements														
Spouse left dirty diaper in toilet														
Child care total														

HOUSEHOLD MANAGEMENT

	1		2		3		4		5		6		7	
	p	d	p	d	p	d	p	d	p	d	p	d	p	d
We ran some errands														
We went grocery shopping														
Spouse helped with shopping														
We planned or prepared a meal together														
Spouse prepared an interesting or good meal														
Spouse carried groceries into the house														
Spouse had dinner ready on time														
Spouse helped with cooking														
Spouse set the table														
Spouse cleared the table and put the food away														
Household subtotal														

HOUSEHOLD MANAGEMENT (*continued*)

	1		2		3		4		5		6		7	
	p	d	p	d	p	d	p	d	p	d	p	d	p	d
Spouse did the dishes														
Spouse helped me do the dishes or other chores														
Spouse straightened up the house														
Spouse swept, dusted, or did other light cleaning														
Spouse mopped the floor or did other heavy cleaning														
Spouse cleaned the bathroom														
We straightened up the house														
Spouse made needed complaints to the landlord, utility companies, garbage collector, etc.														
Spouse appropriately handled a minor household crisis without bothering me about it														
Spouse did household repairs or arranged to have them done														
Spouse put dirty clothes in the hamper														
Spouse set the alarm clock														
Spouse put the newspapers outside														
Spouse turned up the heat in the morning														
Spouse did the laundry														
Spouse chopped wood														
Spouse built a fire														
Spouse turned the lights off, heat down, etc., before we went out														
Spouse fed the pets														
Spouse cleaned up after the pets														
Spouse mowed the lawn or took care of the yard														
Spouse took care of needed car repairs or maintenance														
Spouse washed or cleaned the car														
Spouse put gas in car														
Spouse emptied the car ashtray														
Household subtotal														

HOUSEHOLD MANAGEMENT (continued)

	1		2		3		4		5		6		7	
	p	d	p	d	p	d	p	d	p	d	p	d	p	d
Spouse served leftovers from the night before														
Spouse fixed a food I dislike														
Spouse forgot to buy food we needed														
Spouse left something out of the refrigerator														
Spouse left a sink full of dishes														
Spouse prepared a tasteless meal														
Spouse refused to help with household chores when asked														
Spouse delayed in doing household tasks														
Spouse nagged or became angry about chores I hadn't completed														
Spouse left a chore incomplete														
Spouse left an appliance turned on when he/she left the house														
Spouse did not take care of needed car repairs or maintenance														
Spouse forgot to put gas in car														
Spouse took car when I needed it														
Household total														

FINANCIAL DECISION MAKING

	1		2		3		4		5		6		7	
	p	d	p	d	p	d	p	d	p	d	p	d	p	d
We made a major financial decision														
We worked on the budget														
We balanced the checkbook														
We agreed on a purchase														
We got a "good buy" on something														
Spouse paid the bills on time														
Spouse helped in planning a budget														
Financial subtotal														

	1		2		3		4		5		6		7	
	p	d	p	d	p	d	p	d	p	d	p	d	p	d

FINANCIAL DECISION MAKING (*continued*)

Spouse got a "good buy" on something ....

Spouse agreed to splurge on something ....

Spouse gave me money to spend any way I want ....

Spouse helped make a decision about a purchase ....

Spouse wrote a check without recording it ....

Spouse spent more than the budget allowed ....

Spouse bought something that could have been

    purchased for less at another store ....

Spouse did not pay the bills on time ....

Spouse bought something important without

    consulting me ....

Spouse borrowed money from a friend ....

Spouse wouldn't let me buy something I wanted ....

Spouse made a mistake in balancing the checkbook ......

Spouse wanted to know what I had spent money on ......

_____ Financial total

EMPLOYMENT/EDUCATION

We celebrated a success in work (advancement,

    completion of a project, end of term) ....

We discussed future employment opportunities ....

We figured out ways to meet new job demands ....

Spouse made significant achievement in his/her

    work/school ....

Spouse assisted me with work I brought home ....

Spouse helped me solve a problem I have in my work ......

Spouse earned special recognition at work....................

                  Employment subtotal

	1		2		3		4		5		6		7	
	p	d	p	d	p	d	p	d	p	d	p	d	p	d

EMPLOYMENT/EDUCATION (*continued*)

Spouse consulted me about a decision for work

Spouse showed interest in my work/school

Spouse read my paper (report, etc.)

Spouse showed no interest in my work/school

Spouse interfered with me working on projects I brought from work/school

Spouse made bad decision or behaved inappropriately at work

Spouse remained upset or angry about work after he/she came home

Spouse talked too much about work

Spouse made no efforts to get a job

Spouse worked overtime or brought home work to do

Spouse complained I spend too much time at work

Employment total

PERSONAL HABITS AND APPEARANCE

Spouse paid attention to his/her appearance (shaved, took a bath, etc.)

Spouse dressed nicely

Spouse hung up his/her clothes in the closet

Spouse got a haircut or hairdo

Spouse left clothes lying around

Spouse left dirty dishes around the house

Spouse missed the ashtray with cigarette ashes

Spouse made a mess and didn't clean it up

Spouse left personal belongings lying around the house

Personal subtotal

PERSONAL HABITS AND APPEARANCE (continued)

	1		2		3		4		5		6		7	
	p	d	p	d	p	d	p	d	p	d	p	d	p	d
Spouse mumbled														
Spouse spoke in whining voice														
Spouse smoked during mealtime														
Spouse blew smoke (or coughed) in my face														
Spouse slurped liquid or made other unpleasant noises while eating														
Spouse used poor table manners														
Spouse talked with mouth full of food														
Spouse belched														
Spouse was late in picking me up														
Spouse exceeded the speed limit and drove carelessly														
Spouse made us late for an appointment by not being ready on time														
Spouse hogged the covers														
Spouse wore curlers when I was at home														
Spouse violated his/her diet														
Spouse wore sloppy clothes														
Spouse neglected his/her appearance (did not shave, did not bathe, etc.)														
Spouse used my toilet articles (razor, toothbrush, etc.)														
Spouse left hairs in the sink														
Spouse monopolized the bathroom														
Spouse did not flush the toilet after using it														
Spouse left her/his toilet articles laying out in the bathroom														
Spouse used all of the toilet paper without getting a new roll														
Spouse left the cap off the toothpaste														
Spouse did not clean the tub after using it														
Personal subtotal														

	1		2		3		4		5		6		7	
	p	d	p	d	p	d	p	d	p	d	p	d	p	d
PERSONAL HABITS AND APPEARANCE (*continued*)														
Spouse left the bathroom in a mess														
Spouse used up all the hot water														
Personal total														
SELF AND SPOUSE INDEPENDENCE														
We scheduled independent activities and responsibilities														
We both engaged in independent activities														
We went to different shows that we each wanted to see														
Spouse agreed that we would spend a period of time by ourselves														
Spouse responded favorably to my desire for a night out without her/him														
Spouse supported an independent activity of mine														
Spouse went to a lecture (show, film, etc.) alone														
Spouse read a book														
Spouse is doing a physical activity alone (jogging, biking, etc.)														
Spouse had lunch (dinner) with a friend														
Spouse is taking a night class														
Spouse went to a party alone														
Spouse complained when I wanted to spend time with a friend														
Spouse complained when I wanted time to myself														
Spouse refused to let me have free time for a hobby														
Independence subtotal														

SELF- AND SPOUSE INDEPENDENCE (*continued*)

	1		2		3		4		5		6		7	
	p	d	p	d	p	d	p	d	p	d	p	d	p	d
Spouse left me behind to watch the children or work while he/she went out for fun														
Spouse spoke positively about experience from which I was excluded														
Spouse excluded me from an activity I would have liked to participate in														
Spouse opened my mail or went through my personal papers														
Independence total														

Spouse Observation Checklist
Weekly Summary

Spouse initials
Male _____ Female _____

Serial week: _____

_____

Mo.   Date   Yr.   Day

Day 1 = _____

Day 7 = _____

TIME Together (Hrs) Each Day

MARITAL SATISFACTION RATING

1 — 5 — 9

Very dissatisfied

Neither satisfied nor dissatisfied

Very satisfied

Day

	1	2	3	4	5	6	7

	Day 1		Day 2		Day 3		Day 4		Day 5		Day 6		Day 7		
	p	d	p	d	p	d	p	d	p	d	p	d	p	d	
I. Affection															
II. Companionship															
III. Consideration															
IV. Sex															
V. Communication process															
VI. Coupling activities															
VII. Child care/Parenting															
VIII. Household management															
IX. Financial decision making															
X. Employment/Education															
XI. Personal habits/Appearance															
XII. Independence															
Daily totals															

Example of Client Summary Sheet

Client Summary Sheet: Marriage

Client Identification: _____

Number of years married: _____   Marriage: Husband _____   Wife _____

Number of children: _____   Ages: _____

Age: Husband _____   Wife _____

I. *Precounseling assessment*

	Husband		Wife	
	Pre	*Post*	*Pre*	*Post*
A. Dyadic Adjustment Scale	_____	_____	_____	_____
B. Locke-Wallace	_____	_____	_____	_____
C. Marital Status Inventory	(_____)	(_____)	(_____)	(_____)
D. CES-D (Self-Rating Scale)	_____	_____	_____	_____
E. Areas of Change	_____	_____	_____	_____

Problem areas

Husband

1. _____

2. _____

3. _____

Wife

1. _____

2. _____

3. _____

F. Inventory of Rewarding Activities:
% activities done (% desired increase)

	Husband		*Wife*	
	Pre	*Post*	*Pre*	*Post*
1. total "alone"	( )	( )	( )	( )
2. total "with spouse and family members"	( )	( )	( )	( )
3. total "with partner and other adults"	( )	( )	( )	( )
4. total "with others (nonfamily)"	( )	( )	( )	( )
5. total "with partner"	( )	( )	( )	( )
6. total increase for #2 and #5	( )	( )	( )	( )

Husband   *Wife*

Areas of Strength

1. _____
2. _____
3. _____

G. Negotiation Tapes: Audio _____   Video _____

	Tape #	*Date*		*Topic*	% +	% –
1) Precounseling						
#1		_____		_____	_____	_____
#2		_____		_____	_____	_____
2) Postcounseling	*Tape #*	*Date*		*Topic*	% +	% –
#1		_____		_____	_____	_____
#2		_____		_____	_____	_____

Chapter Eight

Postmodern Theoretical Models

While the previous chapters have oriented the reader to theory groups that helped form the foundation of the family therapy field, this chapter on postmodernist thinking represents the most recent evolution of the field. Many of the ideas that are proposed by constructivist thinkers depart significantly from those held by the early founders of the field. Not least of these is the notion of reality and the therapist's ability to alter it. Social constructivists argue that traditional approaches to family therapy reflect different ways of viewing the same case, whereas constructivists are more concerned with the family's view of the problem that may be hampering a more effective solution.

As applied to a theory of conducting therapy, the term **constructivism** is used by many contemporary systems therapists to describe their view that reality is "constructed" by one's attitudes, beliefs, and cognition about what he or she perceives in his or her world. Even the perceptions themselves are viewed as simply representational constructions that do not represent "true" external reality. The idea that all of reality is constructed leads these therapists to doubt or question the expertise of their therapeutic pronouncements. In other words, who is to say that the therapist's view of the family and their problem is the correct one or that the therapist's interventions are necessarily the appropriate ones? This way of thinking obviously contrasts with some of the other models we have studied so far. Take, for example, the structural therapist who believes he or she knows how a family should be organized and is willing to assign direct interventions to reorganize the family along the lines that the therapist considers more functional. Similarly, imagine how different the strategic therapist might find this orientation. The strategic therapist is so confident of his or her interpretation of the family and the problem that he or she will consider assigning difficult tasks (Haley, 1984) to the family so that family members respond—in spite of themselves—in a way that reflects the therapist's view of how the family needs to change. The transgenerational therapist will want the family to discuss how the past has influenced the present, even if the family does not view the current problem as relating to the past. To place postmodern therapies in their cultural context, we must first briefly discuss what has happened in the social context of Western culture in the latter half of the twentieth century.

The Postmodern World

At the beginning of the twentieth century, families lived in a far more predictable pattern. They grew up in communities with people who had known their family for generations, shared common values, and experienced little change to adjust to throughout their lifetimes. Their sources of information were limited to one or two newspapers, news from travelers, or published texts. Accordingly, the information they had to organize was limited and was shared by the entire community. Collective wisdom about a given subject was easily understood and unquestioned. Truth and reality were not questioned; rather, people relied on them for comfort and guidance.

In the second half of the twentieth century, however, people are likely to be exposed to cultural information from widely disparate sources: television, air transportation, personal computers, global satellites, and the increased role of Third World countries. Not only will the information they encounter be diverse, it also will not be processed; that is, people no longer benefit from collective discourse about a topic because there are too many topics to discuss. Furthermore, the level of discourse can never fully explore in any depth a given topic long enough to understand its connection to other bits of information. With more access to information, individuals and families have lost some of their ability to chart a consistent course based on commonly held values and beliefs.

Another change in twentieth century America has been the increase in households who have no one in the family who can devote all of their time to meeting family needs. The rapid rise in two-income families and single-parent families has meant that the pace of family life is more harried and rushed. There is simply less time to prepare for the needs of others. Although this change has resulted in more options for women to choose careers as well as family work, many more families find it an economic necessity to balance the demands of the work world and those of family life. Added to the options available to all members of the family, many family members find themselves in an almost comical rush to "cover all of the bases." Scheduling transportation, school projects, work-related travel, overtime, and family activities has meant a level of turmoil in family life that previous generations did not face. Boundaries in such families are stretched and stressed because, perhaps, in the midst of such turmoil, some family members actually rely more on others outside the family for support. When knowledge is everywhere, and everywhere knowledge appears equally valid, family members often find it difficult to devote complete allegiance to any given family "truth." The definition of self becomes influenced by many more sources, most of which may be shallow when compared with historical relationships. Yet, in an era in which multiple relationships must "add together" to equal the safety and security provided by only a few relationships in the past, it is understandable how difficult it is for the individual to adhere to his or her own values and beliefs. The fragmentation of input, the lack of coherent belief systems to process the information, and the rapid pace of family life lead to people struggling for ways to adapt to all the stimuli they and their family must face on a daily basis.

Just as families struggle for definition and clarity, so the field of family therapy also struggles to determine what these changes mean for family therapy theory. One result has been the emergence of approaches that reflect a cynicism about what can actually be known and relied upon as real. Practitioners of these approaches are not interested in extending the debate over why a problem exists; rather, they want merely to focus on what will get rid of the problem or reduce its effects. They are concerned about the amount of time treatment takes and are critical of models that insist there is only one way to think about the problem. In the following sections, we will discuss what these emerging postmodern approaches have in common and how they will contribute to the profession's collective knowledge.

Theoretical Constructs and Philosophy

Constructivism is not a unified theory group based on the work of a single individual. Rather, it is a response to the limitations of the more hierarchical theories of individual pioneers in the field. Constructivists share several unifying concepts: (1) reality is subjective, (2) therapy should be less hierarchical, (3) change is inevitable, and (4) change is already occurring. Although the theory is not unified by a single early pioneer, innovative leaders (Anderson, 1993; deShazer, 1985; O'Hanlon & Weiner-Davis, 1989; White & Epston, 1990) have provided significant inspiration and direction on how therapy with families might be practiced within a constructivist perspective.

Reality Is Subjective

The question of the therapist's subjectivity is not new. It has been part of the mental health field ever since Freud, Jung, and Adler launched the modern study of the human personality. To understand the constructivist position on this issue, it is useful to view this concept from a historical perspective.

The early days of the family therapy movement were characterized by efforts to differentiate itself from the dominant approaches of the day. The more prominent medical models emphasized the inner psychodynamic life of the individual, and focused their assessment and treatment on understanding how individual dynamics led to symptom formation. They were reticent to reveal any aspect of their own personality for fear it would reduce the clients' ability to project their inner world onto the therapist (transference). This was generally seen as a careful process that took considerable time and analysis. It was also a process that hid the therapist's reactions to the client and cloistered therapy away behind closed doors. To the pioneers of family therapy, this slow process ignored the significant interactional context of the patient, and unfairly masked the power of the therapist to obtain results. In response, prescriptive approaches developed in the early days of family therapy were aimed at the family system and used the self of the therapists to build intensity for change. In contrast to the decades of psychodynamic therapists, the early systems therapists were more confident in their willingness to experiment with technique.

Additionally, they were not interested in the thoughts of the client, or in getting "bogged down" in the complex convolutions of explaining behavior. They were interested in a simple, observable, action-oriented therapy that could be applied to "all" families, regardless of the presenting problem. Regardless of the systemic model of therapy, they were confident that they knew what was best for the family and were not hesitant to instruct, cajole, or manipulate the family into the desired changes. They also were less interested in what the family believed to be the problem or goal of the therapy, because they saw this as simply part of the problem. In short, they knew what the family's reality was and what needed to change. They would map the current family interaction patterns and strategize how to overcome and master the family's resistance to these plans. They assumed a hierarchical position to the family, believing that their expert role was necessary to initiate change and manage the family's anxiety around that change. In short, they operated in their role as therapist with the confidence that their assumptions about the family were correct and that their view of the family's reality was true.

Few voices questioned the conventional approach. Some of the first to question the conventional were feminist family therapists. While not necessarily adopting the tenets of what would become the constructivist movement within family therapy, they did call into question many of the basic tenets of the field, particularly the presumed gender neutrality of the early models. The early models of family therapy never included gender as an organizing issue in families, nor did they include ethnicity or cultural uniqueness. Families were assumed to operate by the same rules regardless of their cultural influences, and traditional family therapists minimized the effects of gender and cultural issues in resolving the family's problems.

In the late 1980s, the writings of Huberto Maturano influenced many in the field to reconsider whether reality existed outside the stories that individuals and families constructed about their lives. The inventive nature of reality had emerged as a construct that would significantly influence the field of family therapy.

The Meaning of Context

The fact that almost everyone in modern culture is now exposed to multiple ways of looking at similar issues (sometimes referred to as multiple knowledges), explains why those who have moved to a postmodern perspective have adopted "context" as a critical variable, if not the primary variable, influencing how we give meaning to a given experience. This idea has appeared in various theoretical models as punctuating, ascribing noble intentions, or reframing, to name a few. Each of these techniques was based on the idea that it was useful to recontextualize the experience for someone who was suffering from the way they thought about their predicament. For the postmodern constructivist, changing the meaning of an event moves from being one of several techniques to one that occupies central focus as a foundational concept.

Whether through education, rational solutions, or externalization of the problem, the various postmodernists target the meaning their clients ascribe to their situations. This, however, can often mean less attention to the cause of the problem or the circular pattern of interactive symptoms that lead to and maintain the problem. For instance, if the problem being discussed by the client was the trauma experienced from a prior rape, the constructivist would view the trauma of the rape as existing within a language context, a socially agreed upon way of interpreting the experience of rape (Efran, Lukens, & Lukens, 1988). Recognizing that the words and vocabulary people use affect how we interpret our experiences, they work from the premise that changing the contextual meaning of an experience is basic to changing how a person experiences that meaning. In the case of rape, they might change a context that began with the client viewing himself or herself as a victim of a terrible injustice to one in which the client viewed himself or herself as primarily unaffected by the potentially damaging effects of such an experience. Both contexts for interpreting the event are familiar in our culture; however, they would view the latter as having more potential to affect the meaning and therefore the experience of the event.

The Concept of Family

Early family therapy models defined themselves in relation to the long history of individually oriented theories that were predominating the mental health field until the last half of the twentieth century. To the foundational thinkers in family therapy, the unit of attention was strictly the family, and tended to be the traditional two parent nuclear family. It was considered "linear thinking" and "unsystemic" to focus on individuals. The postmodernists, however, with their considerable attention to language and cognitions, have blurred the definitional boundaries of what family therapy used to mean. The constructivists argue for a contextual meaning for family, a shifting community that would involve extended family members, significant others, and may exclude some nuclear family members. They also are quite comfortable working with only an individual, and relying on self reports of who and what represents his or her family.

Therapy as Conversation

The postmodern therapist would argue that therapy is not intervention, it is not treatment, it is not "done" to the client; rather, it is a collaborative process in which both parties must take responsibility for where it inevitably goes. The term often used to describe this relationship is simply *conversation*, a term typically reserved for forms of communication considered omnidirectional and without a specific purpose or goal. This particular concept is not equally shared by all of the postmodernists, yet all subscribe to intentions of working in a non-hierarchical manner. The narrative approach and the solution-focused approach each have very specific agendas to their conversation as we discuss later in this chapter, yet proponents of these models still place a significant importance on developing partnership relationships that allow working closely with the client, teaming up against external forces. Therapy as conversation promotes multiple truths versus a single truth and multiple meanings versus a single meaning. This has led to the question of postmodernists, "Does any idea, any viewpoint have as much validity as any other?" Constructivists respond by saying that we must remember that we don't live in a vacuum, that our constructions interact with others and may cause them or ourselves difficulty, yet clearly the scope of what ideas are acceptable in this form of conversational therapy offers more possibilities than those theory groups that believed they knew what was wrong and what needed to change in the family.

Role of the Therapist

As can be discerned from the concepts previously discussed, the postmodernists adopt a role that is more collegial than directorial. Based on their belief that no one view of reality is intrinsically correct, they approach the therapeutic relationship as an open-ended partnership that may or may not produce change. This role follows a tradition in mental health that goes back to Carl Rogers (1961) yet differs in that the constructivists are motivated not by empathy, but by a belief in the subjective nature of what one considers reality. Empathy would imply that the therapist accepted the client's version of reality and could commiserate with them. The constructivist, on the other hand, assumes that the client's view of reality is in some way defining reality in a way that supports their discomfort. The role of the therapist becomes one of focused inquiry into the world view of the client, as expressed through their language. This world view is then examined from multiple perspectives in an effort to open up alternative views that the client might find more useful to their situation. While theoretically neutral, the constructivist does have intent; that is to say, they are trained therapists and their assistance is being sought by someone.

Therapeutic Practice
Applications

Postmodern therapy has changed the field of family therapy since its emergence and has transformed and expanded the focus of intervention. This theory group has built on the work of the original models of structural, strategic, behavioral, and transgenerational, and has stimulated the field with new ideas and innovative approaches.

The application of postmodern thought has seen several models developed. In this chapter, we will be discussing the *solution-focused* model developed by Steve deShazer, Bill O'Hanlon, and Michele Weiner-Davis, the *narrative* model developed by Michael White, the *conversational* model developed by Harry Goolishian, Lynn Hoffman, and Tom Anderson, and the *psychoeducational* model developed by Carol Anderson and others.

Solution-Focused Family Therapy

Overview

As previously discussed, past models of family intervention were heavily influenced by the disease (dysfunction) model of mental health. In the disease model, families were considered dysfunctional if they experienced symptoms and needed treatment in order to return to a state of health. Problems in families were seen as a manifestation of this dysfunction and were assumed to be a function of the system. That is to say that if the family improved their functioning, the symptoms would disappear and "health" would return. In this disease, or dysfunction, model, the problem had been defined in such a way that it was outside the area of competence of the family. Therapy was used to re-structure the family, in spite of their resistance, by intensifying their focus on the problem. Therapy was thought of as a helping, caring relationship, but not a partnership focused on finding solutions together.

Steve deShazer and Insoo Berg, of the Brief Family Therapy Center in Milwaukee, worked with a group of innovative family therapists throughout the late 1970s and 1980s on a model that shifted its focus from the dysfunctional side of family assessment to assessing what was working in the family. Several therapists studied with them at their center and then built and expanded on their work. Michele Weiner-Davis and Bill O'Hanlon were two that interpreted this model to many in the family therapy field through their writings and popular workshops.

Setting their sights on solutions versus problems, they naturally became more interested in the pragmatics of what might work than in establishing causality. They took the position that people wanted to change, and that resistance was simply a message that the therapist was not approaching them in an effective way. As with other constructivists, they accept the idea that there is no "normal" way of being, that everything is to be defined; thus they developed a strong interest in the use of language to facilitate change. Solution-focused therapists can best be understood by reflecting on their techniques. The following techniques are to assist the reader in understanding how a solution-focused therapist establishes a therapeutic relationship that anticipates and reinforces relatively rapid change.

Creating a Partnership to Find Solutions

In a solution-focused model of family therapy, symptoms are viewed as problems in living, and in particular, problems in accomplishing some specific everyday tasks that all families struggle with when they are in the same life stage. The therapist assumes that the family has made numerous attempts at solving the problem on their own and that they have been unsuccessful. The therapist therefore is very interested in what solutions they have tried and why family members think they didn't work. The family therapist doesn't "treat" the family, but instead works cooperatively with the family to find better solutions that create less discomfort.

The approach recognizes the powerful role an informed outsider can have in assisting a family to identify its resources, internally and externally, identify what is already working in the family, and help them organize themselves and their family to keep their problems manageable. The model does not see symptoms as signs of treatment failure, but as an inevitable part of family development. Health is no longer defined as the absence of symptoms, but the management of expected conflict. The relationship between the therapist and family becomes less hierarchical and moves closer to a problem solving partnership.

Normalizing Family Struggles

Depathologizing the family and the actions of its members will greatly increase their receptivity to exploring new ways of doing things. Solution-focused therapists believe that unnecessary time is wasted and therapeutic relationships weakened by discussions of problems and deficits. Families often begin their relationship with family therapists assuming a defensive posture. This is particularly true of families who have had previous involvement with social service institutions. It doesn't take much for the therapist to trigger more defensive posturing in families during the first meeting. Expecting this, solution-focused therapists working toward a collaborative relationship try to minimize defensiveness by normalizing the family problems as part of the normal developmental process that all families experience. This does not mean the therapist normalizes dangerous behavior that eventually resulted from the normal family conflict, but simply acknowledges what the family views as the problem and what the family therapist views as the unsuccessful solution.

Searching for Exceptions to the Pattern

Only in case files do problems occur in families 100% of the time. Unfortunately, therapists encounter families when they are most in crisis and disarray. Even more unfortunately, by the time families come into contact with services, their sense of discouragement is often very high. They have become so focused on what is wrong in their lives that what is working, or worked before, is difficult for them to see. Clients often make such statements as "He *never* tells the truth," or "She has *always been* a problem child," or "She's an *exact* copy of her mother, who I can't stand." Such expressions, while emotionally correct, clearly do not reflect the total situation. Solution-focused therapists help family members move toward solutions by helping them search for and identify any exceptions to the pattern. Looking for moments when someone didn't lie, or didn't create a problem, or was different than before gives everyone an opportunity to understand what made that exception possible, what unique characteristics of that event made it possible for the pattern to be avoided. The premise is that if it happened once in a different way that was more functional for everyone, then maybe it can happen again if the same conditions were re-created.

For instance, take the case of the couple who "always" argued over money and how it was to be spent. Working with the family therapist, the couple expressed little hope that anything could be different because they "always" argued over money. In search of some exceptions to what was clearly an evolved pattern, the family therapist asked them if there were any times in which the couple found themselves in a high-risk situation and didn't have a big argument. The couple could agree that there must have been those times and with some help they eventually shared several stories and examples. The family therapist then helped the couple search those situations for what they did differently that helped them avoid a blow-up. They shared with each other what the other could do to reduce the tension in those moments. They were able to identify those actions that would trigger them into a deeper cycle and which ones would help them intervene in the cycle. Armed with this knowledge about their individual and couple patterns, they were agreeable to experiment with new behaviors that had at least the potential for helping them get control and avoid further harm to each other. This change process began with a search for exceptions.

Anticipating Change

The solution-focused approaches have made significant contributions to our therapeutic language about change (O'Hanlon & Weiner-Davis, 1989). Rather than accepting the problem as something that may or may not change, the model suggests that solutions come easier to family members who are anticipating that change will occur and that, in fact, has already begun. For instance, a family is more motivated to participate in a conversation about the future when the question is phrased as "What are you looking forward to doing more of in your family once we are past this problem?" There are multiple versions of questions that anticipate change and help create an atmosphere where new behavior patterns are received with expectation of positive outcomes. Two common types of questions solution-focused therapists might use to help clients anticipate change are (1) questions that offer a scale to measure differences by and (2) questions that offer a comparison between one time and another.

Scaling Questions

These questions are extremely useful in highlighting small increments of change or for plotting what outcome is likely if the direction of change is continued. **Scaling questions** (deShazer, 1988) allow the family therapist to ask family members to give their best estimate of where on a scale of a given variable they might fall. While sounding complicated, examples in the box on page 231 may help illustrate how versatile this technique can be and how it can augment some of the other suggestions made in adopting a solution-focused approach. Asking a depressed client how good a parent they are on average, using a scale of 1 to 10 with 1 being the worst parent possible and 10 being the best parent in the world might get an answer that could open the door to examining the pattern the client is trapped in. For instance, their response might be "There are days when I'm a 1, but on average, probably a 2 or 3, maybe a 2.5." The follow-up question could then be, "Are there unusual days when for some reason you are a 3 or 4 or higher as well?" This information would then open the door to explore what is different about a 2.5 day and a 4.0 day. These differences become critical information regarding the individual's pattern, and how other family members interact with the pattern.

Scaling Questions	Time-Oriented Questions
On a scale of 1 to 10, with 1 being the lowest and 10 being the highest: • How would you rate your self-control today? (4) • How would you rate it back three months ago when you started working on it? (2) • What keeps you from slipping back to a 2? • Where do you think you'll be in three more months? (6) • What will you be doing differently when you are not quite a 6, say a 5? • Describe what you are doing on a rare day when you are feeling upbeat . . . say at a 7 or an 8? • How much change does your wife see in you; what would she rate you? (5) • What do you rate yourself? (6) • What does she not see that you do? • What will you have to do to let her see that you are at a 6? • Describe what your husband would be doing on a day that you solved your problem at a level 6?	• If you woke up in the morning and the problem was miraculously solved, what would be different? • What is the first thing you would notice about yourself? • How would you know that a miracle had occurred? • Imagine you are an old person sitting on your front porch, thinking back about this difficult period of your life. What will you say was the turning point? • Let's say I never met you until one year from now, when all this will be behind you. What would be my first impressions of you? • How have you improved over the previous generation in this area? What have you done to keep from repeating their mistakes? • As these changes continue in your family, what will be different one month (one year) from now? • When will your family of origin first notice you have changed? What will they see?

Time-Oriented Questions

Time-oriented questions are another use of question language that allows the therapist to tease out positive change, discover important values that motivate, identify possible goals, or identify first steps of possible change. The box on page 231 offers several examples that illustrate how jumping ahead or back in time helps give people the needed distance to be objective or to gain perspective. The discouraging present can be sidestepped to a promising future. As was the case in the popular movie "Back to the Future," the family therapist can take the client to the future and from that perspective have the client look back and advise himself or herself on what direction to head and what initial steps to take. The purpose of all anticipatory questions is to build a context of hope and encouragement around change as an antidote to the stagnating experience of being overwhelmed by a problem that doesn't want to be resolved.

Solution-oriented therapists find it helpful to use the time in between sessions for more observation and discovery. They may start a session with the question, "What is different or better this week?" The therapist may suggest that the family members see if they can watch themselves over the next week and identify what new things they are learning and applying in times of family stress. It could be that their fists or stomach "tightened up" in the past and now don't tighten up as much, or it could be that their face no longer "feels flushed," or it could be that they start having more positive thoughts. These signs of coming change can be termed early signals that change is occurring. Identifying these early signals could greatly assist them in catching progress before it slips away into discouragement.

In a solution-focused, partnership-type relationship, between-session assignments can be suggested by family members as well. The family may choose to "pretend" to start an incident just to practice their new skills in intervening in their old pattern. For instance, a mother may ask the kids to give her a test the next week to see if she can practice her new response to their high-risk situation. Children love this sort of game, and the pretend nature of the practice goes a long way toward detoxifying the problem pattern. However the between-session tasks are formulated, the family therapist working in a solution-focused mode anticipates change and works actively with the family toward that goal.

The Narrative Approach to Family Therapy

The narrative approach to postmodern family therapy is synonymous with the work of Michael White, a therapist from Adelaide, Australia. He and his wife, Cheryl White, and their colleagues at the Dulwich Center have influenced therapists throughout the world. His powerful impact has been through training workshops and short publications, as well as through feature presentations at national marriage and family therapy conferences in the late 1980s and early 1990s. Like other constructivists, he focuses on the effects and influences problems have on individuals and families, with particular attention to the way the problem takes over and controls an individual or family.

Michael White emphasizes the narrative explanations for human behavior through his belief that people with problems have life stories that have become "problem-saturated" (i.e., they have come to define themselves in such a way that change does not appear possible). Influenced by the writings of Foucault, he would say that stories about oneself and one's family are defined by cultural expectations and restrict options in order to serve society. He mistrusts the subjugating effects of society, viewing cultural norms and expectations as overly controlling and limiting (Foucault, 1980). Negative aspects of a person's life are viewed as a natural consequence of having limited options to realize one's true self. Instead of being self-defining, the individual falls prey to society's message about himself or herself, and begins to exclude information (alternative stories) about himself or herself that does not fit that pattern. Problems in living become self-fulfilling constructs that further confirm the prior message about self. This reiteration of a story about the self becomes self-limiting and self-perpetuating, according to Michael White. Because the way people think about themselves (their story) is so determinative of their options and actions, White's first step is to try to put distance between the person and their problem story. He works at externalizing the problem story through disciplined and detailed use of language.

Externalizing the Problem

One of the ways Michael White, and those influenced by him, **externalize the problem** is to refer to the problem as if it existed outside of the client or family. Saying to the client, "How long have you had to struggle with *this problem pattern*?" or "Has *the yelling problem* been dominating your lives in ways that you all feel is unfair?" or "What would you be doing more of in your family if *this problem* wasn't trying to run your lives?" Such questions move the family slightly outside the actual problem and help them consider more independent action (White, 1988; White & Epston, 1990). If the problem is external to all of them, then they and the family therapist can work together as a team to overcome it. If certain family members have become identified as embodying the problem, then finding ways to externalize the problem is helpful in freeing them to work against the problem rather than spending their energy defending themselves.

Externalizing the problem does not mean minimizing personal responsibility. For instance, even in work with sexual offenders who mask a deep shame for their actions by covering up their destructive patterns with minimizations and distortions, there are helpful ways to give them the room to face their moral responsibility. For instance, a family therapist might frame the problem as external by saying "I understand you are thinking about joining with me to fight this cycle of abuse that you have been caught up in. I wonder what it would take for you to feel honor that you have defeated it and not passed it on to future generations?" The "cycle of abuse" then becomes the enemy and rather than defending himself, the offender can begin to "undermine" the cycle by giving the therapist as much detail as possible about what the cycle's pattern looks like. Some additional examples are offered in the following table:

Presenting Problem	Possible Externalizing Language
Mother who beat her child (prior abuse victim).	"Maybe you would like to put an end to *this cycle of violence* that has been passed on to you. Would you like to be the one to defeat *this monster* and keep it from hurting future generations?"
Mother who neglects her children due to depression.	"This *dark curtain* that you mentioned, tell me about a time when you fought back, or slipped by, or fooled this *dark curtain that descends* on you."
Stepfather who slapped his teenage stepdaughter.	"When you described one of those *episodes* when everybody gets into it and you end up losing it, you seemed to be saying that you hate these *episodes* because they keep you from being the father you really want to be to your stepdaughter."

Externalizing is not limited to rephrasing of family members' problems, but is the natural outcome of the family therapist positioning himself or herself as the family consultant (e.g., partner) in attempting to find solutions to their problem patterns. Working together against a common foe provides the family members with respect: respect for their desire to change, and the room to negotiate without unnecessary loss of personal integrity.

Assessing Problem Pattern Influence

Some problems feel like they influence every part of a person's life. This is particularly true for victims of prior trauma, who may feel they can never escape the events of the past. This burden can get in the way of exploring change and can serve to maintain problem patterns in family members.

Family therapists interested in creating a new reality may find this type of client hesitant to talk about anything other than their problems. In a sense, the problem pattern has become extremely influential in the person's life and in their family's life together. Life outside of the problem takes on less notice as ever increasing amounts of time and energy are spent dwelling on the problem. Families may have little or no awareness of non-problematic times. They may say, "My life is just one big problem." In such cases, it may be helpful to assess the influence the problem has on the family and then assess what influence ιamily members have on the problem.

While the solution-focused therapist might look for exceptions to the problem, the narrative therapist will look for times in which the personal story comes out differently, or in Michael White's terms, has a unique outcome. This effort is noticeably difficult for those people who feel dominated and subjugated by their problems. They are more familiar with talking about examples of when their problem got the best of them versus a time when they were able to minimize the effects of the problem. They assume they have relatively little influence on the problem. But the narrative family therapist can search for examples where the family members stood up to the problem and prevented it from taking undue influence on their lives. The clients may be asked whether their influence on the problem has grown or declined over the past years. Most clients report the problem's influence has always been strong and then downplay their progress. However, if the narrative therapist uses persistent questions to dramatize this difference and to project a trend, then the therapist and family can look into the future when an even higher influence might be possible. They can explore together what the individual and family would be able to do then, or how they would know that they had taken the first step toward more growth. Such questions are similar to the solution-focused questions discussed earlier in the chapter, and similarly can help the therapist and family secure a small but significant growth step. This step is then used to project the next step, and the one after that, until the family members start to include in their definition of themselves (their story) the possibility that they have reduced the influence of the problem in their lives. This creates a good platform for the "team" to solve individual daily aspects of the problem's influence.

Reinforcing Progress Through Credentialing

Reinforcing change has long been a part of effective therapy. Working from a narrative approach affords the family therapist an opportunity to credential change from the earliest moment in therapy. Whether it is acknowledging a client's fortitude in resisting the influence of an old story or certifying expertise in defeating a current problem that has plagued a family for some time, the family therapist moves quickly to claim progress and secure it before old patterns emerge to rediscourage the family members. Since conflict is viewed as normal in this model, it is the management of conflict that is acknowledged and celebrated. The existence of a difficult family situation does not overly concern a narrative therapist, but how the individual family members handled the situation is of utmost concern. Was there any difference in this event that would indicate further growth? Did someone recognize their early warning signals and try to remove themselves? Did the argument stop short of the intensity of the last argument? Did anyone attempt to intervene in ways that had been discussed, even if ineffective? These and countless other questions regarding how the family members managed an alternative response that broke old patterns would highlight small but significant steps of change. The narrative therapist is then quick to credential this change, even in the knowledge that the goal may not yet be reached. The direction is reinforced and secured through acknowledgment. Many techniques are possible to celebrate progress and can range from issuing certificates of accomplishment ("World's Greatest Lip Zipper") to throwing a victory celebration with cake and ice cream.

Conversational Approaches to Family Therapy

Postmodern psychologist Kenneth Gergen (1985) has written extensively about his belief that people's personalities are almost completely shaped by interactions with others, through conversation. If conversation results in someone feeling better about their circumstances, then that conversation was "therapeutic." This conceptual approach has greatly influenced the work of family therapists such as Harlene Anderson, Lynn Hoffman, Tom Anderson, and the late Harry Goolishian. These postmodern therapists take the view that the technological approach of mainstream family therapy placed too much influence on the therapist as an expert, did not respect the knowledge and resources of the client, and encouraged the therapist to be more concerned about curing the client family than caring for them. This approach to postmodern family life places a strong emphasis on egalitarian relationships, on conversational questions, and on the use of reflecting teams for both treatment and training.

Egalitarian Relationships

Frustrated by the cybernetic model, the proponents of a conversational model see traditional family therapy as too focused on doing therapy on a client or to a client rather than with a client. This emphasis on technique and outcome damages the caring quality of the relationship and therefore reduces the opportunities for healing. Since the therapist is no more an expert on the problem than the client in this model, the therapist is more likely to be interested in the client's thinking and views on what needs to change and how it needs to change. Techniques are typically not addressed in this model, which makes it difficult to describe what they actually do in therapy that they consider egalitarian. However, they do share a philosophy about what the therapeutic relationship ought to entail and what they want to avoid in the relationship. It should also be noted that all of the proponents of this approach were fully grounded in mainstream family therapy before choosing to emphasize their nondirective, nontechnique-oriented approach to working with families. It would be unlikely that this earlier training did not influence their work or thinking in some way while conducting conversational therapy. That is to say, those things they discuss would be influenced partially by their previous understanding of family development, family structure, and family histories. However, in constructing their conceptual map, they are in agreement that their relationship with the client is one of respect and equality.

Conversational Questions

Conversational questions are at the heart of this approach. Understanding what a conversational question consists of is a little difficult, however. Anderson (1993) explains that

> conversational questions come from a position of not knowing and are the therapist's primary tool. They involve responsive or active listening, which requires attending to the client's stories in a distinct way, immersing oneself in clients' conversations, talking with them about their concerns, and trying to

grasp their current story and what gives it shape . . . each question . . . comes from an honest, continuous therapeutic posture of not understanding too quickly, of not knowing. (pp. 330–331)

Conversational questions are similar to the Rogerian style of questioning in which the therapist reflects back to the client what they are saying, but it goes further in that the conversational therapist will actively collaborate on generating solutions if that is what the client wishes. The key variable appears to be the way in which opinions or ideas are offered, very tentatively and respectfully, almost as a question. For therapists who have studied family systems and feel the responsibility of their knowledge, such a tentative approach would appear difficult. Training issues therefore has been an area of focus for the conversational family therapists. One of the methods they have written about both to train and level the therapeutic playing field is the use of a reflecting team.

Reflecting Teams

Tom Anderson, a psychiatrist from Norway who trained and practiced traditional family therapy, became disillusioned with the hierarchical nature of the direct styles of structural and strategic therapy. Following his interest in leveling the field between the therapist and client family and influenced by the conversational movement, he began experimenting with radical uses of the one-way mirror (Anderson, 1991), a tool of family therapy that had become almost institutionalized. Rather than maintaining the safe distance and expert position behind the mirror, he began to bring his team into the therapy room to meet with the family, or to change places with them. Instead of conferring about the family "behind their backs," he and his team would discuss their reactions and reflections right in front of them. After the team would share their reflections, the family would have an opportunity to react to what they had heard and proceed with the interview. The process became a widely used technique around the world, regardless of the theoretical models of the participants. Many therapists found the approach useful for generating options and for reducing clients' fear of working in front of a one-way mirror. One of the reasons for the popularity of this technique was also because it turned out to be a very useful technique in training programs around the country, most of which already had been using a one-way mirror and which could use a technique that got the whole team more involved and comfortable with the mirror.

Summary

Conversational family therapy is more of a philosophy than a theoretical model of treatment. Its founders and developers, however, have greatly influenced postmodern family therapy and have seen their ideas echoed in similar approaches that attempt to establish more egalitarian relationships that do not place such a priority on the therapist being an expert. These theorists have balanced a field preoccupation with technique and flair, with a more compassionate, humble, and caring attitude about assisting families in their struggles for change.

Psychoeducational Approaches to Family Therapy

Introduction

As in the other postmodern approaches, a psychoeducational model differs from more traditional family therapy approaches that have focused on alleviating the symptom for solving the problem. The etiology is not of primary concern in psychoeducation. Psychoeducation assumes that the family is healthy and that problems result from ineffective coping. Rather than focusing on how the family can eliminate the problem, this new approach helps the family to cope with the problem. Rather than suggesting that a family causes or needs a problem, psychoeducation helps family members to understand the nature of the problem and get support for coping with it.

Theoretical Constructs and Philosophy

Psychoeducation has its roots in the work of Carol Anderson and her colleagues in the treatment of schizophrenia (Anderson, Reiss, & Hogarty, 1986). Anderson's approach treats schizophrenia as a disease that can best be dealt with using medication and counseling for families faced with the difficulties of coping with a schizophrenic member. McFarlane (1991), in the *Handbook of Family Therapy*, states:

> What has not been so apparent to clinicians, including many family therapists, is that for families of persons afflicted with schizophrenic illness, life is drastically different and in most respects more stressful and more demoralizing than is in the case of most psychiatric disorders and in non-psychotic family dysfunction. This curious absence is largely the result of the dominance of the poorly substantiated belief that family and parental dysfunction are the sole or predominate source of the symptoms and disability of the identified patient. We have been preoccupied with ferreting out the causal transaction patterns, while, to a large degree, ignoring the devastating impact of watching one's child deteriorate into someone who is all but a stranger, and a most incapacitated one. To roughly the same degree, many clinicians have ignored the fact that families have become the de facto caretakers of individuals with schizophrenia, without required knowledge, training, resources or support. (pp. 363–364)

Psychoeducation trains families to create an interactional environment that both compensates for and partially corrects the level of functioning in the family member. More recently psychoeducational programs have been developed for families dealing with alcohol abuse (Joanning et al., 1992); remarriage (Visher & Visher, 1988); obesity (Fischman-Havstad & Marston, 1984), and affective disorders (Clarkin et al., 1990). The primary goals of these programs are to educate family members about the problem and provide a supportive environment for the family. Family members learn to (1) understand the problem and identify potential stressors that might precipitate the problem, (2) identify interactions within the family that produce stress, (3) develop strategies to cope with the stressors, and (4) accept the problem.

Because psychoeducation is provided in a group, family members are able to derive support from each other and thereby reduce blame and guilt for causing the problem. The group provides opportunities for family members to learn from each other's successes. Learning how other family members have coped successfully with a problem will help them be more aware of their strengths when confronting current problems. Family members can also support each other's efforts to try new problem-solving strategies and communication skills. Families are able to provide peer support when they share their life stressors within the group.

Therapeutic Practice

Assessment Psychoeducational assessment is different from other therapeutic approaches in several ways. First, the therapist is primarily interested in the family's experience and reaction to the problem. The therapist attempts to create a collaborative relationship in which family members serve as partners in the treatment process. Assessment may also include members of the family's social network (for example, relatives, friends, and so on) who can support the family's efforts to cope with the problem. McFarlane (1991) states:

> The family clinician needs to have a general sense of interactional style, structural alliances, specific communication patterns, coping strategies, and extended-family and social-network resources of the family as a whole. This will involve taking a brief genogram; asking about who spends time, or tends to interact, with whom; watching for difficulties or strengths in communication (especially clarity of content, ability to listen, and acknowledgment of others' comments and feelings); asking contacts with friends, relatives and outside social or community groups; finding out about sources of enjoyment and distraction; and ascertaining recent life events and changes in household membership, even if these represent desirable outcomes. (pp. 372–373)

The therapist attempts to assess the way the family has coped with the stress and how they have used their own resources to get support. "What have you done to resolve the problem?" "What other people are concerned about your family?" and "Who could help you with this problem?" are questions that engage the family in describing what kind of a program they need to cope with the problem. Psychoeducational assessment guides the specification of goals and the design of the program.

Goals The goals of psychoeducation are based on the needs of the participants. Goals may require a change in attitudes, behavior, or interactional patterns. There should be a clear connection between the goals and the overall design of the program. The process of identifying goals also provides a standard for measuring the effectiveness of the program.

Psychoeducational goals can be classified into two types: general and specific. Each type of goal has a specific function. *General* goals can help the therapist to focus on what they need to do for the target population (for example, to improve children's postdivorce adjustment). *Specific* goals or objectives are measurable and can be used to measure the participants' progress from week to week (for example, to identify dysfunctional family interaction patterns that maintain abusive drug use). Specific goals provide direction and prevent the therapist from claiming effectiveness without demonstrating it.

Goals and objectives Kaplan and Hennan (1992) designed a remarried-education program, *Personal Reflections*, based on Visher and Visher's theory of remarriage family development (1988). The general goals concerned the need to understand and negotiate roles and decision making; the specific goals concerned behavioral expectations in roles and decision making. The goals of the program should match the theoretical content, process, and evaluation of the program. Appropriate assessment measures (such as Likert scales, questionnaires, behavior checklists) correlated with the goals can be used to evaluate the effectiveness of the program.

The Families In Transition Program, Louisville, KY, is a court-mandated divorce adjustment program for parents and children (between the ages of 8 and 16). The purpose of the program is to help parents to help their children to cope more effectively with the effects of divorce. The program is designed for families with older children because research findings related to the age of the child indicate that while younger children may immediately experience more problems following the divorce (Heatherington, Cox, & Cox, 1978), older children (preadolescent and adolescent) may actually experience more problems later.

The general goals of the program are (1) to prevent or reduce children's anxiety, aggression, depression, and behavioral problems; and (2) to increase social competencies critical to children's postdivorce adjustment. The program's five specific objectives are as follows:

- To increase children's competence by teaching specific skills to identify divorce-related feelings in self and others
- To reduce children's feelings of isolation and misconceptions about divorce
- To increase children's awareness of how divorce affects their parents
- To increase appropriate ways children respond to anger
- To develop parental competence by teaching skills to handle children's divorce-related concerns, co-parental relationships, and parent-child relationships

Content The content of psychoeducational programs is based on (1) theory and research, and (2) setting and practice. The *content* of a program is based on sound theory and research. A well-designed program consists of a clearly articulated theoretical prospective in empirical research.

The Families In Transition curriculum has delineated specific content to cover in order to meet its stated goals and objectives: (1) a supportive climate where feelings can be freely explored, (2) acquisition of problem-solving skills for divorce-related problems, and (3) ways for parents and children to develop better relationships with each other.

The program is based on empirical data that suggest specific ways to re-duce risks and symptoms in family members and on the assumption that symp-toms occur at the time of divorce, when individual characteristics of the family members interact with dysfunctional family processes. Each component of the program is designed to address the five factors that make children at risk at the time of divorce: (1) age and sex of the child, (2) predivorce family functioning, (3) postdivorce parent-child relationships, (4) postdivorce parental relationships, and (5) parent-child support systems. There is also extensive evidence that pa-rental separation and divorce is a painful experience for children and that it creates many changes in a child's life. Even given the most positive situation, children experience such feelings as guilt, anger, embarrassment, disbelief, fear, and grief, and even under the best circumstances, a child needs time and sup-port to regain stability felt before the divorce. This content then becomes the specific topics to be covered in the psychoeducational program offered in Ken-tucky to assist divorcing families.

Another example would be the Family Drug Education program designed by Joanning et al. (1992) based on integration of structural (Minuchin & Fishman, 1981) and strategic (Haley, 1976) family therapy. The model was also influenced by the research of Stanton and Todd (1982) on adult addicts. By providing a theoretical perspective, other users can decide whether the psychoeducational program is appropriate for the population they are serving.

The content of effective psychoeducational programs is based on research regarding the content of the program. For example, a psychoeducational pro-gram for parents of a behavior-disordered child is based on the most current knowledge of behavior disorders and interactional processes that are effective with this population. Research findings provide useful guidelines for recom-mendations. Recommendations to families must be clear and accurate and easy to implement. In cases where research is not available, therapists have drawn on their own clinical practice to develop the program.

Settings   A number of *setting* or contextual issues influence the content of a psychoeducational program. For example, a parenting program for divorced parents with primary custody should consider not only the research on parenting, but also issues involving divorced parents with primary custody. Campbell and Patterson (1995) suggest that one must consider social networks and socioeconomic status in developing psychoeducational programs for physi-cal illness. Program designers must also consider setting characteristics such as availability and location of the program: Does the location of the program offer ongoing clinical services? Is the location a place where families are likely to feel comfortable? These questions must be answered when designing a psycho-educational program.

Practice   Effective programs must provide a model of *practice*. Depend-ing on the population, a variety of activities (structured and unstructured) must be provided to accommodate the diversity (culture, gender, and so on) of the population receiving the program. Instructions for presenting the program should be outlined in detail to encourage replication in other settings. Participant objectives and directions for presenting program activities should ensure that the program is carried out effectively.

Implementation   Effective psychosocial programs provide a guide for *implementation*. Programs that are offered in a variety of community settings should provide careful details of program implementation. Details should include characteristics of the target audience, such as age, developmental level, gender, socioeconomic class, and type of family (for example, single parent, divorced, never married, and so on). Knowledge of the target population prevents a program from being implemented with a group for which it is not appropriate.

Effective psychoeducational programs provide training to therapists to implement the program. Programs typically provide an overview of the program and a reading packet to provide some basic background of program content. Most programs require therapists to read the curriculum and attend training sessions before implementing the program. Videotapes that illustrate teaching methods and procedures are also useful in enhancing training. Finally, some programs require observation and supervision before permitting the therapist to conduct the program alone. Some of the techniques the psychoeducational therapist might use to facilitate group process and make the program meaningful for group participants follow:

Assisting with the getting-acquainted process. As participants arrive, the therapist helps them get to know each other and gives them a brief introduction to the program by reviewing the goals and activities for each session.

Structuring the group. The group facilitator begins each session by describing the session goals and activities and answering any questions participants may have from previous sessions. Children are provided structure by establishing rules for acceptable behavior and posting the rules where everyone can see them.

Listening to group members. To lead a group effectively, the group facilitator listens to and understands what the individual members are saying. Therapists accomplish this by reflecting what group members are saying or by commenting on the commonalities among group members' comments.

Praising group member participation. For a group to function effectively, group members must feel free to speak without fear that they will be punished or ridiculed for what they say. One way a group leader can help members to feel comfortable and encourage participation is by praising members' participation. It is important to praise group members as often as possible, particularly members who are reluctant or afraid to speak. The praise should encourage them to speak more frequently.

Encouraging group members to support each other. The group will function most effectively if the group members work together to reach both individual and group goals. This can be accomplished if group members feel free and are willing to help other members of the group by providing support, suggestions, and reinforcement. The group facilitator can encourage this by praising members for helping other members. Praising members' support of each other increases the amount of support for group members and the diversity of ideas and suggestions available for problem solving.

Prompting desired behavior. Group members will often speak in broad, general terms about their experiences and feelings. In order to understand each family member's problems more fully it is often necessary for the group facilitator to focus on what an individual is saying and encourage that member to define problem situations and behaviors more specifically. By asking questions that focus on the specifics of what the family member is discussing, the group facilitator prompts desired verbal behaviors. In prompting desired behaviors it is important to listen for generalizations and vague statements of problem situations. When a family member speaks generally about a problem, the group facilitator might encourage the person to speak more specifically about what he or she is discussing. By prompting desired behaviors the group facilitator encourages members to think more specifically and thereby increases the group members' understanding of the problem.

Responding to undesired member behavior. Group members will sometimes engage in behaviors that interfere with the attainment of group and individual goals and make communication between group members difficult. Children often have difficulty controlling their behaviors or a parent may offer an irrational solution to the problem. Psychoeducational therapists may respond to undesired behaviors by (1) listening for verbal behaviors that are undesirable in the group (such as disinterest or nonconstructive solutions), (2) watching for nonverbal behaviors that interfere with group interaction (such as turning one's chair away from the group), or (3) deciding whether it would be helpful to the individual and the group to ignore the behavior and redirect the group discussion to a more productive area.

Redirecting attention to group members. During a group discussion, the group facilitator may find it useful to refer to previous statements or ideas contributed by group members. When the group facilitator ties in previous members' comments to the present discussion, he or she is redirecting attention to other group members. By redirecting attention to a member's statement, the group facilitator ties in relevant points from previous discussion to make the present discussion more meaningful and cohesive. To redirect attention to members' statements, the facilitator should listen for ideas, themes, complaints, solutions, and so on, that have been expressed in previous discussions. When the group facilitator draws on the ideas of a group member, it involves that group member more actively in the group discussion and encourages the recognition of shared experiences.

Redirecting statements to other members. During a group discussion, the group facilitator may find it relevant or useful to channel the discussion to a group member other than the one who is speaking. When the group facilitator directs the group attention in this manner, he or she is redirecting statements to other members. To redirect statements, the group facilitator should be alert for members who should be drawn into the group discussion. This can occur because the member may seem eager to speak but hasn't had the opportunity or the member can make a useful contribution to the discussion.

Effectiveness of Postmodern Approaches to Family Therapy

Because the postmodern approaches represent a recent trend in family therapy, little comparative research exists to determine the effectiveness of these approaches. Evidence that these approaches work is sparse and anecdotal and often does not live up to claims (Shoham, Rohrbaugh, & Patterson, 1995). With the exception of psychoeducation, none of these approaches have been empirically tested using objective criteria to evaluate their effectiveness. Instead, postmodern therapists (social constructivists) have largely relied on self-report measures that are often subject to experimenter bias when documenting the effects of therapy.

Of the postmodern approaches, psychoeducation is the only approach that measures outcomes under controlled conditions. There is overwhelming evidence that psychoeducation is more effective than routine care (that is, medication management with ancillary crisis intervention) for schizophrenic disorders (Goldstein & Miklowitz, 1995). Moreover, there is evidence from two investigations (Falloon, Boyd, & McGill, 1982; Hogarty et al., 1986) that psychoeducational programs are more effective for two-year periods in laying out and improving social development in individual supportive or skill-oriented approaches. The effectiveness of these programs as an adjunct to medication is in part a function of structure, intervention, and the setting in which they occur (Keith et al., 1989).

The effectiveness of psychoeducation has been demonstrated in other problem areas as well. Brown and Portes (1996) found that parents who completed divorce education programs at the time of divorce showed higher adjustment scores than a control group of parents who did not complete the program. Similar results have been demonstrated with remarriage (Kaplan & Hennan, 1992), drug abuse (Liddle & Dakof, 1996), physical illness (Campbell & Patterson, 1995), adolescent conduct disorders (Chamberlain & Rosicky, 1995), and affective disorders (Prince & Jacobson, 1995).

In contrast, the solution-focused approach evaluates cases by asking clients whether their problem has been resolved. To evaluate the efficacy of their treatment, solution-focused brief therapists have a team member other than the therapist conduct a telephone follow-up with clients three and twelve months after termination. Questions to assess the effectiveness of treatment focus on the following areas: (1) goal attainment, (2) severity of the presenting problem, (3) other areas of improvement not addressed in treatment, and (4) existence of new problems. Based on these questions, deShazer (1991) reports an 80.4% success rate (65.6% of the 164 BFTC clients at the Milwaukee Center attained their goal, and 14.7% showed significant improvement) within 4.6 sessions. Moreover, follow-up contacts at 18 months indicated the success rate had increased to 86%. Unfortunately, it is not clear how the Milwaukee group determines success from their contact with their clients.

There are several limitations with this type of research (Shoham et al., 1995). First, the investigators have not described their methodology in sufficient detail to replicate the study for reliability and validity. Second, the demands of therapists rather than the treatment itself may have influenced the clients to report success. Third, positive bias may exist because the solution-focused therapy team is the final determiner of success, and finally the 80–90% success rate reported by the Milwaukee group exceeds the norms for psychotherapeutic research.

One promising investigation of solution-focused brief therapy examined the immediate impact of a solution-focused family therapy intervention on both the family and the therapist (Adams, Piercy, & Jurich, 1991). This study assessed the formula first-session task (FFST) (deShazer, 1985), plus solution-focused therapy and the structural-strategic intervention model. The authors report that subjects receiving FFST scored significantly higher on measures of family compliance, clarity of treatment goals, and improvement in alleviating the presenting problem. No significant differences were found in therapist or client optimism. The long-term effects of the solution-focused approach are unknown since measurement did not occur beyond the third session. Nevertheless, the formula first-session task appears to be an effective intervention in the initial stages of treatment.

It is rather puzzling why the solution-focused approach has not been subjected to more rigorous investigation. The treatment procedures are quite specific and thus easy to replicate under controlled conditions. The failure to evaluate solution-focused brief therapy under controlled conditions reflects skepticism among social-constructivist and poststructural thinkers about knowledge gained through the objectivist methods of social science (Shoham et al., 1995). One would hope that solution-focused therapists would give the same attention to rigorous evaluation as they do to the efficacy of their treatment procedures.

There also seems to be a trend with the social constructivists to examine the narrative features (storying) of qualitative research as a means of complementing the more reductionistic features of quantitative research (Moon, Dillon, & Sprenkle, 1990). The narrative work of Michael White collaborates with the client in reauthorizing his or her history to create a new narrative that is preferable to the initial problem narrative (Epston & White, 1992). The application of more traditional research methods will help to validate and clarify why these narrative approaches work. We hope that, in the future, postmodern researchers will attempt to use both qualitative and quantitative methods for evaluating the effectiveness of family therapy.

Chapter Summary

The models presented in this chapter are part of a larger movement in the field of family therapy that is based in part on the changes in our postmodern world. The rapid pace of change, coupled with the enormous increase in exposure to new ideas, has left families and individuals struggling to interpret the world around them. Without small, tightly-knit communities to help process all the various ideas that are available, families must construct their own reality. Therapists are less comfortable with the "knowledge" they use to rely on as being enough to define someone else's reality. Because everyone's reality is potentially different, many therapists have looked to models that are based on social construction theories.

Whether looking for solutions, exceptions to the problems, or outcomes that don't fit the old story or providing education to assist adaptation, these new therapists are trying to develop models that are less directive, more supportive, and elicit less resistance and are often quicker and less intrusive than the models that preceded them.

References

Anderson, C. M., Reiss, D. J., & Hogarty, G. E. (1986). *Schizophrenia and the family*. New York: Guilford Press.

Anderson, H. (1993). On a roller coaster: A collaborative language systems approach to therapy. In S. Friedman (Ed.), *The new language of change*. New York: Guilford Press.

Anderson, T. (1991). *The reflecting team*. New York: Norton.

Berg, I. K. (1994). *Family based services*. New York: Norton.

Brown, J. H., & Portes, P. (1996). Evaluation of the Families In Transition Program. Unpublished manuscript, University of Louisville, Louisville, KY.

Brown, J. H., Portes, P. R., & Christensen, D. N. (1989). Understanding divorce stress on children: Implications for research and practice. *American Journal of Family Therapy*, 17, 315–325.

Campbell, T. L., & Patterson, J. M. (1995). The effectiveness of family interventions in the treatment of physical illness. *Journal of Marital and Family Therapy*, 21, 545–583.

Carter, E., & McGoldrick, M. (1980). *The family life cycle: A framework for family therapy*. New York: Gardiner Press.

Chamberlain, P., & Rosicky, J. G. (1995). The effectiveness of family therapy in the treatment of a family of adolescents with conduct disorders and delinquency. *Journal of Marital and Family Therapy*, 21, 441–459.

Clarkin, J. F., Glick, I. D., Hass, G. L., Spencer, J. H., Lewis, A. B., Peyser, J., DeMane, N., Good-Ellis, M., Harris, E., & Lestelle, V. (1990). A randomized clinical trial of inpatient family intervention, V: Results for affective disorders. *Journal of Affective Disorders, 18*, 17–28.

deShazer, S. (1982). *Patterns of brief family therapy: An ecosystem approach.* New York: Guilford Press.

deShazer, S. (1985). *Keys to solutions in brief therapy.* New York: Norton.

deShazer, S. (1988). *Clues: Investigating solutions in brief therapy.* New York: Norton.

deShazer, S. (1991). *Putting differences to work.* New York: Norton.

Duvall, E. (1957). *Family development.* Philadelphia: Lippincott.

Efran, J., Lukens, R., & Lukens, M. (1988). Constructivism: What's in it for you? *Family Therapy Networker, 12,* 26–34.

Epston, D., & White, M. (1992). *Experience, contradiction, narrative and imagination: Selected papers of David Epston and Michael White 1989–1991.* Adelaide, South Australia: Dulwich Centre.

Falloon, I. R. H., Boyd, J. L., & McGill, C. W. (1982). Family management in the prevention of exacerbations of schizophrenia: A controlled study. *New England Journal of Medicine, 306,* 1433–1440.

Fischman-Havstad, L., & Marston, A. R. (1984). Weight loss management as an aspect of family emotion and process. *British Journal of Clinical Psychology, 23,* 265–271.

Foucault, M. (1980). *Power/knowledge: Selected interviews and other writings.* New York: Random House.

Gergen, K. (1985). The social constructivist movement in modern psychology. *American Psychologist, 40,* 266–275.

Goldstein, M. J., & Miklowitz, D. J. (1995). The effectiveness of psychoeducational family therapy in the treatment of schizophrenic disorders. *Journal of Marital and Family Therapy, 21,* 361–376.

Haley, J. (Ed.). (1976). *Problem-solving therapy.* San Francisco: Jossey-Bass.

Haley, J. (1984). *Ordeal therapy.* San Francisco: Jossey-Bass.

Hetherington, E. M., Cox, M., & Cox, R. (1978). The aftermath of divorce. In J. H. Stevens & M. Matthews (Eds.), *Mother/child and father/child relationships.* Washington, DC: National Association for the Education of Children.

Hogarty, G. E., Anderson, C. M., Reiss, D. J., Kornblith, S. J., Greenwald, D. P., Jaine, C. D., & Madonia, M. J. (1986). Family education, social skills training, and maintenance chemotherapy in the aftercare of schizophrenia. *Archives of General Psychiatry, 43,* 633–642

Joanning, H., Thomas, F., Quinn, W., & Mullen, R. (1992). Treating adolescent drug abuse: A comparison of family systems therapy, group therapy, and family drug education. *Journal of Marital and Family Therapy, 18,* 345–356.

Kaplan, L., & Hennan, C. B. (1992). Remarriage education: The personal reflections program. *Family Relations, 41,* 127–134.

Keith, S., Schooler, N., Bellach, A., Matthews, S., Mueser, K., & Haas, G. (1989). The influence of family management on patient stabilization. *Schizophrenia Research, 2,* 224.

Liddle, H. A., & Dakof, G. A. (1995). Efficacy of family therapy for drug abuse: Promising but not definitive. *Journal of Marital and Family Therapy, 21,* 511–543.

Marlatt, G. A., & Gordon, J. R. (1985). *Relapse prevention.* New York: Guilford Press.

McFarlane, W. R. (1991). Family psychoeducational treatment. In A. S. Gurman & D. P. Kniskern (Eds.), *Handbook of family therapy: Volume 11.* New York: Brunner/Mazel.

Minuchin, S., & Fishman, H. C. (1981). *Family therapy techniques.* Cambridge, MA: Harvard University Press.

Moon, S. M., Dillon, D. R., & Sprenkle, D. H. (1990). Family therapy and qualitative research. *Journal of Marital and Family Therapy, 16,* 357–373.

O'Hanlon, W., & Weiner-Davis, M. (1989). *In search of solutions.* New York: Norton.

Pithers, W. D. (1990). Relapse prevention with sexual aggressors: A method for maintaining therapeutic gain and enhancing external supervision. In W. L. Marshall, D. Laws, & H. Barbaree (Eds.), *The handbook of sexual assault: Issues, theories, and treatment of the offender*. New York: Plenum Press.

Prince, S. E., & Jacobson, N. S. (1995). A review and evaluation of marital and family therapies for affective disorders. *Journal of Marital and Family Therapy, 21*, 337–401.

Rogers, C. (1961). *On becoming a person*. Boston: Houghton Mifflin.

Shoham, V., Rohrbaugh, M., & Patterson, J. (1995). Problem and solution-focused therapies: The MRI and Milwaukee models. In N. S. Jacobson & A. S. Gurman (Eds.), *Clinical handbook of couple therapy*. New York: Guilford Press.

Stanton, M., & Todd, T. (1982). *The family therapy of drug abuse and addiction*. New York: Guilford Press.

Visher, E., & Visher, J. (1988). *Old loyalties, new ties: Therapeutic strategies with step families*. New York: Brunner/Mazel.

Wallerstein, J. S. (1984). Children of divorce: Preliminary report of a 10-year follow-up of young children. *American Journal of Orthopsychiatry, 54*, 444–458.

Wallerstein, J. S., & Kelly, J. B. (1980). *Surviving the breakup*. New York: Basic Books.

Watzlawick, P., Weakland, J., & Fisch, R. (1974). *Change: Principles of problem formation and problem resolution*. New York: Norton.

Weiner-Davis, M. (1993). Pro-constructed realities. In S. Gilligan and R. Price (Eds.), *Therapeutic conversations*. New York: Norton.

White, M. (1986). Negative explanation, restraint, and double description: A template for family therapy. *Family Process, 25*, 169–184.

White, M. (1988). *The externalizing of the problem*. Dulwich Centre.

White, M., & Epston, D. (1990). *Narrative means to therapeutic ends*. New York: Norton.

Chapter Nine

Integrative Analysis

Like the family itself, the field of family therapy can be described by studying each part but cannot be fully understood without some synthesis. The majority of practicing family therapists do not draw from a single theory or school of technique (Quinn & Davidson, 1984). Even those clinicians who have been trained under a single mentor usually branch out into other areas once they become more independent in their practice. Each therapist tends to create his or her own eclectic blend of methodologies based on his or her training, personality, and client population. The client population can be particularly influential. For instance, it is doubtful that transgenerational technique would be the initial and primary tool of the therapist who was working with a multiproblemed poor family in acute crisis. In such a case, family-of-origin information may be significant but not critically relevant to the immediate needs of the family. In contrast, the therapist working with a young, depressed college student, away from home for the first time, will not be able to use many of the interactional structural techniques; there are, for example, no spontaneous family interactions to enact in the session.

Family therapists obviously must be creative. By changing, modifying, borrowing, or combining techniques from all the schools, the therapist tailors the technique to a specific client in a specific situation at a specific time. This does not mean, however, that most therapists are simply pragmatic technologists who mix conflicting theory expediently. On the contrary, the general perspective of systems thinking provides a conceptual framework in which clinical diversification can occur, much as diversification developed in the field. The early pioneers would often work together with the same family. Each clinician shared with the others a core perspective of system ideas, yet each approached the task of changing the family from a different point of view. Oftentimes they would use similar techniques for different reasons, or they would use different techniques but for similar reasons. The contemporary family therapist not only can benefit from this history of diversification but may be ethically bound to encompass the breadth of the field. Research continues to indicate that effectiveness of outcome is not exclusive to a specific school but relates, rather, to the use of a specific treatment with a specific family with a specific problem (Gurman & Kniskern, 1978).

This chapter does not propose a universal formula for integrating the various schools of family therapy. Instead, it offers an example of how the theories and techniques might be combined in treating a single family. We hope it will stimulate your own creative integration of the various schools.

Case Illustration

We discussed the Notter family at the end of Chapter 2. *You may find it helpful to return to that chapter and reread the case illustration.* Familiarity with the family's developmental information will aid your understanding of their treatment. Recall that the elder daughter, 13-year-old Kathy, had been throwing temper tantrums, calling her mother names, and refusing to do as she was told. Kathy had been treated previously at an individual-oriented child guidance center, where she stayed three months on an inpatient unit and then saw a counselor on an outpatient basis for about six months. Kathy's mother, Pam, had been seen by the counselor only at intake and occasionally in the waiting room. No other family member was included in treatment. This therapy was not successful, but it did have an effect on the family. Primarily, it solidified the family's collective belief that Kathy was the problem and that if only Kathy would change, the family's life would be less conflictual. The family therefore organized itself not around building on Kathy's strengths and helping her develop, but rather, around avoiding Kathy's disruptive symptoms. Every family interaction had within it the consideration: "Will this set Kathy off?" Obviously, in such a situation, family members become increasingly hostile because they resent having to plan around one person. Their increased hostility in turn contributed to Kathy's symptomatic behavior. So at the point of entering family therapy, Kathy's family was mobilizing its efforts either to find someone who could get through to Kathy or to send her away from home again. The previous treatment did not create this scapegoating, but it did reinforce Kathy's role as symptom bearer.

Circular Interaction

Recall that the Notter family was a blended family that had left many developmental tasks unaccomplished. The incomplete developmental tasks were both individual and systemic, covering both the nuclear family and the family of origin. In Figure 9.1, the therapist has placed the presenting problem within the cycle of family functioning. The sequential pattern presented in Figure 9.1 is only one level of the family cycle. One could take any single point in the cycle and expand on the dynamics in terms of the relations learned in the family of origin, or the reciprocal reinforcers, or the feedback loops, or the lack of choice, or the issues of boundary definition. As a way to lay the groundwork for the integrated treatment plan, we will first illustrate such an expansion. Using the first few interactions in the cycle (Figure 9.2), we will elaborate on the family

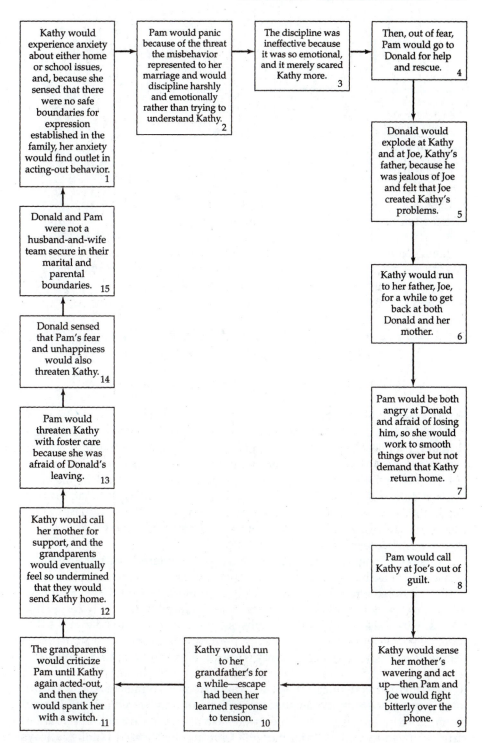

FIGURE 9.1
Cycle of symptoms in the Notter family

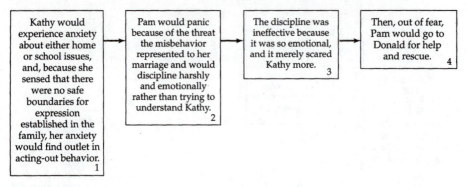

FIGURE 9.2
Cycle of symptoms in the Notter family (detail)

dynamics from each of the major perspectives presented in this book. Through this process, we demonstrate that an integrated eclecticism of *technique* is based first on the therapist's ability to *integrate conceptually* the family's complex dynamics.

The Interaction in Focus

Structural Aspects of the Interaction

From a structural perspective, the primary issues are that the marital subsystem is poorly formed, with little boundary definition, and that the parental subsystem is even less well defined. Pam and Donald are living together without commitment to a shared future. They alternately experience proximity and distance in their relationship as they experiment with what it would be like to be married. In essence, in their relationship, they are particularly attuned to noticing unpleasantness. This characteristic is inherent in any "trial" situation: One tries something for a while to see whether problems arise. In such situations, a person has a rather critical orientation.

This point is significant to the charted series of interactions because Kathy hesitates to voice her unpleasant feelings, regardless of their source, on account of the emotional strain it may place on her mother's trial marriage. Suppressing feelings is not an effective long-term adaptation, particularly for a child who is being raised by a parental subsystem as chaotic as the Notters's. The parental subsystem's boundary was so permeable and fluid that up to seven people would function intermittently within it. Not only were the people intermittently involved, but they were also universally inconsistent. No two people in the entire subsystem could agree on an approach to raising Kathy. Of primary importance was, of course, the fact that not only were Pam and Donald having a "trial marriage," but they were also asking Kathy and her younger sister, Amy, to test out a "trial parent." Children in blended families always have some difficulty with accepting a new parent; however, in Kathy and Amy's case, this new parent could be "gone tomorrow." From a structural perspective, the parenting would certainly be considered weak in terms of executive power, primarily because it was diluted by both numbers and inconsistent commitment.

Strategic Aspects of the Interaction

Looking at the Notter case from a strategic perspective, the therapist asked the questions, "Is the symptom a metaphor for something else in this family?" and "How is this symptom system maintained and system maintaining?" Kathy's metaphorical message to the family through her symptom could be expressed as simply, "No, I won't go along." On one level, her symptoms metaphorically reflected the family's developmental crisis by her refusal to cooperate in what was clearly a dysfunctional system. On another level, however, her unresolved symptoms kept the family from "going along" developmentally.

What system function could these symptoms serve? Possibly, they provided the family members with a defense against their fears and hurts. Kathy's behavior certainly kept the "old" family connected and involved with each other and prevented the "new" family from congealing into a permanent unit. No one in the family had to grieve the loss of the old and face the painful disappointments of years invested in something that didn't work—they were all kept too angry and upset to feel the loss. Pam and Donald also benefitted because Kathy's symptoms provided them a bail-out excuse if their marital experiment didn't work out. Furthermore, it protected them against too much intimacy and their fears connected to intimacy while providing them with a concern around which to relate.

Transgenerational Aspects of the Interaction

Two particularly helpful concepts contributed by transgenerational theorists are (1) that the past is active in the present and (2) that reasoning is easily overwhelmed when the self-concept is poorly defined (when differentiation of self is low). Both concepts are active in the short sequence currently in focus.

First, the past was flooding in upon the present. The therapist had learned that Pam's fears about marriage and intimacy were developed in successive layers, beginning early in her life. Her father was alcoholic, and her mother lived her life through Pam. When Pam's father was drunk, Pam would try to smooth things over to protect her mother. Pam was too close to her mother and too distant from her father. When Pam was about 14, her father began to show an interest in her, and Pam began to think that maybe they could be close. However, her father, in a drunken stupor, made sexual advances toward her, and she successfully pushed him away. He completely abandoned the family a few days later. Pam watched her mother go through the pain, anger, and struggle of being alone.

Pam still felt both guilt and rage over what had happened. Through her past experiences in her family of origin, which were replicated in her first marriage to a heavy drinker, Pam had developed an intense ambivalence about intimacy. She desperately wanted to love and be loved, yet love for her had meant profound pain and hurt. On the few occasions when Pam had taken a stand based on her own feelings (a criterion for the development of self), she had suffered and believed that she caused suffering in others. In the interaction under discussion, Pam panicked when Kathy misbehaved because she was worried about losing Donald. Her worry about losing Donald, however, was made far worse by her unresolved experiences with her own father. Kathy's ambivalent feelings about Donald triggered Pam's memories of ambivalence toward her own father. Those feelings, projected onto Kathy, added even more emotion to Pam's disciplinary measures. In short, Kathy was expressing feelings just like the feelings Pam had tried to repress for so many years. When the discipline failed, Pam would turn to Donald with the hope that he could respond to Kathy as Pam had always hoped her own father would respond to her adolescent self.

Unfortunately, Donald had his own transgenerational history to contend with. He was the son of a couple who had adopted him when they were middle-aged. He never knew his biological parents and had always envied other children who lived with their biological parents. His childhood life was one of love and order. Donald's parents were set in their ways when they adopted Donald and were rather inflexible people anyway, so, although Donald received loving attention, he was also expected to conform in his behavior out of respect for his parents.

His first wife was a woman who fit his parents' ideal rather than his own. The divorce was embarrassing for him and left him feeling very vulnerable in relationships. Before meeting Pam, he had become concerned that he would never again marry or that he would be too old to start a family. In his time as a bachelor, he had become very ordered in his lifestyle. Lonely and discouraged, he had met Pam. Pam and her children became the projected family he had never had as a child and had nearly missed as an adult. He identified with Kathy and Amy because they, too, were "fatherless," and he wanted to fill their void by being their father as he healed his own early wounds. Conflict in his family of origin was unheard of. Conflict in his family of dreams was also unheard of. He also feared that conflict could scare Pam away from marriage, and then he would again have to face failure and aloneness. When Pam asked for Donald's help in disciplining Kathy, he came into the interaction with a full head of steam. He felt threatened and wanted whatever was threatening him to stop. It particularly angered him that Kathy didn't appreciate the fact that he was rescuing her from what he had experienced as a "parentless" child. Her rejection elicited old pains of abandonment. In short, he was in no position to enter the interaction reasonably and minimally.

Although the transgenerational issues were extensive and need not all be discussed, one other issue and person are of note. Kathy also had a history to her role in the sequential interaction. Kathy's father (Pam's first husband) abused Pam. As Kathy grew up, she often would, like Pam, parent her mother; that is, she would be protective of her. Kathy learned not to add anxiety to Pam by keeping her problems to herself. That restraint was possible for her until she encountered the increased problems and tensions of adolescence.

Experiential Aspects of the Interaction

Viewed from an experiential perspective, the personal awareness of each member of the family was extremely low. Pam, Donald, and Kathy all felt one thing but did another. Congruency between their individual needs and their actions was minimal because they were all more concerned about maintaining rather inflexible family roles. Personal growth and freedom of choice had taken a back seat to fulfilling roles and avoiding expression of self. Kathy would act out her concerns rather than telling her mother her fears. Pam would discipline harshly rather than becoming aware of her fear and sadness. Pam could flail out at Donald for his doubt about the future, but she refused to take a self-defining position herself. Donald's avoidance of his existential situation also prevented his further growth. He was in an "as-if" marriage, acting "as if" he were the daddy and husband. Rather than facing his real anxiety, he dealt with a pseudoanxiety created out of his avoidance and lack of awareness of his real anxiety. Individuality, self-expression, freedom of choice, and personal growth were all held in abeyance by the family's overcompensating need to act as if they had family togetherness.

Behavioral Aspects of the Interaction

From a behavioral perspective, the therapist was most interested in how Kathy's behavior was reinforced. Clearly, Pam's overly harsh and emotional discipline was an attempt to control the behavior using aversive stimuli. Equally clear was that periodically Kathy's misbehavior was somehow positively reinforced. Positive reinforcement probably occurred when Kathy was allowed to stay home from school with her grandmother and watch TV after throwing a tantrum. Or maybe it was the reinforcement of hugs from "making up" with Pam after a conflict. Kathy's lack of verbal expressiveness could also be explained in those terms. For example, it was probable that Kathy received aversive reactions from family members when she talked about her problems. Donald's role in the parenting was also aversive. In short, there were no positive contingencies for Kathy's expression of cooperativeness—merely punishment.

Postmodern/Constructivist Aspects of Interaction

From a constructivist's point of view, the family had clearly become over-focused on its problem cycle and had evolved a story of frustration and failure. This story stood unchallenged in the family and had become personalized and polarized. Kathy had acquired a "difficult" reputation, and any exception to that was going unnoticed. Pam had become so sensitized to the problems available responses had diminished, and she could not imagine how her family's situation could improve without Kathy's leaving the family. In short, the family story about Kathy's "difficult" nature had come to dominate family life and even to determine family members' individual responses to family stress. This problem-saturated view of reality left them few good options and further burdened them with feelings of failure.

Each theoretical perspective offered the therapist a related yet different view of the family dynamics. Despite the brevity of these descriptions, it is evident that the perspectives are not mutually exclusive and indeed that each school of thought enhances the therapist's understanding of the problem and expands the alternatives for treatment. In the following section, we will discuss the alternatives chosen by the therapist treating the Notter family, and we will illustrate how the technique of one school can complement the technique of another.

Treatment

In this section, we are interested in how each school's technique was used to help the Notter family. The therapist wove aspects of each orientation into the therapy from the very beginning. There was no attempt made to equalize the use of each therapy in each session; rather, specific issues, concerns, problems, or hurdles appeared to lend themselves to particular intervention strategies. It should again be noted that another therapist treating the same family at the same time would undoubtedly have chosen different perceptual cues on which to focus and therefore would have used different techniques. Therapists would share common systemic outcome goals, although they would differ in process strategy.

Treatment for the Notter family lasted a total of ten sessions. The use of the various techniques employed in the treatment can be best understood by examining the contribution from each school through the various phases of therapy. The discussion of the first session has been divided according to the schools of therapy from which the techniques were drawn. For Sessions 2 through 10, the source of the intervention is noted either in the text or in parenthetical remarks.

Session 1

From Structural Family Therapy

When Pam first telephoned the clinic, she reported that her primary problem was her daughter Kathy. The secretary told Pam that it was important to have the entire family present for the first interview. When the family arrived for the initial session, there was Pam, Kathy, Joe (Kathy's father) and Joe's second wife, Louann. Kathy sat sullenly between her mother and her father, who sat next to Louann. The therapist, confused by the configuration when she walked in, asked, "Which one of you is the mom?" It was a simple informational question, but it became the first structural move to *mark boundaries* around the various subsystems in this blended family. The family responded with a confusing story about who had custody, where Kathy currently lived, where her sister currently lived, and even who was paying the bill for therapy. The therapist listened and understood but chose to respond to the structural confusion by asking Kathy to sit beside her mother, her legal custodian. The therapist continued to mark boundaries by referring to the family's confusion about "who were the parents" as a serious problem.

From Strategic Family Therapy

The therapist spent much of the interview focusing on the interactional sequence of symptoms that would occur when Kathy misbehaved. The therapist asked questions that painted a picture of what occurred during one of their family crises. Here are some examples:

When was the last time Kathy threw a fit?
Where were you, Mrs. Notter?
Who else was around?
What happened prior to the fit?
So what did you do when it started?
Did that work?
What happened next?
Whose idea was that?
Then what happened?
How did her dad get involved?
Did you want to be involved?
Did that help?
So what did you do then?
How long did that last?
And then it settled down?
Did it ever get talked about?
How did it end—or is it over?

This assessment of the interactional sequence occurring before, during, and after Kathy's tantrum allowed the therapist to understand the family better in terms of alignment, power, and hierarchy. Because these concepts are closely related to structural thinking, this discussion also assisted the therapist in her efforts to mark boundaries. Furthermore, it provided the therapist with some rudimentary ideas about what tasks might be assigned for the next session. Finally, this interactional analysis introduced a new piece of important data: that Pam lived with a man named Donald, though Pam and Donald were undecided about marriage.

From Transgenerational Family Therapy

Although Session 1 did not focus on the family's history, the therapist listened for information on how the family's past was active in the present. She noted that Pam would use phrases such as, "I wanted better for *my* daughter," and "I've been treated worse by men before." These phrases indicated to the therapist that Pam was measuring her present experience by her past relationships. The therapist chose not to ask follow-up questions about family history but, rather, to note the matter for later discussion. The reason for her decision was the presence of a structurally confusing array of family members at the first session. The therapist was concerned that such a potentially emotional discussion might undermine future strategies for boundary marking by allowing more distant family members to be privy to information more appropriately shared only with functionally close family members.

From the transgenerational point of view, the therapist also noted how emotionally reactive the family became when discussing conflictual issues. The level of differentiation was extremely low throughout the family. Unable to tolerate their internal stress until it was their turn to speak, family members would frequently interrupt each other to argue a point. The therapist promoted increased objectivity by asking family members to talk directly to her when emotions began to run high.

From Experiential Family Therapy

The therapist both modeled good communication skills and began the process of teaching the family more congruent communication. Specifically, the therapist taught congruency by checking with the family to see if what she intended to say actually came across; in other words, she assessed impact versus intent. While talking with one person or another, she would stop and ask the person to repeat in his or her own words what the therapist had just said in order to let the therapist know if she was being clear. The therapist also attended to nonverbal cues, such as facial expressions or changes in body posture, to obtain the same information. For example, when the therapist was speaking with Pam about Kathy's relationship with her sister, she noticed that Joe was smiling proudly. She asked Joe about the smile, thus eliciting some much-needed positive remarks about Kathy. Occasionally, the therapist would also ask a family member to speak only for himself or herself rather than make continual "we" statements. The therapist did not make a big issue of those requests but did introduce the importance of self-statements so that she could build on it later in therapy.

From Behavioral Family Therapy

The therapist became aware that the family was better at recounting what occurred after an interactional crisis than at recounting what led up to the crisis; that is, they had a hard time pinpointing any pattern of stimulus (antecedent) that triggered the response of misbehavior in Kathy. The therapist also was clearly aware that the consequence Kathy received was attention, albeit negative attention. The rest of the time (when she behaved well), Kathy was ignored (in other words, not reinforced). Additionally, all efforts to extinguish the undesirable behaviors were unpleasant (aversive) in nature. In short, Kathy was not being encouraged toward a certain behavior; instead, she was only being discouraged from her current behavior.

The therapist requested that Pam pay closer attention in the next week to what might be taking place before a family crisis (that is, to begin to make a functional analysis). Pam was assured that her observations would be very useful to the therapist in her efforts to help the family.

From Postmodern/Constructivist Therapy

Once the therapist had an initial understanding of the problem interaction, she asked the family whether there had ever been a time when Kathy felt comfortable coming to her mother to discuss a problem with school or family life. The family thought about this awhile, and, although they had difficulty remembering any exception to the problem, they eventually came up with a time when this was true. The therapist then spent some time exploring what was different about that situation and tried to elicit as many details about the events as possible. This discussion then led to a brief discussion with Pam regarding good days versus bad days. This discussion evolved from Pam's saying that her response was partially explained by whether it was a bad day for her or not.

Summary

By the end of the first session, the family had received the clear message that Kathy should not be allowed to move from house to house and to change parents to avoid changing her behavior. It was decided hat Kathy would return to Pam's home and that Joe and his wife would not attend the next few sessions. These steps helped to clarify one aspect of the confused-boundary question, and Joe was happy not to have to come as long as he was kept informed about what was going on. The therapist asked that both Donald and Kathy's sister Amy be brought to the next session and reminded Pam to work on her notes of observation. In addition to producing some clarification of boundaries, the session helped the family calm down and begin to formulate a plan to improve on its problems. The discussion of exceptions to the problem seemed to introduce some hopeful feelings into the family's view of their situation and gave Pam something to think about (the everyday context for these painful episodes). This lessening of emotional reactivity and definition of boundaries helped to strengthen and elevate the executive hierarchy, Pam in particular.

Session 2

The therapist's primary goal in this session was to assess the functioning of the marital, parental, and sibling subsystems. Of particular concern was how the unsettled marital subsystem influenced the parental subsystem (*structural*). After introductions, the therapist inquired about the functional analysis he had asked Pam to conduct (*behavioral*). Pam reported that there had been no extreme crises during the past week; however, there had been two episodes that had almost escalated to crisis proportions. In both cases, she reported that everything was fine until it was time for Kathy to go to school. Kathy would complain about stomachaches and start crying when Pam said she had to go anyway. In both cases, Pam was afraid that the conflict might escalate to a major scene, and because Donald and Amy were waiting for their breakfast, she had decided not to press Kathy to go. The following dialogue then took place:

Kathy: You should have seen the look she gave when she said, "Stay home, then." She hates me.
Donald: Your mother doesn't hate you, she loves you.
Kathy: Sure, she does. What do *you* know?
Donald: I know your mother, and I know she bends over backwards to please you. If it was up to me, I'd tan your hide. You don't know how lucky you are.
Kathy: [*Sits sullenly, eyes watery.*]

The therapist moved closer to Kathy and gave her a tissue. After a few moments passed, the therapist helped Kathy express her feelings (*experiential*).

Therapist: [*Quietly, to Kathy.*] Does he scare you?
Kathy: [*Crying.*] No, it 's just that he doesn't understand, he always thinks it's my fault.
Therapist: And your mom?
Kathy: She always takes his side, she wants to get rid of me 'cause I just cause trouble, I always cause trouble.
Therapist: And your sister Amy?
Pam: Oh, she's perfect, she's an angel.
Therapist: Does she want to get rid of you, too?
Kathy: No, we're friends. It's just that they don't think she can do wrong.
Pam: That's not true, we—
Therapist: [*Putting his hand up toward Pam.*] Whoa, wait just a minute, it's all right, it's important to let her talk.
Therapist: [*To Kathy, after a few moments of silence.*] Are you OK now? [*Kathy nods.*] Can you and your sister go out in the waiting room for a while and draw? [*Kathy nods.*] Is that OK with you, Amy? [*Amy nods.*] OK, off you go so I can talk with your mother and Donald.

By removing Kathy and Amy, the therapist increased the emotional *intensity* for Pam and Donald (*structural*). Both felt guilt about Kathy's pain, but without her there, they couldn't negate their own discomfort by attacking her for her *misbehavior* (*transgenerational*). In other words, they couldn't restore homeostatic balance to the family by reinstating Kathy as the symptom bearer (*strategic*). The therapist continued to build *intensity* by immediately *expanding the definition* of the problem when Kathy left (*structural*). She did this by not giving them a chance to defend themselves.

Therapist: I know that Kathy's behavior must change, but I'm equally concerned about the burden you have placed upon yourselves as parents.

Pam: What burden? I feel—

Therapist: You two are "trying out" being a parental team—of a teenager no less—before you've even decided whether you are going to be a team! What kind of situation is that? It doesn't make sense; or does it to you?

Pam and Donald just looked at each other. The therapist was challenging the couple's structure and version of reality *(structural)* by expressing her own reactions to their "as-if" family *(experiential)*.

The discussion continued for 15 to 20 minutes. Pam and Donald said that they just weren't ready to make a commitment to each other because they often fought and argued. The therapist responded with, "That's fine, but you're asking Kathy to commit to you two 'as if' you were going to be there tomorrow. Trial marriages are one thing and trial parenting quite another." The discussion was a heated struggle for the definition of what therapy was going to be about. The therapist asked them where they were, on a scale of 1 to 10, on the issue of feeling comfortable with their trial situation *(solution-based)*. Each noted that it really varied, but it was the lowest when they argued about parenting issues. Each could remember an earlier time when they rated their comfort level higher and noted that it was before Donald was asked or chose to become more involved in the parenting. The therapist worked to stay joined with Donald and Pam around their fears of commitment *(structural)*, yet kept them focused on the definition of their relationship dilemma *(structural, strategic,* and *experiential)*. Near the end of the session, she summed up her view from a position of low power.

Therapist: Look, I've given you a hard time tonight. I know it, but you needed to be given a little grief. It isn't easy to trust after what each of you has been through, and maybe you're not ready to tie the knot. But it may be too much to expect Kathy to take up the slack and act as if you two have it all worked out. After all, she is just a teenager, and she hasn't exactly had an easy life either. You seem to agree that Kathy has to get under control—that's a given. But as part of that, you two need to work on your team a little bit, or decide if you are going to be a team. I'd like to spend most of next session with just you two and see if we can work out a way to turn Kathy around. I'd also like you to read some stuff on stepparenting that may help you. What do you think of all this—does this direction make sense?

Donald: I think it's good, no, it's all right. I want to get our relationship resolved—it's a big part of the problem. And if it doesn't get resolved, I don't know how much longer I can put up with it.

Pam: [*Glowering at Donald.*] That's exactly what I don't like. The least bit of trouble and you threaten to walk.

Therapist: Pam, he is just scared, like you're scared. What do *you* think about what I said?

Pam: I think you're right. I don't like it, but we have known for a long time we had to face our relationship.

Therapist: Or face the way you have jumped ahead of yourselves a bit. . . . Next week?

Pam: [*With a sigh and a smile.*] I'll be here.

Therapist: Donald?

Donald: Yep, we'll all be here.

Therapist: Good.

The therapist asked for a few minutes alone with Kathy before ending the session. The therapist felt that Kathy's symptoms were system-maintaining and, in some fashion, an attempt by the system to deal with its problems (*strategic*). She felt she might have some temporary leverage with Kathy if she connected her behavior with the marital conflict and indecision. Alone with Kathy, she made the following strategic task intervention:

Therapist: You did well tonight, you spoke your mind instead of keeping it inside and letting it make you ornery. I know your mom and Donald's relationship is confusing to you; it is to them as well. I'm going to help them work on it, but I need your help. [*Long pause.*] We need to remove the school issue. If you set your mind to it, could you go to school? Because if you keep cutting up, all they'll do is get all stirred up over you, and they won't ever deal with the problems in their own relationship. Besides, you've sacrificed enough for a while. What do you think? Can you do that?

Kathy: Probably. Yeah, if they'd just leave me alone.

Therapist: Great! I'll work on that. Look, I know this will be tough for you, especially if you're sick, but it should really help. Hang in there.

What the therapist did in this session was to redefine the family problem partially as due to the unstable marital relationship. This redefinition could be described in transgenerational terms as the therapist's interpreting the family projection process, or in structural terms as unbalancing and reconstructing reality. The strategic and experiential schools both discuss the need for the therapist to establish control early so as to maximize his or her therapeutic power. The behavioral intervention took secondary importance in this session, but its inclusion here paved the way for returning to it later. Solution-focused questions allowed the couple to identify their feelings about commitment and the connections to parenting. The time alone with Kathy was an attempt to redefine her self-sacrificing role in the family from that of one who stops developing for the good of the family to that of one who goes on developing for the good of the family.

Session 3

The therapist began by asking to see Kathy alone for a few minutes.

Therapist: [*Whispering, as a conspirator.*] Well, how did it go?
Kathy: I went every day.
Therapist: No! You didn't!
Kathy: Yes, and all my detentions are made up.
Therapist: No! You're kidding. That's amazing. Was it hard? I'll bet!
Kathy: Sort of, but Mom's being nicer, so—
Therapist: OK. Well, now I'll try and do my part. Good luck this next week. By the way, I've been thinking that it might be helpful to you if you had someone of your very own to talk to for a while. What do you think?
Kathy: I don't know. Who?
Therapist: A friend I work with. Her parents were divorced when she was in grade school, I think—anyway, someone who might understand a little about what it's like. I'll talk to your mom and we'll see. OK? Let me talk to your folks.

The therapist formed a temporary alliance with Kathy as an interim step toward reducing the enmeshment between Kathy and her mother (*structural*). The therapist was emphasizing needs for autonomy appropriate for Kathy's stage of development. She arranged for a young female student therapist to work with Kathy to further support her during this time of emotional distance between her and her family. The therapist hoped that this adolescent-adult bridge would allow Pam more freedom to focus on her relationship with Donald by stabilizing the mother-daughter relationship. The therapist was thinking spatially (*structural*) in that she was concerned with proximity and distance.

The therapist then met with Donald and Pam. Each was terribly hurt and angry with the other. They had tried to discuss their relationship during the week, and it had ended with both withdrawing into themselves.

Therapist: I know we stirred the waters last week—maybe I pushed too much.
Pam: I was mad at you, but then, you're exactly right, so then I was mad at myself. And he was no help.
Therapist: And you, Donald?
Donald: I've always said we should get married, but when it gets close, something always happens to spoil it.
Therapist: Kathy tells me she went to school this week.
Pam: Thank God for that.
Donald: It's been better this week, except between us.
Therapist: How did you make it better with Kathy?
Pam: [*Pam explains how she listened more and spent more time just hanging out with her but didn't really see that was what made the difference.*]

Therapist: [*After taking some time to congratulate them on the week.*] I take it you're ready to look at where the two of you are—kind of explore that for a little while. [*Pam and Donald nod in agreement.*] I'd like to spend today, and maybe even a couple of sessions, on your own histories. Talk about how you got to where you are today. I think that might be helpful.

The rest of the session was spent on slowly reviewing both Pam's and Donald's early family life. A genogram (diagram of the family tree) was constructed for each, to aid in understanding not only his or her own past but that of the other partner *(transgenerational)*. The therapist used every opportunity she had to ask the couple about how they managed to overcome adversity and difficult times, building a description of their pasts as "histories of courage" *(narrative and solution-focused)*. At the end of the session, the therapist talked to Pam about the young therapy student with whom she was recommending that Kathy work for a while. Pam said that she felt relieved because she knew things were bothering Kathy, but right now she just couldn't seem to help. The therapist also suggested that useful thoughts about their past would come to them in the coming week and that they should keep a small notebook with them for recording purposes *(strategic)*.

Sessions 4 and 5

Two sessions were spent on transgenerational issues. Pam's and Donald's families of origin and histories of early relationships were studied and explored. The therapist took every opportunity to interpret current issues in the light of previous family dynamics, educating the couple about why they reacted to each other the way they did. These sessions often prompted tears or resentment; however, the therapist purposely chose not to elicit or enhance emotions as painful memories were discussed. Instead she worked to stay objective and out of the triangle as she asked each person in turn about his or her reactions to what the other had said. As in Session 3, the therapist used language that helped redefine their histories from stories that were victim-based to stories that were courage-based *(narrative)*. Although Pam and Donald never had a direct conversation during these sessions, each obtained more understanding of and empathy for the other partner's emotional legacy. The therapist used a transgenerational approach rather than confronting their issues immediately because she thought that she needed to increase each partner's ability to reason and empathize before encouraging them to discuss an area of current conflict.

At the end of Session 5, Pam requested that the next session be spent discussing Kathy. Kathy had been much better, but Pam was worried about the upcoming spring vacation. Donald concurred that they needed to talk about Kathy. The therapist understood that that interest may have represented the family's retreat into the position that "Kathy is the problem" due to resistance to dealing with the marital subsystem conflict. Nevertheless, she chose to return with the family to focusing on the symptom, but this time to use the hoped-for progress in the marital subsystem as an approach to dealing with the parenting issues. She was also interested in what the return of attention to the symptom meant metaphorically in the system *(strategic)*.

Session 6

The therapist was concerned that the agenda for the sixth session called for the parental subsystem to focus on changing Kathy's behavior even though the parental hierarchy was still unstable. Of key concern was what role Donald would occupy in this new round of the parental activity. The therapist decided to deal directly with these structural questions at the beginning of Session 6. She started the session with just Donald and Pam. She asked them about their reading on stepfamilies and expressed her interest in what they had read. They discussed their concern that Donald might play too strong a parental role too early as he had done before. Having just covered the transgenerational issues in previous sessions, the therapist was able to expand on this concern that even if Donald did manage to keep himself low-key, Pam might work unwittingly to pull him into the fracas as a consequence of her own history. In this discussion of concerns, the therapist evolved a position of cautioning restraint lest they progress too fast. Her posture of restraining change *(strategic)* allowed Donald and Pam to argue that they could handle their fears. Donald assured the therapist and Pam that he wouldn't feel left out, that he knew it would take time, and that he was more patient than they gave him credit for being. Pam argued convincingly that she could handle Kathy alone, no matter how outrageous Kathy might become. This assertion led to some playful "as-if" discussions, such as "What if she threw a fit in J. C. Penney's?" and "What if she ran to the neighbors screaming bloody murder?" *(experiential)*. The therapist concluded the discussion by "giving in" to their argument that they were ready for this parental test but added that she still felt some concern. At that point, she shifted strategic techniques to work behaviorally, specifically on developing a contract for contingency management between Pam and Kathy. For this work, she invited Kathy to join them.

The rest of the hour was spent developing a contingency contract, following the guidelines presented in Chapter 7. The therapist used herself and physical space to balance the power *(structural)*. She chose to sit next to Kathy, with her hand on the arm of Kathy's chair. This position approximated that of an ally or coach and helped Kathy to avoid feeling threatened. Because Kathy felt supported, through physical arrangement and the earlier "conspiratorial" relationship, she was able to be less emotionally reactive, more adultlike in her negotiations. Her conduct, in turn, allowed Pam more confidence and freedom to be flexible. The therapist aided their bargaining through ideas and suggestions. The session ended with a decision to talk by phone in a week rather than meeting, due to the family's plans, and then to meet again in two weeks.

Session 7

The between-session phone call never occurred. The family reported that all had been going well and they had just forgotten. Both Donald and Pam began the session with, "You didn't think we could do it, did you?" The missed phone call may therefore have been a way to defy the therapist a little bit. Session 7 was characterized by a light and friendly discussion among Donald, Pam, Kathy, Amy, and the therapist; first about how they were able to take further steps toward redefining their situation (*narrative*) and then about household chores. The contract was discussed and expanded. Deals were made between the sibling subsystem and Pam, between the sibling subsystem and Donald, and between Donald and Amy. The family seemed to enjoy using the tool of contracting because it gave them a way to negotiate mutual support from a safe distance. The therapist, while clearly employing behavioral technique, positioned herself much like an experientialist. She enjoyed the friendly atmosphere and used it as an opportunity to play with the rigid family roles and to give voice to the family's submerged fears. For example, when Donald and Kathy were negotiating a special "date" as reward for some household duty, the therapist half-jokingly kidded Kathy: "Careful, Kathy, your mom will get jealous." And then to Pam, "Does he court your favor this much?" These remarks might seem embarrassing out of context, but they allowed the family to act out some of its pent-up feelings. Pam and Kathy responded to the therapist's remarks by making fists at each other and mock-sparring. Donald broke up the mock-fight and then put his arm around Pam and offered her exaggerated "sweet talk." The therapist then returned everybody to the safety of the contingency contracting. This combination of experiential and behavioral technique allowed the family to increase its flexibility without overwhelming itself with premature intimacy.

Sessions 8 and 9

Riding on the successes of Sessions 6 and 7, the therapist suggested to Pam and Donald that it might be good to have a discussion about their relationship, how they felt about each other, and things they liked and didn't like about each other.

Therapist:	Who would like to go first? [*Both point to each other and laugh.*] Is this a little scary?
Pam:	Well, he gets mad when I say something.
Donald:	I do not!
Pam:	You walk away!
Donald:	I do not! [*He leans back and folds his arms and looks out the window with a sigh.*]
Pam:	See!
Therapist:	OK, let's slow this whole thing down and find out what is going on.

The therapist asked them to move their chairs until they faced each other, and she moved her own chair close enough that she could reach out to them if she wanted to *(experiential)*. The therapist then coached them both in communications skills. She emphasized the importance of personal awareness, checking out perceptions, the right to see things differently, and the need to take responsibility for their own thoughts and feelings *(experiential)*. Pam and Donald's conversation for these two sessions was highly emotional but not as reactive as before. Each had a much richer perception of the other one's feelings due to the earlier discussions of family of origin.

Between Sessions 8 and 9 and Sessions 9 and 10, the therapist assigned straightforward tasks that she thought would help them overcome their relationship issues. For instance, one interaction that typically ended in Donald's walking out of the house to his workshop would occur when Pam asked for some cash to buy something. Pam always dreaded asking because Donald would always question her about her budgeting. Because each kept separate accounts, the issue had become a metaphor for the question of whether they would ever unite in marriage.

Therapist: It seems important to you, Donald, that you not feel trapped when you're emotionally overloaded, right? You want the option of walking out to the shop to collect yourself. If you had to put a monetary value on it, what would you say that option is worth—five dollars?

Donald: Ten dollars, at least. I mean, to be able to go and come back later without getting all bent out of shape would be worth ten dollars, easy.

Therapist: OK, I have a plan that will work if you follow it faithfully. Donald, each time you get to the point that you need to take a breather, you need to reach into your wallet, get ten dollars out, and put the money in a cookie jar. Now, Pam, that money will be there for emergency situations if and when you ever need it. How does that sound to you?

Donald: That's crazy, but I like it. Fine.

Pam: Sounds good.

This example of the assignment of strategic tasks may sound absurd; however, Pam and Donald made good use of it. Pam saw how important it was for Donald not to get emotionally trapped when he agreed to pay $10 for the privilege. Paying the money allowed Donald freedom from guilt when he took care of himself, which, in turn, allowed him more flexibility when he returned. And in the first week, Pam had a $30 nest egg for emergencies. It should be noted that they dropped this operation after a week, retaining it only as a joke. Whenever Pam needed money, she would ask Donald if he felt like a walk to his workshop. The therapist used this family success to explore how fast a new story about their relationship was emerging. She did this by returning to scaling questions, by asking them about trends that might continue in the future, and by asking them if others had begun to notice *(constructivist)*.

At the end of Session 9, the therapist suggested a longer time between sessions to give them more of an opportunity to work on their own. Pam and Donald concurred, and it was agreed that they would return with Kathy and Amy in a month.

Session 10

A month later, the session was canceled and rescheduled two weeks later. When the family arrived, Pam and Donald asked to be seen alone first. Alone with Donald and the therapist, Pam apologized for canceling the appointment. She said that at the time they were in the middle of deciding whether to marry or not. As they both smiled, they reported that they had decided to marry in a month. They wanted to talk alone with the therapist first because they hadn't told the children the news yet but would the next weekend. After some shared excitement, the therapist chose to support them by playing the voice of caution (*strategic*).

Therapist: How do you think you'll handle the change, Donald? Do you think it will make you more impatient for that family life you waited for? [*Later.*] Pam, aren't you afraid you'll send him away if he gets too close—that you'll get scared and lash out to protect yourself from getting hurt?

This discussion allowed Pam and Donald one more opportunity to go over the pitfalls to which each was most susceptible. They could review past mistakes and plan future strategies should the old roadblocks reappear. Although they had lived together for nearly two years, they were discussing their future with the hope of a premarital couple.

Later, when Kathy and Amy were brought in, the therapist briefly went through the list of concerns that they had worked on in therapy. With mention of each concern, there was a brief discussion about progress made and progress to be made, with a generous share of compliments for strong effort. Because the contingency contracts were reciprocal, Kathy and Amy had the opportunity to assess Pam's and Donald's progress. They played "as if" they were the adults and graded them with stereotypical colloquialisms. Pam and Donald went along, even going so far as pleading for a second chance (*experiential*). This evidence of renewed flexibility made for an optimistic prognosis.

The therapist suggested that it was time to stop therapy for a while but that her door was always open to them should they wish to touch base again.

Chapter Summary

We have attempted to present both the separate and significant contributions of the major schools of family therapy, as well as to place them in the overall conceptual framework of developing systems. The Notter family system was challenged with developmental issues at almost every level. The treatment they received was formulated by the creative integration of a therapist knowledgeable in each of the major schools. It is our view that most therapists work this way, carefully drawing on such concepts and tools from their base of knowledge as best fit the family with whom they are working. Most therapists probably would not try to cover all of the theory groups in their work and probably would not explain their work from so many different perspectives. Therapists beginning to experiment with postmodern approaches might also tend to apply the newer concepts more consistently throughout the case. This is because postmodern approaches have been defined as partial critiques of earlier approaches, thus making conceptual integration more difficult for practitioners of the newer approaches.

In any case, the treatment offered the Notter family was not presented as a paradigm to be copied; therefore, details of the therapy were deliberately not included. We hope you questioned the appropriateness of certain interventions and thought of alternative approaches and interpretations. Because different schools have different terms for similar concepts and techniques, you may have attributed certain interventions to other schools than did the authors. You may find it useful to outline your own approach to the Notter family and consider some alternative interventions for each stage.

References

Gurman, A. S., & Kniskern, D. P. (1978). Research on marital and family therapy: Progress, perspective, and prospect. In S. Garfield & A. Bergen (Eds.), *Handbook of psychotherapy and behavior change* (2nd ed.). New York: Wiley.

Quinn, W., & Davidson, B. (1984). Prevalence of family therapy models: A research note. *Journal of Marital and Family Therapy, 10*(4), 393–398.

PART THREE

THE PROFESSION
OF FAMILY THERAPY

Chapter Ten

The Practice of Family Therapy in the Community

There are a variety of settings in which to practice family therapy: mental health centers, schools, child-guidance clinics, hospitals, welfare agencies, churches, and private-practice settings. The practice of family therapy is different in each of these contexts because of the characteristics and environmental constraints of the setting. Each setting places a different value on family therapy, depending on the goals of the organization. For example, in a mental health center or hospital, it may be more profitable to see family members separately than as a unit. Furthermore, in these settings third-party payments can be collected only when family members are seen individually by a psychiatrist, thus discouraging treatment of the family as a group.

The characteristics of the setting or system often determine how much control the family therapist has over the care. In many mental health centers and hospitals, for instance, cases are assigned to a case manager and/or a team. Although the therapist may be treating the family, the case manager, team, or both determine the nature of treatment. Biddle (1978) notes that therapists who work in the inpatient settings often are not able to involve families in therapy. Likewise, in child welfare agencies or juvenile courts, the family therapist often does not have control over disposition of the child. In school settings, family therapists do not have control over the educational placement and program of the child. The important consideration here is how the family therapist can work within the system to control certain elements of the case in a way that is beneficial to the family.

A number of practitioners have emphasized the need to work with families in their own contexts. Minuchin (1974) has stressed the necessity of working within the context in which the family is experiencing difficulty. Minuchin and his associates have been successful in intervening in schools (Aponte, 1976), in dealing with child problems in hospitals (Minuchin, Rosman, & Baker, 1978) and in dealing with psychosomatic children.

Working within the System

In their recent book, *Practicing Family Therapy in Diverse Settings*, Michael Berger, Gregory J. Jurkovic, and associates (1984) outline and describe predictable issues confronting therapists who work with families in helping systems such as schools, mental health centers, hospitals, and churches. The authors suggest that one crucial issue a therapist must face is the hierarchy of the system. Just as the therapist must not violate the hierarchy of the family, he or she also should not violate the hierarchy of the social system. Berger, Jurkovic, and associates (1984) advise:

> To do this, the therapist must understand how the helping system is organized (its structure and the hierarchical relationships among the various persons the therapist encounters in the setting) and what its functions are. Understanding the hierarchical relationships among persons in the setting is important so that the therapist will not enter into coalitions that cross levels of the hierarchy. The therapist also needs to take into account the functions of the setting so that he or she will not ask persons in that setting to do something either opposed to the purpose of the setting or irrelevant to it. Different settings have different functions. For example, schools exist to teach students things; special education settings exist to aid students thought to require additional assistance in order to learn; clerical settings exist to help congregation members deal with spiritual issues and correctly carry out the rituals of their religion; and court settings exist to regulate the behavior of felons and, perhaps, to rehabilitate them. Thus, a therapist working in a school setting needs to frame the issues he or she is working on as having something to do with a child's educational performance, while a therapist working in a court setting needs to focus attention on the fact that therapy is helping clients obey the law and court. (p. 11)

The therapist must establish a collaborative relationship with members of the organization to avoid crossing levels of the hierarchy. Collaborative relationships are largely predicated on the problem-solving process. Staff members (teachers, social workers, probation officers, and so forth) are encouraged to define problems and generate solutions. Staff members are thus stimulated by the therapist to participate more fully in the therapeutic program. Staff members are also more likely to work with the therapist in ways that fit their work roles, and a more trusting relationship is likely to exist because the therapist and the staff are mutual partners in the therapeutic program of the family. Finally, therapeutic changes are more likely to be maintained when staff members have become more involved in the program.

There are several things the family therapist can do to maintain a collaborative relationship with staff members in the organization. First, the therapist should try to understand the family problem and how the staff member perceives it. Inherent in this understanding is some discussion of the extent to which the problem is affecting the staff member, as well as the staff member's expectations for the family. In such a discussion, it is possible to determine whether or not the staff member has unrealistic expectations and, if so, to clarify them.

Second, a therapist is more likely to develop collaborative relationships with the frequent use of the term *we*. The use of *we* helps to develop a sense of cooperation and gives the staff member a feeling of support. It is extremely important for the therapist not to confront the staff member and suggest that he or she has contributed to the client's problem.

Third, it is important to know what the staff member has done to remedy the problem. In many instances the staff member may wish to refer the family's problem to the therapist without first doing anything about the problem itself. For example, a teacher who is experiencing problems in the classroom may refer a child (and perhaps the family) to the therapist. Unless the teacher has already tried to do something about the problem, the therapist may not know the severity of the problem or how committed the teacher is to changing it. Furthermore, if the teacher has met with the family and tried to work out a solution and has been unsuccessful, the therapist needs to know the nature of the attempted solution before meeting with the family.

Finally, the therapist must work with individuals within their prescribed work roles. One therapist saw a 23-year-old mother who was trying to maintain custody of her 5-year-old son. The woman had been married twice and had been living with a man who was not accepted by her parents. The parents were overinvolved with their daughter and failed to let her lead her own life. The woman's lawyer requested that the woman live with her parents until final custody was rendered in court. The lawyer felt that living in a closer relationship with the parents would help stabilize the young mother's situation and increase the likelihood that the woman would maintain custody of the child. Although living with her parents might have presented a more stable picture to the courts, such an arrangement discouraged the woman from functioning more independently. The therapist in this case worked with the lawyer to encourage the parents to allow the daughter to take more responsibility as a mother to the child (for example, washing the child's clothes, getting a babysitter for the child, and so forth). These suggestions were presented within the context of proving the mother's competency for the custody hearing. By working closely with the lawyer within his role, the therapist could avoid triangulation between the lawyer and the family, which might have jeopardized the treatment program.

In summary, the therapist must use his or her skills to work within the hierarchy of the system. The therapist should establish a collaborative relationship with individuals and avoid triangles and coalitions that disrupt the process of treatment.

For the remainder of this chapter, we will focus on how these guidelines are realized in the practice of family therapy within hospitals, schools, mental health centers, and child welfare agencies.

Professional Settings
Hospitals

The hospitalization of a family member has a significant impact on the family. The family is often confronted with financial pressures and an alteration of parental and working roles that affect the quality of life. When the needs of the ill member are met at the expense of other family members, tension and disruption are likely to occur. Indeed, chronic illness often disrupts both the developmental life of the family and the attainment of family goals (Nagi & Clark, 1964).

Tension and disruption due to chronic illness appear to be the greatest at the time of diagnosis or hospitalization and at other times in the person's illness when family members must cope with a situation that is changing (Cotter & Schwartz, 1978). Kaplan, Grobstein, and Smith (1976) studied 40 families of children who died of leukemia. The authors found a correlation between the average number of problems identified for each family in the first four weeks following diagnosis and the family's ability to cope in the first three months following the child's death. They concluded that therapeutic intervention would be most beneficial immediately following diagnosis.

The initial diagnosis of an illness is often made in a physician's office. If the patient is hospitalized, then the social worker or family therapist may come in contact with the patient and his or her family, particularly when the physician believes that social and emotional difficulties may be contributing to the physical problem. If the family therapist or social worker is to be successful in working with the patient and family, he or she must understand and respect the hierarchy of the hospital setting.

Hierarchy

In the hospital setting, the physician and the hospital board are at the top of the hierarchy. The nursing services in a hospital also follow a hierarchical pattern. Floor nurses and nurses' aides report to head nurses. Head nurses report to nurse care coordinators or the director of nursing. The head nurse often works with the physician to carry out the treatment program, and thus is in constant contact with the patient. Since the nursing staff plays a role in primary care, it is critical for the therapist to receive support from the head nurse or director of nursing, who is often in a position to recognize family problems.

The therapist may have either a line position or a staff position within the hierarchy (Greiner, 1984). The therapist who holds a line position may have subordinates for whom he or she has administrative responsibilities and superiors to whom he or she must be accountable. The family therapist who holds a staff position reports directly to a superior, such as head nurse or director of nursing, but has no subordinates. The clearer the lines of authority, the easier it is for the family therapist to receive referrals and consult with staff members on individual cases.

Focus of Intervention

The intervention should focus on the points of major stress for the family. The stress points of any major illness involve diagnosis, hospitalization, discharge, and aftercare. It is important for the therapist to recognize how the family copes with the illness at each of these points so the therapist can intervene to move the family through the transitional process.

Diagnosis The need for family intervention first begins when the patient is diagnosed for a chronic disease. When first told by the physician, the patient and family often experience shock and discouragement. Family members often react by denying the severity of the illness. At this point it is common for family members to experience high levels of anxiety.

Stress levels are often highest in family members who are poorly differentiated. When family members are not individuated and are overly dependent on one another, they are unable to accept help from each other. Family members who are poorly differentiated are not objective enough, and thus they have difficulty knowing how to negotiate what is to be done about the illness. Feelings of dependency are often frightening and often render the patient and family helpless, particularly when separation and loss are imminent.

At this point, the family therapist tries to help the family manage the illness. The family is assisted in getting in touch with the strengths that helped them cope with previous situations. Each family member is encouraged to express his or her feelings about how the illness affects him or her. The therapist facilitates problem solving so that family members can support each other and the patient. The therapist may serve as a source of stability for the family in dealing with anxiety.

Hospitalization Hospitalization may be particularly stressful when the ill member is separated from his or her family. Family members must adopt new roles and functions and change their activities. They must recognize that their lives have at least temporarily changed. The family must share time in an unfamiliar environment, functioning in unfamiliar roles.

There is particular stress when an ill member is hospitalized for a diagnosis. Family members face uncertainty while they await the final result. Family stress is exacerbated by hospital rules and policies, which often separate the family from the patient. The patient and the family may become upset when the diagnosis is confirmed. When the patient fails to respond immediately to treatment, the family grows increasingly frustrated. The extent to which family members are individuated will determine how successful the family members will be in coping with the separation and change (Fine, 1980).

The family therapist often intervenes at the time of hospitalization. The therapist must accept family denial while holding to reality. The therapist must help family members express the difficulties they are having in adjusting to the loss. Each family member should be encouraged to identify personal issues relating to the hospitalization of the ill family member. If necessary, the family therapist helps family members adopt new roles and responsibilities to improve the functioning of the family.

Death The death of a family member generally produces stress in the entire family system. Family members often experience conflict, role confusion, and unresolved feelings of guilt. Family members may find it difficult to accept even small changes in their life out of a desire to keep things as they were prior to the loss. The family therapist helps family members express their feelings of sadness, anger, guilt, relief, or sorrow. If the therapist works with the grieving family at the time of death or shortly thereafter, there is less chance that dysfunctional interactions will become patterned into family structure (Christensen, 1983). The therapist must also deal with his or her own unresolved issues surrounding death so that he or she can tolerate working closely with the family in its pain (Hare-Mustin, 1979).

Discharge It is easy to understand a family's difficulty in dealing with the death of one of its members. However, stress also occurs for the family whose member gets well enough to be discharged. Dysfunctional families often become resistant to cooperating with the physician and hospital staff. Families may be unwilling to discuss the discharge plan or come to the hospital. Family members may be angry with the patient and refuse to participate in the discharge plan.

According to Fine (1980), there are three essential tasks for the therapist when dealing with families who fail to participate in the discharge plan: (1) to remind the family that the patient must leave the hospital because he or she does not need acute care, (2) to identify specific issues related to the separation of the patient from the family, and (3) to separate such issues from issues relating to the discharge plan. The therapist must also help the family decide whether it is able to care for the patient. Families may be unwilling or unable to care for the patient but at the same time reluctant to admit the patient to a nursing home or rehabilitation center.

Aftercare One of the difficult times for the family and patient is the aftercare period. The family experiences particular stress when the patient fails to make a full recovery from the illness. Special problems arise when the family fails to recognize that full recovery is not possible. When the family fails to adopt new roles and functions, the patient is often unable to accept his or her new developmental changes. In severely disturbed families, permanent changes often threaten family members' sense of well-being and produce fear and anxiety (Lewis, Beavers, Gossett, & Phillips, 1976).

In the aftercare stage, the therapist must help family members understand the patient's disability. Each member is asked to identify sources of anger and helplessness. Each member is helped to recognize that these feelings are normal and often accompany disabling illness. The patient and family are encouraged to work out problems; when the patient is no longer able to perform a specific role or function, then that role or function must be transferred to another person. In short, the therapist helps the family reorganize to carry out its new tasks and functions.

Case Illustration

The following case illustrates how a therapist can work with a family in a hospital setting.

> Rob and Sandy Paul approached the family therapist for help three months after Mr. Paul's mother, Violet, had been hospitalized for a stroke. Violet was a dominant figure in the family and had a great deal of influence with her children. She was confined to a bed, was adamantly opposed to being placed in a nursing home, and expressed a desire to live with her son. Rob and Sandy had reservations, but they decided to keep Violet at their home.
>
> When Rob brought his mother home, the situation presented several problems. First, Rob and Sandy assumed all responsibility for hiring someone to care for Violet during the day. On days when the person could not come to the home, Sandy would stay home from work. Second, Rob had two sisters who agreed to care for their mother on weekends. However, because they lived some distance away, they often were not available. Because Violet refused to let the family use her money, her children were left with the financial responsibility for her care. Finally, Rob and Sandy's teenage children became resentful when they couldn't invite their friends to the home. When Rob suggested to his mother that she would be better off in a nursing home, she said she would die if he moved her.
>
> The family therapist helped the family to recognize the problems it faced in caring for Violet. Each family member was able to help other family members understand that Violet's reaction to placement in the nursing home was normal. All family members were able to express sadness and regret for the painful decision. The family therapist helped the family select a nursing home. It was decided that Rob, with the support of his sisters, would explain the decision to his mother.

This case illustrates the difficulty a family may experience in caring for an ill member. If the therapist had been contacted at the time of discharge, rather than three months later, then issues related to the placement could have been dealt with immediately. The therapist's main functions in this case were (1) to help the family recognize the burden placed on Rob and Sandy, (2) to help the family recognize that Violet's reaction was normal and that they were doing what was best for her, (3) to help members deal with feelings of sadness and guilt surrounding the placement, and (4) to assist Rob in taking over the executive role once played by his mother.

Schools

Schools play a significant role in the life of a family. With an increase in after school day-care programs and extracurricular activities, a child may spend as many hours at school as he or she does at home. A child's problems at school may place a great deal of pressure on the family system. School problems, social, academic, or otherwise, are commonly referred to family therapists.

Schools, like families, are social systems with overlapping functions. Both schools and families are charged with the socialization and protection of children. Yet the natures of these functions differ. In families, the socialization and nurturing roles are treated with equal importance, whereas in schools the socialization function takes precedence over the nurturing function (Lightfoot, 1978).

Indeed, because the two systems carry out similar functions, the boundaries often become blurred and functional responsibilities unclear (Lightfoot, 1978). Either system is unable to carry out its functions when there is interference from the other. For example, parents cannot fulfill their functional responsibilities when schools attempt to dictate what the child should be doing in the home. Likewise, teachers who allow parents to become too involved in the child's classroom behavior have failed to protect the classroom boundary around the teacher and child.

Boundaries between the school and family are likely to be violated under stressful conditions. Suppose that a husband and wife have a very conflictual relationship. When stress increases in their relationship, the child may stay home to protect the mother. Often, such a child is labeled by the school as "phobic"; however, from a systems perspective, the child's phobic behavior serves two purposes. First, the phobia shifts the focus of the parents' attention toward the child and away from their own conflict. Second, the child is able to stay at home and receive more attention.

In some cases, learning problems in the classroom may produce boundary problems at home. For example, parents may feel responsible for the child's learning problems and overprotect him or her. Each parent may be confused and uncertain about how to deal with the child. In some cases, one or both parents may violate generational boundaries by competing for the child's affection. In other cases, if marital conflict occurs, the child's learning problem may be seen as the source of the problem. One parent will then usually defend the child against the other parent, in which case the child's problems may be exacerbated both at home and at school.

Hierarchy

The organizational structure of the school is often determined by the hierarchy. In administrative terms, superintendents are over principals, who, in turn, are over teachers. A hierarchy also exists in the classroom. The teacher is in charge of the class. The hierarchy may become complicated by various staff personnel, such as psychometrists, school psychologists, counselors, curriculum coordinators, and supervisors. How well these various roles are defined will affect how clear the hierarchy is.

The principal has a major influence on how well the roles of various personnel are defined (Foster, 1984). Principals who are centrally involved in the instructional program are more likely than others to become involved with child problems, and when they do, hierarchical boundaries become more diffuse and roles unclear. A principal who is more removed from the instructional program is more likely to leave child problems to the teachers. The more detached administrative style allows for clearer roles and reduces the likelihood that hierarchical boundaries will be violated.

Within the school, the principal is the authority. Aponte (1976) suggests that the principal should participate in the family/school interview. Aponte (1976) further states that when a school needs to alter a policy in order to alleviate a problem, the principal's permission should be obtained. A principal who understands the plan of treatment is better able to support school staff who carry it out. The therapist respects the hierarchy in the school by including participants who are related to the problem.

Focus of Intervention

The intervention in the school begins when the therapist first makes contact with the school system. The therapist's focus will depend on whether the referral is made by the school or by the family. When the school makes the referral, the therapist should immediately call the school to gather relevant information. Aponte (1976) suggests an initial interview with both school personnel and family. The initial interview avoids misinterpretation of the school's position and premature identification of the child as a client.

Family/school interview Harry Aponte (1976) describes the nature of the initial family/school interview:

> The first step in response to the school's referral is to explore the problem where the request for help has originated. Because the pressure for a solution has originated in the school, the therapists have never been refused an interview at the school. In the clinic's experience, the usual sequence begins with a mother calling the clinic to ask for an appointment for her son or daughter, usually the former. When asked to describe the problem, she explains that the school is complaining about her son, but that he is not a problem at home. The therapist then asks her whether he and the family could meet with the school staff to find out more about the problem. When the mother agrees—and she always has, in our experience—the therapist calls the school counselor to arrange the interview. The counselor is usually willing, but occasionally there is a question of freeing the teacher from class, and, more often, the principal's reluctance to take part in the interview. The therapist may call the principal personally, with the explanation that the family can see no problem and that, since the school knows the problem first hand, it would help both the family and the clinic if all concerned parties talk together. The clinic is quite prepared to wait until school personnel can arrange their schedules so that all can attend the interview. We

have found that when we compromise and have the first interview with the child and family in the clinic, we are apt to meet greater resistance to a school interview. Our leverage diminishes as we lose the momentum of the school's initial pressure. This is not to say, however, that such interviews are never held after treatment has begun at the clinic, but only that they are often more difficult to arrange. (pp. 464–465)

The family/school interview provides a mechanism for gathering information related to the problem. Aponte suggests that the therapist should focus on solving the problem rather than searching for the cause of the problem. Those personnel—teachers, psychologists, and so on—related to the problem should be present at the interview.

Changing the hierarchy Therapeutic intervention in these meetings is often directed at changing the hierarchy. Hierarchical problems often develop when the child's school behavior deteriorates. School authorities may request that parents take responsibility for the problem. Phone calls and notes are directed to the parents. When such efforts fail, parents and school personnel tend to blame each other (DiCocco & Lott, 1982). Therapeutic efforts must be directed at altering the cycle of negative communication and altering the hierarchy so that both the parents and teachers assume responsibilities within their respective domains (DiCocco & Lott, 1982).

DiCocco and Lott (1982) suggest that one way to alter the hierarchy is to put the parents in charge of developing a treatment plan. This type of approach will work best if school personnel feel that there is nothing more they can do to handle the child's problem. To implement the treatment plan, the teacher must be willing to allow the parent to provide suggestions concerning the child's behavior in the classroom. Parents are able to use consequences within the home and classroom to manage the program.

DiCocco and Lott note several conditions that must be present for this sort of intervention to be successful. First, parents must be willing to provide direction to the teacher. The therapist should be understanding if parents do not wish to take such responsibility. Second, children should be aware that the parent is directing the teacher so "new behavioral sequences can begin to transpire between the child and teacher, between child and parents, and between the two sets of adults" (1982, p. 101). Third, parental disagreements about how to handle the child should be resolved so that the child and teacher do not get caught in the triangle. Finally, once the behavior is under control, the teacher should take over responsibility for the child.

Triangles

Therapeutic intervention should also focus on triangles that are likely to occur among children, parents, and teachers. Foster (1984) lists three types of triangles that are common in dealing with home/school problems.

Parent/teacher/child When tension occurs between parents and teachers, the child is often triangulated. Parents who are too protective of the child may try to save the child from the teacher. Parental statements such as "the teacher always picks on Jimmy" or "if anyone else had done this, the teacher wouldn't have done anything" often indicate that the parent has entered a coalition with the child against the teacher.

The family therapist must intervene to resolve disagreements between the teacher and parent in order to detriangulate the child (Foster, 1984). The therapist might set up a conference to discuss areas of agreement and disagreement. If a history of extremely negative interaction exists, the family therapist might initially ask the parent and teacher to talk to him or her. In such cases, it is best for the therapist to request that the parent and teacher not communicate outside the session. The therapist marks boundaries by requesting that each party control the child's behavior within his or her own particular setting. A statement of responsibilities can be drawn up in the form of a contract and presented to the child for his or her written acknowledgment. When the parents and teacher unite, even if only through the family therapist, the child is no longer caught in the middle and his or her behavior is brought under control (Haley, 1976).

Mother/father/teacher   Carl and Jurkovic (1983) report that when parents disagree about how to handle a child, each may attempt to get the teacher to take his or her side. Before talking to the teacher, the therapist must first work with the parents alone to get agreement about how to deal with the child. If there is a strong alliance between the teacher and one parent (typically the mother), then a special session should be established between the teacher and the other parent to break the alliance (Foster, 1984). If one parent has been inactive, the therapist encourages that parent to take a more active role in the child's education.

Teacher/teacher/child   Foster (1984) notes that, in some cases, teachers or other school personnel may disagree about how to handle the child's behavior. Such conflicts often arise between the child's homeroom teacher and another teacher or professional who has different views about how to handle the child. A child may do quite well in a highly structured classroom but have difficulty in an unstructured classroom. A teacher who is having difficulty with a child may sometimes feel that the counselor or school psychologist is taking the child's side against the teacher. The therapist must mark boundaries by ensuring that teachers and counselors do not interfere with each other's domain.

Thus, when a child is having a problem in the classroom, the therapist should explore the following questions:

1. What are the patterns of interaction in the family?
2. What are the boundaries within the family system?
3. What kind of interaction exists between the parent or parents and teacher?
4. What triangles exist between the parents, teacher, and child?
5. What is the power hierarchy within the family and the school?

By assessing each of these areas, the therapist is in a position to determine (1) the relationship between the child's problem at school and his or her position in the family and (2) the appropriate intervention to alleviate the problem.

Case Illustration

The following case example illustrates how a therapist can work with a family when the child is having a problem at school.

> Sarah Thomas and her 9-year-old son, Jerry, were referred to a family thera-
> pist by the school. Jerry was an only child with above-average intelligence.
> The presenting problem was Jerry's failure to comply with the rules in his
> fourth-grade classroom. Jerry did not complete assignments and frequently
> talked out in class. Moreover, the school reported that Jerry fought with
> other children and seemed socially immature for his age.
>
> In the initial interview, the therapist learned that Jerry did not like his
> teacher, who often punished him for things he said he didn't do. Sarah
> reported that she had had few problems with Jerry until that year. She indi-
> cated that her husband, Jake, had recently changed shifts at the factory,
> thus placing most of the parental responsibilities on her. Recently, Jerry had
> been disobedient around the house. He often became angry with his mother
> and said that nobody liked him. Sarah reported that she and Jerry would
> often engage in intense arguments. When the arguments would get out of
> hand, Sarah would ask Jake to discipline Jerry. However, when Jake at-
> tempted to strongly correct Jerry's behavior, Sarah would intercede and tell
> him he was "too severe." Jake would then withdraw, and the struggle would
> begin.
>
> Following the interview with the family, the therapist arranged a sec-
> ond session that included both the family and teachers at the school. Jake
> could not attend this session because he had to work. During the interview,
> Sarah appeared surprised to learn that Jerry did not complete his work
> because he had always done well at school before. The teacher felt that
> Sarah did not believe her, whereas Sarah felt that the teacher was picking
> on her son.
>
> Jerry continued to misbehave, and two weeks later, the therapist re-
> quested another session with Jake, Sarah, Jerry, the teacher, and the school
> counselor. Sarah was reluctant to include her husband because of his work
> schedule but agreed to do so anyway. At the session, Sarah said that al-
> though Jerry didn't do his chores, he had not been a serious problem at
> home, and she couldn't understand why he was such a problem at school.
> She also stated that she did not want to bother her husband because he was
> working long hours and needed his rest. Jake reported that he was not aware
> of his son's problems at home and school. Jake also indicated that he could
> spend more time with Jerry to help him with his homework. Sarah voiced
> the opinion that Jerry should complete his work without any help.
>
> At that point, the therapist asked the teacher to show Jerry's home-
> work to his parents for their inspection. Jake agreed with the teacher that

Jerry needed help. Sarah felt that with Jake's work schedule, he would not have the time to give to Jerry. Whenever Jake and Sarah began to raise their voices, Jerry would interject a comment to detour the conversation. This pattern of communication continued throughout the session.

To understand this problem better, one must examine how Jerry *interacted* with others in both the school and family systems. When Jerry misbehaved in the classroom, other children often laughed at him, which resulted in Jerry's gaining the teacher's attention. When the teacher reprimanded Jerry, the children gave him more attention, which escalated his misbehavior. At home, Jerry often failed to complete his chores; his mother would complain but also would often do his chores for him. Whenever Jerry began to argue with his mother, she would become frustrated and ask his father to discipline him.

The interactional sequence that expresses this boundary problem consists of the following elements:

1. Mother is in an intense relationship with the son, which is characterized by both affection and frustration.
2. Son fails to respond to the mother's directions.
3. Mother continues to plead with the son to do his work.
4. Mother asks father to get the son to complete his work.
5. Father attempts to get the son to do his work.
6. Mother criticizes the father because he is too harsh with the son and doesn't know how to handle him.
7. Father withdraws.
8. Mother and son continue intense relationship.

This interactional sequence is also descriptive of the boundary problems in the classroom. The teacher and child are engaged in an intense struggle. When the teacher is unable to control Jerry's misbehavior, she asks his mother to control him. When Jerry's mother attempts to intercede, the teacher blames the mother and threatens to remove Jerry from the classroom. The mother then becomes angry and withdraws, and the teacher and Jerry continue their intense struggle.

This pattern of communication continues to exist, because the parents are arguing through their children. Father often says mother is too "permissive" and mother feels that he is too "harsh." The same kind of complementary pattern exists at school: The teacher perceives the mother to be too "soft," while the mother perceives the teacher to be too "strict." The mother and teacher are engaged in an intense struggle, with Jerry caught in the middle of the triangle. The result in this case is a cross-generational coalition that excludes both the father and the teacher from a role of authority and traps the mother in an overinvested role.

When a parent is too invested in or enmeshed with a child, he or she is unable to exercise appropriate control, as Sarah's overinvolvement with Jerry prevents her from teaching him to obey rules or respect authority. Likewise, a teacher may see a child's behavior as a reflection of his or her competence and have difficulty establishing boundary control. Children in such confused hierarchies are often disobedient and disruptive and have difficulty complying with rules.

These repetitive interactional patterns reflect both the family's and the classroom's hierarchical structure. The child's problems indicate that there is no power hierarchy: it is not clear who is in charge. The child's problem can be viewed as an effort to solve the family's organizational problems—namely, the intense involvement of the mother-child relationship, mirrored in the teacher-child relationship, and the concomitant exclusion of the father-child relationship.

The structures of the family and school systems were stressed when the father changed his work schedule and the child was assigned a stricter teacher. The family did not realign itself to adapt to the changing circumstances. Mother assumed all the parenting responsibilities and involved the father when she could no longer tolerate the child's misbehavior. Moreover, when the child began to experience problems at school, the family failed to provide adequate support—both to the child and to the teacher. Thus, the child's problems at school became an extension of the problems at home.

When there is a change in the family system, new rules must be established. In the Thomas family, new rules were not established when the father changed his work schedule. The mother, attempting to be helpful, assumed total control of the child rather than relinquishing control to the father on weekends or to the teacher during the week. New rules were not established for the child in the father's absence.

Moreover, the teacher's rules may have been too demanding, given that the child had not been required to follow rules at home or previously at school. In the classroom, the child served as the scapegoat for the teacher's frustrations with the child's antagonistic parent.

It is important to note that in family systems, roles are reciprocal. If someone is to play a permissive role, then someone else must play a strict role, and vice versa. In this case, the father and teacher felt the need to be strict because the mother was seen as permissive. Similarly, the mother felt that she needed to be more permissive because the father and teacher were too strict.

The therapist made the following recommendations:

1. Bimonthly meetings would be established between Jake and Sarah, the teacher, and Jerry.
2. No critical comments about the parents or teacher would be permitted in the sessions.
3. The three members of the executive hierarchy (teacher, mother, and father) were to support each other's efforts to help the child.
4. A daily homework form was to be sent home with Jerry.
5. Jake would inspect the homework each night and sign the form if the work was satisfactorily completed.
6. Jake would help Jerry on weekends in any areas that required remediation.
7. The teacher would award privileges to Jerry for appropriate progress in the classroom.

Child Welfare Agencies

Child welfare agencies are established for the protection of children against abuse and neglect. The agencies are often encompassed by protective services, which assist in cases of abuse and neglect, teenage pregnancy, and foster care and adoption. The various branches have overlapping functions, which often create hierarchical problems with case workers and families.

Tension arises when agencies view problems as residing within individuals rather than within families. In such cases, family members are often divided up for assessment and treatment. Adults may be seen by one agency and children by another agency. Moreover, workers from still other agencies may provide special services to family members. Thus, each worker may see only one aspect of the problem rather than seeing how the problem functions within the family system.

Hierarchy

Protective service workers often work in groups under a staff supervisor. Each case worker is responsible for a large number of families. Case workers are responsible for assessing abuse and neglect, monitoring the families in the home, and assisting the family in getting help from community agencies. In addition, protective service workers have the legal mandate from the courts that require treatment for the family. Thus, case workers are responsible to both case supervisors and the court. All other professionals (for example, school personnel, family therapists, and physicians) are responsible to other case workers within their own domain of expertise. It is critical that these professionals work in a cooperative manner.

The family therapist must work within this hierarchy in order to be effective with the family. The therapist must work with the entire system as the unit of treatment. The therapist must be aware of the professionals who are involved and how they function in the case. The therapist should be in direct communication, whether by letters, telephone calls, or visits, with those professionals to ensure that the hierarchy is maintained and the treatment program is properly implemented.

Lewis (1984) suggests four ways in which the therapist can support the position of the protective service worker within the hierarchy. First, the therapist should respect the protective service worker's knowledge of environmental and institutional demands on the family. The therapist should ask the worker to help him or her understand those demands and how they affect the family. By gaining some understanding of environmental and institutional issues affecting the family, the therapist and worker will have a more complete knowledge of the family system.

Second, the family therapist should attempt to support the worker's position in the hierarchy without condescension. For example, the therapist might say, "You know a lot about child abuse and can determine whether the child is safe." Lewis further suggests that the therapist encourage other professionals, such as physicians and police, to support the protective service worker's efforts.

Third, the therapist should become knowledgeable about issues relating to child abuse. Lewis (1984) suggests that the family therapist can gain valuable information on child abuse in the journals *Child Welfare* and *Family Process*. The therapist should make his or her views known to the protective service worker and be willing to work with families when not all members can be present.

Fourth, the therapist should avoid technical language when communicating with professionals in other fields, particularly professionals such as physicians who view pathology from an individual perspective.

The ultimate goal is to place the parents in an executive position in the hierarchy. When child abuse occurs, the family often gives its power away to other professionals: case workers, police officers, and others. When parents believe that they cannot handle a problem, they turn to professionals and expect them to solve it. The therapist must support the parents' ability to handle their own problems.

When protective service workers and other professionals fail to respect the parents' executive role, the therapist must intervene. The therapist might, for instance, coach the parents on how to respond to stressful situations. Lewis (1984) suggests that parents may need to be coached on how to express anger or how to discuss private matters. In addition, parents must learn to identify their strengths and know how and when to ask professionals for information.

Some families are powerless because they are socially isolated and lack environmental supports (Baldwin & Oliver, 1975). Abusing families are often isolated from the community and their extended families. Families who receive little support from relatives may have difficulty handling stress effectively. These parents commonly have little support for their child-care role and feel overloaded and powerless to handle their children.

When the family lacks environmental supports, the therapist takes on the role of an ombudsman to empower the family. Minuchin (1974) states:

> If [the therapist] analyzes the family organization and determines that it is basically viable but is overloaded by the impingement of many uncoordinated agencies, he may act as the family's ombudsman. He may teach the family how to manipulate the institutions for its own benefit. Or he may work to coordinate the efforts of the agencies vis-à-vis the family. With a Puerto Rican family overwhelmed by relocation, the family therapist would do well to locate Puerto Rican resources in the community—the church, schools with a large Puerto Rican enrollment, Puerto Rican parents active in the PTA, or social and civic agencies dedicated to helping this ethnic group. His functions as a family therapist will be complemented by his actions as a social matchmaker. (p. 63)

In addition to his or her therapeutic and ombudsman's roles, the therapist also has legal responsibilities. If family members abuse one another or fail to attend sessions, the therapist should immediately get in touch with a protective service worker. In some cases, a change in circumstances (for example, if a family member loses a job or becomes ill) will produce an unstable situation that warrants contact with the case worker. The therapist has the responsibility to make written recommendations to the protective service worker. The court considers the recommendations when making its decision. The effective therapist can empower parents by eliciting their suggestions in drawing up the recommendations. When responsibilities and power are clearly delegated, then the hierarchy is maintained and the treatment program may be more successfully carried out.

Case Illustration

The following case illustrates how the therapist can work with a family referred by a protective service agency.

Frank and Donna had two children: Mary (age 11) and Steven (age 3). Mary was Donna's child by a previous marriage; Steve was the biological child of Frank and Donna. The couple was referred by protective services because Frank had physically abused Mary. Frank had a history of violence, and his records indicated that he was epileptic and alcoholic. However, Frank had been abstinent for nine months and was currently attending AA.

In the first interview, Frank admitted that he had trouble controlling his emotions. Frank also said that he had difficulty getting along with others on the job, and he often came home at night angry. Donna reported that she was afraid of Frank because she never knew when he would "blow up." Frank complained that Mary was "whiny" and "would never do what she was told." Donna protected Mary and indicated that she often cleaned Mary's room for her so Frank would not get angry with Mary. Donna felt that Frank was "too hard" on Mary and devoted all his attention to Steven. Donna would often leave Mary at her mother's—something that disturbed Frank. Both agreed that Mary should be at home (safely) and that they should agree on how to handle her when she failed to do her work.

The therapist also learned that Frank trusted the protective service worker, possibly more than he trusted the therapist. The couple had had other case workers, but this one was different: "She seemed to understand our problems and gave us some ideas about handling Mary." The therapist encouraged the couple to listen to the case worker's suggestions on how to handle Mary.

Following the initial session, the therapist called the protective service worker. They agreed that Frank and Donna needed to greatly improve their parental teamwork. The therapist suggested that, in addition to the parents' coming to some agreement about Mary's behavior, it made structural sense for Donna to carry out any disciplinary actions. Furthermore, he suggested that Frank be encouraged to develop a positive, nondisciplinary relationship with Mary. The therapist also told the worker that because she seemed to have a lot of credibility with the family, they might be more receptive to her suggestions than to his own. The therapist agreed to work on those issues in the session, and the protective service worker agreed to discuss and monitor weekly progress in the home.

The therapist also called Frank's physician. The therapist was concerned that Frank's medication might be producing side effects that made it difficult for him to control his emotions. The physician felt that Frank's medication should not be producing any negative side effects but agreed to reduce his dosage as a precautionary measure.

After two months, the case was mandated to the courts. The protective service worker asked the therapist to write a progress report and a list of recommendations. Before writing the report, the therapist asked each family member to indicate what had changed since they had come to therapy. The therapist also asked what areas still needed to be improved and let the family know that the information would be included in his report to the court.

The report stated that "Frank and Donna are in general agreement about how to discipline Mary." The family was also "doing more things together and having fun." Because Frank reported that he still was having difficulty controlling his anger, the therapist recommended that the family attend therapy sessions until Frank's reactions were confidently under control. The report further recommended that "Frank continue to spend more time with Mary to establish a positive relationship and prevent further abuse."

This example illustrates how the therapist can work with a family referred by protective services. The therapist was able to work cooperatively with both the protective service worker and the physician to carry out the treatment program. The therapist made use of the protective service worker's credibility to empower the family. The therapist treated the family in the sessions and the worker reinforced the changes in the home. The family was put in charge of its own treatment and asked to participate in the recommendations made to the court. The entire system thus became the unit of treatment.

Mental Health Centers

Mental health centers have been slow to adopt a family systems perspective. There are several reasons why mental health centers do not practice family therapy. First, many community mental health centers are attached to hospitals, which are based on a medical model. The supervisory staff are often psychiatrists, and the staff has an individual, rather than a systems, orientation.

Second, community mental health centers require individual diagnosis. The diagnosis is typically derived from the *Diagnostic and Statistical Manual of Mental Disorders, Fourth Edition* (DSM-IV) and often figures in third-party payments to insurance companies. Although a few diagnostic labels (for example, parent-child problems) are tailored to a systems classification, an individual diagnosis is often required for the identified patient. Unfortunately, such labels do not help us to understand how the client functions in his or her environment.

Third, many mental health centers must justify their existence by the number of clients treated. Carl (1984) elaborates:

As with any bureaucratic system, one of the purposes of the community mental health center is to increase or at least maintain its own domain. Therefore, systemic thinking and the therapeutic work deriving from it must be presented in such a way that they are not threatening to the institution's resources and domain. Unfortunately, many mental health appropriations tie funding to head count, which means that the system becomes invested in helping clients, not discharging them. The life of a typical chronic, adult mental-health client revolves around visits to the mental health center, short hospitalizations and medication. The central events in life concern past hospital stays, schizophrenic breaks, and the specter of craziness. Sometimes we see a client, hospitalized once, ten, fifteen years ago, whose life still revolves around that hospitalization and the prevention of a recurrence. Clients who "do well" may be given the opportunity to become volunteers at the program. As mentioned earlier, we have succeeded in substituting institutionalized outpatients for institutionalized inpatients, but we feel happy because they look better and are "functioning" in the community. (p. 88)

Finally, systems approaches are seen as just another kind of treatment. A systems perspective is not considered as the primary treatment modality (Haley, 1975) and is often used to augment the primary individual treatment (Carl, 1984). Because these perspectives are incompatible, seeing the family while thinking "individual" rarely works. Failure is then often used to justify the practice of individual models alone.

Hierarchy

The family therapist working inside a mental health center must be sensitive to hierarchical issues within the organization. First, the therapist must be aware of the hierarchical roles of each staff member. The therapist may report to a supervisor who reports to a clinical director or case manager. The therapist must be aware of the decision-making powers belonging to persons at each level of the hierarchy. The therapist should be sensitive to triangles in which a family may be caught between the therapist and another professional inside or outside the agency. For example, if the therapist and supervisor disagree on whether the client should take medication, the family may regress or drop out of therapy. In such cases, the therapist must be aware of how the family, and in some cases the therapist, can become trapped between members of the professional staff in the center.

Perhaps the only way a therapist can practice a systems approach in a mental health center is to have some control over the intake process, which in turn requires that intake workers have a systems orientation. Carl (1984) suggests that one must often "sell" a family on being seen as a unit rather than individually. Persuading an entire family to seek treatment is easiest to accomplish during the initial contact. If a family is first referred to a psychiatrist who medicates, the identified patient, then family members, are likely to see the patient as the problem and become less willing to enter therapy as a family. Thus, it is critical that the family therapist hold a position in the hierarchy that permits him or her control over intake procedures.

Case Illustration

The following case illustrates how a therapist can work with a family in a mental health center.

Mrs. Wells was a 42-year-old woman who was referred to the family therapist by a supervising psychiatrist. The psychiatrist had prescribed an antidepressant and tranquilizers for Mrs. Wells but felt that she would also benefit from therapy. The psychiatrist said that Mr. Wells had moderate paralysis in one arm but saw an occupational therapist once a month and seemed to be doing fine.

Mrs. Wells began the first session by praising her psychiatrist and complaining about how little respect she received from her husband. She felt that her husband didn't care about her and showed no affection for her. Mrs. Wells reported that it had been nine months since the couple had had sexual relations. Mrs. Wells said that she cried often and that, although the medication helped, she still felt that no one cared for her. The therapist stated that she wanted to talk with the psychiatrist about the wisdom of involving Mr. Wells in treatment. Mrs. Wells said he would never come.

The family therapist talked with the psychiatrist about what she had learned and suggested that marital therapy might be appropriate but that Mr. Wells would probably resist. The psychiatrist volunteered to call Mr. Wells and prescribe marital therapy. The psychiatrist also suggested that the therapist inform the occupational therapist about the change in treatment and solicit his support.

Mr. Wells did attend the second session and was seen alone. He reported that his wife was sick and needed more medication. He denied that anything was wrong in the marriage and insisted that any problems they might be having were due to his wife's illness. He seemed surprised that his wife would seek therapy when the psychiatrist had given her medication for her depression. The therapist reframed Mrs. Wells's action as an attempt to protect Mr. Wells from her stress. Mr. Wells did not understand why she would protect him but expressed the wish that his wife were her old self. He agreed to return because everyone thought it important.

In the third session, the couple was seen together, and the therapist suggested that Mrs. Wells was acting depressed because she was afraid that if she really expressed herself, she would offend Mr. Wells. Mr. Wells was very critical of his wife, but she always accepted his criticism. Following the session, the therapist consulted with the psychiatrist about Mrs. Wells's medication. The therapist reported that Mrs. Wells seemed slow and sedated and needed to be more active. The psychiatrist agreed to eliminate the tranquilizer and prescribe only the antidepressant.

In the next session, the couple reported that they had had a serious argument and then had held each other. Shortly thereafter, they had gone to the bedroom and made love. The therapist cautioned against too rapid a change and suggested that it was important for them to argue because that was a way to get close and foster improvement in their sex life. In subsequent sessions, the couple learned through typical marital therapy to express affection without first having had an argument.

The case of the Wells family illustrates how a family therapist can work within a mental health care setting, with its medical model. The therapist managed the case effectively by working with the psychiatrist and the occupational therapist to coordinate the treatment program. She avoided becoming triangulated between the supervisor and the occupational therapist, as well as between the two partners, thus positioning herself to be effective and to treat the couple effectively.

References

Aponte, H. (1976). The family-school interview. *Family Process, 15,* 464–477.

Baldwin, J., & Oliver, J. (1975). Epidemiology and family characteristics of severely abused children. *British Journal of Preventive and Social Medicine, 29,* 205–221.

Berger, M., & Jurkovic, G. J. (1984). Introduction: Families, therapists, and treatment settings. In M. Berger & G. Jurkovic (Eds.), *Practicing family therapy in diverse settings.* San Francisco: Jossey-Bass.

Berger, M., Jurkovic, G. J., & associates (Eds.). (1984). *Practicing family therapy in diverse settings.* San Francisco: Jossey-Bass.

Biddle, J. R. (1978). Working with families within inpatient settings. *Journal of Marriage and Family Counseling, 4,* 43–51.

Carl, D. (1984). Community mental health centers. In M. Berger & G. Jurkovic (Eds.), *Practicing family therapy in diverse settings.* San Francisco: Jossey-Bass.

Carl, D., & Jurkovic, G. (1983). Agency triangles: Problems in agency-family relationships. *Family Process, 22,* 441–452.

Christensen, D. (1983). Postmastectomy couple counseling: An outcome study of a structured treatment protocol. *Journal of Sex and Marital Therapy, 9,* 266–275.

Cotter, J., & Schwartz, A. (1978). Psychological and social support of the patient and family. In A. Altman & A. Schwartz (Eds.), *Malignancies of infancy, childhood and adolescence.* Philadelphia: Saunders.

DiCocco, B., & Lott, E. (1982). Family/school strategies in dealing with the troubled child. *International Journal of Family Therapy, 4,* 98–106.

Fine, J. (1980). Family treatment in a medical hospital setting. In C. Janzen & O. Harris (Eds.), *Family treatment in social work practice.* Itasca, IL: F. E. Peacock.

Foster, M. (1984). Schools. In M. Berger & G. Jurkovic (Eds.), *Practicing family therapy in diverse settings.* San Francisco: Jossey-Bass.

Greiner, D. (1984). Hospitals and outpatient clinics. In M. Berger & G. Jurkovic (Eds.), *Practicing family therapy in diverse settings.* San Francisco: Jossey-Bass.

Haley, J. (1975). Why a mental health center should avoid family therapy. *Journal of Marriage and Family Counseling, 1,* 3–13.

Haley, J. (1976). *Problem-solving therapy: New strategies for effective family therapy.* San Francisco: Jossey-Bass.

Hare-Mustin, R. (1979). Family therapy following the death of a child. *Journal of Marital and Family Therapy, 5,* 51–59.

Kaplan, D. M., Grobstein, R., & Smith, A. (1976). Predicting the impact of severe illness in families. *Health and Social Work, 1,* 71–82.

Lewis, H. (1984). Child welfare agencies. In M. Berger & G. Jurkovic (Eds.), *Practicing family therapy in diverse settings.* San Francisco: Jossey-Bass.

Lewis, J. M., Beavers, W. R., Gossett, J. T., & Phillips, A. V. (1976). *No single thread: Psychological health in family systems.* New York: Brunner/Mazel.

Lightfoot, S. (1978). *Worlds apart: Relationships between families and schools.* New York: Basic Books.

Minuchin, S. (1974). *Families and family therapy.* Cambridge, MA: Harvard University Press.

Minuchin, S., Rosman, B., & Baker, L. (1978). *Psychosomatic families: Anorexia nervosa in context.* Cambridge, MA: Harvard University Press.

Nagi, S. Z., & Clark, L. D. (1964). Factors in marital adjustment after disability. *Journal of Marriage and the Family,* 215–216.

Chapter Eleven

Contemporary Professional Issues in Family Therapy

Family therapy as an approach to treatment has developed into a major force in the mental health field. Family therapy has become an international movement, with clinicians lecturing and demonstrating their work throughout the world. National and international meetings are held to exchange new ideas. Training programs are rapidly developing, and professional associations are setting standards for accrediting such programs (Goldenberg & Goldenberg, 1983). This chapter describes the role of professional organizations, issues in licensure and certification, professional ethics and law, and training. Finally, we discuss possible future trends in the field of family therapy.

The Role of Professional Organizations

One of the first professional organizations for family therapists was the American Association of Marriage Counselors (AAMC). This organization consisted of an interdisciplinary group of counselors, psychologists, and psychiatrists led by Nathan Ackerman, Don Jackson, and Lyman Wynne. Although AAMC offered an opportunity for exchange of information, its scope did not attract those whose primary interest was family therapy. The new organization eventually became known as the American Association of Marriage and Family Counselors (AAMFC). In 1978, AAMFC changed its name to the American Association for Marriage and Family Therapy (AAMFT).

AAMFT is one of the fastest-growing mental health organizations. Currently, AAMFT has over 20,000 members and more than 45 regional, state, and provincial divisions in the United States and Canada. The number of states certifying or licensing marriage and family therapists has more than tripled in the last ten years—growing to 35 states. In 1978, the Department of Health, Education, and Welfare designated AAMFT as the official body to establish certification standards for training programs in marriage and family therapy.

AAMFT publishes a brochure *(AAMFT: What it is . . . What it does . . .)* that describes the major functions of the organization:

1. *Professional standards.* AAMFT sets rigorous membership standards covering specialized academic training and supervised professional experience. These standards help elevate the entire profession of marriage and family therapy and discourage unqualified practitioners to ensure that skilled, effective therapy will be available to couples who need it. AAMFT also has a code of professional ethics to which each member subscribes. AAMFT's goal is to ensure that every person who practices marriage and family therapy will meet these professional standards and code of ethics.

2. *Specialized training.* AAMFT examines and accredits training centers in marriage and family therapy. These centers, located in major universities and educational institutions, offer advanced training programs and supervised clinical internships to meet the growing demand for qualified marriage and family therapists.

3. *Professional publications.* The *Journal of Marital and Family Therapy* is published quarterly by AAMFT to advance the professional understanding of marriage and family behavior and to improve the psychotherapeutic treatment of marital and family dysfunction. The journal publishes articles on clinical practice, research, and theory in marriage and family therapy. AAMFT members receive the journal as a membership benefit. Paid subscriptions are available to nonmembers and institutions.

4. *Professional meetings.* AAMFT and its regional divisions conduct frequent regional, national, and international conferences to provide members with new ideas, techniques, and developments in the field of marriage and family therapy.

5. *Cooperation with other professions.* AAMFT maintains close contact with professional groups in allied fields for exchange of information and cooperation on programs of mutual benefit. AAMFT works closely with other professional groups to establish and revise state laws pertaining to marriage, divorce, licensing of marriage and family therapists, and related subjects. AAMFT has held cooperative conferences with the American Academy of Family Physicians, American College of Obstetricians and Gynecologists, the National Council on Family Relations, the American Bar Association, the American Psychological Association, and many other organizations.

6. *Public education.* AAMFT carries on intensive educational programs to help people understand more about marriage and family problems, and the role of professional counseling in preventing and solving these problems, as well as the dangers of unscrupulous or unqualified persons who pose as marriage and family therapists. Public education also helps persons learn to solve their own marital and family difficulties and to build healthier family relationships. AAMFT staff and members provide factual material on marriage and family problems to newspapers, television, radio, and magazines. Members speak to many citizen groups and write extensively for periodicals and professional journals.

In 1977, a group of members of the editorial board of *Family Process* organized another association, called the American Family Therapy Association (AFTA). The first officers of AFTA were Murray Bowen (president), John Spiegel (vice president), Gerald Birenson (executive vice president), James Framo (secretary), and Geraldine Spark (treasurer). AFTA's membership has doubled in the last decade, from 500 to 1,000 members. AFTA provides a forum for small-group interaction.

Each year, there are four national conferences for marriage and family therapists. The largest is AAMFT's national conference, which is held in October in a major metropolitan area. Over 4,000 MFTs participate in this annual event. The Family Therapy Network Symposium meets in the spring in Washington, D.C. The conference is sponsored by the *Family Therapy Networker* magazine and often includes special topics that are not addressed at the AAMFT conference. AFTA's annual meeting is much smaller (300 to 500 attendees) and emphasizes teaching, clinical practice, and research. Finally, the American Orthopsychiatry Association is an interdisciplinary body whose annual conference covers a wide range of subjects (medicine, psychiatry, and so on) related to families.

Issues in Licensure and Certification

The regulation of mental health professionals has become a major professional issue in the past ten years. The various professions are regulated through professional organizations and boards of certification and licensure. Mental health professions such as psychiatry, psychology, counseling, and social work have established, within their respective organizations, standards for accreditation of professional training programs. Trainees who complete a prescribed course of study under an approved program in one of these disciplines are then eligible to sit for an examination or apply for membership in a particular organization.

Licensure and certification are processes used by state governments to ensure that individuals have met specified standards of education and training. Licensure allows the individual to practice. Doctors and lawyers are not permitted to practice medicine or law without a license. Likewise, most licensure laws prevent the individual from using a professional title (such as psychologist or doctor) if he or she is not licensed as such. Engelbert and Hiebert (1982) note that certification is less restrictive than licensing. Unlike licensure, certification does not prevent a noncertified individual from practicing, but it does restrict the use of a particular title. Certification helps to assure the client that the individual has met certain professional standards for practice.

Other licensed mental health practitioners are permitted to provide marriage and family therapy as long as their services fall within the licensed regulations of their practice. Licensure laws for marriage and family therapists also include practice exemptions for other mental health practitioners (such as social workers and psychologists), grandparenting for experienced therapists, and alternative tracks for practitioners in other disciplines who wish to become licensed marriage and family therapists.

In the field of family therapy, an individual can earn credentials in one of two ways. An individual can complete an advanced degree in one of the traditional disciplines, such as clinical psychology, counseling, pastoral counseling, expressive therapies, social work, or psychiatry. Either within the course of study for that degree or after completing the degree, the student must complete specific course work that meets AAMFT's education requirements (AAMFT, 1997), which are as follows:

- Human development (3 courses minimum). Human development, personality theory, human sexuality, and psychopathology-behavior pathology.
- Marriage and family studies (3 courses minimum). Family development; family systems; and marital, sibling, and gender and cultural issues in families.
- Marriage and family therapy (3 courses minimum). Major marital and family therapy treatment approaches, such as systems, new-analytic (object relations), communications, behavioral, structural, and systemic sex therapy.
- Research (1 course minimum). Research design, methodology, statistics, and research in marital and family studies and therapy.
- Professional studies (1 course minimum). Ethics and family law.
- Practicum (minimum of 1 year, 300 hours of supervised direct client work with individual couples and families). Applicants who do not complete a clinical practicum can record their first 300 post-master's client contact hours supervised by an AAMFT-approved supervisor, supervisor in training, or alternate supervisor accepted by the AAMFT.

The individual must also complete a specified period of clinical practice during which he or she conducts family therapy under the supervision of an experienced family therapist. On completion of the course of study, the person may apply for clinical membership in the American Association for Marriage and Family Therapy.

The second route to gaining credentials is completion of a graduate training program at a post degree clinical training center approved by AAMFT. The student attending such a program is assured that the curriculum has met AAMFT's standards for the course of study. On graduation, the individual will need to complete his or her supervised clinical practice.

In 1981, a separate Commission on Accreditation for Marriage and Family Therapy Education was approved by the United States Department of Education. The commission is now approved as the accrediting agency for graduate degree programs and postdegree clinical training centers in marriage and family therapy. The commission has developed policies and standards for accreditation, which are set forth in the *Manual on Accreditation*.

There appears to be a great deal of controversy surrounding the matter of credentials for marriage and family therapists. The traditional mental health professions such as psychiatry and psychology take the position that marital and family therapy is but one branch of the psychotherapy they practice and is not an independent discipline (Levant, 1984). Psychologists and psychiatrists often create strong opposition to the establishment of accrediting procedures and challenge the authority of AAMFT. Marital and family therapists take the position that family therapy is not a technique but a separate field of study with its own theoretical base and orientation. They also argue that the traditional professions do not fulfill the certification and training requirements for marriage and family therapy. Mental health professionals who wish to obtain credentials must seek traditional training in family therapy and apply for licensure and certification as marital and family therapists (Levant, 1984).

The major issue surrounding licensure and certification is the collection of third-party payments. Professional journals and conferences allocate a great deal of time and space to this issue. Those professionals who have adopted the medical model are able to collect third-party payments, whereas those who practice the nonmedical model have had difficulty collecting third-party payments. The Commonwealth of Massachusetts has recently adopted a family intervention code whereby licensed psychologists who practice family therapy may collect third-party payments. Okun and Rappaport (1980) note that marital and family functioning is part of one's mental health and argue that if third-party payments can be collected for mental health treatment, then more than one subspecialty within this domain should therefore be eligible for insurance benefits.

Thus, the issue of whether to license family therapists is related to the whole controversy about collection of insurance. Who is really qualified to practice family therapy is not the only question being considered. Unfortunately, this controversy is likely to continue, given the competition and guarding of turf of the various mental health professions.

Professional Ethics

The most recent Code of Ethical Principles for the American Association for Marriage and Family Therapy was approved in 1991 (AAMFT, 1991). The code consists of eight principles for family therapists. These principles are concerned with responsibility to clients; confidentiality; professional competence and integrity; responsibility to students, employees, and supervisees; responsibility to research participants; responsibility to the profession; financial arrangements; and advertising. A statement of each principle and a brief discussion follow.

1. *Responsibility to clients. Marriage and family therapists advance the welfare of families and individuals. They respect the rights of those persons seeking their assistance, and make reasonable efforts to ensure that their services are used appropriately.* This principle reflects an overall concern for the welfare of clients. Family therapists are not allowed to discriminate or refuse services to anyone on the basis of sex, national origin, race, cultural or sexual orientation, or religion. All services must be in accordance with AAMFT standards. Professional decisions should be shared with the client. It is critical that the therapist not overstep his or her boundary and make a decision that is within the purview of the client (concerning, for example, marriage, divorce, or separation). A therapist's relationship with a client should be maintained only as long as the client is benefiting

from the relationship. Marriage and family therapists should assist persons in obtaining other therapeutic services if the therapist is unable or unwilling to provide professional help.

2. *Confidentiality. Marriage and family therapists have unique confidentiality concerns because the client in a therapeutic relationship may be more than one person. Therapists respect and guard confidences of each individual client.* If the family therapist is to maintain an effective relationship with the family, it is critical that he or she maintain confidentiality. In some instances, a family member will request that specific information not be revealed to other family members. However, if the therapist is to maintain the trust of the family, he or she should encourage the individual to share the confidential material when the individual is ready (Okun & Rappaport, 1980). A request like this commonly comes from a marital partner who is having an affair but wishes not to reveal the fact to the other partner. Family therapists should communicate a client's information only after obtaining permission from the client, unless the client is dangerous to someone or to society.

Confidentiality must also be maintained in the use of audiotapes or videotapes. When the family therapist wishes to audiotape or videotape a session, he or she must obtain written permission from all participants prior to the session. The consent statement should state how the tape will be used. If the tape is to be used only by the therapist's supervisor, then this fact should be stated. However, if the tape is to be used for instructional purposes in the classroom or at conferences, then its intended use should be made clear.

In some cases, however, confidentiality must be broken. For example, in most states therapists are required to report child or spouse abuse to the appropriate protective services agency. Many supervisors suggest that the therapist inform the family of his or her position and encourage the family to report the problem. The therapist should follow up to make sure that it has been reported and carry out his or her responsibilities if it has not. Placing the matter before the family often puts the family in control, helps the family to take responsibility for the problem, and maintains the quality of the therapeutic relationship. Similarly, in custody disputes, family therapists often do not have the right to privileged information because they must testify. The family therapist attempts to maintain the welfare of the family and support children when custody issues cannot be resolved (Everett & Volgy, 1983).

Likewise, it is important for marriage and family therapists to store client records to protect the client. File cabinets and offices should be locked. Videotapes should be erased and written waivers should be obtained if the therapist wishes to use these materials for teaching or public presentations.

3. *Professional competence and integrity. Marriage and family therapists maintain high standards of professional competence and integrity.* A family therapist who is experiencing personal problems or conflicts that interfere with therapy should seek professional assistance from a supervisor or colleague. Therapists should not attempt to assess or treat a problem outside their level of competence. Therapists should attempt to assess their competence through peer consultation or supervision and be prepared to refer cases beyond their level of competence.

Therapists should seek appropriate professional assistance for problems that may impair performance or clinical judgment.

Integrity ensures that family therapists will be honest in representing themselves and their services to the public. Family therapists must not list professional qualifications beyond those that they have received from accredited institutions or programs. Any inaccurate information given by others concerning the qualifications or services of the family therapist must be corrected by the family therapist. Likewise, any employee of the family therapist must accurately represent his or her qualifications.

The principle of integrity also calls for family therapists to be responsible for the professional conduct of other family therapists. When family therapists violate ethical principles, they should be informed and the violation should be brought to the attention of the ethics committee. Such matters must be handled confidentially.

4. *Responsibility to students, employees, and supervisees. Marriage and family therapists do not exploit the trust and dependency of students, employees, and supervisees.* Marriage and family therapists must avoid exploiting the trust and dependency of students, employees, and supervisees. Dual relationships must be avoided to reduce the risk of exploitation. If a dual relationship (business or close personal relationship) is unavoidable, precautions must be taken to ensure that judgment is not impaired. Therapy should not be provided to students, employees, or supervisees. Marriage and family therapists must perform professional services within their level of training and experience. Supervisees' confidences must not be revealed unless it is legally mandated or there is a need to prevent immediate danger to a person or persons.

5. *Responsibility to research participants. Investigators respect the dignity and protect the welfare of participants in research and are aware of federal and state laws and regulations and professional standards governing the conduct of research.* Family therapists who conduct research must abide by the laws and regulations governing the use of human participants. Research should be conducted in an ethical manner and reported accurately. Participants should be informed on all aspects of the research that might influence their willingness to participate. Respect should be given to participants who decline or withdraw from the study. Members of the research team should avoid dual relationships that increase the likelihood of exploitation.

6. *Responsibility to the profession. Marriage and family therapists respect the rights and responsibilities of professional colleagues and participate in activities that advance the goals of the profession.* The principle refers to the roles of practitioner, researcher, and teacher covered by the code. Family therapists who publish manuscripts are obligated to assign credit to contributors where appropriate. Appropriate references should be cited for original ideas. Authors of books and publications should ensure that the publisher advertises the materials accurately. Marriage and family therapists should contribute to their community by volunteering or allocating a portion of their professional time where there is little or no financial gain. Efforts should also be made to develop or alter laws that serve the public interest.

7. *Financial arrangements. Marriage and family therapists make financial arrangements with clients, third-party payers, and supervisees that are reasonably understandable and conform to accepted professional practices.* Marriage and family therapists should not accept financial payment for referrals and should not charge excessive fees. Fees and information should be disclosed at the beginning of therapy and to third-party payers.

8. *Advertising. Marriage and family therapists engage in appropriate informational activities, including those that enable persons to choose professional services on an informed basis.* Advertising should accurately reflect the therapist's competence, education, training, and experience. Advertisements and publications (brochures, business cards, directories) should convey information that is essential for the public to make an appropriate choice of professional services. Information might include fees, office information, office hours, professional credentials, and a description of professional practice.

In addition to the AAMFT *Code of Ethical Principles,* the professional would do well to become familiar with the American Psychological Association (APA) *Standards for Providers of Psychological Services* (American Psychological Association, 1977), APA *Ethical Standards of Psychologists* (American Psychological Association, 1979), AAMFT *Code of Professional Ethics and Standards for Public Information and Advertising* (American Association for Marriage and Family Therapy, 1982), and *Procedures for Handling Complaints of Violations of the Code of Ethical Principles for Family Therapists* (American Association for Marriage and Family Therapy, 1981).

Issues in Family Law

It is critical that the family therapist have an understanding of family law. Little has been written on the legal aspects of family therapy, but there appears to be an abundance of information on family law. Family laws vary from state to state. Therefore, it is important that the family therapist become familiar with the statutory laws of the state in which he or she practices. The family therapist should become familiar with the principles and practices of the legal system. It is recommended that the family therapist develop a relationship with a competent local attorney regarding changes in statutory law (Piercy & Sprenkle, 1983). Most members of the legal profession are more than willing to assist family practitioners.

There are certain areas of the law in which family therapists should be knowledgeable, including (1) malpractice and legal liability, (2) courtroom testimony, (3) divorce and custody, and (4) lawyer-therapist relationships.

Malpractice and Legal Liability

Family therapists should have a basic knowledge of malpractice and legal liability. Family therapists who are found negligent may find themselves legally liable. American Jurisprudence (1971) defines negligence "as the failure to exercise the degree of care demanded by the circumstances, or as the want of that care which the law prescribes under the particular circumstances existing at the time of the act or omission which is involved." (57 Am. Jur. 2nd 333, Sec. 1). Thus, a current standard of care must be maintained for practice.

How is standard of care determined? Standard of care must be consistent with the average level of skill of a professional in a similar context. It is becoming more difficult to prove that such a standard has been maintained. In the past, local practitioners were used for normative comparison. Currently, national standards for care are being established that often exceed local standards. Expert testimony is used to determine standard of care; thus, the courts will call on the expert family therapist to define standard of family therapy (Bernstein, 1981). A family therapist who has not established a minimum standard of care (for example, in prescribing a program of treatment that cannot be supported by established clinical experience or scientific evidence) is vulnerable to a malpractice suit.

Negligence cases are sometimes based on breach of confidentiality. Information about a client should not be shared without the consent of the client. However, when there is danger to the client or others, then the therapist must exercise professional judgment. Privileged communication is determined by state statutory law, which specifies to which communications the law applies. In many states, privileged communication does not apply to marriage and family therapists. The court has power of subpoena in cases in which a benefit to society may be derived from the therapist's giving testimony (Woody & Weber, 1983).

The family therapist can also be found negligent if he or she fails to warn others when there is imminent danger. If someone is suspected of being violent and dangerous to another person, the therapist has a responsibility to warn the other person. In such cases, breach of confidentiality is necessary to protect the endangered party as well as the therapist, who may be sued by an injured party (Bernstein, 1981). Therapists who are aware of physical threats must inform clients that the threats must be reported (Woody & Weber, 1983). Family therapy training programs need to make trainees sensitive to the legal consequences surrounding confidentiality and their duty to warn others.

Family therapists should protect themselves against liability through malpractice insurance. This type of insurance is inexpensive and can generally be purchased through professional associations. In addition, therapists should familiarize themselves with their state's statutes and consult an attorney in questions surrounding malpractice.

Courtroom Testimony

Family therapists are often called upon to give expert testimony. Increasingly, family therapists are asked to testify in cases involving custody, disposition of juvenile offenders, and institutionalization. Family therapists must apply their therapeutic skills to be effective (Meyerstein & Todd, 1980). A brief description of these skills follows.

The family therapist should have expertise and professional training for the case in question. Traditional disciplines such as psychology and psychiatry often carry more status in court cases than does family therapy, which is less familiar to many courts than the traditional disciplines. The family therapist must overcome this lack of familiarity by demonstrating his or her expert knowledge of the case.

The family therapist must also learn to function in the adversarial role rather than the accustomed mediation role. The ground rules and assumptions are different under the adversary system. Family therapists should consult with attorneys to become more familiar with those rules, even to the point of role-playing a cross-examination.

Meyerstein and Todd (1980) suggest that family therapists can be more effective on the witness stand if they remember that the courts are a kind of system just like the family. If the therapists can remember that an individual's behavior is a reaction to the interpersonal setting, he or she will be more confident on the witness stand. When the therapist is challenged by the prosecutor, he or she should recognize the challenge as similar to aggressive resistance and avoid overreacting. Family therapists can also use their therapeutic skills to alter perceptions of the judge and jury. Finally, family therapists can often reframe a problem to show how the interactional patterns in the family contribute to the problem. The therapist must often hold his or her position and present an alternative meaning for the same set of facts (Watzlawick, Weakland, & Fisch, 1974).

If the family therapist is to be an effective witness, according to Meyerstein and Todd, he or she must be able to respond to resistance. The family therapist must be conscious of the accuracy of his or her testimony. Any discrepancies may give leverage to the opposing attorney and put the therapist who is testifying on the defensive. An opposing attorney who is unable to challenge the family therapist's testimony may raise doubts about the family therapist's qualifications. When such resistance occurs, the family therapist should redirect it by agreeing with the opposing counsel, thus defusing the attorney's argument.

The family therapist who wants to be an effective witness should meet the following conditions: (1) participate in pretrial coaching in legal procedures, (2) prepare documents for his or her testimony, (3) assume the role of expert witness, and (4) employ effective communications skills on the witness stand (Brodsky & Roby, 1972). Only when the therapist has prepared for his or her legal role will he or she be an effective witness.

Divorce and Custody

There is a growing body of literature on the role of the family therapist in disputes in divorce cases and in cases of custody and visitation. Everett and Volgy (1983) recently described a family assessment model for family dissolution and child custody disputes. Similar papers have been written to assist the family therapist in the legal process of divorce and custody (Chasin & Grunebaum, 1981; Steinberg, 1980; Thomas, 1981).

The rate of legal disputes regarding child custody and visitation has increased dramatically. Changes in parental roles and lifestyles have contributed to the rapid increase. Mothers are often caught in the dilemma of motherhood versus career. Fathers are becoming more active in the parenting role and often want custody of the child. Adultery, homosexuality, and mental instability are being given less and less emphasis in custody decisions. The result of these changing attitudes is that it is less likely that one person is seen as "unfit," and thus a custody and visitation agreement must be worked out by the parents (Chasin & Grunebaum, 1981). Family therapists are often called upon to assist the court in reviewing previous decisions in such matters.

The systemic model   There are a number of guidelines that can be helpful to family therapists consulted in divorce and custody/visitation arrangements. It is of paramount importance to use a systemic model in the evaluation process (Everett & Volgy, 1983). The evaluation process should examine the major features of the family organization. The evaluation must take into account the power struggles, triangles, coalitions, alliances, and family boundaries. Everett and Volgy note that a family therapist who makes a custody evaluation without considering these systemic issues may be engaging in self-deception about his or her ability to assist in the process of dissolution. A systemic evaluation of the family will help family members and legal professionals to understand the changes occurring in the organization of the family.

Objectivity   It is essential that the family therapist remain objective during the legal process. When the therapist allows a coalition with one client to form, then the therapist's effectiveness in the decision-making process is hampered (Cohen & Jones, 1983). Such a coalition often leads to other parties' resistance to the final divorce or custody evaluation. Similarly, when the therapist provides an evaluation for only one party, the therapist may actually be contributing to the adversarial process.

There are several ways in which the therapist can maintain objectivity. One way is to avoid serving as evaluator for only one client in the dispute. Chasin and Grunebaum (1981) recommend serving as an impartial evaluator for the entire process, if both parties and their attorneys consent. Grunebaum and Chasin require both parties to sign an agreement that outlines the process of evaluation for making recommendations. Both parents are free to present information bearing on the custody decision. Participation on a family assessment team helps the therapist to maintain a neutral position. Team members can assist each other to maintain appropriate emotional distance so that recommendations are completed in an objective manner (Everett & Volgy, 1983).

Valid information   It is critical that the family therapist collect valid information in the evaluation. In an effort to elicit a candid response, Chasin and Grunebaum (1981, p. 45) pose the following questions to each parent separately:

1. What is the legal custody arrangement for your family? Why?
2. How would it affect you if the other parent got custody?
3. Joint custody involves equally shared decision-making and may or may not involve equally shared child care. What would be its benefits and drawbacks for your family?
4. What aspects of your ideal arrangement would you be willing to negotiate?
5. For each child, describe his/her daily routine, friends, teachers, likes, dislikes, interests, fears, skills, and problems. For each problem, describe the remedy you feel would be most effective.
6. What are your strongest assets as a parent? What are your weaknesses?
7. What are the strengths and weaknesses of the other parent?

Interviews should also be conducted with relevant family members, such as grandparents, new spouses, or live-in companions. Interviews may also be conducted with school personnel, housekeepers, babysitters, neighbors, day-care operators, and members of the family's network.

When gathering information from children, the therapist must discover what troubles them about the divorce. The family therapist should talk with each child privately and then in the presence of their parents determine their preferred living arrangements and how they interact with each parent (Cohen & Jones, 1983). During the interviews, the therapist notes the child's social cognitive functioning. The therapist also gathers an understanding of the family's systemic process on the basis of the child's perceptions (Everett & Volgy, 1983). Interviews may also be conducted with siblings and relatives of the child or children.

If possible, it is useful to observe the child and parents in a playroom setting. Play materials should be appropriate to the child's age. The therapist can provide tasks to elicit parent-child interactions. For example, the parent and child may be instructed to play a game or build a house together. Parents with young children might bring familiar play materials from home. Parents might be instructed to feed or diaper an infant to permit assessment of their skills in that area. During these activities, the therapist observes patterns of interaction, attentiveness, nurturance, control, and the ability of the parent to relate to the child on the child's level. The therapist must also apply therapeutic skill to make the assessment procedure nonthreatening and natural. Otherwise, the data collected will reflect anxiety about the assessment procedure rather than the real family dynamics.

Once the assessment has been completed, the therapist writes a report based on the creative functions of family members in the family system. Everett and Volgy (1983) base their recommendations on four systemic issues: "(1) the relative enmeshment or cohesion in each parent's family of origin loyalties, (2) the relative degree of each spouse's success in structural decoupling, (3) patterns of 'structural coupling' achieved by each parent, and (4) the parents' potential for healthy recoupling" (p. 350). Recommendations should provide for postassessment follow-up on the custody/visitation arrangements. When one parent is awarded custody, the other parent may be frustrated and angry, particularly when the father is awarded custody. Bernstein (1977) suggests that in such cases the father make sure that the children visit at the times stated in the court order. The therapist can be helpful in making sure that visitation is carried out under peaceful conditions.

Divorce Adjustment Programs

Educational programs for divorcing parents are proliferating because courts are not the proper forum to settle issues that affect the well-being of children. Parent education programs provide a climate for building positive parent-child and co-parental relationships. According to Blaisure and Geasler (1996) there are currently 541 court-connected education programs for divorcing parents. Effective parent education programs should emphasize (1) a supportive climate where feelings can be freely explored, (2) acquisition of problem solving skills for divorce-related problems and (3) ways for parents and children to develop better relationships with each other (Brown, Portes, Cambron, Zimmerman, Rickert, & Bissmeyer, 1994). As the popularity of these programs increases, there will be an increased need for family practitioners who are interested in contracting with the courts to run these programs.

The Lawyer-Therapist Relationship

The importance of a strong relationship between therapist and lawyer has been stressed in the literature (Bernstein, 1977, 1979, 1981, 1982). Bernstein emphasizes the need for the therapist to become familiar with the law. Bernstein (1982) elaborates:

> If the therapist is not familiar with the law that affects the client's problems, the evolving attitudinal and behavioral changes will be short-lived. Unless the legal problems are faced along with the personal and psychological problems, the attitudinal changes may revert back to pre-therapy days, thus recreating old problems. Family therapists must be aware of the laws that affect particular individual clients. They must recognize the law not to practice it, but to recognize problem areas and to make referrals where appropriate. They cannot make a referral if they are not aware that a legal problem exists. Ignorance of the law may be an excuse in the malpractice area in the sense that therapists are not liable for failure to offer legal advice nor would they be liable for failure to refer a client to an attorney. (p. 100)

One way therapists can become better informed about the law is to work closely with attorneys. Although such cooperation has been minimal in the past, therapists and attorneys have recently been working more closely with each other. Such collaboration is most likely due to the increased number of divorces, changes in family law, and awareness of the advantages of interdisciplinary cooperation (Cohen & Jones, 1983). The net result is that therapists and attorneys are beginning to cooperate in ways that serve the best interests of the family.

The therapist may also be helpful to the family in choosing a lawyer. The therapist should help the family find a lawyer that is compatible with their style. The family should be encouraged to interview more than one lawyer and to select one who will work in the best interest of the entire family. In the case of divorce, is the lawyer concerned about the welfare of children and working cooperatively with the other's side? Is the lawyer willing to consider mediation and other methods for resolving conflict? The therapist can be helpful to the family in framing questions about these issues. When families are better informed, they will be more likely to choose a lawyer that will be an advocate for the entire family.

Training

The development of family therapy training programs that meet standard criteria for professional development is a major task of the 1980s (Woody & Weber, 1983). Training is currently offered in a variety of programs and institutions. This section will include a discussion of the various kinds of training programs, the educational methods of family therapy programs, and the evaluation of training.

Family Therapy Training Programs

There has been a recent upsurge in the number of family therapy training institutions. Bloch and Weiss (1981) found that 60% (77 programs) of the training programs in their master list of training programs in the United States had been developed between 1971 and 1980. Currently, the American Association for Marriage and Family Therapy has 78 accredited programs; 46 masters and 12 doctoral programs. In addition, there are 20 accredited, nonacademic postdegree training centers, the most prominent of which include the Acherman Institute for Family Therapy in New York City; the Philadelphia Child Guidance Clinic; the Family Institute of Cambridge in Massachusetts; the Family Therapy Institute of Washington, D.C.; the Georgetown Family Center in Washington, D.C.; the Family Institute of Westchester in Mount Vernon, N.Y.; and the Brief Family Therapy Center in Milwaukee.

Following training the young therapist is free to choose a variety of ways to enhance his or her skills. Workshops and supervision are critical for the development of new ideas. Marriage and family therapists who wish to receive supervision may do so by contacting their state division of the American Association for Marriage and Family Therapy and obtaining a list of approved supervisors. Supervision and additional training help to integrate clinical experience with one's own model and style of doing therapy.

Methods of Family Therapy Training

According to Kniskern and Gurman (1979), all family therapy training programs employ three methods of training: didactic, experiential, and supervisory. The preference of the instructor governs the relative degree of emphasis on each of these methods. In view of the wide variety of training programs, it is not too surprising to find varying emphasis in clinical methods. The problem, however, is that methodology is often left up to the intuition of the instructor, rather than being based on empirical research that shows what teaching method is most effective (Kniskern & Gurman, 1979). Given the diverse settings in which family therapy is practiced, one could predict that emphases on learning methods and training issues would vary (Liddle & Halpin, 1978).

Didactic methods Classroom lectures, extensive reading, and group discussions are among the didactic methods used in teaching theory of marital and family therapy. There is some discussion in the field about what theoretical content should be covered. Kniskern and Gurman (1979) raise the issue of whether trainees should be exposed to a range of approaches to family therapy or receive intensive instruction in one approach. Programs that focus on one approach run the risk of producing a practitioner who lacks flexibility and creativity. Programs that present a variety of approaches take the chance of confusing the trainee.

There has been a proliferation of books and articles that present a comprehensive and integrated view of family therapy. Such reading material offers trainers of family therapists an opportunity to present a comparative analysis of several approaches. Kniskern and Gurman (1979) suggest that researchers should examine various ways of sequencing instruction: What are the training and learning costs and benefits of beginning didactic family therapy training from a broad base, and offering advanced training in more focal models, versus reversing this order of exposure (p. 87)?

More recently, Howard Liddle (1991) cites publications that address therapists' conceptual development. Experienced clinicians, such as Anderson (1984), Carter (1982), and Minuchin (1984), describe their developmental detours in working with families. These publications outline different theoretical models while dealing with the conceptual life and development of the therapist (Liddle, 1991, p. 651). In contrast to edited videotapes, these publications provide a more realistic picture of therapeutic practice.

Experiential methods Kniskern and Gurman (1979) classify experiential methods into three categories: personal therapy, sensitivity training and role-playing, and working with family of origin. The first category, personal therapy for trainees, may facilitate personal growth. Some believe that personal therapy enables the trainee to become aware of transference and countertransference (Kniskern & Gurman, 1979). Nevertheless, Haley (1976) and Minuchin (1974) question the desirability of personal therapy for family therapy trainees.

Their view tends to see countertransference as bad technique. There appears to be no conclusive research to support the efficacy of personal therapy as a training method. Few programs make use of the method, despite the fact that the American Association for Marriage and Family Therapy (1979) recommends personal therapeutic experiences for family therapy trainees.

Role-playing has been used effectively with simulated families (Weingarten, 1979). Role-playing provides the opportunity for the trainee to develop therapeutic skills under simulated conditions. Trainees can also learn how to work on issues related to their families of origin through the use of role-playing. Role-playing is quite helpful in developing insight, overcoming resistance, and working through unresolved issues (Satir, 1972).

The third type of experiential method involves working with one's own family of origin. Working on one's family of origin may involve constructing a genogram of the family or visiting one's family to increase differentiation (Kniskern & Gurman, 1979). Although there are no empirical studies that assess the effectiveness of working with one's family of origin, Bowen (1971) reported that his psychiatric residents found that working with their families of origin enabled them to relate more effectively to families they saw in clinical practice.

Supervision   Supervision is an important tool in teaching family therapy. Family therapists have been effective in developing a wide variety of supervisory methods. Supervisory methods are heavily influenced by one's theoretical orientation. For example, structural therapists (Minuchin, 1974) will focus on the therapist's techniques for changing the structure in the family. Behavioral (Margolin, 1981) and problem-oriented therapists (Haley, 1976) will focus primarily on reduction of symptoms. Thus, differences in the theoretical orientation of the supervisor will probably influence the style of the therapist (Kniskern & Gurman, 1979).

The supervisory process has been greatly influenced by the advent of the one-way mirror (Hoffman, 1981). Live supervision involves having an individual or peer group standing behind a one-way mirror. The supervisor provides instant feedback to the supervisee during the interview. Supervision may take place through several media: a bug-in-the-ear wireless microphone, a CB radio, a telephone, or a supervisor's entry into the counseling room to confer with the supervisee (Birchler, 1975).

Coopersmith (1980) has developed several uses of the telephone: The team behind the one-way mirror sends a strategic message to the therapist or a message directly to the family. Family members are also allowed to call the team behind the one-way mirror.

Berger and Dammann (1982) list a number of advantages of live supervision:

> Live supervision has a number of advantages for the supervisor, too. As opposed to traditional supervision, in which a therapist describes a case to the supervisor, live supervision permits the supervisors to see at first hand what the therapist and family do with one another. Live supervision also permits

the supervisor access to the nonverbal components of the interaction, which is not possible when supervision is based on the audiotapes of a session. Finally, as compared with videotape supervision, live supervision permits the supervisor to see how the therapist uses data from outside the system (that is, from the supervisor). (p. 34)

Behind the one-way mirror, the supervisor can observe patterns of interaction between the supervisee and the family without necessarily influencing the nature of that interaction.

Despite the benefits, there are no clear methodologies for supervision. Instead, supervision has been dependent on the personal style of the individual supervisor (Everett, 1980). There is a corresponding lack of research that examines the effects of various types of supervision on therapeutic behavior and on the client families. The originators of live supervision did not have to learn family therapy from behind the one-way mirror. Family therapists who have been on both sides of the one-way mirror and recognize its importance may offer our best hope for developing an empirical base for a clear methodology of supervision.

The feminist movement has also had a profound impact on supervision. Avis (1986) cites several gender issues that are relevant to training and supervision: (1) the failure to include gender and power issues in training and supervision, (2) teaching theories that undermine women's role in the family, (3) addressing goals of training that may be at odds with the socialization processes and outcomes with women, and (4) the interactional process in supervision between men and women. Recent critiques of family therapy models (Luepnitz, 1988) provide a more contextually and gender-sensitive direction for supervision.

Evaluation of Family Therapy Training

It is unfortunate that there is no empirical evidence yet to support any one training method. There is very little research to support the efficacy of family therapy training programs (Kniskern & Gurman, 1979). A number of family therapy educators have called for more research addressing the effectiveness of marriage and family therapy training (Avis & Sprenkle, 1990; Figley & Nelson, 1990). However, Kniskern and Gurman (1979) suggest that we not ask the broad question, "Does family therapy training work?" but that we ask more specific questions that examine the effects of specific training methods. They list some important questions (p. 90):

With regard to selection, some of the crucial questions are the following:

- What type of previous training best prepares a trainee for family therapy training?
- Are there any types of previous training that inhibit family therapy training?
- What personality factors predict success in training, and do these vary as a function of emphasizing different theoretical orientations to family therapy?

- Does the developmental stage of the trainee (that is, never married versus married) influence success?
- Can success be predicted without a personal interview? Based on what criteria?
- Does a sample of therapy behavior improve selection?

Some controversial questions about *didactic* methods would be:

- Is it better to present one view or many?
- Does reading about families help the trainee learn therapy?
- Should reading be done before, after, or during the bulk of therapy training practice?
- Does the live observation of experts help or hinder development of skills?

With regard to *supervision*:

- When are audio or videotapes most helpful? When are they harmful?
- What are demonstrable advantages and disadvantages of co-therapy supervision?
- What are the measurable strengths and weaknesses of problem-oriented supervision and of therapist-oriented supervision?
- Should all cases be supervised?
- What differences do different forms of supervision make on different trainees?

Some questions related to *experiential* methods would be:

- What specific changes are produced by different types of personal therapy?
- What are the positive and negative effects of personal therapy when it is required?
- At what point in one's training in family therapy are personal experiences most beneficial, and when may they be harmful?
- Does working with one's own family, via family genograms, facilitate cognitive (conceptual) change more than it facilitates personal emotional change?
- When working with one's own family becomes the primary method of training, what is the effect on outcome for the families in treatment with such trainees?
- Are role-playing experiential methods more effective in producing technical skill than in reducing neophyte family therapists' anxieties about their competence?

Training programs should evaluate (1) the knowledge acquired by the trainee, (2) the level of the skills demonstrated by the trainee in therapy, and (3) the ability of the trainee to produce desirable outcomes in families in treatment. Knowledge can be measured by pencil-and-paper tests prior to and following training. Trainees' acquisition of skills can be measured by trainee, observer, and supervisor rating scales or skills checklists. The success of efforts in treating families can be measured by self-report of the families prior to and following treatment. In addition, videotapes may be used to assess the family's changes in cognitive functioning, patterns of communication, and subsystem and system functioning.

In a recent investigation, Hines (1996) surveyed 205 graduates from degree-granted marriage and family therapy training programs accredited by the Commission on Accreditation for Marriage and Family Education. The graduates reported that they were well prepared in marital and family therapy and individual therapy with adults, but minimally to moderately prepared in individual therapy with children, individual psychological assessment, and diagnosis. They also felt they needed more emphasis in their training in alcoholism, substance abuse, sexual abuse, and domestic violence. The author suggests that future researchers might pay closer attention to the work roles of their graduates (that is, should marriage and family therapy programs be expected to provide training in specific aspects of work commonly engaged in by graduates?) (Hines, 1996, p. 193). To the extent that family therapy training is linked to practice, the quality of training will be maintained.

References

American Association for Marriage and Family Therapy. (1979). *Marriage and family therapy manual on accreditation.* Upland, CA: Author.

American Association for Marriage and Family Therapy. (1981). *Procedures for handling complaints of violations of the code of ethical principles for family therapists.* Upland, CA: Author.

American Association for Marriage and Family Therapy. (1982). *Code of professional ethics and standards for public information and advertising.* Upland, CA: Author.

American Association for Marriage and Family Therapy. (1983). *Membership requirements: Clinical member, associate member, student member.* Washington, DC: Author.

American Association for Marriage and Family Therapy. (1991). *AAMFT code of ethics.* Washington, DC: Author.

American Association for Marriage and Family Therapy. (1997). *Membership requirements and applications.* Washington, DC: Author.

American jurisprudence (2nd ed.). (1971). Vol. 57. Rochester, NY: Lawyers Co-Operative.

American Psychological Association. (1977). *Standards for providers of psychological services.* Rockville, MD: Author.

American Psychological Association. (1979). *Ethical standards of psychologists* (rev. ed.). Washington, DC: Author.

Anderson, H. (1984). *The new epistemology in family therapy: Implications for training therapists.* Ann Arbor, MI: University Microfilms International.

Avis, J. (1986). Feminist issues in family therapy. In F. P. Piercy, D. H. Sprenkle, et al. (Eds.), *Family therapy sourcebook.* New York: Guilford Press.

Avis, J. M. & Sprenkle, D. H. (1990). Outcome research on family therapy training: A substantive and methodological review. *Journal of Marital and Family Therapy, 16,* 241–264.

Berger, M., & Dammann, C. (1982). Live supervision as context, treatment, and training. *Family Process, 21,* 337–344.

Bernstein, B. E. (1977). Lawyer and counselor as an interdisciplinary team: Preparing the father for custody. *Journal of Marriage and Family Counseling, 3,* 29–40.

Bernstein, B. E. (1979). Lawyer and therapist as an interdisciplinary team. *Journal of Marital and Family Therapy, 5,* 93–100.

Bernstein, B. E. (1981). Lawyer and counselor as an interdisciplinary team: Problem awareness in the blended family. *Child Welfare, 60,* 211–220.

Bernstein, B. E. (1982). Ignorance of the law is no excuse. In J. C. Hansen & L. L. L'Abate (Eds.), *Values, ethics, legalities, and the family therapist.* Rockville, MD: Aspen Systems Corporation.

Birchler, G. R. (1975). Live supervision and instant feedback in marriage and family therapy. *Journal of Marriage and Family Counseling, 3,* 53–60.

Blaisure, K. R., & Geasler, M. J. (1996). Results of a survey of court-connected parent education programs in U.S. counties. *Family & Conciliation Courts Review, 34,* 23–40.

Bloch, D., & Weiss, H. (1981). Training facilities in marital and family therapy. *Family Process, 20,* 133–146.

Bowen, M. (1971). Towards the differentiation of self in one's family of origin. In F. Andres & J. Ford (Eds.), *Georgetown family symposia (Vol. 1).* Washington, DC: Georgetown University Department of Psychiatry.

Brodsky, S. L., & Roby, A. (1972). On becoming an expert witness: Issues of orientation and effectiveness. *Professional Psychology, 1,* 173–176.

Brown, J. H., Portes, P., Cambron, M. L., Zimmerman, D., Rickert, V., & Bissmeyer, C. (1994). Families in transition: A court-mandated divorce adjustment program for parents and children. *Juvenile and Family Court Journal, 45,* 27–31.

Carter, E. (1982). Supervisory discussions in the presence of the family. In R. Whiffen & J. Byng-Hall (Eds.), *Family therapy supervision.* New York: Grune & Stratton.

Chasin, R., & Grunebaum, H. (1981). A model for evaluation in child custody disputes. *American Journal of Family Therapy, 9,* 43–49.

Cohen, S. N., & Jones, F. N. (1983). Issues of divorce in family therapy. In B. B. Wolman & G. Stricker (Eds.), *Handbook of marital therapy.* New York: Plenum.

Coopersmith, E. (1980). Expanding uses of the telephone in family therapy. *Family Process, 19,* 411–417.

Engelbert, S., & Hiebert, W. J. (1982). Family therapy licensure versus certification. *Family Therapy News, 13*(2), 4.

Everett, C. (1980). Supervision of marriage and family therapy. In A. Hess (Ed.), *Psychotherapy supervision.* New York: Wiley Interscience.

Everett, C. A., & Volgy, S. S. (1983). Family assessment in child custody disputes. *Journal of Marital and Family Therapy, 9,* 343–353.

Figley, C. R., & Nelson, T. S. (1990). Basic family therapy skills, II: Structural family therapy. *Journal of Marital and Family Therapy, 165,* 225–239.

Goldenberg, I., & Goldenberg, H. (1983). Historical roots of contemporary family therapy. In B. B. Wolman & G. Stricker (Eds.), *Handbook of family and marital therapy.* New York: Plenum.

Haley, J. (1976). *Problem-solving therapy.* San Francisco: Jossey-Bass.

Hines, M. (1996). Follow-up survey of graduates from accredited degree-granting marriage and family therapy training programs. *Journal of Marital and Family Therapy, 22,* 181–194.

Hoffman, L. (1981). *Foundations of family therapy: A conceptual framework for systems change.* New York: Basic Books.

Kane, C. M. (1996). An experiential approach to family-of-origin work with marital and family therapy trainees. *Journal of Marital and Family Therapy, 22,* 481–487.

Kniskern, D. P., & Gurman, A. S. (1979). Research of training in marriage and family therapy: Status, issues, and directions. *Journal of Marital and Family Therapy, 5,* 83–96.

Levant, R. F. (1984). *Family therapy: A comprehensive overview.* Englewood Cliffs, NJ: Prentice Hall.

Liddle, H. (1991). Training and supervision in family therapy: A comprehensive and critical analysis. In A. S. Gurman & D. Kniskern (Eds.), *Handbook of family therapy: Volume II.* New York: Brunner/Mazel.

Liddle, H., & Halpin, R. (1978). Family therapy training and supervision literature: A comparative review. *Journal of Marriage and Family Counseling, 4,* 77–98.

Luepnitz, D. (1988). *The family interpreted: Feminist theory in clinical practice.* New York: Basic Books.

Margolin, G. (1981). A behavioral systems approach to the treatment of marital jealousy. *Clinical Psychology Review, 1,* 469–487.

Meyerstein, I., & Todd, J. C. (1980). On the witness stand: The family therapist and expert testimony. *American Journal of Family Therapy, 8,* 43–51.

Minuchin, S. (1974). *Families and family therapy.* Cambridge, MA: Harvard University Press.

Minuchin, S. (1984). Stranger in a strange land: An interview with Salvadore Minuchin. (By R. Simon). *Family Therapy Networker, 8,* 20–31.

Okun, B. F., & Rappaport, L. J. (1980). *Working with families: An introduction to family therapy.* Pacific Grove, CA: Brooks/Cole.

Piercy, F. P., & Sprenkle, D. H. (1983). Ethical, legal and professional issues in family therapy: A graduate level course. *Journal of Marriage and Family Therapy, 9,* 393–401.

Satir, V. (1972). *Peoplemaking.* Palo Alto, CA: Science and Behavior Books.

Steinberg, J. L. (1980). Towards an interdisciplinary commitment: A divorce lawyer proposes attorney-therapist marriages or, at the least, an affair. *Journal of Marriage and Family Therapy, 6,* 259–268.

Thomas, R. (1981). The family practitioner and the criminal justice system: Challenges for the 80s. *Family Relations, 30,* 614–624.

Watzlawick, P., Weakland, J., & Fisch, R. (1974). *Change: Principles of problem formation and problem resolution.* New York: Norton.

Weingarten, K. (1979). Family awareness for nonclinicians: Participation in a simulated family as a teaching technique. *Family Process, 18,* 143–150.

Woody, R. H., & Weber, G. K. (1983). Training in marriage and family therapy. In B. B. Wolman & G. Stricker (Eds.), *Handbook of family and marital therapy.* New York: Plenum.

Glossary

Accommodation: The technique of joining with the family by behaving in ways similar to the family's style, pace, and idiosyncrasies.

Antecedent behavior: An event that precipitates a behavior.

Asymptomatic: Exhibiting no symptom.

Blended family: A reconstituted family formed by the union by marriage of two separate families, wherein stepparents and stepchildren form a new family.

Boundaries: Rules governing family interaction that serve to separate parts of a system or subsystems.

Boundary marking: Application of therapeutic technique to the changing of boundaries between or among individual family members or subsystems.

Circular feedback: A reciprocal pattern of interaction in which an event can be both the effect of an earlier event and the cause of a later event.

Circular feedback loop: Relationship of two or more events in which information flows in a circular pattern.

Closed system: A family system whose boundaries are impermeable to outside input so that the family interacts only within the system.

Coalition: An alliance between or among family members for a specific function or purpose.

Communications theory: A theory that focuses on the contradictory overt and covert messages sent by family members.

Complementarity: A condition in which spouses reciprocally supply what each other lacks or needs.

Conductor: A family therapist who is active, directive, and central in the family's pattern of communication.

Conjoint marital therapy: Therapy in which the therapist works with both spouses simultaneously.

Constructivism: Applied to a theory of conducting therapy, constructivism involves describing a view that reality is "constructed" by one's attitudes, beliefs, and cognition about what he or she perceives in his or her world.

Conversational questions: Questions that allow a therapist to come from a position of not knowing and that involves the therapist's actively listening to the client's stories in a distinct way.

Countertransference: The therapist's unconscious reaction to a family or family member that is similar to the way the therapist reacted in previous personal relationships.

Cross-generational coalition: An alliance (see *Coalition*) formed between members of different generations, as between a child and parent or grandparent against a parent.

Differentiation: (1) The distinguishing of self from other in a relationship. (2) The ability to distinguish emotional from intellectual processes and thus become more independent and less emotionally reactive.

Disengaged families: Families in which there is little interaction, causing members to feel a sense of isolation and lack of connection.

Double bind: A no-win situation in which a person receives two contradictory messages from the same person but cannot respond appropriately to either message.

Dyad: A relationship between two people, such as spouses or parent and child.

Ego: (From psychodynamic theory) The rational, problem-solving component of the personality that mediates between the demands of instinctual drives (id) and social prohibition (superego).

Empty nest: A family at the stage when the children have left home, thus leaving the husband and wife to themselves.

Enactment: A therapeutically induced replay of a genuine interaction among family members to determine the function of the problem in the family.

Enmeshed behavior: Behavior that is typical of family members who are over-involved or overprotective and of subsystem boundaries that have become diffuse.

Equifinality: The capacity of a system to reach the same final state under a variety of conditions.

Extended family: The total family, consisting of the nuclear family (parents and children), the parents' parents, and other relatives, such as aunts, uncles, and cousins.

Externalizing the problem: Referring to the problem as though it existed outside of the client or family.

Extinction: The reduction or elimination of a behavior by separating it from a reinforcing event.

Extrafamilial members: Individuals who have a significant relationship with one or more members of the family but are not members of the nuclear family.

Family of origin: Family in which one is born and reared.

Family organism: The family as an entity, a single being, as opposed to a collection of beings.

Family projection process: The mechanism by which parents project or transmit their conflict to one or more of their children, thus making them symptomatic.

Family sculpting: A therapeutic technique in which family members graphically represent their experience in the family through body language.

Feedback: Return of information about the consequences of an event in a system.

First-order change: An adjustment in the system to maintain stability without changing the structure of the system or the way it maintains stability.

Focus: The technique in structural family therapy of selecting an area of family interaction to explore for structural elements.

Functional analysis: A study of behavior and the conditions that precipitate and maintain that behavior.

Fused relationship: A relationship of two people who are so emotionally close that they lose their own sense of self-identity.

General systems theory: A biologically based theory that focuses on the interrelationships among parts of a system.

Generational legacy: Previous generations' expectations of offspring.

Homeostasis: The tendency of a system to seek stability and equilibrium.

Horizontal stressor: Stressor produced by the family as it moves through transitions of the family life cycle.

Identified patient: The symptom bearer or family member identified as having the problem.

Intensity: Tension or pressure created by' the therapist in order to produce a meaningful impact on the client.

Intergenerational relatedness: Connectedness between generations' relationships and loyalties.

Intrapersonal: Occurring within the individual.

Intrapsychic: Occurring within the mind; used in reference to psychological events.

Introject: Primitive form of identification by which aspects of others are taken to form part of oneself.

Linear causality: Relation between events such that one event is the cause of the next event, without reciprocity.

Marital schism: Extreme division or conflict in a marriage; term developed by Theodore Lidz.

Marital skew: Extreme domination of one partner by the other in the marital relationship; term developed by Theodore Lidz.

Marital subsystem: The subset of the family system that is governed by interactional rules pertaining only to marital transactions.

Metaphor: A therapeutic analogy to characterize family relationships; or, a condition, such as a symptom, that represents another condition by analogy.

Mimesis: A therapeutic technique by which the therapist appears similar to family members through imitation of body language, style, and idiosyncrasy.

Modeling: Performance of behavior for another person, so that he or she can learn by imitation.

Negative cooperative tasks: Tasks that family members agree to complete but that the therapist expects the family not to accomplish.

Negative feedback: Information that flows back to the system to reduce deviation from a state of equilibrium; information that corrects the current course.

Network therapy: A therapeutic approach in which friends, neighbors, and relatives all assemble to support the treatment of family member or members.

Nuclear family: A family unit consisting of husband, wife, and their children; may include grandparents if they act as immediate caregivers to the children.

Object relations: Relationships with external objects (other persons) that have been internalized and thus affect the way one relates to others.

Operant conditioning: A type of learning that is governed by the consequences of behavior.

Paradoxical directive: Request by the therapist that the family member or members continue behaving in a symptomatic manner, thus exposing the secondary gain produced by the symptom.

Parental child: An older child who has been granted the authority of a parental role to take care of the younger children.

Parental subsystem: The subset of the family system that is governed by interactional rules pertaining to parent-child transactions.

Permeability: The property of system and subsystem boundaries that permits family members to move across them.

Positive cooperative tasks: Tasks that family members agree to complete and that the therapist anticipates their performing.

Positive feedback: Information that counteracts negative feedback and leads to deviation from the system's norm, with consequent loss of stability.

Positive label: A connotation given to a family member to alter family perceptions of that member in a positive direction.

Positive reinforcement: An event that follows a behavior and that increases the probability of that behavior's recurrence.

Pseudoindependence: The superficial appearance of independence in a relationship that is really very dependent.

Pseudomutuality: A façade of harmonious relationship among family members that allows the family to avoid close relationships.

Punishment: An aversive stimulus that follows a behavior.

Reactor: A therapist who acts as a facilitator and clarifier of family interaction rather than being directive.

Reciprocity: Equitable exchange of rewarding behaviors among family members.

Reinforcement: An event that follows a behavior and increases the probability of occurrence of a certain response.

Scaling questions: Questions that allow a therapist to ask family members to give their best estimate of where on a scale of a given variable they might fall.

Scapegoating: Displacement of family conflict onto a single member and labeling of him or her as the identified patient.

Second-order change: A change in the structure and functioning of a system and the way the system maintains stability.

Sibling subsystem: The subset of the family system that is governed by interactional rules pertaining to transactions among siblings.

Social exchange theory: A theory that views social exchanges in terms of the individual's attempt to maximize rewards and minimize costs.

Social learning theory: A theory that views a person's behavior as being a result of the social conditions under which the behavior was learned.

Stimulus: Event that triggers or controls specific behavior in family members (plural *stimuli*).

Straightforward tasks: Tasks that the family is intended to accept and perform as stated.

Subsystems: Organizations of component parts that have their own autonomous functions within the system.

Symptom: Behavior of a family member that indicates dysfunction in the family.

System: A set of interrelated elements that make up a whole.

System-maintained symptoms: Symptoms in a family member that are perpetuated by conditions in the family system.

System-maintaining symptoms: Symptoms in a family member that serve to maintain homeostasis in the family system.

Time-oriented questions: Questions that allow a therapist to elicit positive changes, motivating values, possible goals, or first steps of possible change.

Time out: Brief isolation of a person in a neutral environment rather than a reinforcing environment.

Tracking: Remaining attuned to the family's style of communication in order to follow its discussions.

Transference analysis: Analysis of family members' emotional reactions to current relationships based on past unresolved family relationships.

Triangulation: The tendency for two people who are in conflict to involve a third person or entity in order to reduce the stress in the dyad.

Unbalancing: A therapeutic technique to alter the hierarchy of the family by the therapist's forming a coalition with one or more members.

Vertical stressor: Stressor transmitted down through previous generations.

Wholeness: The integrality of consistent elements combined in a system such that the entity is greater than the sum of its parts.

Name Index

Subject Index

Credits

This page constitutes an extension of the copyright page. We have made every effort to trace the ownership of all copyrighted material and to secure permission from copyright holders. In the event of any question arising as to the use of any material, we will be pleased to make the necessary corrections in future printings. Thanks are due to the following authors, publishers, and agents for permission to use the material indicated.

Chapter 2: 33, Excerpt from "Structural family therapy with drug addicts," by M. D. Stanton and T. C. Todd. In E. Kaufman & P. Kaufman (eds.), *The Family Therapy of Drug and Alcohol Abuse.* Copyright © 1979 Gardner Press. Reprinted by permission.

Chapter 4: 83–84, 86, excerpts from *Strategic Family Therapy,* by C. Madanes, pp. 225–226. Copyright © 1981 by Jossey-Bass, Inc. Reprinted by permission. **88, 89, 90,** excerpts from *Problem-solving Therapy,* by J. Haley. Copyright © 1976 by Jossey-Bass, Inc. Reprinted by permission. **91, 96,** excerpts from "The Greek Chorus and Other Techniques of Paradoxical Therapy," by P. Papp, *Family Process,* 1980, *19,* 45–57. Copyright © 1980 Family Process, Inc. Reprinted by permission.

Chapter 6: 138, 139, 141, 144, 145, 146, excerpts from "Symbolic-Experiential Family Therapy," by C. A. Whitaker and D. V. Keith. In A. S. Gurman and D. P. Kniskern (eds.), *Handbook of Family Therapy.* Copyright © 1981 by Brunner/Mazel, Inc. Reprinted by permission. **141–142, 147–148,** excerpts from *Peoplemaking,* by V. Satir. Copyright © 1972 by Science & Behavior Books, Inc. Reprinted by permission of the author and publisher.

Chapter 7: 156, 171, 177–179, 185–186, excerpts from "Behavioral Marital Therapy," by N. S. Jacobson. In A. S. Gurman and D. P. Kniskern (Eds.), *Handbook of Family Therapy.* Copyright © 1981 by Brunner/Mazel, Inc. Reprinted by permission. **163, 165,** list from "Toward Comprehensive Behavioral Family Intervention," by E. A. Blechman, *Behavior Modification,* Vol. 5, No. 2, 1981, pp. 221–236. Copyright © 1981 by Sage Publications, Inc. Reprinted by permission. **164,** Figure 7.1 from "Family Problem-Solving Training," by E. A. Blechman, *American Journal of Family Therapy, Vol. 8, 1980, pp. 3–21.* Copyright © 1980 by Brunner/Mazel, Inc. Reprinted by permission. **176,** Figure 7.2 from *Marital Interaction Coding System,* by H. Hops, T. A. Wills, G. R. Patterson, and R. L. Weiss.

TO THE OWNER OF THIS BOOK:

We hope that you have found *Family Therapy: Theory and Practice,* Second Edition, useful. So that this book can be improved in a future edition, would you take the time to complete this sheet and return it? Thank you.

School and address: ——————————————————————————

Department: ——————————————————————————

Instructor's name: ——————————————————————————

1. What I like most about this book is: ——————————————————

———————————————————————————————

———————————————————————————————

2. What I like least about this book is: ——————————————————

———————————————————————————————

———————————————————————————————

3. My general reaction to this book is: ——————————————————

———————————————————————————————

4. The name of the course in which I used this book is: ———————————

———————————————————————————————

5. Were all of the chapters of the book assigned for you to read? ———————

   If not, which ones weren't? ——————————————————————

6. In the space below, or on a separate sheet of paper, please write specific suggestions for improving this book and anything else you'd care to share about your experience in using the book.

———————————————————————————————

———————————————————————————————

———————————————————————————————

———————————————————————————————

———————————————————————————————

Optional:

Your name: _____ Date: _____

May Brooks/Cole quote you, either in promotion for *Family Therapy: Theory and Practice,* Second Edition, or in future publishing ventures?

Yes: _____ No: _____

Sincerely,

Joseph H. Brown
Dana N. Christensen